HOUGHTON MIFFLIN HARCOURT

JOURNEYS

Program Authors

James F. Baumann · David J. Chard · Jamal Cooks
J. David Cooper · Russell Gersten · Marjorie Lipson
Lesley Mandel Morrow · John J. Pikulski · Héctor H. Rivera
Mabel Rivera · Shane Templeton · Sheila W. Valencia
Catherine Valentino · MaryEllen Vogt

Consulting Author

Irene Fountas

HOUGHTON MIFFLIN HARCOURT
School Publishers

Cover illustration by Mike Wimmer.

Printed in the U.S.A.

ISBN 10:   0-54-725157-2
ISBN 13:   978-0-54-725157-8

3 4 5 6 7 8 1421 16 15 14 13 12 11 10
4500234396

HOUGHTON MIFFLIN HARCOURT

JOURNEYS

HOUGHTON MIFFLIN HARCOURT

School Publishers

School Spirit!

Big Idea We never stop learning.

Unit 2

WILD ENCOUNTERS

Big Idea Nature deserves our respect.

Unit 3

Revolution!

Big Idea History is made by individuals.

Unit 4

What's Your Story?

Big Idea Everyone has a story to tell.

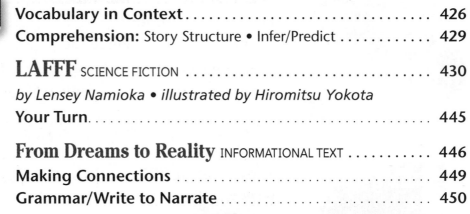

Under Western Skies

Big Idea Our country is always changing.

Welcome, Reader!

You are about to set out on a reading journey that will take you from a virtual ride on a space shuttle to the countryside of Spain, where a knight battles a windmill. On the way, you will learn amazing things as you become a better reader.

Your reading journey begins in a school that is unlike any you have ever seen.

Plenty of other reading adventures lie ahead. Just turn the page!

Sincerely,

The Authors

School Spirit!

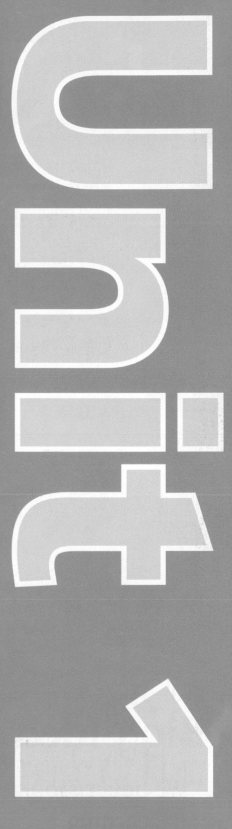

Unit 1

Big Idea

We never stop learning.

Paired Selections

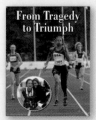

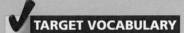

specialty

disturbing

collapsed

squashing

shifted

numb

staggered

struggled

wobbled

interrupted

Vocabulary
Reader

Context
Cards

Vocabulary in Context

1 specialty

A schoolroom may be set up for one skill, or specialty. In this room, students use computers.

2 disturbing

Loud noises are disturbing students working in the library. Please be courteous.

3 collapsed

After a hard practice, you might find a tired team collapsed onto benches in the gym.

4 squashing

It's not unusual to see students squashing, or pressing, clay into shapes in the art room.

- **Study each Context Card.**
- **Use a dictionary or a glossary to verify the meanings of the Vocabulary words.**

5 shifted

These students shifted, or moved, their attention to the first question on the test.

6 numb

Wear mittens on cold, numb hands. When your fingers warm up you will feel them.

7 staggered

Wearing heavy backpacks, these students staggered unsteadily to class.

8 struggled

These science students struggled to make their difficult chemistry experiment work.

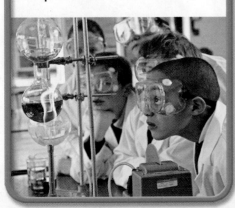

9 wobbled

This girl held her stack of books steady when it wobbled. She kept it from falling over.

10 interrupted

This band teacher interrupted, or briefly stopped, the band to ask them to start over.

Background

✔ **TARGET VOCABULARY** **Types of Humor** Have you ever interrupted your reading to giggle or to laugh out loud? Most people would rather read a funny story than one that left them feeling numb after they had struggled to get through it.

To create humor, some writers use absurdity, or ridiculous events. Others use exaggeration, such as a character who has staggered under the weight of a feather or collapsed when scared by a butterfly. Understatement is another specialty of humor writers. Here is an example: "Walking through poison ivy barefoot was disturbing Sam a bit." Writers might also use wordplay, such as tongue twisters: "Sheila's sheepdog shifted on the sand, squashing her seashells" or "The wall wobbled when Wilbur the walrus whacked it."

In the next selection, look for examples of these types of humor.

Comprehension

Story Structure

The structure of a story includes the important elements of the plot. Make a graphic organizer like the one below for "A Package for Mrs. Jewls." It will help you keep track of a character's problem, events surrounding the problem, or conflict, and the solution to the problem. Make sure that you list the events in sequential order.

Setting:	Characters:
Plot	
Problem (Conflict): Events: Solution (Resolution):	

Summarize

Use story structure and the graphic organizer above to write a summary of "A Package for Mrs. Jewls." A summary is a brief recap. It includes only a story's main ideas and most important details or events. As you summarize, use your own words. Make sure you do not change the story's meaning or its order of events.

Main Selection

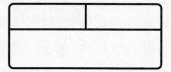
TARGET VOCABULARY

specialty	numb
disturbing	staggered
collapsed	struggled
squashing	wobbled
shifted	interrupted

✔ TARGET SKILL

Story Structure Examine details about characters, setting, and plot.

✔ TARGET STRATEGY

Summarize Briefly tell the important parts of the text in your own words.

GENRE

Humorous fiction is a story that is written to entertain.

Set Purpose Before reading, set a purpose for reading based on what you know about the genre and your own experience.

MEET THE AUTHOR

Louis Sachar

While working as an elementary school aide, Louis Sachar wrote some stories and read them to his students. The kids loved his stories, and he's been writing ever since. Sachar says, "I want kids to think that reading can be just as much fun, or more so, than TV or video games or whatever else they do."

MEET THE ILLUSTRATOR

Bruce MacPherson

Bruce MacPherson's illustrations have appeared in newspapers and magazines nationwide. Although his own children are now grown, he also loves illustrating for kids. His humorous, colorful artwork has appeared in the books *Josefina Javelina* and *Thank You, Aunt Tallulah!*

A PACKAGE FOR MRS. JEWLS

from Wayside School Is Falling Down

by Louis Sachar

selection illustrated by Bruce MacPherson

Essential Question

What funny events lead Louis to Mrs. Jewls's classroom?

Louis, the yard teacher, frowned.

The school yard was a mess. There were pencils and pieces of paper everywhere. How'd all this junk get here? he wondered. Well, I'm not going to pick it up!

It wasn't his job to pick up garbage. He was just supposed to pass out the balls during lunch and recess.

He sighed, then began cleaning it up. He loved all the children at Wayside School. He didn't want them playing on a dirty playground.

As he was picking up the pencils and pieces of paper, a large truck drove into the parking lot. It honked its horn twice, then twice more.

Louis ran to the truck. "Quiet!" he whispered. "Children are trying to learn in there!" He pointed at the school.

A short man with big, bushy hair stepped out of the truck. "I have a package for somebody named Mrs. Jewls," he said.

"I'll take it," said Louis.

"Are you Mrs. Jewls?" asked the man.

"No," said Louis.

"I have to give it to Mrs. Jewls," said the man.

Louis thought a moment. He didn't want the man disturbing the children. He knew how much they hated to be interrupted when they were working.

"I'm Mrs. Jewls," he said.

"But you just said you weren't Mrs. Jewls," said the man.

"I changed my mind," said Louis.

The man got the package out of the back of the truck and gave it to Louis. "Here you go, Mrs. Jewls," he said.

"Uhh!" Louis grunted. It was a very heavy package. The word FRAGILE was printed on every side. He had to be careful not to drop it.

The package was so big, Louis couldn't see where he was going. Fortunately, he knew the way to Mrs. Jewls's class by heart. It was straight up.

Wayside School was thirty stories high, with only one room on each story. Mrs. Jewls's class was at the very top. It was Louis's favorite class.

He pushed through the door to the school, then started up the stairs. There was no elevator.

There were stairs that led down to the basement, too, but nobody ever went down there.

The box was pressed against Louis's face, squashing his nose. Even so, when he reached the fifteenth floor, he could smell Miss Mush cooking in the cafeteria. It smelled like she was making mushrooms. Maybe on my way back I'll stop by Miss Mush's room and get some mushrooms, he thought. He didn't want to miss Miss Mush's mushrooms. They were her specialty.

He huffed and groaned and continued up the stairs. His arms and legs were very sore, but he didn't want to rest. This package might be important, he thought. I have to get it to Mrs. Jewls right away.

He stepped easily from the eighteenth story to the twentieth. There was no nineteenth story.

Miss Zarves taught the class on the nineteenth story. There was no Miss Zarves.

STOP AND THINK

Summarize What has happened in the story so far? Include only the most important events in your summary.

At last he struggled up the final step to the thirtieth story. He knocked on Mrs. Jewls's door with his head.

Mrs. Jewls was in the middle of teaching her class about gravity when she heard the knock. "Come in," she called.

"I can't open the door," Louis gasped. "My hands are full. I have a package for you."

Mrs. Jewls faced the class. "Who wants to open the door for Louis?" she asked.

All the children raised their hands. They loved to be interrupted when they were working.

"Oh dear, how shall I choose?" asked Mrs. Jewls. "I have to be fair about this. I know! We'll have a spelling bee. And the winner will get to open the door."

Louis knocked his head against the door again. "It's heavy," he complained. "And I'm very tired."

STOP AND THINK
Author's Craft This story uses **third-person omniscient point of view** to tell thoughts, words, and actions of more than one character. How does this point of view help make the action on these pages funny?

"Just a second," Mrs. Jewls called back. "Allison, the first word's for you. Heavy."

"Heavy," said Allison. "H-E-A-V-Y. Heavy."

"Very good. Jason, You're next. Tired."

"Tired," said Jason. "S-L-E-E-P-Y. Tired."

Louis felt the package slipping from his sweaty fingers. He shifted his weight to get a better grip. The corners of the box dug into the sides of his arms. He felt his hands go numb.

Actually, he *didn't* feel them go numb.

"Jenny, package."

"Package," said Jenny. "B-O-X. Package."

"Excellent!" said Mrs. Jewls.

Louis felt like he was going to faint.

At last John opened the door. "I won the spelling bee, Louis!" he said.

"Very good, John," muttered Louis.

"Aren't you going to shake my hand?" asked John.

Louis shifted the box to one arm, quickly shook John's hand, then grabbed the box again and staggered into the room.

"Where do you want it, Mrs. Jewls?"

"I don't know," said Mrs. Jewls. "What is it?"

"I don't know," said Louis. "I'll have to put it down someplace so you can open it."

"But how can I tell you where to put it until I know what it is?" asked Mrs. Jewls. "You might put it in the wrong place."

So Louis held the box as Mrs. Jewls stood on a chair next to him and tore open the top. His legs wobbled beneath him.

"It's a computer," exclaimed Mrs. Jewls.

Everybody booed.

"What's the matter?" asked Louis. "I thought everyone loved computers."

"We don't want it, Louis," said Eric Bacon.

"Take it back, Jack," said Terrence.

"Get that piece of junk out of here," said Maurecia.

"Now, don't be that way," said Mrs. Jewls. "The computer will help us learn. It's a lot quicker than a pencil and paper."

"But the quicker we learn, the more work we have to do," complained Todd.

"You may set it over there on the counter, Louis," said Mrs. Jewls.

Louis set the computer on the counter next to Sharie's desk. Then he collapsed on the floor.

"Now watch closely," said Mrs. Jewls.

Everyone gathered around the new computer.

Mrs. Jewls pushed it out the window.

They all watched it fall and smash against the sidewalk.

"See?" said Mrs. Jewls. "That's gravity."

"Oh, now I get it!" said Joe.

"Thank you, Louis," said Mrs. Jewls. "I've been trying to teach them about gravity all morning. We had been using pencils and pieces of paper, but the computer was a lot quicker."

✔ **STOP AND THINK**

Story Structure How do the events in the story foreshadow the story's ending? Was the ending of this story a surprise? Why or why not?

YourTurn

Look Out Below

Short Response Mrs. Jewls pushes a computer out the window to teach her students about gravity. Imagine that you are one of Mrs. Jewls's students and that she has asked you to come up with your own creative way to teach a lesson on gravity. Write a paragraph describing how you would do it. PERSONAL RESPONSE

Spelling Bee

Perform a Play During the spelling bee, Mrs. Jewls's students sometimes spell synonyms instead of the given words. In a group, act out the scene. Make a list of spelling words. Have a student play Mrs. Jewls by calling out the words. The rest of the group should take turns spelling synonyms of the words. SMALL GROUP

Cold. I–C–Y. Cold.

Lots of Laughs

Turn and Talk With a partner, discuss the humorous events that happen to Louis during the story. Which events would not have happened if the story had taken place in a typical school? STORY STRUCTURE

✔ **TARGET VOCABULARY**

specialty	numb
disturbing	staggered
collapsed	struggled
squashing	wobbled
shifted	interrupted

GENRE

Readers' theater is a text that has been formatted for readers to read aloud.

TEXT FOCUS

An **interview** uses a question-and-answer format to give information in a person's own words.

Questioning Gravity ✳

by Katie Sharp

Cast
Dr. Gene E. Us
Alex
Sara
Ed

Dr. Gene E. Us: Greetings students! I hope I'm not disturbing your work.

Alex: Who are you?

Dr. Gene E. Us: That's a great question. And it tells me I have come to the right class. Good scientists always ask questions.

Sara: So, who are you and why are you here?

Dr. Gene E. Us: Ah . . . another scientist! My name is Dr. Gene E. Us, and my specialty is science. Your teacher asked me to come here to answer your science questions. Ask me anything!

Ed: Yesterday, I was carrying a big stack of books home from the library. There were so many that the top one wobbled and crashed to the ground. Then I staggered and fell trying to catch it. That got me thinking. If the Earth has such strong gravity, why isn't everything in space falling onto Earth and squashing us?

Dr. Gene E. Us: Ah, when I was your age, I struggled with that question, too. You see, gravity gets weaker with distance. But without any gravity, the Moon would fly off into space and we might never see it again. It makes me numb just thinking about it.

Sara: All this talk about Earth and the Moon makes me wonder something. Where did the planets come from in the first place?

Dr. Gene E. Us: Another good question! Most scientists believe that about 4.6 billion years ago, dust and gas came together to form a huge cloud. They came together because of our good friend gravity. At first the core of the cloud started to spin around slowly. But as the cloud collapsed, the core spun faster and faster and eventually became the Sun. The stuff left over cooled and became the planets, asteroids, and other objects in space.

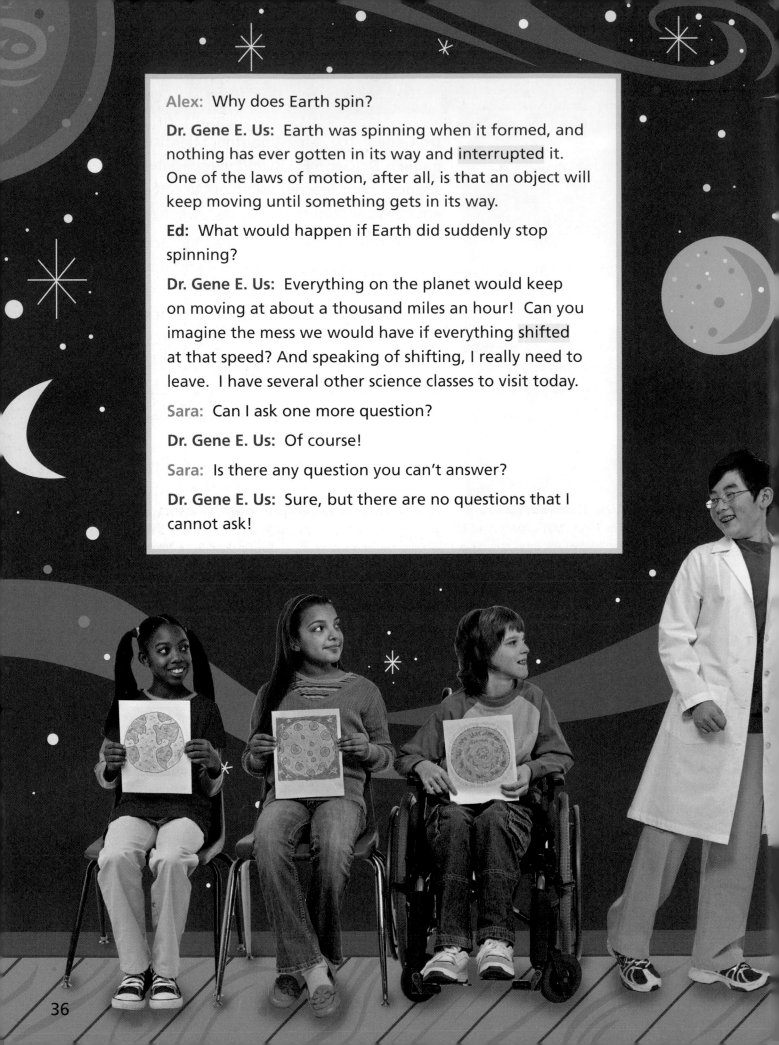

Alex: Why does Earth spin?

Dr. Gene E. Us: Earth was spinning when it formed, and nothing has ever gotten in its way and interrupted it. One of the laws of motion, after all, is that an object will keep moving until something gets in its way.

Ed: What would happen if Earth did suddenly stop spinning?

Dr. Gene E. Us: Everything on the planet would keep on moving at about a thousand miles an hour! Can you imagine the mess we would have if everything shifted at that speed? And speaking of shifting, I really need to leave. I have several other science classes to visit today.

Sara: Can I ask one more question?

Dr. Gene E. Us: Of course!

Sara: Is there any question you can't answer?

Dr. Gene E. Us: Sure, but there are no questions that I cannot ask!

Making Connections

Text to Self

Describe a Scene The author of "A Package for Mrs. Jewls" uses third-person omniscient point of view to tell a humorous story. Write about a time when something extraordinary happened to you. Then explain how a different point of view might have changed your story.

Text to Text

Make Comparisons Think about some of the ways in which students learn from Mrs. Jewls and Dr. Gene E. Us. Write a paragraph comparing their teaching methods. Provide at least two examples from "A Package for Mrs. Jewls" and "Questioning Gravity" to support your answer.

Text to World

Research a Science Question The students in "Questioning Gravity" learn some surprising scientific facts. Create a list of questions you would ask if you had a chance. What valid sources could you use to find your own answers to your questions?

1. Why is the sky blue?

2. Why is

Grammar

What Is a Sentence? A **sentence** is a group of words that expresses a complete thought. To be complete, a sentence must have both a subject and a predicate. The **simple subject** is the word or words that name the person or thing the sentence is about. The **simple predicate** is the main word or words that tell what the subject is or does.

Complete Sentences

simple subject   simple predicate

A large truck entered the parking lot.

---

simple subject   simple predicate

A teacher ran to the truck.

A group of words that does not express a complete thought is a **fragment**.

Sentence Fragments

A package for Mrs. Jewls. (does not tell what the subject does)

Handed the package to a teacher. (does not tell who did the action)

Try This! **Identify each of the following as a sentence or a fragment. List on a sheet of paper the simple subject and the simple predicate in each complete sentence. Then rewrite each fragment as a complete sentence.**

❶ Carrying a heavy package up the stairs.

❷ The teacher knocks on the door with his head.

❸ The happy students compete in a spelling bee.

Sentence Fluency Always check the sentences you write to make sure they are complete. Fix any fragments you find. Sometimes you can fix a fragment by adding it to a complete sentence.

Complete Sentence	Fragment
Mrs. Jewls put her hands on the computer.	Shoved it out the window.

Complete Sentence + Fragment

Mrs. Jewls put her hands on the computer and shoved it out the window.

Connect Grammar to Writing

As you revise your writing, make sure each sentence has a subject and a predicate. Change any fragments you find into complete sentences.

Write to Express

In "A Package for Mrs. Jewls," Louis *huffed* and *groaned* up the stairs. The author's words bring the event to life. You can make a **narrative paragraph** clearer by adding specific details and strong, active verbs.

Eduardo drafted a narrative paragraph that showed someone doing a difficult task. Later, he added vivid details to add more action to his story.

Writing Traits Checklist

✓ **Ideas**
Did I tell the events clearly, using specific details?

✓ **Organization**
Does each event help build the story structure?

✓ **Sentence Fluency**
Did I use complete sentences and combine them when I could?

✓ **Word Choice**
Did I use strong, active verbs?

✓ **Voice**
Do my words help reveal the mood of the story?

✓ **Conventions**
Did I use correct spelling, grammar, and punctuation?

Revised Draft

Aldo's basement was a mess. Last week, he had been ~~working with wood.~~ *sawing and hammering furiously* ~~Scraps of~~ wood *scraps and sawdust* had scattered everywhere. ~~Sawdust everywhere.~~ Now paint was ~~getting~~ *splattering* all over the floor as Aldo ~~tried to finish~~ *raced to complete* his project. The school's Medieval Fair was tomorrow, and he had promised to bring in a big surprise.

Aldo's Surprise

by Eduardo Martinez

Aldo's basement was a mess. Last week, he had been sawing and hammering furiously. Wood scraps and sawdust had scattered everywhere. Now paint was splattering all over the floor as Aldo raced to complete his project. The school's Medieval Fair was tomorrow, and he had promised to bring in a big surprise. After four hours of painting, Aldo stood back to admire his creation. He had built a model of a medieval castle, complete with a drawbridge that really worked and two tall turrets. In the morning, he'd be ready to reveal his masterpiece to the world. Suddenly, Aldo saw a slight problem. His wood and cardboard castle was much too big to fit up the stairs!

In my final paper, I added some details and strong, active verbs. I also combined fragments to form complete sentences.

Reading as a Writer

Which details and strong verbs make Eduardo's story come alive? Where can you add details and strong verbs to your own narrative writing?

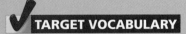

function

operator

tethered

version

axis

simulate

acute

flawed

delicate

adjusted

Vocabulary Reader   Context Cards

Vocabulary in Context

1 function

For a successful liftoff, all parts of a space shuttle must function, or work, properly.

2 operator

An astronaut must be an operator of complex machines. He uses each one on his job.

3 tethered

This astronaut is tethered to a spaceship. Tied to the spacecraft, he can't drift away.

4 version

The space station is an orbiting version, or type, of very advanced laboratory.

- **Study each Context Card.**
- **Use context clues to determine the meaning of each Vocabulary word.**

5 axis

Earth turns on its axis, or imaginary line of rotation, creating day and night.

6 simulate

Astronauts train in swimming pools to simulate, or imitate, conditions in space.

7 acute

Astronauts need an acute sense of balance to work in the weightlessness of space.

8 flawed

If any shuttle part is flawed, it must be repaired so it is perfect before takeoff.

9 delicate

From space, some astronauts see Earth as a delicate, easily damaged planet.

10 adjusted

The shuttle's flight path is adjusted, or changed, as it nears the space station.

Background

✔ **TARGET VOCABULARY** **What Is Gravity?** Here's one version of the definition: gravity is a force of attraction, or pull, between any two masses. But how does gravity function on Earth and in space?

Here, gravity pulls objects toward Earth's center. Gravity can vary between planets and other bodies in space. It is adjusted upward as the body's mass increases. The Moon, although smaller than Earth, exerts a gravitational pull on our planet. As Earth turns on its axis, the Moon's gravity causes ocean tides.

A planet's gravity grows weaker over distance, so Earth's is weak in space. If delicate repairs to flawed parts are needed outside a spaceship, the astronaut doing the repairs will be tethered to keep from floating away. An astronaut who will be the operator of tools in space must have acute vision and practice in conditions that simulate zero gravity.

- Review the table below. What would be the difference in your weight on Earth from your weight on Mercury and on Neptune?

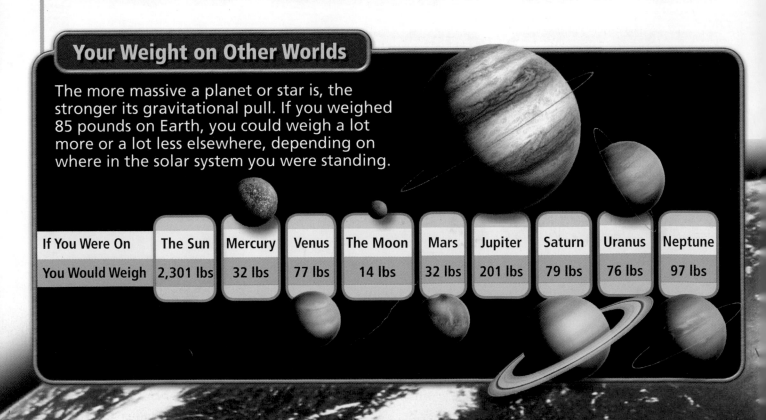

Your Weight on Other Worlds

The more massive a planet or star is, the stronger its gravitational pull. If you weighed 85 pounds on Earth, you could weigh a lot more or a lot less elsewhere, depending on where in the solar system you were standing.

If You Were On	The Sun	Mercury	Venus	The Moon	Mars	Jupiter	Saturn	Uranus	Neptune
You Would Weigh	2,301 lbs	32 lbs	77 lbs	14 lbs	32 lbs	201 lbs	79 lbs	76 lbs	97 lbs

Comprehension

✔ **TARGET SKILL** **Text and Graphic Features**

As you read, use text and graphic features, such as headings and subheadings, to better understand what happens at Space Academy. These features will help you gain an overview of the selection and locate important information. Make a graphic organizer like the one below to help you identify text features in "Ultimate Field Trip 5: Blasting Off to Space Academy."

Text/Graphic Feature	Purpose
• • •	• • •

✔ **TARGET STRATEGY** **Question**

Use your graphic organizer to ask questions about what you are reading. Questioning helps you understand what the author is trying to say. It also helps you realize what more you would like to know.

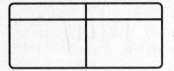

MEET THE AUTHOR

SUSAN E. GOODMAN

Before writing *Ultimate Field Trip 5: Blasting Off to Space Academy,* Susan Goodman went to adult Space Camp and learned what it feels like to walk on the moon in the 1/6 Gravity Chair. She enjoys writing nonfiction because it gives her the opportunity to learn new things and to have great adventures!

MEET THE PHOTOGRAPHER

MICHAEL J. DOOLITTLE

Michael Doolittle has collaborated with Susan Goodman on all the books in the *Ultimate Field Trip* series. To get good photos, he has dangled from rain forest trees and plunged into freezing cold water, but his most exciting experience was taking a photo while plummeting downward on the Space Shot.

BLASTING OFF to SPACE ACADEMY

FROM ULTIMATE FIELD TRIP 5

by Susan E. Goodman • photographs by Michael J. Doolittle

U.S. SPACE CAMP
FLORIDA

Essential Question

How can graphics help you learn about space?

Countdown to Adventure

What's the best part of being an astronaut? Is it the thrill of rocketing out of Earth's atmosphere at 25,000 miles per hour? Is it the chance to make new scientific discoveries? Or is it the adventure of leaving the familiar behind and going, as someone once put it, "where no man has gone before?"

Few people actually get to answer these questions by traveling into space. But some kids take the first step by going to the U.S. Space Academy at the United States Space and Rocket Center in Huntsville, Alabama.

The Habitat, where kids sleep at Space Academy, was designed as an earthbound space station with stairs and handrails to get from floor to floor. In space, you'd float where you need to go.

For almost a week they used the same simulators that real astronauts use and learned how to walk on the Moon and work without gravity. They built their own rockets and visited the ones scientists used to launch the Apollo astronauts to the Moon. They tried tasting space food and wearing space suits. They learned how to eat in space and sleep in space.

During their training they became a team, Team Europa, named after one of Jupiter's seven moons. Then, Europa blasted off on a mission of its own . . .

Amazing Space Facts

The last time astronauts walked on the Moon was in 1972, but all of their footprints are still there. Since the Moon does not have an atmosphere, there is no wind to blow the prints away.

On the Training Floor

"Europa, the training center is a dirt-free zone," said Paul. "Gum and drinks can create disasters here."

Paul, one of Europa's team leaders, led the kids through a maze of strange-looking machines. As they walked, the kids peeked at other teams jumping high enough to dunk a basketball and spinning in what looked like a giant gyroscope. Paul explained that astronauts trained for years before going into space. It takes lots of practice to learn how to function in such a different environment. On space walks, for example, they must make delicate repairs while floating upside down. In their ships they must learn how to drift rather than walk through the air.

How do they learn these things while anchored by Earth's gravity? To find out, Europa tried some of the simulators that astronauts have used.

"I felt like I was on a trampoline," said Lindsay, "but I didn't go down—just up!"

The 1/6 Gravity Chair

"The Moon has only one-sixth of our gravity," explained Paul. "If you weigh one hundred twenty pounds here, you'd only weigh twenty pounds on the Moon. And you'd have to learn to walk differently because there isn't as much traction."

To practice this movement, the kids used a 1/6 Gravity Chair similar to the Apollo astronauts'. In fact, Europa learned from the astronauts' experiences. The best ways to get around were a slow jog and the bunny hop.

John waited impatiently while Paul adjusted the chair to offset five-sixths of his weight.

"Bunny hop for me," said Paul.

"You've got to be kidding," answered John. "I can barely reach the ground."

Soon, however, he was leaping across the training floor.

"This looks like good practice for the high jump," said Stephanie.

"It shouldn't be; you want to jump for distance, not height," said Paul. "Astronaut Charlie Duke of *Apollo 16* tried to set a height record. But his life-support pack changed his center of gravity. He landed on his back and couldn't get up, just like a beetle. If John Young hadn't been around to help him, he could have been stuck there until *Apollo 17*!"

> **STOP AND THINK**
> **Question** What question would you ask a friend to make sure he or she understands the information on this page?

The Multi-Axis Trainer (MAT)

"Remove everything from your pockets," said Bethany, Europa's other team leader. "Take off your necklaces, too, so you don't get whacked in the face."

To get ready for the MAT, some kids took off jewelry; others just took a few deep breaths. The MAT looks like an atom gone wild, with each of its three outer circles spinning separately and you as its whirling nucleus. The Mercury astronauts used it to learn how to regain control of a tumbling spacecraft.

The MAT never turns more than twice in the same direction, which is supposed to keep you from feeling sick. That didn't keep a lot of kids from getting nervous. But once they tried it, the glint of silver braces flashed through their smiles.

"It was terrific," said Stacy, "but next time, I'll tie my hair back so it doesn't keep hitting my face."

"It's awesome," Stephanie agreed.

When asked how she'd feel doing it for a ten-minute stretch in a spaceship, Stephanie added, "Your head spins like crazy, but it doesn't feel bad."

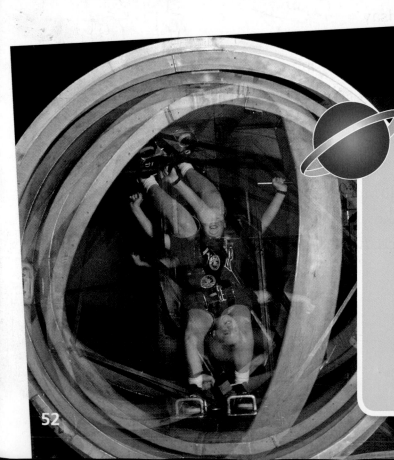

"I couldn't help smiling all the time because it was so much fun," said Lindsay.

Amazing Space Facts

NASA's first space suits were silver colored. They only protected Mercury astronauts if their capsule depressurized. Today's version shields astronauts from space's deadly environment and keeps them comfortable. An astronaut can get hungry working in space, so the suit has a granola bar mounted at the shoulder along with a straw for water. The other shoulder has an emery board to scratch an itchy nose. A stream of air flows from the top of the suit to below the neck to keep the effects of sneezes and space sickness from blocking an astronaut's vision.

The Five Degrees of Freedom (5DF) Chair

On Earth, when you jump up, gravity pulls you back down. In space, you just keep going up. If you push away from a wall, you keep going backward. Bending quickly to grab something could make you do somersaults. To get used to the weightless tumble of space, the Gemini and Apollo astronauts—and the kids at Space Academy—used the 5DF Chair. This chair glided over the floor on a cushion of air like the puck in an air hockey game.

"This is what an EVA, an extravehicular activity, or space walk, feels like," Bethany said, tipping and rolling the chair in all directions to give the kids a taste of the different movements.

Bethany held on to the 5DF chair to keep it safe. In space, astronauts are tethered to their ship. It's a good thing, too. When astronaut Pete Conrad went on his space walk, he lost hold of *Skylab*. That tether was the only thing that kept him from floating away.

In the 5DF Chair, kids practiced inching their way along a wall. Once Lindsay pushed herself away by accident, she had a hard time getting back.

"Swim, Lindsay, swim," Courtney called out.

Lindsay tried to breaststroke her way back to the wall—it was hopeless.

"Oh, well," said Charles, "she's *Lost in Space*!"

✓ STOP AND THINK

Text and Graphic Features These pages include headings and a sidebar. What different kinds of information do these text features provide?

Space Shot

"This is your last chance to change your mind," said the operator. "Once the generator has been charged, we cannot stop."

In just seconds, the kids were blasting off on the Space Shot. They would rocket skyward with a force of 4 Gs, one more than astronauts experience during their launches. All that force meant that, for a few seconds at the top, before gravity pulled them back, the kids could feel what it was like to be weightless.

NASA doesn't use the Space Shot to simulate weightlessness; it trains astronauts aboard its KC-135 airplane. The plane climbs sharply and then free-falls straight toward the ground, up again, then down again, and again. For twenty-five seconds, at the top of each roller-coaster ride, the plane's passengers are weightless. But many astronauts have paid a price for this amazing experience. The KC-135 is nicknamed the "Vomit Comet" for good reason.

"I wish I hadn't eaten so much breakfast," said Erin S. as she waited for her turn on the Space Shot. "I'm going to scream. It helps you not throw up."

Before her second ride, Erin was too excited to feel sick. "I love that feeling of just shooting up there," she said.

"Then you rise up out of your chair and float there for a second," said Stacy. "Weightlessness, I wish it lasted longer."

Amazing Space Facts

Skylab was America's first space station, launched in 1973. While taking a shower during his mission, astronaut Alan Bean suddenly stopped hearing the hum of Skylab's electronics. Since they controlled life support, he started to investigate immediately. The answer was quite a relief. In this weightless environment, blobs of water had stuck to his ears.

This is the way Frank and most kids feel going up on the Space Shot . . .

. . . and they feel this way coming down. Devin was amazed that one kid in line thought the experience would cure his fear of heights.

Some people call the Space Shot "an elevator with an attitude."

STOP AND THINK

Author's Craft Sometimes an author's **purpose** is to create a certain mood, or feeling, for readers. Look at the details included in the Space Shot section. How well do they work to achieve the author's purpose of creating a feeling of excitement?

The Pool

Another way the earthbound astronauts simulate working in weightlessness is by going underwater. At Houston's Lyndon B. Johnson Space Center, astronauts practice in a huge water tank holding a full-scale model of the Shuttle's payload bay. At Space Academy, the kids went to a swimming pool.

"Your job is to build a cube underwater as fast as possible," said Bethany. "It takes teamwork, an ability to work in weightlessness, and—something astronauts don't need, I hope—an ability to hold your breath."

Each strut, or tube, belonged in a specific place.

Amazing Space Facts

At least half the astronauts experience space sickness at the beginning of their voyage. That's why John Young didn't do Gus Grissom any favor when he smuggled him a corned beef sandwich on the Gemini 3 mission. The story is Grissom threw up; in weightless conditions, that's a difficult cleanup job.

The water started boiling as kids grabbed struts and dove underwater. It kept boiling as they came up for air again and again, slowly realizing they needed a better plan . . .

"Ten minutes and fifty-six seconds," Bethany said when they finally finished. "Well, every astronaut has to start somewhere. How could you have gone faster?"

"Talk more to each other?" said Isabelle.

"That's right," Bethany agreed. "Communication, letting your leaders lead, and teamwork. It's true in the pool, and it will be even more important when you work to make your own space mission a real success."

Amazing Space Facts

Flawed when it went into orbit in 1990, the Hubble Space Telescope was repaired in 1993 during a spectacular mission that required five space walks. Located above our hazy atmosphere, the Hubble sees deep into the universe to reveal black holes, new galaxies, the birth of some stars and the death of others. Its "eagle-eyed vision" is so acute that if the Hubble were on Earth, it could spot a firefly ten thousand miles away!

Once the kids started working together, the cube was built quickly.

Blast Off!

As the kids at Space Academy learned, you don't have to be a pilot to work in the space program. Astronauts can be chemists or biologists or medical doctors. Engineers and technicians build the machinery that gets the astronauts up there and home safely. Then there are the mathematicians, psychologists, nutritionists, astronomers, radio operators . . .

Going to Space Academy is only one way to get ready for a career in aerospace. Education is also important, so take as many math and science courses in high school as you can. Learn to work with computers. And (especially if you want to be an astronaut), keep physically fit with good eating habits and regular exercise.

Your Turn

Out of This World

Write About Being an Astronaut

Think about what takes place at the Space Academy. What traits do you think a successful astronaut should have? Use this information to write about whether you would want to become an astronaut yourself. In your explanation, include any traits you have that might make you a successful astronaut. PERSONAL RESPONSE

Space Trainer

Illustrate a New Invention

The Space Academy has the 1/6 gravity chair, the MAT, the 5DF chair, and other machines to help kids learn what it feels like to be in space. With a partner, brainstorm a new type of machine that could help future astronauts train for weightlessness. Then illustrate your new invention. PARTNERS

Talk About Visuals

Turn and Talk

With a partner, discuss the different kinds of graphic features in "Blasting Off to Space Academy." Which one did you find most helpful in explaining space travel? If you could add to the selection another graphic feature, such as a graph, chart, or diagram, what would you include? What would your graphic feature explain? TEXT AND GRAPHIC FEATURES

✓ **TARGET VOCABULARY**

function	simulate
operator	acute
tethered	flawed
version	delicate
axis	adjusted

GENRE

Informational text, like this magazine article, gives facts and examples about a topic.

TEXT FOCUS

Informational text may include a **diagram**, or a drawing with labels, that explains how something works or how parts relate to each other.

Set a Purpose Set a purpose for reading based on the genre and your background knowledge.

PROFILE OF A SPACEWALKER

by Carole Gerber

Astronaut Michael Lopez-Alegria's job is truly out of this world! On February 7, 2007, he set the U.S. record for most spacewalks (ten) and most time in space (215 days). Lopez-Alegria was the commander for Expedition 14 to the International Space Station. He was also the science officer in charge of experiments on a mission to learn the effects on humans of long space flights.

Michael Lopez-Alegria

The Making of a Space Walker

Growing up in California, Lopez-Alegria learned a little about a lot of things. He developed an acute sense of what he could and could not do, and he adjusted his expectations accordingly. His version of his accomplishments is modest. "I couldn't play the piano like a concert pianist. I couldn't do . . . any one thing really, really well," he says. "But I could do a handful of things reasonably well."

After graduating in 1976 from high school in Mission Viejo, California, Lopez-Alegria went to the U.S. Naval Academy. There he earned two degrees in engineering. He then trained to be a Navy test pilot. Later, he joined NASA's astronaut training program, and he has been with NASA ever since.

Helping to assemble the International Space Station has been a career highlight. "When you look at the task-by-task challenges, we've had very few surprises," he says. "I think we have a good shot at completing the station at or on the timetable that's been laid out."

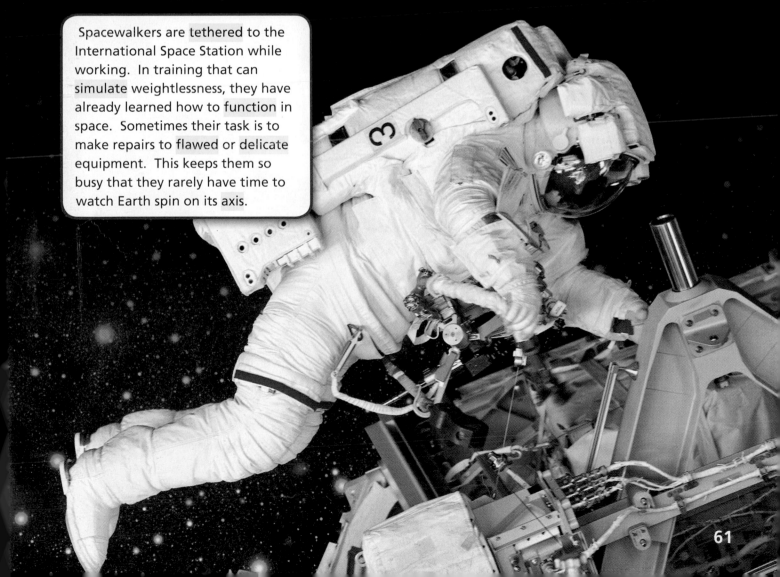

Spacewalkers are tethered to the International Space Station while working. In training that can simulate weightlessness, they have already learned how to function in space. Sometimes their task is to make repairs to flawed or delicate equipment. This keeps them so busy that they rarely have time to watch Earth spin on its axis.

ninety minutes, is the largest manned object in space. It will span more than three hundred feet when completed, and represents the work of sixteen nations.

The Johnson Space Center in Houston, Texas, has been the headquarters of NASA's Mission Control since 1963. Here astronauts train for their missions. Once in space, they communicate with NASA officials at the Space Center. In 1973 the Center was renamed for President Lyndon Johnson, a Texan and longtime supporter of the space program.

• Review the diagram of the Space Station. Approximately how big is the living unit?

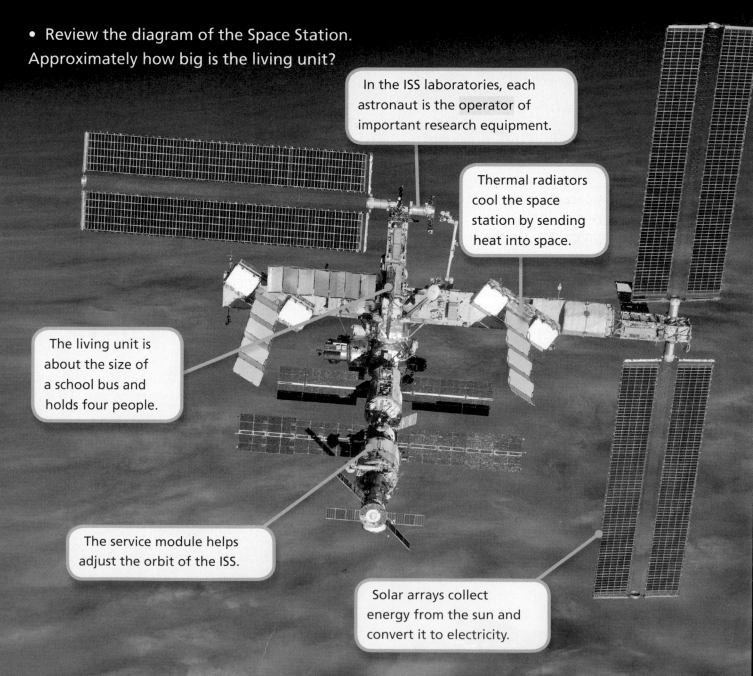

In the ISS laboratories, each astronaut is the operator of important research equipment.

Thermal radiators cool the space station by sending heat into space.

The living unit is about the size of a school bus and holds four people.

The service module helps adjust the orbit of the ISS.

Solar arrays collect energy from the sun and convert it to electricity.

Making Connections

 Text to Self

Write About Your Experiences Think about what Michael Lopez-Alegria studied and did to prepare for his career. What kinds of things have you had to study and prepare for in your life? Write a brief narrative about a time when you were successful because of studying, training, or practicing. Be sure to include details that will make your narrative interesting to your readers.

 Text to Text

Practice First The students at Space Academy practice before their simulated space mission, just as astronaut Michael Lopez-Alegria practices for a real one. Why do you think that is? Work with a partner to explain the kinds of things people can learn from hands-on practice. Use information from "Blasting Off to Space Academy" and "Profile of a Spacewalker" to help you.

 Text to World

View the Space Station The International Space Station (ISS) is visible to the naked eye from many locations in the U.S. Work with a group to visit the NASA website and research when it is visible from your community. Create a handout with facts you learn about the ISS from the selection and your research. Discuss the dates and times when your group could view the ISS.

Grammar

What Are the Four Kinds of Sentences? A sentence that tells something is a **declarative sentence**. It ends with a period. A sentence that asks something is an **interrogative sentence**. It ends with a question mark. A sentence that gives an order is an **imperative sentence**. It ends with a period. A sentence that expresses strong feeling is an **exclamatory sentence**. It ends with an exclamation point.

Academic Language

declarative sentence

interrogative sentence

imperative sentence

exclamatory sentence

Sentence	Kind of Sentence
period Astronauts fly into space.	declarative
question mark How long do they train?	interrogative
period Fill out these forms.	imperative
exclamation point This will be an incredible experience!	exclamatory

 **Work with a partner. Read aloud each sentence below. Then tell which kind of sentence it is.**

1. Try this simulator.

2. It looks as if it will be fun.

3. How does it feel to be weightless?

3. What a strange sensation it is!

Sentence Fluency You know that there are four kinds of sentences—each kind doing a different job. Using a variety of sentence types can make your writing more lively and interesting.

One Sentence Type	Varied Sentence Types
The last light is leaving the sky. I wonder if it can get any darker. Standing in the dark and the cold will be worth it if we get a clear view of the satellite passing overhead. I want you to keep a close eye on the northwest part of the sky. I see it. Wow.	The last light is leaving the sky. Can it get any darker? Standing in the dark and the cold will be worth it if we get a clear view of the satellite passing overhead. Keep a close eye on the northwest part of the sky. I see it! Wow!

Connect Grammar to Writing

When you revise your descriptive paragraph, vary the kinds of sentences in your writing. Using a variety of sentence types will help you hold the interest of your audience. Be careful not to overuse exclamatory sentences.

Write to Express

The author of "Blasting Off to Space Academy" creates a mood of excitement by describing the MAT as "an atom gone wild." A good **descriptive narrative** often describes things in a vivid way to reveal the author's attitude or feelings.

Natalie drafted a paragraph about a somewhat scary place. Later, she added words and phrases to give the reader a clearer sense of her feelings about it.

Writing Traits Checklist

✔ **Ideas**
Did I use specific details to describe the setting?

✔ **Organization**
Did I present the details in an order that makes sense?

✔ **Sentence Fluency**
Did I use varied sentence types?

✔ **Word Choice**
Did I use sensory words?

✔ **Voice**
Do my words reveal an attitude or feeling about the place?

✔ **Conventions**
Did I use correct spelling, grammar, and punctuation?

Revised Draft

Each stroke of my canoe paddle created
a dark swirl in the water. The air ~~was~~
   sludgy   warm, sticky
                        humming with
~~warm and sticky. It~~ was ~~full of~~
              Ugh!
mosquitoes. It smelled like rotten eggs!

My nature group was exploring the

Oxbow Nature Reserve with Terry, our

guide.

66

The Bog Slog

by Natalie Sheng

Each stroke of my canoe paddle created a dark swirl in the sludgy water. The warm, sticky air was humming with mosquitoes. Ugh! It smelled like rotten eggs!

My nature group was exploring the Oxbow Nature Reserve with Terry, our guide. The area was once a lake that is slowly becoming land. What does that make it now? It is a swamp, and a frustrating place for canoeing.

"Don't go near the shore!" called Terry. Too late! My friend Erin and I were already stuck. We got out to free the canoe, and our feet sank into the muddy bottom. As we slogged through mud up to our knees, we truly understood what it means to feel "bogged down." We now call that famous field trip the "bog slog."

> In my final paper, I added sensory words that showed my attitude. I also added different sentence types.

Reading as a Writer

What words help you know how Natalie feels about her setting? How can you change your narrative to make your feelings clear?

TARGET VOCABULARY

debate

prodded

gradually

decorated

beckoned

scanned

inflated

stalled

shaken

hesitated

Vocabulary Reader

Context Cards

Vocabulary in Context

1 debate
This class held a debate to discuss which project helps their school the most.

2 prodded
No one needed to be prodded, or pushed, to buy an item at this class bake sale.

3 gradually
The graph shows that gradually, or little by little, the class will get funds for a field trip.

4 decorated
Students decorated this room with crepe paper and balloons for the graduation ceremony.

- **Study each Context Card.**
- **Break the longer words into syllables. Use a dictionary to check your work.**

5 beckoned

The cheerleaders beckoned, or signaled, the fans to join them in a cheer for the team.

6 scanned

This library aide scanned the shelves, looking carefully for a certain book.

7 inflated

This student inflated balloons to decorate the classroom for a party.

8 stalled

When traffic in the halls has stalled, a hall monitor may need to move people along.

9 shaken

Although shaken by the height of the microphone, this boy gave a good speech.

10 hesitated

This student hesitated, or hung back, before she tried to answer her teacher's question.

Background

School Elections Has anyone ever beckoned to you and urged you to run for a school office? Perhaps the thought left you so shaken that you hesitated to get involved, but don't wait. Working in school government is a *good* thing.

If you are a student leader, you have a say in issues that affect everyone at school. You can help raise money for field trips, make rules of conduct, and organize community service. Gradually, over time, you can get things done. If a project is stalled, you can get it moving again. If you have made a list of issues and scanned it for important ones, you will know what to do.

If you run for office, you'll be prodded to take part in a debate. You'll have to speak from a stage decorated with balloons that your friends have inflated. Is that so bad, though? Think of the good you can do if elected!

Even if you don't run for office, be sure to vote!

Comprehension

✔ **TARGET SKILL** **Compare and Contrast**

As you read "Off and Running," compare and contrast the thoughts and behaviors of characters. Look for ways in which they are alike and different. Make a graphic organizer like the one below to help you compare and contrast characters.

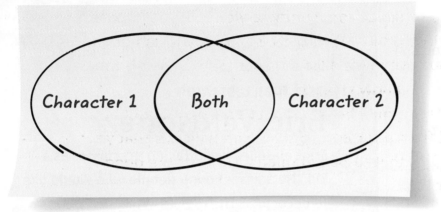

✔ **TARGET STRATEGY** **Infer/Predict**

Use your graphic organizer to help you infer what a character thinks, or to help you predict how he or she might act. Inferring and predicting will help you better understand the characters.

debate	scanned
prodded	inflated
gradually	stalled
decorated	shaken
beckoned	hesitated

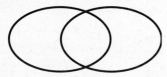

✔ **TARGET SKILL**

Compare and Contrast
Examine how two or more details or ideas are alike and different.

✔ **TARGET STRATEGY**

Infer/Predict Use text clues to figure out what the author means or what might happen in the future.

GENRE

Realistic fiction is a present-day story with events that could take place in real life.

MEET THE AUTHOR

Gary Soto

When Gary Soto was a boy, he thought he would grow up to study dinosaurs. Then in college he discovered poetry and started writing poems of his own. He has been a writer ever since. He gets his ideas from his own experiences, his Mexican-American heritage, and his imagination.

MEET THE ILLUSTRATOR

Eric Velasquez

Eric Velasquez loved taking art classes as a kid. He advises young people who would like to become artists to "draw, draw, draw, paint, paint, paint, read, read, read." He also loves old movies, which have inspired many of his illustrations.

Off and Running

by Gary Soto

selection illustrated by Eric Velasquez

Essential Question

What can our differences teach us?

Miata Ramirez is running for fifth-grade class president with her best friend, Ana, as her running mate. Also running is Rudy Herrera with his friend Alex. Miata has good ideas to improve the school, but Rudy is funny and popular. It will be a close race. Both students try to convince their classmates to vote for them when election speeches are held in front of the entire class.

Miata scanned the audience sitting on the floor in the multipurpose room, which was still decorated with banners for the sixteenth of September, Mexican Independence Day. The heads of the fifth-graders wagged like apples on a branch. Miata was nervous about the debate. But this was her big chance to tell the students why they should vote for her and not for Rudy.

Miata looked at Rudy sitting next to her. She could see that he was chewing gum, which was against school rules. He was smacking his lips and waving to the boys in the audience.

Blowing a bubble, Rudy turned to Miata. The bubble grew as large as a fist and popped like a fist in a baseball glove. He laughed and asked, "You want some gum?"

"No, it's against school rules," Miata said. "I'm not going to get in trouble just before elections."

"Oh yeah, that's right," Rudy said. He swallowed the bubble gum and opened his mouth like an alligator's. His throat blared "Ahhhhhhhhhh." He closed his mouth and said, "See, it's all gone."

"That's ugly, Rudy." Miata grimaced.

Rudy shrugged his shoulders. He turned his attention to the audience. Someone was yelling at Rudy to ask if he wanted to exchange his sandwich for a burrito during lunch. Rudy gave him a thumbs-up response.

Miata's nervous knees shivered, and the lines on her palms ran with sticky sweat. She looked down at the five MIATA AND ANA badges on the front of her blouse. Earlier they had seemed so neat, but now they just got in her way.

"People—fifth-graders—let's settle down," Mrs. Castillo, the vice principal, yelled above the noise. She repeated her command and gradually the bobbing heads stopped moving.

"Yeah, let's knock it off," Rudy yelled, getting to his feet. His gaze locked on two boys who were pushing each other. "Carlos, leave Jaime (HI meh) alone. Save it for the playground."

Carlos stopped shoving his friend and sat up as straight as an angel, which he was not.

"That's better," Rudy said. He then returned to his seat.

"Thank you, Rudy," Mrs. Castillo said.

"No problem," he said.

Mrs. Castillo turned to Miata and, with a smile, said sweetly, "We're going to hear from Miata first. She's in room six. Let's hear what she has to say."

STOP AND THINK

Author's Craft An author may use an **idiom**, a phrase whose meaning is different from the meanings of its individual words, to make dialogue more realistic and lively. Find the idiom Rudy uses when he speaks to the students. What does it mean?

There was light applause as Miata rose from her chair and approached the podium. She climbed onto a box that was set there for her. She adjusted the microphone.

"Good morning," Miata said.

"It's almost afternoon," Carlos yelled.

Miata looked at the clock on the wall and then at Carlos. She decided to ignore him. She continued with a bright chime in her voice. "I'm seeking your votes next Tuesday. I want to be your president."

"President of the United States?" Carlos yelled through the funnel of his hands.

With that, Mrs. Castillo, now stern faced, shook a finger at him. He returned to sitting as straight as an angel.

Miata breathed in as she gathered strength. She inflated her lungs and boomed, "If elected, I plan to beautify the school grounds. I want to get rid of all that *cholo* graffiti and put some flowers in by our fifth-grade rooms."

Some of the students, mostly girls, applauded.

"I'm sure you're tired of a *cochino*[1]-looking (koh CHEE noh) school," Miata boomed even louder.

There was more applause, but not enough to make Miata confident. She eyed Ana in the audience. Ana hadn't clapped that hard. Miata clicked her tongue and thought, Come on, Ana, let's get with it.

[1] *cochino*: dirty

"Those are good ideas," Ana remarked, not too bravely. She looked around at the audience. No one was applauding.

Miata paused, somewhat shaken. She had practiced with Ana on the school grounds, but now behind the podium the words didn't seem as powerful.

"I plan to get parents involved," Miata continued. "I want them to help with the cleanup."

Only one student applauded. It was Carlos. He was applauding as hard as rain on a car roof. He wouldn't stop until Mrs. Castillo beckoned him with a finger. He was being called out of the room. He rose to his feet and said, "I'll vote for you, Miata. You're nicer." Then, looking at Rudy, Carlos stepped over his classmates sitting on the floor. "Nah, I better vote for Rudy. I owe him a quarter." He was prodded from the multipurpose room toward the principal's office.

"Just think," Miata said, her voice weak. She was losing her confidence. "We can put some really nice azaleas and pansies outside our windows. The walls will be all clean, not like they are now." She looked at her scribbled notes, then up toward the audience. "It'll be work, but we can do it."

The audience scrunched up their faces.

"And I have plans for a school trip," Miata countered quickly, sensing that she was losing her listeners. "And I have a fund-raising idea for how we can get computers."

The audience yawned. Two posters that said VOTE FOR MIATA AND ANA sank down.

"I have a question," a boy said, his hand as tall as a spear.

"Yes."

"Are we gonna get paid to work?" His face was lit with a grin. He knew he was being silly.

"No, we're not getting paid. It's for our school."

The students muttered but applauded lightly. A few of the posters went up again in a rattle but quickly sank down.

"Please think of me when you vote on Tuesday," Miata said. Her voice was now as faint as a baby bird's chirp.

She sat down, exhausted. She wanted to shake her head in defeat but knew that she had to sit up bravely. She waved at the audience, but only a few students waved back. Not one of them was a boy.

Then Rudy stood up. He approached the podium and leaped up onto the box.

"Hey, I like this," he laughed. As he held on to the podium, he wobbled the box and said, "It's like a skateboard!"

The audience laughed. From where she sat, Miata could see that more than one boy was chewing bubble gum.

Rudy then became serious. He looked at Miata and said, "She's got some ideas. Miata would make a good prez, but I think I would make a truly great one."

The audience laughed.

"And you know why?" Rudy asked.

STOP AND THINK

Compare and Contrast How is the audience's reaction to Rudy different from its reaction to Miata?

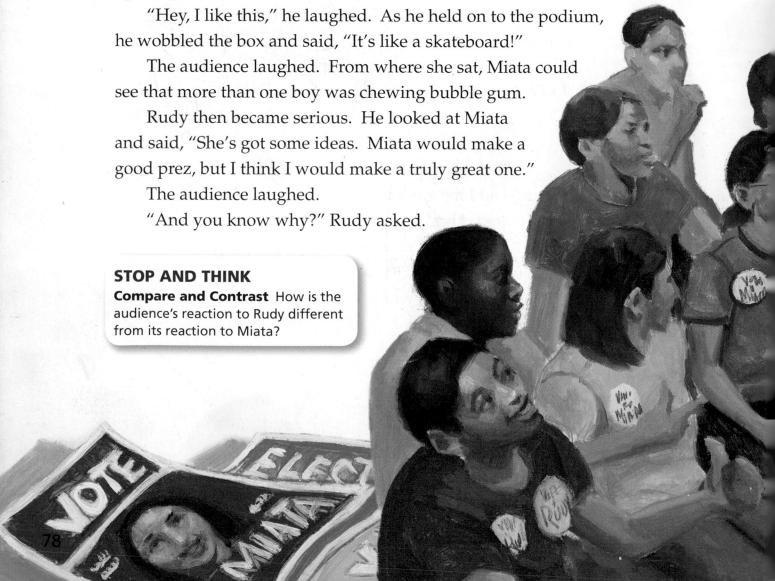

"Why?" some of the boys in the audience repeated.

Rudy turned a cupped ear to the audience. "I can't hear you."

"Why?" yelled a mixed group of boys and girls.

"Still can't hear you." Rudy smiled.

"*Why*?" the entire audience yelled.

Rudy nodded his head, smiling. He had their attention. "It's because . . . I'm going to work to get us more recess time."

The audience applauded and chanted, "More recess! More recess! More recess!"

"Yeah, *gente!*[2] (HEHN teh) Instead of just fifteen minutes, I'm going to ask the principal for twenty—at least! Maybe even half an hour, homeboys!"

[2] *gente*: people

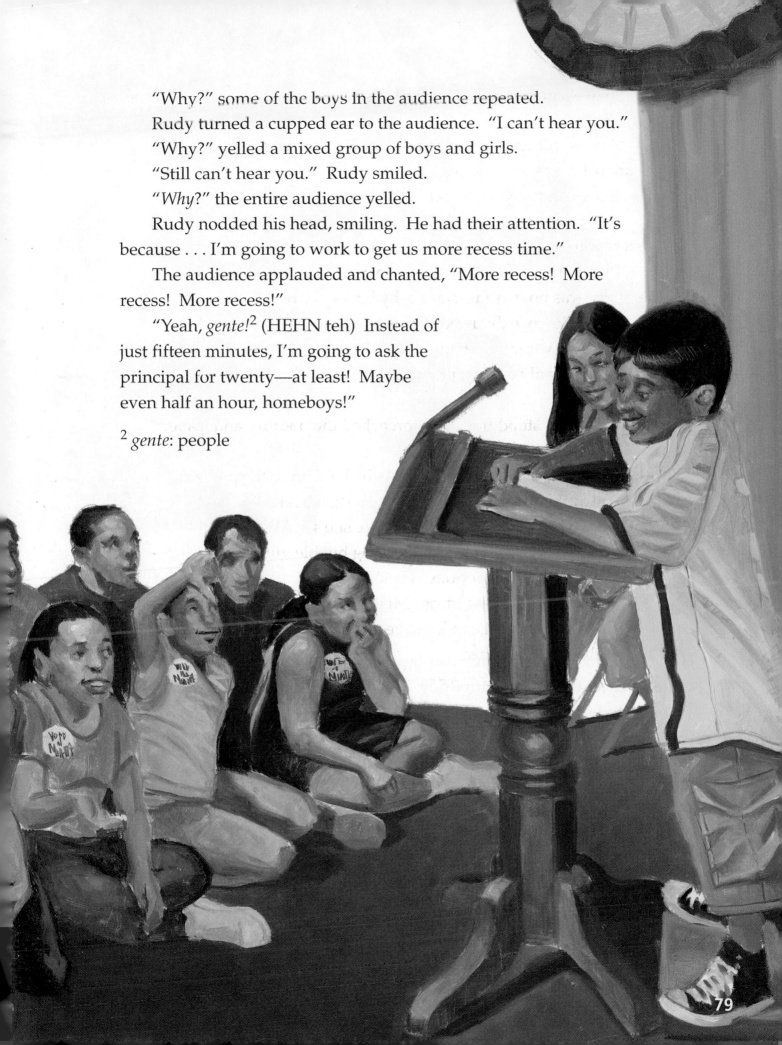

79

"Why not an hour?" someone yelled from the audience.

"We can't push our luck, dude," Rudy responded.

Miata wanted to cover her face. It was obvious that the audience was siding with Rudy.

Rudy raised his hands and asked for silence.

"Plus," he continued as he slowly scanned the audience. "Plus I'm going to ask for Ice Cream Day every day. Not just on Fridays."

The audience roared as Rudy wobbled the box and then jumped off. He returned to his seat, pushing a fresh piece of bubble gum into his mouth.

"You got good ideas," Rudy said with confidence. "Good luck. *Buena suerte*." (BWEH nah SWER teh) He extended a hand.

"Yeah, thanks. I'll need it," Miata said in a whisper as she stood up and shook Rudy's hand, which was as cool as a lizard's. "Good luck to you, too, Rudy."

After the debate, the students returned to their classrooms. Miata tried to put on a good face. Most of the girls knew that Rudy was a joker. They knew he could never get that extra five minutes of recess or Ice Cream Day five days a week. But the boys might believe him. Miata needed a new strategy.

STOP AND THINK
Infer/Predict Describe what happens in the story that makes Miata think she needs a new strategy. What do you think she will do?

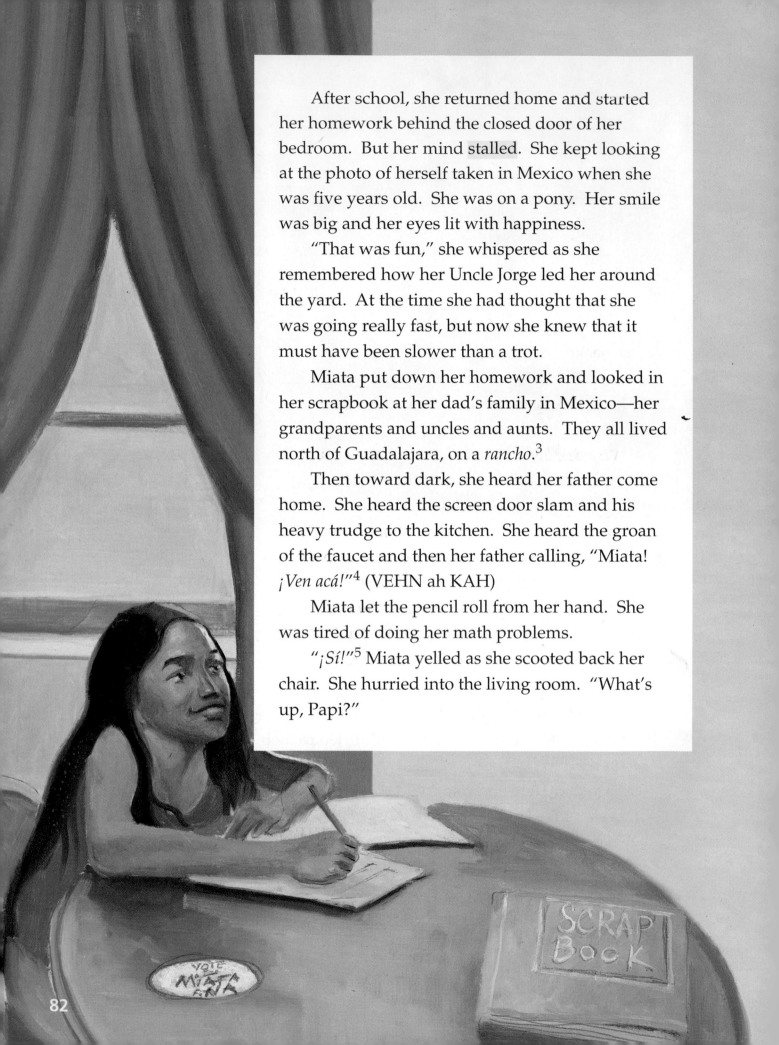

After school, she returned home and started her homework behind the closed door of her bedroom. But her mind stalled. She kept looking at the photo of herself taken in Mexico when she was five years old. She was on a pony. Her smile was big and her eyes lit with happiness.

"That was fun," she whispered as she remembered how her Uncle Jorge led her around the yard. At the time she had thought that she was going really fast, but now she knew that it must have been slower than a trot.

Miata put down her homework and looked in her scrapbook at her dad's family in Mexico—her grandparents and uncles and aunts. They all lived north of Guadalajara, on a *rancho*.[3]

Then toward dark, she heard her father come home. She heard the screen door slam and his heavy trudge to the kitchen. She heard the groan of the faucet and then her father calling, "Miata! *¡Ven acá!*"[4] (VEHN ah KAH)

Miata let the pencil roll from her hand. She was tired of doing her math problems.

"*¡Sí!*"[5] Miata yelled as she scooted back her chair. She hurried into the living room. "What's up, Papi?"

"I found something at work."

"What?"

"A most unusual thing."

"What is it? Tell me."

He was holding a small white box in his hand.

"It scared me when I found it." Her father's face was dark with worry and dust from his long hours at work.

Miata furrowed her brow. She was curious.

Slowly her father lifted the lid from the box. Miata peeked in, standing on her tiptoes. In it stood an adult index finger that was as gnarled as a root. She eyed her father and clicked her tongue.

"Where do you think it came from, *mi'ja*[6] (ME hah)?" her father asked seriously. He petted the finger with his free hand.

"From your left hand, Papi," Miata answered, hands on her hips. "That's where it came from."

A sudden smile brightened his face. He wiggled the finger in the box and screamed, "*Ay,*[7] (EYE) it's coming alive. I better put it down the garbage disposal." He ran into the kitchen laughing, and Miata followed her father. But he only got himself another glass of water.

[3] *rancho*: ranch or large farm

[4] *¡Ven acá!*: Come here!

[5] *¡Sí!*: Yes!

[6] *mi'ja*: my dear; my daughter

[7] *Ay*: Uh-oh

"Dad?" Miata asked, taking his large work-stained hand into hers.

"Yeah, *mi'ja*." He wiped his mouth with the back of his free hand.

"Do you think I should run for office?" She hesitated and then continued. "I mean, I'm not as popular as Rudy or his friend Alex."

"Well, popularity is one thing, but service is another. *¿Entiendes?*" [8] (ehn TYEHN dehs)

Miata shook her head. She was confused.

"I mean, it's OK to have a lot of people who like you, but it's far better to help people, to get things done." He gave her a light hug. "Don't worry. Just go for it. If it doesn't happen, *pues*,[9] (PWEHS) you can still do good."

Miata liked that. She had plans for the school, and they were good ones.

[8] *¿Entiendes?*: Do you understand?
[9] *pues*: then

Your Turn

What It Takes

Reflect and Write In "Off and Running," a candidate's popularity seems nearly as important as his or her ideas for improving the school. If you were voting for class president, which would be more important to you—a candidate's popularity or his or her ideas for school improvement? Write a paragraph explaining your answer. PERSONAL RESPONSE

Campaign Talk

Give a Speech Work with a partner to play the roles of a person running for class president and his or her running mate. Brainstorm a list of appealing but impossible promises you might make to your classmates. Then hold a debate with another pair of classmates to see whose promises are more outrageous.

PARTNERS

Just Go for It

Turn and Talk Think about the strategies Miata and Rudy use in their campaigns for class president. Then discuss the strategies with a partner. Compare and contrast the two candidates and how they work to gain the support of their classmates. COMPARE AND CONTRAST

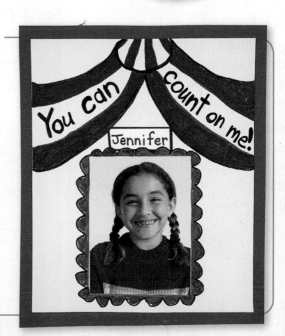

✓ **TARGET VOCABULARY**

debate	scanned
prodded	inflated
gradually	stalled
decorated	shaken
beckoned	hesitated

GENRE

Persuasive text, such as these campaign advertisements, seeks to convince the reader to think or act in a certain way.

TEXT FOCUS

Persuasive techniques are ways an author tries to convince a reader to think or act in a certain way.

Media Literacy The techniques used in a persuasive text may be different from the techniques used in a persuasive commerical.

VOTE FOR ME!

by Pamela Zarn

A class election debate is not the only method candidates have to convince other students to vote for them. If you have hesitated to run for office because public speaking leaves you feeling shaken, or if you feel your campaign efforts have stalled, try creating election advertisements to catch people's interest.

Posters are a great way to advertise your strengths. Use short sentences and bold, clear lettering so that your message can be easily scanned by students as they pass on the way to class. Posters are also a great way to reach those students who may need to be beckoned or prodded into going to the polls to vote.

Read the campaign posters below and on page 88. Think about how the candidates' posters persuade you to vote for them. How do the techniques differ from a commercial on television?

The candidate provides a call to action. It is short and punchy. A few words are better than a paragraph.

The poster is decorated with an eye-catching image of a pizza, which helps to associate the candidate with something kids like.

She makes a generalization.

She makes a promise. You should ask yourself if it is an exaggerated promise.

She asks a question with emotional appeal. Most ads want you to feel before you think.

IF YOU LIKE PIZZA, VOTE NATASHA!

Everybody loves pizza! Wouldn't you like pizza for lunch EVERY day? If you vote for Natasha, our cafeteria will never be without pizza again!

He begins with a short, eye-catching campaign slogan. The easier it is to remember, the better.

The candidate's poster includes inflated balloons in the school colors for emotional appeal.

He gives supporting examples of his strengths. Always check to see if the information in ads is true.

He lists his strengths.

He makes a promise. His promise is one that will make students feel good about him.

VOTE JARED
HE HAS WHAT IT TAKES!

- Leadership: soccer team co-captain
- Communication: member of student-teacher council
- Action: leader in the class fund-raiser

I will listen to fifth-graders and do what it takes to get what they want!

Whom would you vote for?
Did one of these posters catch your eye right away, or did you gradually decide which candidate you favor?

Making Connections

Recognize Exaggerated Statements Many candidates running for office exaggerate what they will do when elected. In "Off and Running," which candidate exaggerates what he or she will do? Give examples from the text. Then write a brief campaign speech for class president telling what changes you would make and why classmates should vote for you. Deliver your speech to a small group. Maintain eye contact to make your points effectively.

 Text to Text

Make a Poster Review Rudy's and Miata's campaign speeches in "Off and Running." Think about which candidate would be most likely to get your vote. Then choose one of them and create a campaign poster for him or her. Use the posters and information in "Vote for Me!" to help you develop your candidate's message.

 Text to World

Connect to Social Studies The candidates in "Off and Running" want to take a leadership role in their school. With a partner, use print resources or the Internet to gather information about two important elected leaders. Note the leadership qualities that have made them successful. Then compare and contrast their leadership qualities.

Grammar

What Is a Compound Sentence? A **compound sentence** is a sentence made up of two shorter sentences joined by a comma and the word *and, but,* or *or.* Each part of a compound sentence has its own **complete subject** and **complete predicate**.

complete subject	complete predicate	comma	complete subject	complete predicate

Miata sits quietly, but her opponent yells to the crowd.

In each part of a compound sentence, a present-tense verb and its subject must agree in number. This agreement is known as subject-verb agreement.

plural subject	plural form of verb	singular subject	singular form of verb

Two boys scuffle, and Rudy hollers at them.

Try This! **Find the errors in these compound sentences. Which do not contain proper subject-verb agreement? Where should commas be placed? Write the sentences correctly on another sheet of paper.**

❶ Miata presents her plan and students clap.

❷ Ana and Carlos disappoints Miata and she feels sad.

❸ Some boys chew gum but no one stop them.

Sentence Fluency In your writing, you might find pairs of sentences that are related in some way. Try combining the sentences using a comma and the word *and*, *but*, or *or*.

Related Sentences

Several girls supported Jeanne.

Eddie was popular with almost everyone.

Compound Sentence

Several girls supported Jeanne, but Eddie was popular with almost everyone.

Connect Grammar to Writing

As you revise your writing, look for related sentences that you can rewrite as compound sentences, using a comma and the word *and, but,* or *or.* Be sure to use proper subject-verb agreement.

Write to Express

☑ Word Choice Good **dialogue** in a narrative sounds natural and expresses the personalities and feelings of the characters who are speaking. Dialogue can make your narrative more realistic.

Brad drafted a narrative in which two or more characters provoke a reaction in each other. Later, he changed some words to make the dialogue sound more natural. Use the Writing Traits Checklist below as you revise your writing.

Writing Traits Checklist

☑ Ideas
Does the dialogue reveal a problem or conflict?

☑ Organization
Do the words of one speaker cause a reaction in another?

☑ Sentence Fluency
Do details show more about my characters?

☑ Word Choice
Did I choose words that reveal different feelings and personalities?

☑ Voice
Do the speakers' words sound natural?

☑ Conventions
Did I use correct spelling, grammar, and punctuation?

Revised Draft

"Writing history skits is a blast!"
~~"You will enjoy writing skits,"~~ said

Ms. Ghose, the fifth-grade social

studies teacher.
                "In your dreams,"
~~"I don't think I will like it much,"~~

muttered Evan as he sat down with

his group. He could see that he would

have to be the leader.

History Superhero
by Brad Baumgartner

"Writing history skits is a blast!" said Ms. Ghose, the fifth-grade social studies teacher.

"In your dreams," muttered Evan as he sat down with his group. He could see that he would have to be the leader. "Okay, let's decide who we'll be. How about George and Martha Washington?"

"That is so pathetic," said Derek, who thought everything was pathetic and who rarely smiled. Kalil yawned. Nothing interested him except superheroes. Jolene sketched in her notebook and didn't look up.

"Wait!" said Evan. "How about making George a superhero with secret powers, but nobody knows it, not even Martha. Kalil could be George."

"Okay," said Kalil. "I could go with that." Jolene stopped sketching and looked up. Best of all, Derek actually smiled.

> In my final paper, I changed words to sound more like my characters. I also used a comma and the word *but* to combine sentences.

Reading as a Writer

How does Brad show his characters' personalities? What dialogue could help your narrative show more about your characters?

competition

identical

routine

element

intimidated

unison

recite

qualifying

uniform

mastered

Vocabulary Reader

Context Cards

Vocabulary in Context

1 **competition**
A contest between evenly matched teams makes for an exciting competition.

2 **identical**
The clothing worn by members of a team is often exactly alike, or identical.

3 **routine**
This coach is explaining a routine, or set course of action, that the team must learn.

4 **element**
Speed is an important part, or element, of many team sports, such as hockey.

- **Study each Context Card.**

- **Make up a new context sentence that uses two Vocabulary words.**

---

5 intimidated

Smaller players might be intimidated, or frightened, by larger players.

---

6 unison

These rowers must work in unison to win. They must move their oars as one.

---

7 recite

Cheerleaders recite a cheer to urge the team to win. Then they shout out another.

---

8 qualifying

This team won three earlier races, qualifying them to take part in the finals.

---

9 uniform

Professional baseball fields are uniform in size. Bases are always ninety feet apart.

---

10 mastered

The medals these girls won show that they have mastered their athletic skills.

Background

✔ TARGET VOCABULARY **What Is Double Dutch?** Double Dutch is a game of jump rope with a twist. There are *two* ropes, identical in length, that are turned in different directions.

A double Dutch team has at least three or four members, including two rope turners and one or two jumpers. Teams practice long and hard to perfect a fancy routine. Two jumpers can hop with different footwork and tricks or in unison. Turners often recite rhymes to help jumpers keep a uniform rhythm.

Teams that have mastered double Dutch may want to try qualifying for a competition. This sport is difficult, but don't be intimidated. It also has an element of art to it. It's as much fun to watch as it is to do!

• Read aloud with a partner the directions for "Turning the Ropes." Describe the positions of your wrists and hands as you turn the rope.

Turning the Ropes

❶ Turning partners face each other.

❷ Hold the end of a rope in each hand.

❸ Hold the ropes waist high, shoulder-width apart.

❹ The middle of each rope should just touch the floor.

❺ Stand straight with legs shoulder-width apart.

❻ Turn the right-hand rope counterclockwise and the left-hand rope clockwise.

❼ Keep wrists locked and hands closed in a fist, with the thumbs up.

Comprehension

✓ **TARGET SKILL** **Sequence of Events**

Sequence is a text structure that nonfiction authors can use to organize text. Events are written in chronological order. As you read "Double Dutch," notice how the selection follows a sequential order. Look for time-order words and phrases, such as *years ago*, *first*, and *Friday*. Then make a graphic organizer like the one below to show the sequence of events in the selection.

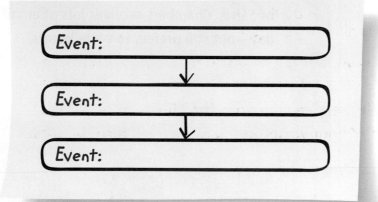

Event:

↓

Event:

↓

Event:

✓ **TARGET STRATEGY** **Monitor/Clarify**

Use sequence of events and your graphic organizer to help clarify events and actions that you don't understand in a selection. Monitoring and clarifying help you understand the order of events and their importance.

DOUBLE DUTCH
A Celebration of Jump Rope, Rhymes, and Sisterhood

VERONICA CHAMBERS

✔ TARGET VOCABULARY

competition	unison
identical	recite
routine	qualifying
element	uniform
intimidated	mastered

✔ TARGET SKILL

Sequence of Events
Identify the time order in which events take place.

✔ TARGET STRATEGY

Monitor/Clarify As you read, notice what isn't making sense. Find ways to figure out the parts that are confusing.

GENRE

Narrative nonfiction gives informational text by telling a true story.

Set Purpose Set a purpose for reading based on what you know about the genre and your background knowledge.

MEET THE AUTHOR

Veronica Chambers

Veronica Chambers was born in Panama. When she was five, she moved to New York City, where she got her first library card and learned to jump double Dutch. She loves to travel and learn new languages. She can speak English, Spanish, Japanese, and French. Her books for young people include novels about best friends Marisol and Magdalena, and the biography *Celia Cruz, Queen of Salsa*. Chambers receives lots of email each day—but still prefers to write letters.

DOUBLE DUTCH

A Celebration of Jump Rope, Rhyme, and Sisterhood

by Veronica Chambers

Essential Question

What events lead a team to learn double Dutch?

ROCKETT GIRLS

It's early Saturday morning, and five girls gather in the gymnasium of Reed Junior High School in Central Islip, Long Island. They are a multiracial group: white, black, and brown, but each girl is dressed in a matching red tracksuit. When they jump into the double-Dutch ropes, each head bobs with an identical ponytail. They are a team. And what's more, each girl, averaging only thirteen years old, knows what it's like to be a winner. The Snazzy Steppers, as this team is called, are the New York City champions. They are also ranked fifth in the world.

As they unfold their ropes and begin to jump, they are intensely silent. They don't sing songs; they don't recite rhymes. Peggy and Debbie jump in to rehearse their doubles routine. They move in unison, which isn't easy, and they execute even the most complex moves with a uniform grace. It's as if they were rowers on the same boat, their arms and legs slicing and curving together. The two turners offer up tips and criticism. "Don't go faster than the rope," Lanieequah reminds her teammates. Sometimes, the entire team catches a case of the giggles, prompting their coach to insist they focus harder. "I'm not laughing," Peggy mutters. "Yes, you were," whispers Debbie. "I smile and then you laugh."

In the ropes, it seems that the Steppers defy gravity. They do handstands and back-flips. They bend to touch their feet and kick their legs as high as Radio City Rockettes. But they are something even better. They are astronauts of the asphalt, rocket girls limited only by their imagination and their unbelievably limber, athletic bodies.

Coach Rockett

Life for the Snazzy Steppers wasn't always so sweet. It was only five years ago that these girls couldn't jump double Dutch at all. Their coach, David Rockett, started the team eight years ago when he became frustrated with the lack of positive activities for kids in the public school where he teaches. "One recess, I was looking out the window of my classroom," says Coach Rockett. "Some of the kids were doing double Dutch on the playground. I was fascinated by the call-and-response element, the rhythms, and the movement." The very next day, Rockett went to the local hardware store and bought a couple hundred yards of clothesline. He made a flyer inviting students to form a double-Dutch team. Forty girls showed up!

Coach Rockett was thrilled but intimidated. Most of the girls had no double-Dutch experience. He'd have to teach them; but first, he had to learn himself! No small feat for a forty-something white guy from the 'burbs. But Coach Rockett was determined to see his girls fly. He visited other schools and playgrounds, asking kids for lessons. He studied books about jump rope and scanned the Internet for competition tips and news. In just a few short months, he had mastered the game. Coach Rockett even wrote a song to help teach his girls how to jump:

✔ STOP AND THINK
Sequence of Events What are the steps Coach Rockett took to create a double-Dutch team? List the steps in sequential order.

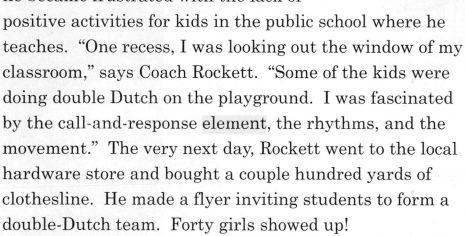

My name is Franny.
I'm the rainbow frog.
Inside the ropes
I'm a double-Dutch star!

Bring three friends together,
who share the same dream.
Two turners and one jumper
make a winning jump-rope team!

Let's start with two ropes,
turners hold the ends.
Don't drop the ropes,
or you'll have to start again.

Bend your knees slightly,
with your feet set apart.
Spin those ropes round and round,
you're off to a good start.

Can you imagine an eggbeater
as it spins round and round?
That's how the ropes look
as they slap on the ground.

Come gather around, friends.
We're going to have some fun
singing and jumping
double Dutch.

Coach Rockett taught the girls all he knew, and then they attended their first competition in Harlem. The girls were pulverized. Back in Central Islip, it had seemed that they were so talented! Everyone at Reed Junior High School was impressed by the way they could do flips and somersaults in the rope. Sure, at home, the Snazzy Steppers were so baaaaad, they were good, but the teams in Harlem were faster, bolder, smoother, and sassier. The girls left Harlem with no trophies and their confidence ripped to pieces. "It was the most painful thing to watch. They thought they were all that," remembers Coach Rockett. "Then they saw double Dutch for the first time. The girls hid in the bathroom at the competition, feigning illness. They were so scared. They knew they were one of the weakest teams in the league."

STOP AND THINK

Monitor/Clarify How did the team turn themselves into champions? Read ahead to the next paragraph to see if you can find the answer.

I had a little puppy.
His name was Tiny Tim.
I put him in the bathtub,
to see if he could swim.

He drank all the water,
he swallowed a bar of soap.
Next thing you know,
it was halfway down his
throat.

In jumps the doctor.
In jumps the nurse.
In jumps the lady with
the alligator purse.

Out jumps the doctor.
Out jumps the nurse.
Out jumps the lady with
the alligator purse.

STOP AND THINK
Author's Craft Notice the rhythm,
or the way you stress words, in
the poem above. Why is rhythm
important in double-Dutch rhymes?

The Snazzy Steppers were down but by no means out. Each year, they returned to competition a little stronger. First, they won fifth place, then fourth, then third, then second. Finally, after a lot of hard work, they grabbed the number-one spot in New York City, qualifying for the world championships. They've been flying high ever since. They've also become the best of friends. "It's a funny math," says Coach Rockett. "In double Dutch, one plus one plus one doesn't equal three. One plus one plus one equals one. You have to be tight. If you and I are turning and we have even the tiniest bit of animosity toward each other, it comes out on the ropes. You're trying to get kids to care about each other, to learn about each other, to nurture each other. When it works—when a team comes together—it makes for a powerful group of young women."

Each of the Snazzy Steppers has her favorite element of competition:

"Speed is my favorite thing. The challenge of it," says Debbie.

"Freestyle. It's where you get to express yourself," says Erika.

"My favorite thing is . . . the trophies!" says Katelyn.

"My best moment was when I learned the karate kick, when I was in the third grade. It's such an easy trick, but it was my first trick. The first time I ever showed some style in the rope," says Peggy.

"I'm the only girl on the team who came in knowing street double Dutch. It's different from competitive jumping. In street rope, you jump long and fast. In competition, you're slowing down the rope so you can catch the trick. It was almost harder than learning from scratch. My style had to change," says Lanieequah.

DOUBLE DUTCH IS . . .

"**. . . fearlessness.** The audacious willingness to jump in and mix things up when life is sweeping over you from all sides in incessant, overwhelming waves. The skill—ultimately, the thrill—is not in stopping the flow, but in keeping pace with rhythm."

> —Lynette Clementson,
> reporter for the *New York Times*

"**. . . confidence in motion.**
Double Dutch is bodies in motion, not decoration: strong, glorious, exultant.

Double Dutch is glorious."

> —Peggy Orenstein,
> award-winning author of *School Girls*

Your Turn

✎ Being Number One

Short Response What do you think it takes to become really good at something? Write a paragraph summarizing the experiences you have had while trying to master a sport, hobby, or skill. Explain what you learned about yourself from those experiences.

PERSONAL RESPONSE

💡 Jump, Jump

Tricky Routines Work with a group to create a routine for the Snazzy Steppers, highlighting the footwork and tricks you would like to see them use in a competition. Then perform the routine for the class, either with or without jump ropes.

SMALL GROUP

Face the Challenge

Turn and Talk Think about the Snazzy Steppers' defeat at the team's first competition. Discuss with a partner how this painful experience contributed to the Snazzy Steppers' later success. What steps did the team take to master double Dutch?

SEQUENCE OF EVENTS

Poetry

competition	unison
identical	recite
routine	qualifying
element	uniform
intimidated	mastered

GENRE

Poetry uses the sound and rhythm of words in a variety of forms to suggest images and express feelings.

TEXT FOCUS

Rhyme Poets often use rhyming words to create a rhythm, focus on an image, or heighten certain feelings.

• As you read "Deanie McLeanie" on page 112, think about how the poet's use of rhyme makes you feel about the poem's subject and meaning.

SCORE!

Winning is not the only element of sports. Many people love to watch a pair of figure skaters spinning in unison. Some are awed by the precision of a gymnast's balance beam routine. For others, teamwork on the basketball court brings them the greatest satisfaction.

Though no two athletes are identical, they all share one thing: the love of sports. The following poems celebrate the joy, beauty, and sportsmanship of athletics in its many forms.

Good Sportsmanship
by Richard Armour

Good sportsmanship we hail, we sing,
It's always pleasant when you spot it.
There's only one unhappy thing:
You have to lose to prove you've got it.

This poem by Jane Yolen shows that karate is much more than a
competition. Those who have mastered karate must also have grace
and discipline, and they must know how to use their skill wisely.

Karate Kid

by Jane Yolen

I am wind,
I am wall,
I am wave,
I rise, I fall,
I am crane
In lofty flight,
Training that
I need not fight.

I am tiger,
I am tree,
I am flower,
I am knee,
I am elbow,
I am hands
Taught to do
The heart's commands.

Not to bully,
Not to fight,
Dragon left
And leopard right.
Wind and wave,
Tree and flower,
Chop.
      Kick.
            Peace.
                  Power.

111

Deanie McLeanie

by Walter Dean Myers

Deanie McLeanie is a basketball genie
Six foot seven from his sneakers to his beanie

He wears a fourteen jersey and a fifteen shoe
And there's nothing on the court that the kid can't do

He can scoop, he can loop
He can put it through the hoop

He can ram, he can slam
He can do the flying jam

He can tap, he can rap
He can snatch it with a slap

He can dunk, he can plunk
He can stop and make the junk

He can shake, he can bake
He can lose you with a fake

He can pin, he can win
He can do the copter spin

Cause Deanie McLeanie's a basketball genie
Six foot seven from his sneakers to his beanie

He wears a fourteen jersey and a fifteen shoe
And there's nothing on the court that the kid can't do.

WRITE A SPORTS POEM

Write a poem based on a memory of a sporting event you participated in or watched. Think about the feelings you had. Perhaps you felt intimidated by an opponent or excited when your favorite team won a qualifying event. As you write, use the poems in this lesson for inspiration. Include rhyme, repetition, or a uniform rhythm to emphasize emotion and action. Recite your poem to a friend when you are finished.

Making Connections

 Text to Self

Write a Poem You have read several poems relating to sports and athletes. Write a poem or song about your favorite freetime activity. Try to use rhyme, rhythm, and sound to show how you feel about the activity. Remember that rhyme is a sound device that can create rhythm or a certain feeling.

 Text to Text

Compare Poems With a partner, choose one poem from "Double Dutch" and one from "Score!" Take turns reading the poems aloud. Notice the sound effects the poets use, such as rhyme, rhythm, and repetition. Then make a list of similarities and differences between the sound elements used in the two poems. For each poem, write a sentence about how the rhyming words reinforce the poem's meaning.

 Text to World

Summarize a Sports Article "Double Dutch" originally appeared as an article in *The New York Times*. Look through a local newspaper and choose a sports article that interests you. Note the main ideas and supporting details from the article, and summarize those points for a classmate.

Grammar

What Is a Common Noun? What Is a Proper Noun?
When you talk or write about a general person, place, or thing, you use a **common noun**. When you talk or write about a particular person, place, or thing, you use a **proper noun**. Capitalize every proper noun.

Common Nouns	Proper Nouns
boy	Al Moniz
street	Century Boulevard

The name of an organization is a proper noun. Capitalize every important word in the name. Some organizations use a name made up of **initials,** or the first letter of each important word. If a name made from initials can be read as a word, it is called an **acronym**. Acronyms and other names made of initials are written with all capital letters. An **abbreviation** is a shortened form of a word. An abbreviation of a proper noun begins with a capital letter and usually ends with a period.

Name of organization: Uptown Jump Rope Club
Organization name made up of initials: SCA (Sports Clubs of America)
Acronym: NATO [NAY toh] (North Atlantic Treaty Organization)
Abbreviation: Mr. (Mister)

Turn and Talk **Work with a partner. In the sentences below, find a common noun, a proper noun, the name of an organization, a name made up of initials, and an acronym.**

❶ My sister wants to work for NASA or the FBI.

❷ She is a member of the Lubbock Junior Scientists Club.

❸ Her hero is Sally Ride.

Conventions You have learned to capitalize important words in names of organizations. You have also learned to capitalize all letters in acronyms and in other names made of initials. When you proofread your work, make sure you have capitalized each of these correctly.

Incorrect Capitalization	Correct Capitalization
Wed. Oct. 8 7:00 P.M.	Wed. Oct. 8 7:00 P.M.
Come to a lecture by dr. Roberta price of the American double dutch Association. You may know it by its acronym, Adda. Dr. price has appeared many times on programs on Pbs, the Public Broadcasting system.	Come to a lecture by Dr. Roberta Price of the American Double Dutch Association. You may know it by its acronym, ADDA. Dr. Price has appeared many times on programs on PBS, the Public Broadcasting System.

Connect Grammar to Writing

As you revise your fictional narrative, look for proper nouns of all kinds. If you find a proper noun that you have not capitalized correctly, rewrite it with correct capitalization.

Write to Express

☑ **Ideas** Good writers explore their topic before they write a draft. As you prepare to write your **fictional narrative**, ask yourself questions such as *Who? Where? What?* Write down words and phrases that you might build into a story.

Chermaine decided to write about a school event. While thinking about her topic, she made notes about her characters, setting, and events. Later, she organized her ideas into a story map. Use the Writing Process Checklist below as you prewrite.

Writing Process Checklist

▶ **Prewrite**

☑ Do I have enough ideas for a story?

☑ Who are my characters?

☑ Where and when does my story take place?

☑ What are the most important events?

☑ Did I include a problem and a solution?

Draft

Revise

Edit

Publish and Share

Exploring a Topic

Who? two kids from one basketball team
two kids from another team

Where? school playground basketball court

What? argue about using the hoop
compete in the playoff game

Story Map

Characters	Setting
Jed and Elly: good kids Ike and Chantal: bullies	School playground with one basketball hoop

Plot

Problem: Some players can't practice because bullies hog the basketball hoop.

Event 1: Jed and Elly are chosen to lead their class team.

Event 2: Ike and Chantal won't let them use the hoop.

Event 3: Jed and Elly ⋀secretly practice early every morning.

Solution: Jed and Elly's team wins the big game. Everyone is surprised!
⋀

I got some new ideas as I was making my story map. I started adding details about the plot.

Reading as a Writer

How did Chermaine's story map help her develop new ideas? What ideas could you add to your story map?

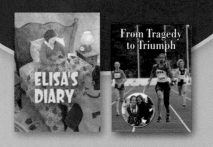

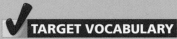

TARGET VOCABULARY

opponents

brutal

supposedly

gorgeous

embarrassed

obvious

typically

preliminary

sweeping

officially

Vocabulary Reader	Context Cards

Vocabulary in Context

1 opponents

There must be at least two opponents, or rivals, in any competition.

2 brutal

Harsh, or brutal, weather can make running on the field very difficult.

3 supposedly

A school is supposedly, or thought to be, where children learn about the world.

4 gorgeous

Male parrots have gorgeous feathers. The rich colors help them compete for mates.

- **Study each Context Card.**
- **Use a dictionary or a glossary to help you pronounce the Vocabulary words.**

5 embarrassed

Don't be embarrassed or ashamed if you have tried your best but failed to win.

6 obvious

A clear photo of the finish line makes the winner of the race obvious.

7 typically

Plants compete for light. Typically, or usually, those that get more light grow faster.

8 preliminary

When strangers meet, shaking hands may be the preliminary, or first, thing they do.

9 sweeping

The winner of the election made a broad, sweeping gesture to thank her supporters.

10 officially

The judges officially declared this lamb to be the winner of the first-place blue ribbon.

Background

✔ **TARGET VOCABULARY** **Newcomers** In the next story, Elisa moves to the United States from Puerto Rico. She has to overcome her fears about fitting in at a new school and speaking English.

The first weeks at school in a new country can be a brutal experience. Some students might take a sweeping glance at their new classroom and feel as if their new classmates are opponents, but, typically, students are curious to learn about one another—the hobbies they have or the gorgeous places they may have visited. The new country's customs may not be obvious, and new students may feel embarrassed if they fail to follow them. Learning a supposedly easy language that is officially spoken in a new country can be a real challenge. It is important to remember what it is like to be a newcomer.

Ways to Make Newcomers Feel Welcome

1. Introduce yourself to newcomers.

2. Invite them to sit with you at lunch or join in a game.

3. Give new students a preliminary tour of the school to help them feel at home.

- Which of the three ways listed above would make you feel most comfortable? Why?

Comprehension

✔ **TARGET SKILL** **Theme**

You can determine the theme, or main message, of a story by analyzing the main character's qualities, motives, and actions. Qualities are personality traits that make a character think and act in certain ways. A character's motives are the reasons for his or her behavior. A character's actions show how he or she responds to conflict and to other characters in the story. As you read "Elisa's Diary," ask yourself what important life lesson the main character learns. This lesson is the story's theme. Use a graphic organizer like the one below to help you determine the story's theme.

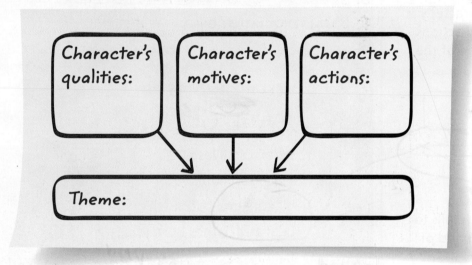

✔ **TARGET STRATEGY** **Visualize**

As you read, remember to pause and visualize, or form a picture in your mind of, what you are reading. Use sensory details in the selection to help you create a vivid mental picture of characters or events as you read.

✔ **TARGET VOCABULARY**

opponents	obvious
brutal	typically
supposedly	preliminary
gorgeous	sweeping
embarrassed	officially

✔ **TARGET SKILL**

Theme Examine character's qualities, motives, and actions to recognize the theme of the story.

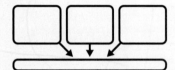

✔ **TARGET STRATEGY**

Visualize Use text details to form pictures in your mind of what you are reading.

GENRE

Realistic Fiction is a story with events that could happen in real life.

Set a Purpose Set a purpose for reading based on the genre and your background knowledge.

MEET THE AUTHOR

Doris Luisa Oronoz

Doris Luisa Oronoz and her family moved from Puerto Rico to the United States. Afterwards her children went through experiences and feelings very similar to those that Elisa goes through. Oronoz has said that although this story is not based on real events, the emotions of Elisa's character are drawn from her memory. They are a meditation on the joys and difficulties children encounter when they move to a new place.

MEET THE ILLUSTRATOR

Byron Gin

Byron Gin lives near Chicago, Illinois with his wife and two cats, Bear and Kathe. Born in California, Gin worked as an illustrator and printmaker before becoming a full-time painter. One group of his paintings, Street Series, captures people Gin has glimpsed while walking through downtown Chicago.

ELISA'S DIARY

by Doris Luisa Oronoz
Illustrated by Byron Gin

Essential Question

How does a character learn an important lesson?

"Today is the saddest day of my life," Elisa wrote in her diary on March 25th. She was going to continue, but her father knocked on the door and said, "It's nine o'clock, dear. Turn off the lights and go to sleep." Elisa put her pen and notebook away in her backpack and promptly obeyed.

In the semidarkness she could just make out the objects in her room. She had been here before, but it seemed to her as though it were the first time. The bright, vivid colors of her bedspread, which she liked so much, now seemed cold and muted.

Elisa looked at the little porcelain squirrel and remembered the day it was given to her. It was the first time she visited this country. She had come to spend some time with her grandmother. One night she heard a sound like something scratching under the eave of the house. She became frightened thinking that it might be mice and she ran to ask her grandmother.

Grandma took her to the patio and motioned to her to be very quiet. When they reached the back, she saw two squirrels playing on the roof right above her room. They were sliding down a branch and jumping onto the roof tiles to gather acorns. Then they would run back to the branch and do it all over again.

There were no squirrels in her country. This was something new, and she enjoyed it so much that when her vacation was over, Grandma bought her the squirrel figurine and put it on her night table.

"It will be right here waiting for you when you get back."

"I'll be back soon, Grandma. I love this place. Maybe some day I'll come and live with you."

But that was then and this is now.

"Who needs squirrels?" she asked herself.

She closed her eyes and breathed deeply. She was tired. It had been a long day that for some reason had gone slowly. That morning she had been in Puerto Rico and now she was in the United States of America. Except that this time, supposedly, it was forever. A tear rolled down her cheek and hit the pillow.

Elisa was ten years old. Her brother Francisco was twelve. She would have liked to have gone to the same school as he. That way she would feel protected. But of course, boys at that age typically don't want anything to do with their little sisters.

"He's unbearable," she thought aloud. Just then, her brother came in.

"Who's unbearable?" asked Francisco.

"You," answered Elisa, holding nothing back.

"Oh? Why is that?" asked her brother, surprised.

"Because you leave me alone all day while you're out running around."

"It's obvious that you're afraid to go out," answered her brother. "Look, I've met some neighbors and they're nice."

"And in what language do you speak to them, huh?"

"Well, in English."

"I can imagine the crazy things you come up with."

"But at least I try," answered her brother. "What you have to do is make an effort. If they don't understand me, I talk with my hands until something happens."

"I write well in English. And when I read, I understand a lot. But now, when they talk to me, I don't understand a word."

"Listen, the woman who lives in the house on the corner—"

"Which one?" interrupted Elisa.

"The one who gave me two dollars to take care of her cat."

"What about her?"

"She told me that she used to listen to the news on the radio and got used to hearing English that way. And then, little by little, she understood English better and better."

"I don't like the radio," declared Elisa.

"Turn on the TV, then. But not to those lovey-dovey soaps in Spanish and all that silly stuff you like."

"What do you want me to watch, then?"

"Things from here, like baseball, football . . ."

"Football is brutal. I hate sports!"

"Oh well, if you'd rather be ignorant . . ."

"O.K., forget it."

Elisa regretted ever having wanted to be in the same school as her know-it-all brother. She'd have to solve her problem on her own, but how?

The summer came to an end and the school year began. That's when she met José. That day she wrote in her diary,

I met a student from Guatemala. He's very quiet. He spends all his time with his head down, drawing in a notebook. He has sad, dark eyes. I thought he was going to talk to me once, but he didn't. He just smiled and kept on drawing.

She read what she had written and added, "I think I'm going to like this school after all."

The fact is that she didn't like the school one bit. The second day of classes, the English teacher called her name, which sounded more like "Alisha" than "Elisa." She got up from her desk expecting a disaster. And that's exactly what happened. She was asked a question that she didn't understand. When it was repeated, she understood even less. She was so nervous that she could only stammer a few syllables *"eh, ah, ah, uh."* She couldn't continue and she collapsed in her seat in front of those forty faces—her opponents—some disbelieving, some mocking. How embarrassing!

Around noon, José's turn came. He got up and he spoke shyly of the customs and traditions of his country. He mentioned the quetzal—a bird with soft feathers, a green crest, and a red chest. He told how this gorgeous bird was the symbol of power for the Maya and that today it is officially the national bird of Guatemala. Finally, he showed them a color drawing and told them proudly that the quetzal on the Guatemalan flag was an emblem of national liberty.

Everyone clapped. He sat down, and, as always, he put his head down and went back to drawing.

STOP AND THINK

Visualize How does the imagery in Elisa's description of José help you understand why Elisa adds the last line to her diary entry?

In the afternoon each student wrote a composition. Elisa wrote about her home, Puerto Rico. Like José, she described its customs and traditions and explained the symbolism of Puerto Rico's shield—a lamb, the emblem of peace and fraternity, appears in the green center. Above the lamb is a bundle of arrows, symbols of the creative force. And above these is a yoke which represents the joining of forces necessary to attain success. She thought it turned out pretty well, but writing was one thing and talking was another.

That night she didn't open her diary. She was tired of complaining, even if it was only to her diary.

The next morning Elisa smiled for the first time since classes had started. She got a good grade on her composition. She wanted to show it to everyone so that they'd see that she wasn't so dumb, but she didn't do it. Maybe she'd show it to José, though. Yes, to him. So during recess she called to him and proudly showed him her paper. He looked at it and, lowering his eyes, he said with a brief smile, "Congratulations."

"Thanks." said Elisa. "And how did you do?"

"O.K."

"No doubt you got an A and you don't want me to be embarrassed."

"No, it's not that, Elisa. It's that...I picked up English by listening. You know, 'on the street.' I never took English in school. I write it like I hear it, and everything comes out wrong."

Elisa read the paper that he handed her and in one sweeping glance she saw what he meant. She didn't know what to say.

"But you speak it very well," Elisa tried to console him.

"Speaking is one thing and writing is another."

"And vice-versa," said Elisa.

"And the opposite."

"And the other way around."

They laughed so hard that the rest of the kids came over to see what was so funny. But they didn't tell anyone their secret. That afternoon, they made a deal. She would help him with writing, and he, in turn, would help her with pronunciation.

Twelve years later, Elisa was getting ready for work. She pulled down a box of shoes from the top shelf of her closet. In the rush, several things fell on top of her. One of them was her old diary. It fell open to the last page. She picked it up and read,

Today I received my high school diploma. When I looked at myself in the mirror with my cap and gown and my gold honors tassels, I remembered the little girl who arrived here confused, scared, and sad. I'm happy now.

STOP AND THINK

Author's Craft In the fourth paragraph, José uses the idiom "on the street." How does the idiom help him explain the way in which he has learned English?

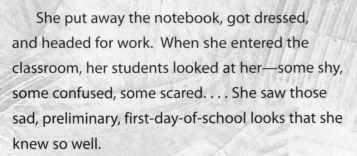

She put away the notebook, got dressed, and headed for work. When she entered the classroom, her students looked at her—some shy, some confused, some scared. . . . She saw those sad, preliminary, first-day-of-school looks that she knew so well.

She opened her lesson planner, thought a moment, and then shut it. She stood up and wrote on the board, "The joining of forces."

Then she said, "I'm going to tell you the story of a quetzal that came down to the plain with the gentleness of a lamb, and a lamb that soared to great heights on the wings of a quetzal."

☑ **STOP AND THINK**

Theme How does Elisa's introduction to "The joining of forces" show the lesson she learned when she was a student? Why might she want to share the story with her students?

Your Turn

Share Your Talents

Short Response Elisa's school life changes when she meets José. Think about how Elisa and José are able to learn from and help each other. Then write a paragraph describing a time when you and a friend joined forces to help each other.

PERSONAL RESPONSE

Show the Flag

Design a Flag or Shield In "Elisa's Diary," Elisa and José tell about their countries' customs, symbols, and traditions. Work with a partner to choose a symbol that represents your community. Design and illustrate a flag or shield that incorporates the symbol. Then create a list of customs or traditions celebrated in your community. PARTNERS

Learning Life Lessons

Turn and Talk Think about the moment when Elisa reads her diary entry about receiving her high school diploma. With a partner, discuss another selection, book, or real-life experience in which someone overcomes a challenge and finds happiness or success. Identify the important life lesson that these characters or people learn. THEME

Social Studies

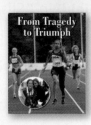

✓ TARGET VOCABULARY

opponents	obvious
brutal	typically
supposedly	preliminary
gorgeous	sweeping
embarrassed	officially

GENRE

Informational text, such as this newspaper article, gives details, facts, and examples about a topic.

TEXT FOCUS

Informational text may include **graphic sources** that give additional information and show how different facts and numbers relate to each other and the text.

Media Literacy Newspaper articles and websites about the same topic use different types of language. Newspapers often use more formal words than do website articles or blogs.

TODAY'S

From Tragedy to Triumph

by Jennifer Johnson

One day, while waiting for a train in Philadelphia, twenty-seven-year-old April Holmes fell onto the tracks. The oncoming train ran over her left leg, which had to be amputated below the knee.

For most people, a brutal accident like that would mean the end of a running career; for Holmes it was the start. Holmes had been a track star in high school and college, specializing in the short races known as sprints. At the time of the accident, she no longer ran competitively. Inspired by magazines about Paralympics athletes that a doctor gave to her in the hospital, she decided to run again. She was not embarrassed or ashamed to wear a prosthetic leg. She began training as a sprinter only seven months after her accident.

"When you fall down in life you need to get back up and keep on going," Holmes says. "Whether that be with a prosthesis, with crutches or with a wheelchair, my spirit is still the same."

NEWS

Community
Find out about
your neighbors.

Classifieds
Buy, sell, and help
wanted section

FROM THE PAGES OF
WEEKLY READER

*April Holmes overcame personal
tragedy to triumph on the track.*

Triumph on the Track

Today, Holmes bills herself as
"the world's fastest amputee." Is that
officially true? It is hard to say. What
is obvious is that she is a top athlete by
any standard.

In 2002, Holmes entered her first
Paralympics track meet. On a gorgeous
spring day, her arms pumping in a
sweeping motion at her side, she took
first place in the 100-meter dash and
second place in the 200-meter race.

Later that year, Holmes competed
in the International Paralympics
Committee (IPC) championships. She
set two new records for American
athletes! In 2003, she sprinted past her
opponents to two new world records.

In 2004, Holmes competed in
the Paralympics Games in Athens,
Greece. They take place in the same
year as the Olympics and typically in
the same place. She made it through
the preliminary rounds of the 100- and
200-meter sprints. She ran in the final
rounds of both races. She also won a
bronze medal in the long jump.

SPORTS

Helping Others

When April Holmes is not racing or training, she is busy with the April Holmes Foundation. Holmes started the foundation in 2002 to help other people with disabilities. Losing a limb is supposedly a handicap, but Holmes says it does not have to be. "Your dreams shouldn't change," she says.

Through her foundation, Holmes raises money for special sports equipment for people with disabilities. She also pays personal visits to people who have lost limbs. She shares her story and helps them see how they, too, can lead physically active lives. "Everybody has a purpose in life," Holmes says, "and I've always felt that my purpose is to help people."

• Examine the graph below. What is the difference between the record Holmes set in 2002 and the record she set in 2006?

Holmes devotes much of her time to helping others with disabilities.

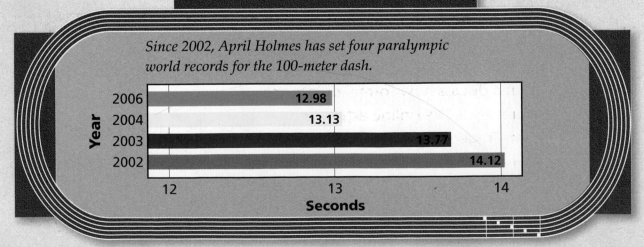

Holmes Sets 100-Meter Records

Since 2002, April Holmes has set four paralympic world records for the 100-meter dash.

Year	Seconds
2006	12.98
2004	13.13
2003	13.77
2002	14.12

Making Connections

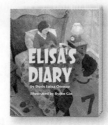
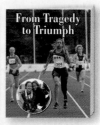

Write About a Challenge Both Elisa in "Elisa's Diary" and April Holmes in "From Tragedy to Triumph" had to overcome challenges in order to be successful. Think of a challenge you have had to overcome. Write a short composition describing the challenge you overcame, your feelings, and what you learned about yourself.

Discuss Points of View "Elisa's Diary" is narrated in third-person limited point of view with a focus on Elisa. "A Package for Mrs. Jewls" is narrated in third-person omniscient point of view with a focus on the thoughts and feelings of many characters. With a partner, discuss why you think each point of view is appropriate for each story. What might change about the selections if the points of view were reversed?

Read Online News Find and print an online article about April Holmes or another athlete. Circle examples of informal or formal language used in the article. With a partner, discuss how formal or informal language is used differently in the online article and the newspaper article, "From Tragedy to Triumph."

Grammar

How Are Plural Nouns Formed? A noun that names only one person, place, or thing is a **singular noun**. A noun that names more than one person, place, or thing is a **plural noun**. Most plural nouns are formed by adding *-s* or *-es*. A few are formed in other ways.

Singular Nouns	Plural Nouns
Robin made one shot in the first half.	She made a total of five shots in both halves.
The coach spoke at a rally.	The coaches spoke at rallies.
The man runs like a deer.	The men run like deer.

A **collective noun** names a group of people, animals, or things that act as a unit. A collective noun is treated as a singular noun, unless it names more than one group or collection.

singular collective noun

Our local team wins the tough games.

plural collective noun

Our local teams win the tough games.

 **Copy each sentence onto another sheet of paper. Change underlined singular nouns to plural nouns.**

❶ The new <u>student</u> greeted the teachers.

❷ During recess, friends sat on the <u>bench</u>.

❸ The frisky <u>squirrel</u> gathered acorns.

❹ The new books are on the <u>shelf</u>.

Word Choice You have learned how to use singular and plural nouns to show exactly what you mean. Using exact nouns in your writing will create clear pictures for your readers. It also will help make your writing interesting and easy to understand.

Less Exact Noun	More Exact Noun
A fan brought his pet to the track meet.	A fan brought his iguana to the track meet.

Connect Grammar to Writing

As you revise your fictional narrative, look for nouns that you can replace with more exact nouns. Remember that exact nouns can be singular or plural. They create clear pictures in your writing.

Write to Express

✔ Voice When you revise a **fictional narrative**, use dialogue to give characters their own distinct voices and show what they are like. What characters say and how they say it can reveal their feelings and personalities.

Chermaine drafted her story, using the story map she had made. Later, as she revised the story, she added dialogue to bring her characters to life and make her story seem more realistic.

Writing Process Checklist

Prewrite

Draft

▶ **Revise**

✔ Did I begin at the end and then flash back?

✔ Did I include only events that are important to my plot?

✔ Did I use natural-sounding dialogue and exact details?

✔ Did I include a variety of sentence types?

Edit

Publish and Share

Revised Draft

"I can't believe those losers won," Ike moaned. He looked stunned.

~~When Mrs. Mack's class won the Grade 5~~
~~Basketball Playoff, the other team looked~~
He and his team
~~stunned. They~~ had never fought so hard in their lives. With only two minutes left in the game, the score had been tied. Ike was dribbling the ball when elly managed to steal it. She turned and shot from the middle of the court—a three-point shot!

Beating the Basketball Bullies

by Chermaine Jones

"I can't believe those losers won," Ike moaned. He looked stunned. He and his team had never fought so hard in their lives. With only two minutes left in the game, the score had been tied. Ike was dribbling the ball when Elly managed to steal it. She turned and shot from the middle of the court— a three-point shot! From that moment on, it was no contest. Elly's team won the Grade 5 Basketball Playoff, and the crowd went wild.

That was not the ending most students expected. When Elly and Jed were chosen to lead the team for Ms. Mack's class, they made a plan to practice every day at recess. There was just one problem: the kids from Mr. Day's class were hoop hogs.

"We don't play with losers," Chantal sneered at Elly and Jed.

"Go play four-square," jeered Ike. "You're too short to shoot hoops."

In my final story, I added dialogue to give my characters a voice. I also capitalized proper nouns.

Reading as a Writer

What did you learn about the characters from the dialogue? Where can you add dialogue to give your characters a voice?

Unit 1 Wrap-Up

The Big Idea

Learning Can Be Fun Think about a time when you thought you were doing something or going somewhere just for fun, but instead you found yourself learning something new. Describe what you were doing and where you were. What did you learn?

The Ultimate Field Trip Washington, D.C.

Listening and Speaking

Each Can Teach Do you know how to solve a tricky puzzle? Can you make a greeting card on the computer? Have you learned a new dance step? Find a group of classmates who do not have your special skill. Share your knowledge with them.

Wild Encounters

Unit 2

Big Idea

Nature deserves
our respect.

Paired Selections

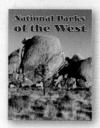

Lesson 6

✓ **TARGET VOCABULARY**

marine

basking

stunned

intensive

ordeal

treating

fatal

analyzing

juvenile

calling

Vocabulary Reader | Context Cards

Vocabulary in Context

1 marine
We go to the seashore to see marine life in the tidal pools.

2 basking
This turtle is basking in the warm morning sun.

3 stunned
It may take a stunned bird several moments to recover from its fall.

4 intensive
This vet performs an intensive exam of the sick animal.

146

- **Study each Context Card.**
- **Use a dictionary or a glossary to clarify the part of speech of each Vocabulary word.**

5 ordeal

These wet hikers are going through an unpleasant ordeal.

6 treating

Doctors suggest liquids and rest for treating a cold.

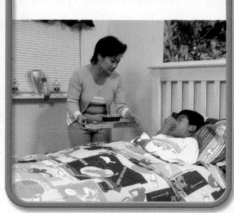

7 fatal

Pollution can be fatal to sea creatures. It can cause their death.

8 analyzing

After analyzing the water, these scientists say it is safe for animals.

9 juvenile

A juvenile bear stays close to its mother.

10 calling

This girl feels it is her calling in life to take care of animals.

Background

Sea Turtles Sea turtles are reptiles that have adapted to a marine environment. All sea turtles are threatened or endangered, but the Kemp's ridley turtle is most at risk. After analyzing an old video, scientists estimated that 40,000 of these turtles nested on one beach in Mexico in 1947. By the mid-1980s, the number was down to 700.

There are many reasons why the turtles' population has decreased. Turtles basking in warm coastal waters often get caught in fishing nets or collide with boats. Such an ordeal can be fatal. Stunned turtles, close to death, often wash ashore. Some are rescued by people who are trained in treating injured turtles, but many turtles do not survive. Luckily, intensive efforts are being made to protect the Kemp's ridley. People have found their calling in saving these turtles.

One way you can help protect turtles is by keeping balloons from flying away. Many juvenile turtles have died from eating balloons that ended up in the sea. Another way to help protect turtles is by keeping the turtles' nesting areas free of litter.

Comprehension

✔ **TARGET SKILL** **Cause and Effect**

Nonfiction authors sometimes use a cause-and-effect text structure to organize the ideas they present. Causes and effects in a nonfiction text can be directly stated or implied. As you read "Interrupted Journey: Saving Endangered Sea Turtles," look for implied causes and effects. Keep in mind that sometimes a single cause will have more than one effect. At other times, several causes will have a single effect. Make a graphic organizer like the one below to help you keep track of causes and effects in "Interrupted Journey: Saving Endangered Sea Turtles."

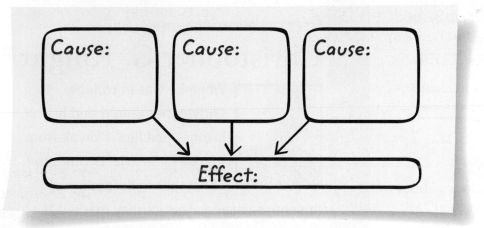

✔ **TARGET STRATEGY** **Question**

Ask questions about what you are reading. Your graphic organizer can help you answer some of the questions you have about saving sea turtles. Questioning helps you better understand the information and the points an author makes in a text.

Main Selection

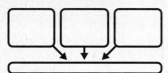
MEET THE AUTHOR

Kathryn Lasky

As a child, Kathryn Lasky often made up stories. One day, her mother told her that with her love of words, she should become a writer. For the first time, she gave the idea serious thought. Kathryn Lasky is equally comfortable writing fiction and nonfiction. She is married to Christopher Knight, a photographer who takes the pictures for many of her books, including *Shadows in the Dawn: The Lemurs of Madagascar* and, of course, *Interrupted Journey*.

MEET THE PHOTOGRAPHER

Christopher G. Knight

When he was in college, Christopher Knight and his brother paddled a kayak from Alaska to Seattle, Washington. Christopher photographed the entire voyage. This journey marked the beginning of his career as a professional photographer. He and his wife, Kathryn Lasky, have traveled the world together, working on books. Their book topics include monarch butterflies, a fossil dig, and the birth of a volcanic island near Iceland.

INTERRUPTED Journey

Saving Endangered Sea Turtles

by Kathryn Lasky
photographs by Christopher G. Knight

Essential Question

What effect can one person have on a stranded sea turtle?

STRANDED

The young turtle has been swimming for three months now in the same warm shallow bay, grazing on small crabs and plankton, basking in an endless dream of calm water and plentiful food. But as the days begin to shorten and the light drains out of the sky earlier and earlier, the water grows colder. It drops to fifty degrees Fahrenheit. The turtle is confused. Swimming is harder. Its heartbeat slows—and almost stops.

Ten days before Thanksgiving, on a beach where Pilgrims once walked, Max Nolan, a ten-year-old boy, and his mother begin their patrol. The Nolans are among volunteers who walk Cape Cod's beaches during November and December to search for turtles who are often cold and stunned and seem dead—turtles whose lives they may be able to save.

STOP AND THINK

Question What questions do you have about the turtle and Max Nolan after reading this first page? Write your questions on a sheet of paper. Look for the answers as you read on.

It is a blustery day on Ellis Landing Beach. At twenty-five knots the bitter northwest wind stings Max's face like sharp needles. It makes his eyes water but he keeps looking—looking above the high-water mark through the clumps of seaweed, looking below the tide line where the sand is hard and sleek and lapped by surf—looking for a dark greenish-brown mound about the size of a pie plate, looking for a Kemp's ridley turtle that is dying and perhaps can be saved.

Max and his mother and the other volunteers work for a vital cause. All sea turtles are threatened or endangered; Kemp's ridleys are the most endangered of all. Right now on our planet there are fewer than eight thousand Kemp's ridley turtles left. They are a vanishing species.

On Ellis Landing Beach, snow squalls begin to whirl down. The waves are building, and as they begin to break, the white froth whips across their steep faces. So far there is no sign of a turtle.

Max is far ahead of his mother when he sees the hump in the sand being washed by the surf. He runs up to it and shouts to his mom, "Got one!" The turtle is cold. Its flippers are floppy. Its eyes are open, but the turtle is not moving at all. It might be dead, but then again, it might not.

Max remembers the instructions given to all rescuers. He picks up the turtle, which weighs about five pounds, and moves it above the high-tide mark to keep it from washing out to sea. Then he runs to find seaweed to protect it from the wind. He finds a stick to mark the spot, and next, he and his mother go to the nearest telephone and call the sea-turtle rescue line of the Massachusetts Audubon Society.

Within an hour the turtle has been picked up and taken to the Wellfleet Bay Wildlife Sanctuary on Cape Cod. Robert Prescott, the director of the Sanctuary, examines the turtle. "It sure does look dead," he says softly. "But you never can tell." If the turtle is really alive, it must be brought out of its cold, stunned condition. That is a task for the New England Aquarium with its medical team who, over the years, have made a specialty of treating turtles.

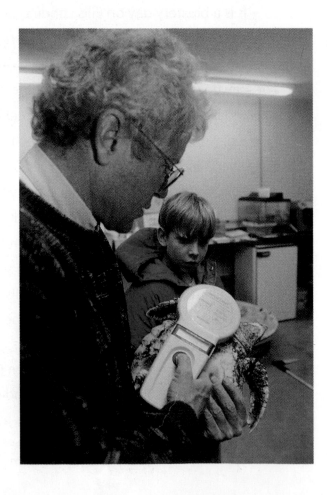

Robert puts the new turtle in a plastic wading pool with another turtle that is quite lively. Max crouches by the edge and watches his turtle. It is as still as a stone. He gently touches a flipper. Nothing moves. Then after about twenty minutes, he thinks he might see a flicker in the turtle's left eyelid. He leans closer. "Hey, it's moving!" It wasn't just the eyelid. He saw the right rear flipper move a fraction of an inch. Over the next five minutes, he sees the turtle make three or four microscopically small motions with its right rear flipper. Soon, the rescue team from the New England Aquarium arrives.

✔ STOP AND THINK
Cause and Effect Do you think Max's actions and observations will help the rescue team save the turtle's life? Explain.

EMERGENCY

Beth Chittick is a vet at the New England Aquarium. When the turtles arrive she is ready for them. The turtles are taken immediately into the examination room. Beth is joined by head veterinarian, Howard Crum. The temperature of the turtle Max found is fifty degrees Fahrenheit. Normal temperature for a turtle is usually about seventy-five degrees. Howard next tries to find a heartbeat. He listens intently. "I think I can hear a faint sound . . ." He holds the stiff turtle against his ear as one might hold a seashell. "Why, gee whiz, I can hear the ocean," he jokes.

Howard is still not convinced that the turtle is dead. "With turtles," Howard says, "death is a relative term." Turtles can operate, can survive, even when their hearts slow down for periods of time. Events that might damage the larger, more complicated brains of other animals will not always prove fatal to turtles.

In fact, a turtle's heartbeat naturally slows down at times to just one or two beats per minute in order to conserve oxygen and keep vital organs like the brain working. So Howard won't give up on this turtle yet. The turtle does not seem dehydrated. The skin on its limbs is not wrinkled—a good sign.

An assistant swabs down an area on the turtle's neck, from which a blood sample will be taken. By analyzing the blood, Howard and Beth will be able to see how the turtle's kidneys and other organs are functioning.

STOP AND THINK

Author's Craft What science words does the author use on this page? How does the author's **word choice** help clarify the turtle's chances of survival?

Next the turtle is cleaned. The algae are washed and wiped from its shell. The doctors detect movement in its tail and then see some of the same movements that Max saw in its flippers. They are the motions a turtle makes when it swims. They do not necessarily mean that it is alive, though.

Nonetheless, the vets hook up the turtle to an intravenous needle through which fluids will be pumped very slowly at a temperature slightly higher than the turtle's body. Beth and Howard have learned much about the condition of this turtle but they are still not sure if it is really alive or dead.

Finally the turtle is tagged with a yellow-blue band. It will be known as Yellow-Blue. It is put in the Intensive Care Unit, a large temperature-controlled stainless steel box with a glass window. Inside, the turtle is placed on a soft pile of towels so its shell is supported and it will not have to rest on its ventrum, or bottom shell.

RELEASE

On a windy spring morning in April, five months after it was found, Yellow-Blue is taken from its small tank in the New England Aquarium and put into a plastic box with wet towels. Yellow-Blue has recovered from its ordeal. But for the first leg of its journey it will not swim—Yellow-Blue will fly. A small cargo jet will take the turtle to The Turtle Hospital in Marathon, in the Florida Keys.

Richie Moretti is the owner, director, and founder of the hospital. He is not a veterinarian. He is not a marine biologist. He is a man who loves turtles, and his calling in life is to help injured animals. In order to do this, Richie runs Hidden Harbor, a motel. With the money he makes from the motel, he runs the hospital.

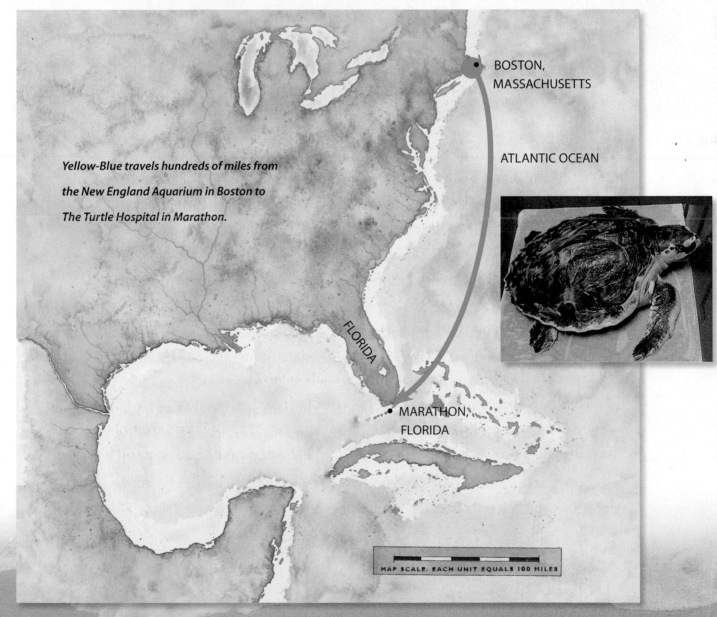

Yellow-Blue travels hundreds of miles from the New England Aquarium in Boston to The Turtle Hospital in Marathon.

BOSTON, MASSACHUSETTS

ATLANTIC OCEAN

FLORIDA

MARATHON, FLORIDA

MAP SCALE: EACH UNIT EQUALS 100 MILES

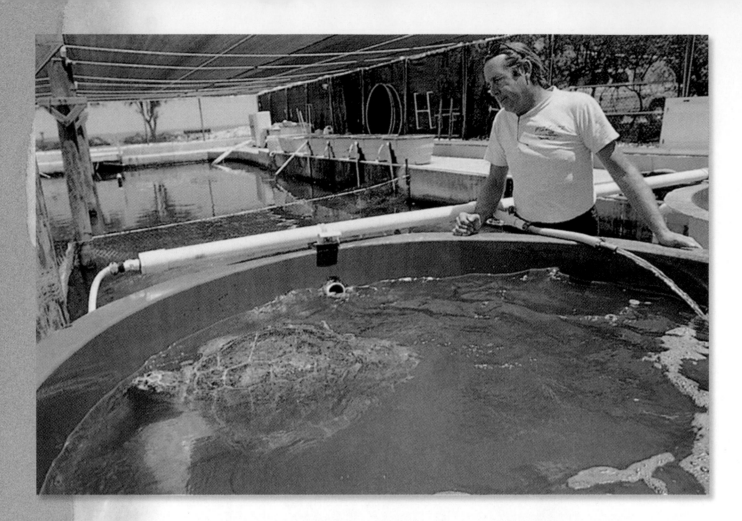

The people who come to the motel can no longer swim in
the motel pool. It is filled with injured sea turtles—loggerheads,
green turtles, Kemp's ridleys, and hawksbills. Guests cannot even
sunbathe or sit around the pool, for there are smaller tanks for baby
and juvenile turtles not big enough, or too sick, to swim in the big
pool. Veterinarians and volunteers come to the hospital to work
with the turtles.

On the day of the release, Richie and his assistant remove Yellow-
Blue from the tank and attach a permanent metal tag to its flipper
so that the turtle can be tracked throughout its sea voyage. The
turtle is feisty and flaps its flippers, perhaps sensing that something
exciting is about to happen. Richie and his crew load Yellow-Blue
and several larger turtles into his high-speed, shallow-bottomed
boat. Before departing from the pier, Richie checks the charts of
the waters around the southern keys. He wants to take Yellow-Blue

to the quietest, calmest, and safest waters he knows—a place where there are no tourists racing around in speedboats or fishing boats or shrimp trawlers. He wants this turtle to have a fair chance of swimming out to the Sargasso Sea without getting hit by a boat, chopped by a propeller, or tangled in the deadly nets and lines of fishermen. They put Yellow-Blue in a box, cover its shell with wet towels, and then roar out into Florida Bay.

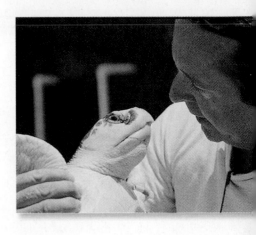

The boat goes fast, close to sixty miles an hour. Soon they are forty miles to the south and west. They are on the very most outlying keys of the Gulf side. The waters are shallow and calm. They cut the boat's engine and now the water is so shallow that Richie raises the outboard motor and poles in to what he considers the perfect place to release Yellow-Blue. It is in the still waters of a cove off a key named Content. Susan, a volunteer, lifts Yellow-Blue from its box and holds it half-in, half-out of the water. "Oh, you want to go! You want to go! Hang on, fella! Let's get used to things!"

Then she lowers Yellow-Blue so it is completely underwater. The flippers beat, and finally Susan's hands let go! Yellow-Blue streaks through the turquoise water, leaving a curling wake of bubbles. "So long, buddy," Richie calls.

Your Turn

Rescue!

Short Response As Max makes his way down Ellis Landing Beach, snow squalls swirl and the northwest wind stings his face. Write a paragraph explaining why you think people such as the Nolans spend their time and energy working in harsh conditions to help endangered animals. PERSONAL RESPONSE

Cold or Warm?

Exploring Species Think about the differences between cold-blooded and warm-blooded animals. Work with a partner to make a poster showing several animals, such as mammals, reptiles, and fish. Then share your poster with another pair of students, and have them label the animals as either warm-blooded or cold-blooded. Discuss what characteristics make the animals one kind or the other. PARTNERS

Follow Your Dreams

Turn and Talk Think about the last stop in Yellow-Blue's rehabilitation, the Turtle Hospital in Florida. With a partner, discuss how Richie Moretti's efforts to help injured animals have affected his life and the turtles he rescues. CAUSE AND EFFECT

Social Studies

Skywoman
and Turtle

✔ TARGET VOCABULARY

marine	treating
basking	fatal
stunned	analyzing
intensive	juvenile
ordeal	calling

GENRE

A **myth** is a story that tells what a group of people believes about the world.

TEXT FOCUS

Animal characters in myths act like people. They often have one special trait, such as bravery or wisdom.

• As you read, note what natural event, or phenomenon, the myth describes. What details in the myth help explain the phenomenon? Is the explanation believable? Why or why not?

Skywoman and Turtle

Retold by Alan Felix

Many Native American groups have myths about the origin of the world. Here is a retelling of a myth told by the Haudenosaunee (hoh deh noh SHAW nee) people of northeastern North America.

In the beginning, people lived among the clouds. Below the clouds there was no earth, only a dark, watery world where birds and animals lived. In the center of the clouds stood a single, giant tree. For the Sky People, the tree was a source of life.

The Chief of the Sky People had a wife named Skywoman. She was expecting a baby, and one night she fell ill with fever. The most intensive efforts could not cure her. While ill, Skywoman dreamed of a great hole in the clouds. She told the Chief of her dream. Stunned by the powerful image, he sat alone in deep thought. At last, he decided to make the dream come true.

The Chief wrapped his powerful arms around the tree's trunk. He began to pull it from the ground. With a mighty heave, the Chief uprooted the tree. There was the hole Skywoman had seen in her dream. She peered down at the watery darkness below, and her foot slipped on the edge of the clouds. With a cry, she grabbed for something to stop her. She caught hold of a handful of seeds among the roots of the great tree as she fell.

The marine animals below saw Skywoman falling. They knew such a fall would be fatal to her. A pair of geese flew up and caught Skywoman between their wings. Meanwhile, the other animals sought the advice of Turtle, eldest and wisest of them all. Turtle had a calling for solving problems. She knew how illnesses should be treated. Now she cocked her head to the left and right, analyzing the situation thoroughly.

"Toad," Turtle called out finally, "swim below and bring up mud from the water's bottom. Then spread the mud across my back."

The juvenile Toad croaked grumpily. He had been basking in the cool waters, hoping to take a nap. But he did as Turtle asked. The geese arrived with Skywoman between them, and they gently dropped her upon the soft mud on Turtle's back.

With the fever and the ordeal of falling gone, Skywoman opened her hand that held the seeds. The seeds fell into the mud. The mud spread from Turtle's back until it became the earth, teeming with life. Skywoman gave birth to twins upon that landmass. Thus, people walked the earth for the first time.

Making Connections

Write as a Journalist In "Interrupted Journey: Saving Endangered Sea Turtles," a rescued sea turtle called Yellow-Blue travels from Cape Cod to Florida in order to reach its new ocean home. Imagine that you are a journalist writing a newspaper article about Yellow-Blue's rescue. Describe Yellow-Blue's experiences and journey. Use the information in the selection's map and the photographs to help you write your article. Then share and discuss your article with a partner.

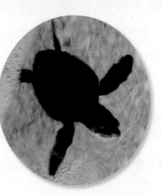

 Text to Text

Compare Representations of Turtles Make a two-column chart showing factual and fictional information about turtles. In one column of the chart, list the facts you learned about sea turtles in "Interrupted Journey: Saving Endangered Sea Turtles." In the other column, list the qualities or traits Turtle displayed in "Skywoman and Turtle." Then work with a group to discuss the different representations of turtles in the two texts.

 Text to World

Analyze an Origin Myth With a partner, review "Skywoman and Turtle," a Native American origin myth. Retell the myth and discuss the events it explains. Work with your partner to find other origin myths. Then compare and contrast the phenomena they each describe.

Grammar

What Is a Verb? A **verb** is a word that can show action or a state of being. When a verb tells what people or things do, it is called an **action verb**. When a verb tells what someone or something is, or what someone or something is like, it is called a **linking verb**. Most linking verbs are forms of the verb *be*.

Action Verbs	Linking Verbs
The turtle dug a hole.	Those turtles are hawksbills.
She laid eggs in the nest.	That species is scarce now.

Sometimes the verb in a sentence is made up of more than one word. The **main verb** is the most important verb. The **helping verb** comes before it and adds detail to the main verb.

helping verb main verb   helping verb main verb
The eggs will hatch.   The babies must walk into the sea.

Turn and Talk   **Work with a partner. Find two sentences that have linking verbs. Then find three sentences with action verbs. Tell which sentence has a main verb and a helping verb.**

❶ The turtle is the only reptile with a shell.

❷ Some land turtles stay in a small area all their lives.

❸ Many sea turtles migrate thousands of miles.

❹ Most land turtles are slow movers.

❺ At least one species can outrun a human being!

Word Choice You can make your writing clearer by choosing vivid, exact verbs. Exact verbs also will help make your writing interesting.

Sentence with Vague Verb	Sentence with Exact Verb
 A ranger walks the beach twice a day.	 A ranger patrols the beach twice a day.
 The newly hatched turtle walks from the nest toward the ocean.	 The newly hatched turtle stumbles from the nest toward the ocean.

Connect Grammar to Writing

As you revise your cause-and-effect paragraphs, replace vague verbs with exact verbs to show readers what you mean. Exact verbs will help clarify the actions and events you write about.

Write to Respond

Writing about causes and effects is one way to respond to literature. In **cause-and-effect paragraphs**, use signal words and phrases such as *because, so,* and *as a result* to make clear the relationships between causes and their effects.

Barry drafted a response to this question: *What are some causes and effects related to a sea turtle becoming stranded?* Then he revised his writing to include transitions that connect his ideas.

Use the Writing Traits Checklist below as you revise your writing.

Writing Traits Checklist

✔ **Ideas**
Did I clearly identify causes and effects?

✔ **Organization**
Do my paragraphs contain transitions that connect my ideas?

✔ **Sentence Fluency**
Did I vary the structure of my sentences?

✔ **Word Choice**
Did I use signal words to clarify cause-and-effect relationships?

✔ **Voice**
Does my writing sound clear and informative?

✔ **Conventions**
Did I use correct spelling, grammar, and punctuation?

Revised Draft

Sea turtles can have problems. For example,
If a turtle stays in northern waters too
late in the season, the water can turn cold.
As a result,
A turtle may become confused. Its heart beats
~~goes~~ more slowly. It isn't able to swim
well. It can ~~end~~ wash up on a beach.
Because of that,

170

Saving Sea Turtles
by Barry Williams

Sea turtles can have problems. For example, if a turtle stays in northern waters too late in the season, the water can turn cold. As a result, a turtle may become confused. Its heart beats more slowly. It isn't able to swim well. Because of that, it can wash up on a beach.

There are ways in which people can help stranded turtles. A person can take a turtle past the high-tide line so the tide will not wash the turtle back out to sea. Covering the turtle with seaweed is important because the seaweed will act as a blanket and keep the turtle warm. Calling a turtle rescue group is also important. Someone in the group might take the turtle to a doctor. As a result, the turtle might be saved. Then the doctor can transport it to warm waters.

> In my final paper, I used transitional words to connect my ideas. I also used exact verbs to make details more clear.

Reading as a Writer

What transitional words did the writer use to connect causes and effects? Where in your writing can you signal causes and effects and connect ideas more clearly?

romp

strained

picturing

wheeled

shouldered

frantic

lunging

checking

stride

bounding

Vocabulary Reader

Context Cards

Vocabulary in Context

1 romp

For many kids in the 1800s, the trip West was a romp. For adults, it was a serious task.

2 strained

Gold-rush miners strained to sift gold from mounds of heavy soil.

3 picturing

In their imagination, many pioneers were picturing owning big cattle ranches.

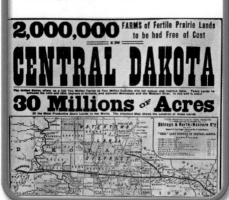

4 wheeled

Teams of oxen wheeled the wagons around to form a circle for protection.

- **Study each Context Card.**
- **Use a thesaurus to find a synonym for each Vocabulary word.**

5 shouldered

Pioneers may have shouldered newborn animals to carry them, just like this farmer.

6 frantic

Frightened by the storm, this frenzied herd of buffalo began a frantic stampede.

7 lunging

These goats, like the ones on farms, enjoy lunging, or dashing, at each other.

8 checking

Stopping, or checking, the wandering ways of sheep is the job of these farm dogs.

9 stride

Pioneers who walked had to match their stride, or step, to the pace of the wagons.

10 bounding

This man is cheered by his happy dog bounding forward to greet him.

173

Background

✓ TARGET VOCABULARY **Frontier Life** Try picturing what frontier life was like in the 1800s. The journey west itself must have been very hard. Imagine lunging down a riverbank in a loaded wagon toward rushing water. As you walked along, you might have had to quicken your stride to escape a coyote. Would you have wheeled around if you'd heard a rattlesnake? Checking their fear when they faced danger must have been a challenge for pioneers.

There was probably little time for a romp after settlers arrived at their destination. They must have been frantic as they strained to plant crops and build homes. Children, like the adults, shouldered the tools needed to build fences, cut wood, and plow the soil. They had little time for bounding happily across the prairie. Could you have survived life as a pioneer?

• Review the map below. If you traveled the Gila Trail, which states would you have traveled through?

Pioneers could follow one of several trails into the Southwest, depending on their destination.

Map showing states: NEVADA, UTAH, COLORADO, IOWA, CALIFORNIA, ARIZONA, KANSAS, OKLAHOMA, NEW MEXICO, TEXAS, MEXICO. Cities: Los Angeles, San Diego, Fort Yuma, Tucson, Santa Fe, Independence. Sonoran Desert labeled.

Legend:
- ----- Santa Fe Trail
- —— Southern Trail
- —— Gila Trail

Comprehension

Understanding Characters

You can understand characters by the things they do, say, and think. In "Old Yeller," the main character, Travis, tells the story in his own words. Use a graphic organizer like the one below to help you compare Travis's thoughts, actions, and words to better understand his motives and how he really feels.

Thoughts	Actions	Words
•	•	•
•	•	•
•	•	•

✓ TARGET STRATEGY **Visualize**

As you read, use sights, sounds, and other details to picture the scenes that Travis describes. By visualizing what Travis experiences, you can better understand his motives and behavior.

It is the late 1860s. Travis lives with his family on the Texas frontier. When Papa leaves home to drive their cattle to market in Kansas, Travis must take over Papa's responsibilities. All goes well until a stray yellow dog shows up. Travis's younger brother, Little Arliss, loves the dog, but Travis thinks the mangy animal is nothing but a "meat-stealing rascal." Then one day something happens that changes Travis's feelings about the dog forever.

Swinging that chopping axe was sure hard work. The sweat poured off me. My back muscles ached. The axe got so heavy I could hardly swing it. My breath got harder and harder to breathe.

An hour before sundown, I was worn down to a nub. It seemed like I couldn't hit another lick. Papa could have lasted till past sundown, but I didn't see how I could. I shouldered my axe and started toward the cabin, trying to think up some excuse to tell Mama to keep her from knowing I was played clear out.

That's when I heard Little Arliss scream.

Well, Little Arliss was a screamer by nature. He'd scream when he was happy and scream when he was mad and a lot of times he'd scream just to hear himself make a noise. Generally, we paid no more mind to his screaming than we did to the gobble of a wild turkey.

But this time was different. The second I heard his screaming, I felt my heart flop clear over. This time I knew Little Arliss was in real trouble.

I tore out up the trail leading toward the cabin. A minute before, I'd been so tired out with my rail splitting that I couldn't have struck a trot. But now I raced through the tall trees in that creek bottom, covering ground like a scared wolf.

Little Arliss's second scream, when it came, was louder and shriller and more frantic-sounding than the first. Mixed with it was a whimpering crying sound that I knew didn't come from him. It was a sound I'd heard before and seemed like I ought to know what it was, but right then I couldn't place it.

Then, from way off to one side came a sound that I would have recognized anywhere. It was the coughing roar of a charging bear. I'd just heard it once in my life. That was the time Mama had shot and wounded a hog-killing bear and Papa had had to finish it off with a knife to keep it from getting her.

My heart went to pushing up into my throat, nearly choking off my wind. I strained for every lick of speed I could get out of my running legs. I didn't know what sort of fix Little Arliss had got himself into, but I knew that it had to do with a mad bear, which was enough.

The way the late sun slanted through the trees had the trail all cross-banded with streaks of bright light and dark shade. I ran through these bright and dark patches so fast that the changing light nearly blinded me. Then suddenly, I raced out into the open where I could see ahead. And what I saw sent a chill clear through to the marrow of my bones.

There was Little Arliss, down in that spring hole again. He was lying half in and half out of the water, holding on to the hind leg of a little black bear cub no bigger than a small coon. The bear cub was out on the bank, whimpering and crying and clawing the rocks with all three of his other feet, trying to pull away. But Little Arliss was holding on for all he was worth, scared now and screaming his head off. Too scared to let go.

How the bear cub ever came to prowl close enough for Little Arliss to grab him, I don't know. And why he didn't turn on him and bite loose, I couldn't figure out, either. Unless he was like Little Arliss, too scared to think.

But all of that didn't matter now. What mattered was the bear cub's mama. She'd heard the cries of her baby and was coming to save him. She was coming so fast that she had the brush popping and breaking as she crashed through and over it. I could see her black heavy figure piling off down the slant on the far side of Birdsong Creek. She was roaring mad and ready to kill.

And worst of all, I could see that I'd never get there in time!

Mama couldn't either. She'd heard Arliss, too, and here she came from the cabin, running down the slant toward the spring, screaming at Arliss, telling him to turn the bear cub loose. But Little Arliss wouldn't do it. All he'd do was hang with that hind leg and let out one shrill shriek after another as fast as he could suck in a breath.

Now the she bear was charging across the shallows in the creek. She was knocking sheets of water high in the bright sun, charging with her fur up and her long teeth bared, filling the canyon with that awful coughing roar. And no matter how fast Mama ran or how fast I ran, the she bear was going to get there first!

STOP AND THINK

Visualize What do the visual details provided by the author help you "see" in this scene?

I think I nearly went blind then, picturing what was going to happen to Little Arliss. I know that I opened my mouth to scream and not any sound came out.

Then, just as the bear went lunging up the creek bank toward Little Arliss and her cub, a flash of yellow came streaking out of the brush.

It was that big yeller dog. He was roaring like a mad bull. He wasn't one-third as big and heavy as the she bear, but when he piled into her from one side, he rolled her clear off her feet. They went down in a wild, roaring tangle of twisting bodies and scrambling feet and slashing fangs.

As I raced past them, I saw the bear lunge up to stand on her hind feet like a man while she clawed at the body of the yeller dog hanging to her throat. I didn't wait to see more. Without ever checking my stride, I ran in and jerked Little Arliss loose from the cub. I grabbed him by the wrist and yanked him up out of that water and slung him toward Mama like he was a half-empty sack of corn. I screamed at Mama. "Grab him, Mama! Grab him and run!" Then I swung my chopping axe high and wheeled, aiming to cave in the she bear's head with the first lick.

STOP AND THINK

Author's Craft The author uses words such as *lunging*, *roaring*, *scrambling*, and *slashing* to provide sensory details. How do these words help you picture what is happening?

But I never did strike. I didn't need to. Old Yeller hadn't let the bear get close enough. He couldn't handle her; she was too big and strong for that. She'd stand there on her hind feet, hunched over, and take a roaring swing at him with one of those big front claws. She'd slap him head over heels. She'd knock him so far that it didn't look like he could possibly get back there before she charged again, but he always did. He'd hit the ground rolling, yelling his head off with the pain of the blow; but somehow he'd always roll to his feet. And here he'd come again, ready to tie into her for another round.

I stood there with my axe raised, watching them for a long moment. Then from up toward the house, I heard Mama calling: "Come away from there, Travis. Hurry, son! Run!"

That spooked me. Up till then, I'd been ready to tie into that bear myself. Now, suddenly, I was scared out of my wits again. I ran toward the cabin.

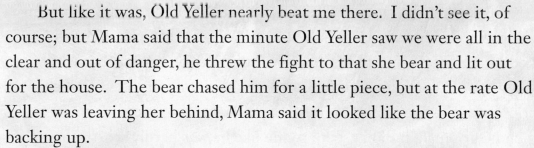

But like it was, Old Yeller nearly beat me there. I didn't see it, of course; but Mama said that the minute Old Yeller saw we were all in the clear and out of danger, he threw the fight to that she bear and lit out for the house. The bear chased him for a little piece, but at the rate Old Yeller was leaving her behind, Mama said it looked like the bear was backing up.

But if the big yeller dog was scared or hurt in any way when he came dashing into the house, he didn't show it. He sure didn't show it like we all did. Little Arliss had hushed his screaming, but he was trembling all over and clinging to Mama like he'd never let her go. And Mama was sitting in the middle of the floor, holding him up close and crying like she'd never stop. And me, I was close to crying, myself.

Old Yeller, though, all he did was come bounding in to jump on us and lick us in the face and bark so loud that there, inside the cabin, the noise nearly made us deaf.

The way he acted, you might have thought that bear fight hadn't been anything more than a rowdy romp that we'd all taken part in for the fun of it.

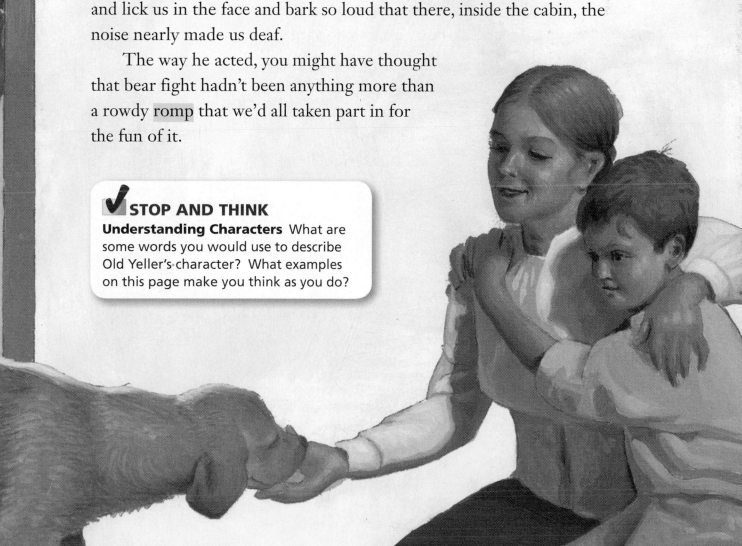

> ✔ **STOP AND THINK**
> **Understanding Characters** What are some words you would use to describe Old Yeller's character? What examples on this page make you think as you do?

Till Little Arliss got us mixed up in that bear fight, I guess I'd been looking on him about like most boys look on their little brothers. I liked him, all right, but I didn't have a lot of use for him. What with his always playing in our drinking water and getting in the way of my chopping axe and howling his head off and chunking me with rocks when he got mad, it didn't seem to me like he was hardly worth the bother of putting up with.

But that day when I saw him in the spring, so helpless against the angry she bear, I learned different. I knew then that I loved him as much as I did Mama and Papa, maybe in some ways even a little bit more.

So it was only natural for me to come to love the dog that saved him.

After that, I couldn't do enough for Old Yeller.

Your Turn

No Time to Think

Short Response Travis and Arliss reacted differently to the dangerous encounter with the bear at the river. What do you think makes some people ignore their fear and stand up to a threat? Write a paragraph explaining your thoughts and telling how you might have responded in such a situation.

PERSONAL RESPONSE

Illustrate It

Draw a Scene The fight with the bear was filled with intense action. Work with a small group to reread the description on pages 180–184. Then create a series of illustrations showing the encounter with the bear. Include captions and arrows to clarify each character's actions. Display the illustrations in the classroom.

SMALL GROUP

Changes Over Time

Turn and Talk Think about how Travis's feelings toward his brother change during the story. Discuss with a partner how the incident with the bear affects Travis. Then evaluate whether Travis's change in perspective is believable, based on what you know about how a real person might react and feel.

UNDERSTANDING CHARACTERS

Lester Year: Now wait a minute! That fight between Old Yeller and the bear was exciting, I admit. But what makes the movie truly great is its historical accuracy. If Travis had broken his stride, wheeled around and seen the bear, then dialed 9-1-1 on a cell phone, you would not believe it.

But he does not carry a cell phone. He has shouldered an ax. I hope you noticed the ax. It was an excellent example of an important 1860s tool. Living on the frontier was no romp on the playground, and pioneers depended on their tools for survival.

Ah, now that scene of Old Yeller licking Arliss after checking the bear's attack may be very accurate as far as dog behavior is concerned. But more important, the cabin looks very realistic, down to the notches holding the logs in place. If the cabin had wallpaper, you would have strained to believe the scene. That is why historical accuracy is more important.

Host: We are almost out of time. Let's summarize. *Old Yeller* is a good movie because it is . . .

Kay Nyne: Scientifically accurate.

Lester Year: Historically accurate.

Host: Well, they may never agree. Audience, I guess you have to decide for yourself what makes it good!

Making Connections

 Text to Self

Write About an Animal Think about an experience you have had with an animal. Write a narrative paragraph about the experience. Include details that convey your thoughts and feelings. Draw a picture to accompany your paragraph, and provide a caption for your drawing.

Always view wildlife from far away.

 Text to Text

Analyze Viewpoint In "What Makes It Good?", Lester Year makes a clear argument about "Old Yeller" and provides evidence to support it. Identify Lester Year's viewpoint. Then make a list of the ideas and text details from "Old Yeller" that support his viewpoint. Include those that he mentions, as well as those you discover in the selection. Use your list to write a sentence about how the ideas and details work together to form a solid argument.

 Text to World

Connect to Science In the 1860s, when "Old Yeller" takes place, bears lived in many parts of the United States. Work with a partner or small group to make a plan for researching where one type of bear, such as the black bear or the grizzly bear, lives today. Then use print or online resources to find information about the type of bear you selected. Use the information to create a map of the bear's habitat. Share your map with another group.

Grammar

What Is a Direct Object? A **direct object** is the word in the predicate that receives the action of the verb. It can be a noun or a pronoun, a word that takes the place of a noun. A **compound direct object** is made up of two or more words that receive the action of the same verb.

Verbs and Objects	What Receives the Action
action verb direct object The boy swung his axe.	*Axe* receives the action of the verb *swung.*
action verb compound direct object He chopped big logs and small branches.	*Logs* and *branches* receive the action of the verb *chopped.*

An **indirect object** usually tells to *whom* or to *what* the action of the verb is done. The indirect object comes between the verb and the direct object.

action verb indirect object direct object
The boy gave his brother a treat.

Brother tells to whom the treat was given.

Turn and Talk **The action verb in each sentence is printed in bold type. Find the direct object. Then find the indirect object, if one is used.**

❶ Mom **wrote** Dad a letter.

❷ She **described** the big fight.

❸ Our dog **protected** my brother and me.

❹ We **gave** our dog great praise.

Sentence Fluency You can improve the flow of your writing by combining sentences in which the direct objects receive the action of the same verb. First, identify the subject, verb, and direct object of each sentence. Then combine the sentences, using *and* or *or* to join the direct objects.

Separate Sentences

A brave dog will fight a bear.

A brave dog will fight a mountain lion.

Combined Sentence with Compound Direct Object

A brave dog will fight a bear or a mountain lion.

Connect Grammar to Writing

As you revise your poem, check to see whether you can create compound direct objects to combine sentences. Combining sentences will help make your writing smoother.

Write to Respond

Writing a response to literature can give you a chance to express your thoughts and feelings about a character through poetry. A good poet uses figurative language, poetic techniques, or graphic devices to tell about a character.

Stefania wrote a **poem** about her little sister in response to "Old Yeller." When she revised her draft, she used onomatopoeia, alliteration, and metaphors to create vivid images. She also varied line length for rhyming and rhythm.

Use the Writing Traits Checklist below as you revise your poem.

Writing Traits Checklist

✔ **Ideas**
Did I express the traits, feelings, or motives of a character?

✔ **Organization**
Did I connect my response to the events and details in the story?

✔ **Sentence Fluency**
Did I vary the structure of my sentences?

✔ **Word Choice**
Did I choose words that create vivid sounds or images?

✔ **Voice**
Did I express my feelings about a character?

✔ **Conventions**
Did I use correct spelling, grammar, and punctuation?

Revised Draft

If a bear woke up my sister,

I'll tell you what I'd do.
I would tell ~~her~~ the bear to run!
I would tell the bear to ~~go!~~ shoo!

Because even a ~~large mean~~ big brown bear

Is really not a match
For my ~~little~~ baby sister Sarah

When she's woken from her nap.

She's the siren on a fire truck,
She's ~~a crash~~ the smash of broken glass,
She's the ~~shrill lawn~~ sound of a mower mowing

Miles and miles of tall green grass.

194

If a Bear Woke Up My Sister

by Stefania Almeida

If a bear woke up my sister,
I'll tell you what I'd do.
I would tell the bear to run!
I would tell the bear to shoo!

Because even a big brown bear
Is really not a match
For my baby sister Sarah
When she's woken from her nap.

She's the siren on a fire truck,
She's the smash of broken glass,
She's the sound of a mower mowing
Miles and miles of tall green grass.

It's not that I don't love her,
It's not that I don't care,
But if a bear woke up my sister,
I'd feel sorry for the bear.

In my final poem, I added words that create vivid sounds and images. I also included examples of figurative language.

Reading as a Writer

Which words help Stefania's poem express more about her sister? What words could you replace to make your own poem come alive with sights, sounds, and rhythm?

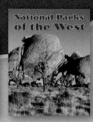

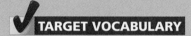
conserving

restore

regulate

vegetation

endangered

responsibility

attracted

adapted

unique

guardians

Vocabulary Reader   Context Cards

Vocabulary in Context

1 conserving

Saving, or conserving, natural habitats is a main goal of our national park system.

2 restore

Park workers restore harmed habitats by bringing them back to their original state.

3 regulate

Managers regulate, or control, access to an area. Fewer people cause less harm.

4 vegetation

Many animals survive by feeding on the vegetation, or plant life, in a habitat.

- **Study each Context Card.**
- **Use a thesaurus to find an alternate word for each Vocabulary word.**

5 endangered

Damaged habitats put endangered animals at risk of dying out.

6 responsibility

Humans have a duty, or responsibility, to preserve and protect wild habitats.

7 attracted

Birds are attracted, or drawn to, habitats that can hide their nests from predators.

8 adapted

Gills are specially adapted features that let fish breathe in the water.

9 unique

Many habitats support unique plants and wildlife that are not found elsewhere.

10 guardians

One day some of these students may become guardians, or caretakers, of wild habitats.

Background

The National Park Service The original responsibility of the National Park Service, founded in 1916, was to protect our nation's unique natural wonders. Today, the Park Service's job is to regulate nearly four hundred areas, including parks, monuments, historic sites, wild rivers, and seashores.

Rangers are guardians of our country's natural and historical treasures. Most rangers who work in national parks spend their days protecting the wildlife and vegetation. They are devoted to conserving the parks' scenic beauty and trying to restore damaged areas. They give tours and lectures about plant and animal species, including endangered ones. They explain the adapted traits that help living things thrive in park habitats.

Might you be attracted to a career as a park ranger?

Rangers in national parks work in some of the most beautiful places in the world, such as Colorado's Mesa Verde National Park.

Comprehension

Persuasion

The author of "Everglades Forever" gives us information, but her goal is to persuade. She uses interesting facts about the Everglades to convince us that the area is worth saving. Use a graphic organizer like the one below to help you see how she builds her argument.

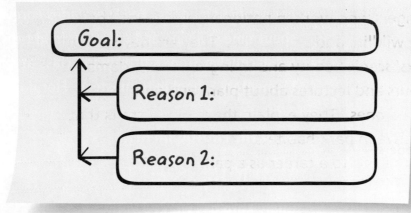

Goal:

Reason 1:

Reason 2:

✔ **TARGET STRATEGY** **Analyze/Evaluate**

Use your graphic organizer to identify facts, opinions, and arguments the author uses to persuade. Ask yourself questions as you read to determine your feelings about the author's arguments. Analyzing and interpreting each question and answer will help you understand your response to the topic and the author's position on it.

conserving responsibility
restore attracted
regulate adapted
vegetation unique
endangered guardians

✔ **TARGET SKILL**

Persuasion Examine how an author tries to convince readers to support an idea.

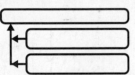

✔ **TARGET STRATEGY**

Analyze/Evaluate Think carefully about the text and form an opinion about it.

GENRE

Narrative nonfiction gives factual information by telling a true story.

MEET THE AUTHOR

Trish Marx

Trish Marx travels to the people and places she writes about to get firsthand information for her nonfiction books. For *Everglades Forever*, she spent time studying and going on field trips with Ms. Jacquelyn Stone's fifth-grade class at Avocado Elementary School in Homestead, Florida.

MEET THE PHOTOGRAPHER

Cindy Karp

Cindy Karp has worked with Trish Marx on several books for children. She is also a photojournalist whose pictures have appeared in national magazines and newspapers. Karp is a resident of Miami, Florida, and has spent many days exploring the Everglades.

EVERGLADES FOREVER

RESTORING AMERICA'S GREAT WETLAND

by Trish Marx • photographs by Cindy Karp

Essential Question

What persuades us to protect the environment?

In Homestead, Florida, the students in Ms. Stone's fifth-grade class have been learning about the Everglades, a vast natural wetland located on the southern tip of Florida. Since 2000, the Comprehensive Everglades Restoration Plan has helped to preserve this wetland and its natural water system. Now all of Ms. Stone's students are visiting the Everglades to experience this amazing place and learn what they can do to preserve it. The map on the right shows where Everglades National Park is located in Florida and the areas Ms. Stone's class explored.

On the morning of the field trip, the bus traveled west from Avocado School. The students saw the landscape change from houses and shopping centers to a flat, grassy prairie that met the horizon miles away. Soon they arrived at the Royal Palm Visitor Center, part of Everglades National Park.

South Florida

Lake Okeechobee

Miami

Gulf of Mexico

Pinelands · Homestead

Anhinga Trail

Florida Bay

ATLANTIC OCEAN

Key West

0   25   50 Miles
0   25   50 Kilometers

Legend

Everglades Agricultural Area

Water Conservation Area

Big Cypress National Preserve

Everglades National Park

■ Visited by Ms. Stone's Class

Overlooking sawgrass on Anhinga Trail

Ms. Stone had arranged for the class to meet Ranger Jim at the visitor center. From there the ranger led them to the start of the Anhinga Trail, a boardwalk circling into a slough (sloo). It was the dry season, which lasts from December through April, so the water levels were low. But there is a deep part of the slough at the beginning of the trail that never dries up. Around the edge of this part, large waterbirds called Anhingas sunned their wings. Anhingas hold out their wings to thermoregulate (thur moh REHG yuh layt), or regulate their body temperature, by soaking up the sun's energy to keep their bodies warm. An Osprey, a fish-eating hawk, waited in a tree for a flash of fish in the water. In the distance an egret stood in the sawgrass, and a flock of endangered wood storks flew overhead.

Great Blue Heron feeding on fish

"Right now you'll see many animals close together around the deeper water areas," said Ranger Jim. Fish and smaller water animals had migrated to these deep water areas to search for food. Wading birds, alligators, Ospreys, and Cormorants (large diving birds with bright green eyes) followed to feed on the fish and smaller animals. Alligators also use their tails, snouts, and feet to dig deep holes, which fill with water. These holes are places for alligators to cool off while they wait for a meal of the small animals that are attracted to the water-filled holes. During the wet season, which lasts from May through November, water covers much of the land. Then the animals spread out because the water that carries their food is spread out.

The Everglades has wet and dry seasons, but it also has wetter and drier areas caused by how high the land is above the water level. Even a few inches of elevation can make a difference in how wet or dry the soil remains throughout the year. These differences in moisture help create unique habitats, each with its own special set of plants and animals.

Mangrove trees

One of the lowest Everglades habitats is the mangrove swamp, which is named for the mangrove trees that line the islands and bays leading into the ocean. Fresh rainwater flows toward these areas and mixes with the salty ocean water, making the water in mangrove swamps brackish. The mangrove trees have specially adapted roots and leaves so they can live in this salty, muddy water. The swamps also serve as nurseries for shrimp, bonefish, and other marine animals that need a protected place to grow before they head to the ocean. If the brackish water in mangrove swamps changes, these animals cannot survive. Since two goals of the Restoration Plan are to allow Everglades water to flow more naturally to the ocean and to regulate the amount of freshwater flowing during each season, animals of the mangrove swamps—including pelicans, sea turtles, and the endangered American crocodiles and manatees—will be helped to survive.

STOP AND THINK

Analyze/Evaluate How does the author feel about the Everglades mangrove swamps? Which details make you think so?

The class was too far from the ocean to see a mangrove swamp, but as they walked the Anhinga Trail, the students saw several of the Everglades habitats. The slough filled with slow-moving water stretched in the distance. A sawgrass prairie covered the shallow parts of the slough, and in the distance the rounded domes of hardwood hammocks rose above the surface of the water.

As the students came to the end of the Anhinga Trail, Ranger Jim pointed out a gumbo limbo tree. "It's also called a tourist tree," he said, "because the bark of the tree peels off, just like the skin of sunburned tourists." Then he directed the students back to the bus for a short ride to a pine forest called the Pinelands.

Ranger Jim took the class on a hike through the Pinelands, one of the driest habitats in the Everglades. The sunlight filtered through the trees. Everything was quieter than on the Anhinga Trail. The floor of the Pinelands is covered with cabbage palms, marlberry bushes, blue porter flowers, and other vegetation that help absorb sounds from the outside world.

"This is where you'll find solution holes," Ms. Stone told the students. They searched the forest for the large holes that have been carved out of the limestone by tannic acid, a chemical formed when rainwater mixes with the pine needles and other leaves in the forest. Small animals live, feed, and raise their young in the solution holes. The students also watched as a tiny yellow tree snail nestled under the bark of a tree, eating a growth on the tree called lichen. They saw a Red-Shouldered Hawk swirl in the sky, and they waited for a golden orb spider to catch its next meal in its web close to the ground.

Hiking through the Pinelands

"Perhaps even in this last hour . . . the vast, magnificent, subtle and unique region of the Everglades may not be utterly lost."
Marjory Stoneman Douglas

207

As they walked through the Pinelands, the students talked with Ms. Stone and Ranger Jim about the circle of life—the Miccosukee (MIHK uh SOO kee) belief that all plant and animal and human life is connected. They had seen this today in the habitats they visited. The students also realized how terrible it would be if the habitats in this part of the Everglades were not protected from the effects of farming and development that were still putting the Everglades in danger. What would happen to all the unique plants and animals they had seen? Ranger Jim said they could help by conserving water, even when brushing their teeth or washing their faces, because most of the water used in southern Florida comes from the Everglades. With responsible water conservation, the Everglades Restoration Plan could, over the next thirty years, restore a healthy balance so all living things—plants, animals, and people—will be able to live side by side in the only *Pa-hay-okee*, "Grassy River," in the world.

It was the end of a long day for the class, but there was one more part of the Everglades to visit. Ms. Stone and Ranger Jim led the students into an open space hidden at the end of the hiking trail.

 **STOP AND THINK**

Persuasion On this page, what does the author say people should do to help the Everglades? How does this show you how she feels about the Everglades?

Flock of White Ibis

208

"This is a finger glade," Ms. Stone said. "It's a small part of the sawgrass prairie that does not stay wet all year." During the wet season, the finger glade would be filled with water and fish. But now the ground, which is higher than the larger sawgrass prairies, was dry and hard.

"For a few minutes you can walk as far as you like and enjoy the finger glade," said Ms. Stone.

The students fanned out. Some pretended they were birds, flying low overhead. Others studied the sawgrass, pretending to be explorers discovering the glade. Still others talked about how the hard ground on which they were walking would turn into a lake deep enough for fish to swim through during the wet season. And some just lay on their backs, looking at the sky and the ring of trees around the glade.

When the students came back, they sat in a circle close to Ms. Stone.

"Close your eyes," said Ms. Stone, "and listen."

"Do you hear cars?" she whispered.

"Do you hear sirens?"

"Do you hear people?"

"What do you hear?"

Silence.

"You are not going to find silence like this anyplace else in the world," Ms. Stone said quietly. "This glade is protected by a circle of trees and marshes and natural wildlife. It is far from the noise of the outside world. It's full of *silence.* Any time you are in a sawgrass prairie like this one, stop and listen to the silence."

STOP AND THINK

Author's Craft An author's **word choice** can shape a reader's perception, or understanding, of a subject. How does the word *silence* shape your understanding of the Everglades? Based on the information the author gives here, what kinds of conclusions can be drawn about the noise of everyday life?

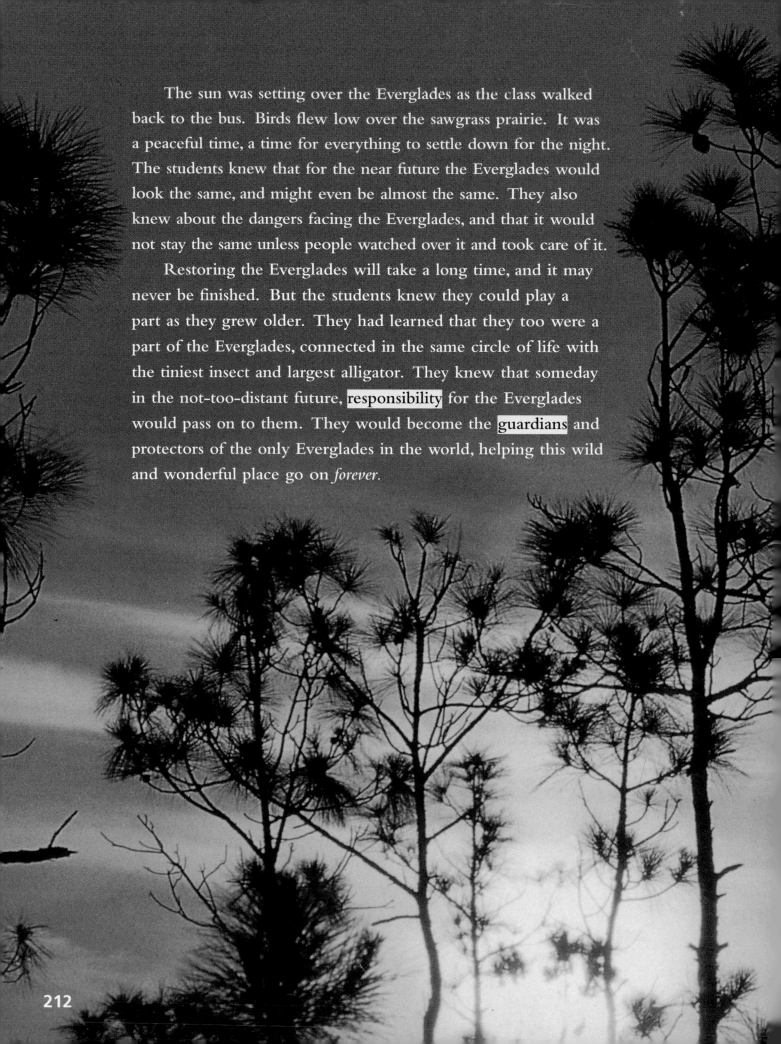

The sun was setting over the Everglades as the class walked back to the bus. Birds flew low over the sawgrass prairie. It was a peaceful time, a time for everything to settle down for the night. The students knew that for the near future the Everglades would look the same, and might even be almost the same. They also knew about the dangers facing the Everglades, and that it would not stay the same unless people watched over it and took care of it.

Restoring the Everglades will take a long time, and it may never be finished. But the students knew they could play a part as they grew older. They had learned that they too were a part of the Everglades, connected in the same circle of life with the tiniest insect and largest alligator. They knew that someday in the not-too-distant future, responsibility for the Everglades would pass on to them. They would become the guardians and protectors of the only Everglades in the world, helping this wild and wonderful place go on *forever*.

Your Turn

You Were There

Short Response The author of "Everglades Forever" describes a real-life experience, a fifth-grade class field trip to Everglades National Park. Imagine that you had been on that field trip. Write a paragraph explaining what experiences and information you found most meaningful, and tell why. PERSONAL RESPONSE

Add Some Drama

Write a Script During the trip, Ranger Jim shows Ms. Stone's students many habitats filled with plants and animals. Work with a small group to choose a scene from the selection. Use details from the scene to write a script. Make up a new event to include in the scene. Add characters, including Ranger Jim, and dialogue. Read the script to the class. SMALL GROUP

It's a Group Effort

Turn and Talk Think about the author's message on the last page of the selection. Discuss with a partner what facts and details the author uses to persuade people to watch over and care for the Everglades.

PERSUASION

Science

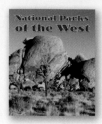

✓ TARGET VOCABULARY

conserving	responsibility
restore	attracted
regulate	adapted
vegetation	unique
endangered	guardians

GENRE

Informational text, such as this website, gives facts and examples about a topic.

TEXT FOCUS

Graphic Sources Informational text may include a graph, which shows how different facts and numbers relate to each other and to the text.

File   Edit   View   Favorites

National Parks of the West

Big Bend National Park: Texas

Big Bend National Park is located along the Rio Grande, also called the Rio Bravo, the river that forms the boundary between Mexico and the United States. The park is open year-round. <u>more</u>

Wildlife and Vegetation

Big Bend is the home of more than 1,200 plant species, including 60 kinds of cactus, and more than 4,000 animal and insect species. This diversity is due to the park's many natural habitats, from the Chihuahuan Desert to the Chisos Mountains. <u>more</u>

search

ACTIVITIES

Hiking in Big Bend National Park

Big Bend's 150 miles of trails have attracted hikers for years. Many choose the easy Window View Trail. Others prefer the challenge of a hike to the summit of 7,832-foot Mt. Emory. more

Hikers' Guidelines

Thousands of hikers visit Big Bend every year. National park rangers, guardians of the park, regulate the hiking. They ask hikers and backpackers to follow these tips:

- Your safety is your responsibility. Do not start your hike without the right supplies and equipment.
- Clean up after yourself.
- Do not climb within 50 feet of any Native American rock art.
- Do not harm or disturb nature. Conserving the environment is important!

A hiker in Big Bend National Park

Yellowstone National Park: Wyoming, Montana, and Idaho

Yellowstone National Park is the first and oldest national park in the United States. It was established in 1872. Yellowstone has at least 150 geysers. The most famous geyser is Old Faithful. This natural wonder shoots hot water as high as 200 feet in the air. <u>more</u>

A gray wolf running

Wildlife

Yellowstone has dozens of animal species. Today, wolves are among them, but in 1994, Yellowstone had no wolves. Humans had killed off the park's native gray wolves.

In the 1990s, scientists decided to restore this endangered wolf species to the park. In 1995 and 1996, scientists captured thirty-one gray wolves in Canada and brought them to Yellowstone. At first, the wolves lived in three large pens. In time, they were released into the wild.

The wolf restoration program is not unique. It was modeled after other similar programs. But it is one of the most successfully adapted programs of its kind. In 2006, 136 gray wolves lived in Yellowstone. They live in thirteen different areas of the park.

Analyze the graph below. In what year was the wolf population the highest? The lowest? How many wolves were there in each of these years?

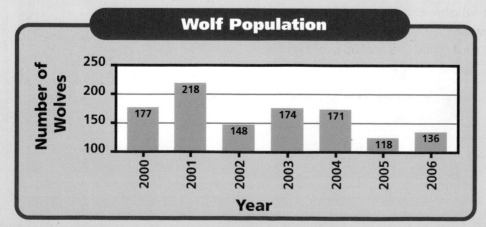

Wolf Population

Number of Wolves — Year

2000: 177, 2001: 218, 2002: 148, 2003: 174, 2004: 171, 2005: 118, 2006: 136

Making Connections

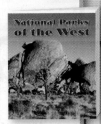

Text to Self

Write an Informal Letter Which national park would you most like to visit—the Everglades, Big Bend, or Yellowstone? Write a letter to your classmates to persuade them to plan a field trip to this park. Use facts from the selections to make a strong case.

Text to Text

Role-Play a Panel Discussion Work in a group. Have group members play these roles: host or hostess, Ranger Jim, Big Bend ranger, Yellowstone ranger. Hold a mock panel discussion in which the park rangers answer questions about their parks. Use information from the selections, including details from photos, captions, or other graphic sources.

Text to World

Identify Point of View Review the website featured on pages 214–216. What point of view is presented? Think about how that point of view affects your interest in national parks. Then search the Internet for a website about another wildlife preserve similar to Yellowstone. Discuss with classmates your thoughts about the website's information and its point of view.

STORM WARRIORS

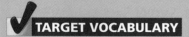
✓ TARGET VOCABULARY

critical

demolished

elite

commotion

bundle

annoyance

secured

squalling

clammy

realization

Vocabulary Reader

Context Cards

SAVED from the SEA

Vocabulary in Context

1 critical

Rescue workers can provide critical, or vital, aid when a hurricane strikes.

2 demolished

These people returned to search the ruins of their home after a tornado demolished it.

3 elite

Medals for bravery are given to an elite group of the best and most skilled lifeguards.

4 commotion

Rescue dogs are trained to stay calm in spite of chaos and commotion.

- **Study each Context Card.**
- **Break each Vocabulary word into syllables. Use your glossary to check your answers.**

5 bundle

Rescuers bundle, or wrap, injured skiers in blankets for warmth or to prevent shock.

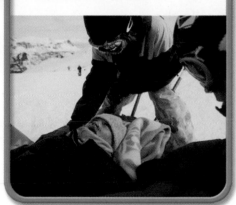

6 annoyance

During a fire, people who get too close can distract firefighters and cause them annoyance.

7 secured

In mountain rescues, one person is secured to another by safety fasteners.

8 squalling

The squalling of a child can lead rescuers to the frightened, crying victim.

9 clammy

The protective clothing worn by firefighters can make them feel clammy and damp.

10 realization

The realization, or understanding, that rescuers save lives makes families proud.

Background

The Outer Banks The chain of islands off North Carolina's coast is called the Outer Banks. The islands protect the mainland because of their critical location in the path of many hurricanes. Huge storms have demolished parts of the islands. One storm cut Hatteras Island in two! So many ships have sunk in storms there that the area is called "The Graveyard of the Atlantic."

In the 1870s, lifesaving stations were set up on the Outer Banks. Elite crews, often secured to the shore by ropes, swam out to grounded ships to rescue those aboard. They would bundle the clammy victims, including children, in blankets. They kept working through the commotion of wind, waves, and the children's squalling.

Not everyone reacts to the Outer Banks' winds with annoyance. Today, a realization of the islands' beauty attracts thousands of tourists each year.

• Examine the map below. Which islands make up the Outer Banks?

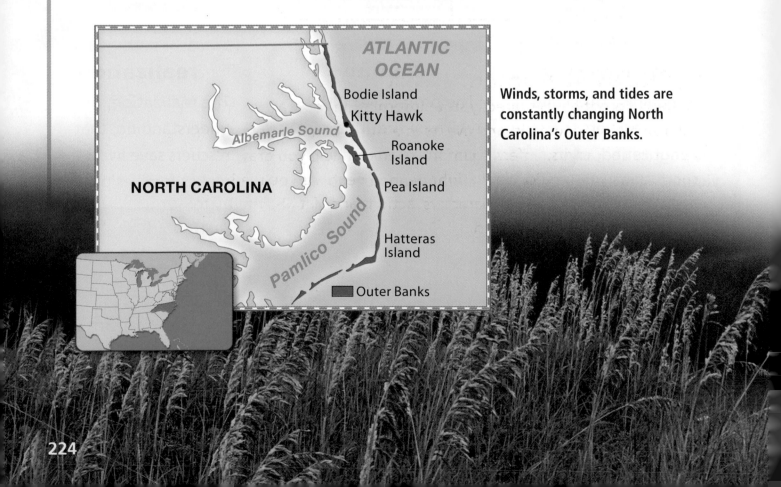

ATLANTIC OCEAN

Bodie Island

Kitty Hawk

Albemarle Sound

Roanoke Island

NORTH CAROLINA

Pea Island

Pamlico Sound

Hatteras Island

■ Outer Banks

Winds, storms, and tides are constantly changing North Carolina's Outer Banks.

Comprehension

✔ **TARGET SKILL** **Conclusions and Generalizations**

As you read "Storm Warriors," notice the details that the author
provides about the men who rescue the passengers aboard the *E. S.
Newman*. Their actions and words can help you draw conclusions
and make generalizations about the job the surfmen once did. Use
a graphic organizer like this one to record a conclusion about the
surfmen and the details you used to draw your conclusion.

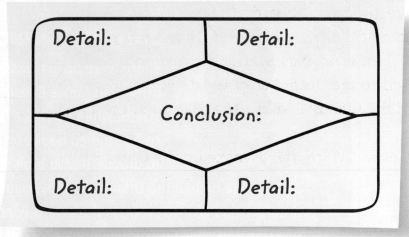

✔ **TARGET STRATEGY** **Infer/Predict**

Authors do not always directly state information for readers. You
can use dialogue, details, and events in a story to infer information
about its characters. Inferring information can help you draw
conclusions and predict what might happen next. As you read,
make inferences based on characters' actions and details, and try to
predict how the story will end.

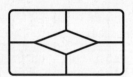

STORM WARRIORS

✓ **TARGET VOCABULARY**

critical	annoyance
demolished	secured
elite	squalling
commotion	clammy
bundle	realization

✓ **TARGET SKILL**

Conclusions and Generalizations Use details to explain ideas that aren't stated or are generally true.

✓ **TARGET STRATEGY**

Infer/Predict Use text clues to figure out what the author means or what might happen in the future.

GENRE

Historical fiction is a story whose characters and events are set in a real period of history.

MEET THE AUTHOR
Elisa Carbone

To research *Storm Warriors*, Elisa Carbone went to North Carolina's Outer Banks to experience a storm for herself. She says, "I would go out onto the beach for as long as I could stand it, feeling the force of the wind, taking in all of the sensations. Then I'd . . . write it all down."

MEET THE ILLUSTRATOR
James Ransome

There were no art classes offered in James Ransome's school when he was a boy, so he studied books on how to draw. Then in high school and college he had the chance to study painting, drawing, and film. Now he is the award-winning illustrator of over twenty-five books for children.

STORM WARRIORS

by Elisa Carbone
selection illustrated by James Ransome

Essential Question

What conclusions can we draw about the sea?

It's 1896 on Pea Island, part of North Carolina's Outer Banks. Nathan dreams of becoming a fearless surfman with Pea Island's elite African American lifesaving crew. However, his father, a fisherman, doesn't want Nathan to risk his life rescuing people from shipwrecks. Nevertheless, Nathan studies medical books and learns critical lifesaving skills. Then a hurricane hits the Outer Banks. The E.S. Newman runs aground in the storm. This is Nathan's chance to help the surfmen. As the storm rages, he begins to realize that knowledge is as important as bravery.

I stumbled forward and caught my balance on the side of the beach cart. I faced the sea and the wind. There was the sunken ship, hardly thirty yards from us. She was a mass of dark hull and white torn sails against the foaming sea, rocking on her side, her cabin and much of her starboard already demolished by the heavy surf. As I stood with my mouth open, panting, the wind blew my cheeks floppy and dried my tongue.

A cheer went up from the sailors aboard the ship. They'd spotted us and had high hopes that they would soon be rescued. I expected to hear the command "Action," to begin the breeches-buoy rescue, but heard nothing. It took me a moment to realize what Keeper Etheridge must already have figured out: our equipment was useless. There was no way to dig a hole for the sand anchor under these rolling waves, nowhere to set up the Lyle gun.

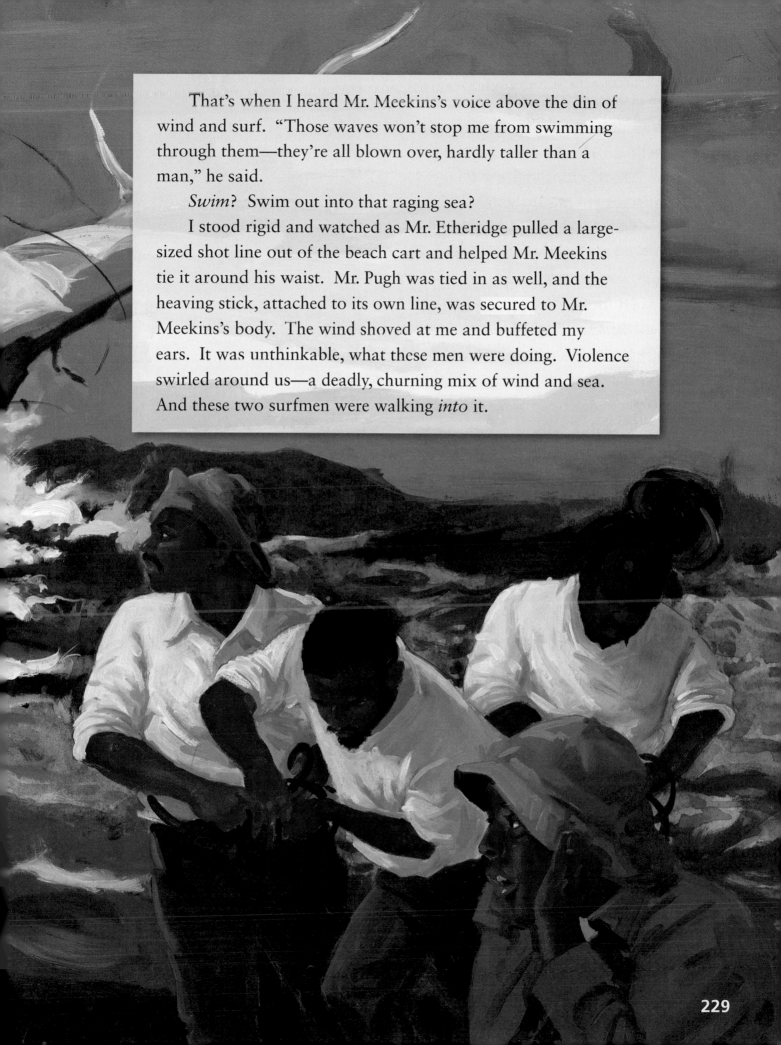

That's when I heard Mr. Meekins's voice above the din of wind and surf. "Those waves won't stop me from swimming through them—they're all blown over, hardly taller than a man," he said.

Swim? Swim out into that raging sea?

I stood rigid and watched as Mr. Etheridge pulled a large-sized shot line out of the beach cart and helped Mr. Meekins tie it around his waist. Mr. Pugh was tied in as well, and the heaving stick, attached to its own line, was secured to Mr. Meekins's body. The wind shoved at me and buffeted my ears. It was unthinkable, what these men were doing. Violence swirled around us—a deadly, churning mix of wind and sea. And these two surfmen were walking *into* it.

"Man the ropes," shouted Mr. Etheridge. "One of them goes down, we'll haul them both back in."

Mr. Meekins and Mr. Pugh were dark forms against the white foam, plodding into the surf. Powerful waves smacked them in the chest. They ducked their heads down and pushed forward.

I watched with a sick feeling in my stomach as the realization crept over me: I would never be able to do what these men were doing. The words of their motto ran through my head: "You have to go out, but you don't have to come back." In that moment I knew, with not a shred of doubt, that I did not have the courage to risk my life that way. The dream, and all the months of hoping, blew away as quickly as the foam off the waves. William and Floyd and Daddy were right. I would never be a surfman.

STOP AND THINK

Infer/Predict Do you think the rescue crew will be able to rescue the sailors? What makes you think as you do? Use the text to support your answer.

There was no time for me to wallow in my loss. The men were paying out the ropes, and I was a fisherman—here to help. I took hold of one of the ropes. I turned my face sideways to the wind, but still it made my eyes blurry with tears. Blindly, I let the rope out, hand over hand, then squinted out toward the ship. A ladder had been lowered, and the sailors leaned over the side, waiting. Mr. Meekins and Mr. Pugh were almost there.

I heard another cheer from the men on the ship. When I peered out, Mr. Meekins was swinging the heaving stick and line. He let it fly and it landed on deck. The sailors would tie the line to the ship so that the rope could help steady the surfmen as they made their way from ship to shore and back again.

Soon we were hauling rope back in. The surfmen would be carrying one of the sailors between them now. I squinted into the spray. Where was the rescued sailor? Mr. Meekins and Mr. Pugh were on their way back, but without a third man between them. Mr. Meekins was carrying something a little larger than a Lyle gun.

231

What in the world could be more important to save off that ship than the lives of the men on board? I shook my head and hauled rope. The surfmen were half walking, half swimming, pushing forward, the waves smacking against their backs and seeming to want to spit them out of the sea.

As the surfmen drew closer, I heard what sounded like the squalling of an alley cat. Mr. Meekins handed over his bundle and shouted, "Get it into dry blankets before it goes blue!" The bundle was passed from man to man, until it was handed to me and I found myself looking into the terrified eyes of a screaming child.

Daddy put his arm around my shoulders. "The driving cart," he shouted over the din of the waves and wind. In the driving cart, which was nothing more than an open wagon, dry blankets were packed under oilskins.

We crouched next to the cart, and it gave us some protection from the storm. The child clung to my neck. He was drenched and shivering miserably. I tried to loosen his grip so I could get his wet clothes off, but he just clung tighter. He was crying more softly now. "Mamma?" he whimpered.

I gave Daddy a pleading look. What if his mother had already been washed overboard and drowned? Daddy stood, cupped his hands around his eyes, and looked in the direction of the ship. "They're carrying a woman back now," he said.

"Your mamma is coming," I told the child. He looked to be about three or four years old, with pale white skin and a shock of thick brown hair. "Let's get you warm before she gets here."

We had the boy wrapped in a dry blanket by the time his mother came running to him, cried, "Thomas!" and clutched him to her own wet clothing with such passion that she probably got him half drenched again.

The lady, who told us her name was Mrs. Gardiner, said she'd be warm enough in her wet dress under blankets and oilskins. No sooner had we settled her with Thomas than we heard the cry "Ho, this man is injured!"

STOP AND THINK

Author's Craft The author uses **first-person point of view,** which tells the story from the narrator's perspective. How would the story change if it were told from Mr. Meekins's (third-person limited) point of view?

233

I ran to see. A young sailor had just been delivered by the surfmen. Blood dripped from his head and stained his life preserver. His lips were a sickly blue. He took two steps, then collapsed face first into the shallow water. Mr. Bowser dragged him up by his armpits and pulled him toward the driving cart.

"George, take over my place with the ropes," he shouted to Daddy. "Nathan, come help me."

The sailor looked hardly older than me, with dirty blond hair that had a bloody gash the size of a pole bean running through it.

"Treat the bleeding first, then the hypothermia," I said as I recalled the words from the medical books and they comforted me with their matter-of-factness.

Mr. Bowser grunted as we lifted the sailor into the driving cart. "You did study well, Nathan," he said.

Mr. Bowser sent me for the medicine chest, then I held a compress against the man's head wound while Mr. Bowser began to remove his wet clothes. That's when Mr. Bowser seemed to notice Mrs. Gardiner for the first time.

"Ma'am, we're going to have to . . ." He cleared his throat. "This boy's hypothermic, so his wet clothes have to . . ."

Mrs. Gardiner rolled her eyes in annoyance. "Oh, for heaven's sake!" she exclaimed. She immediately went to work to pull off the man's boots, help Mr. Bowser get the rest of his clothes off, and bundle him in a dry blanket.

"Are there any other injured on board?" Mr. Bowser asked as he wrapped a bandage around the man's head.

"No, only Arthur," she said. "He took quite a fall when the ship ran aground."

Arthur groaned and his eyes fluttered open. "I'm cold," he complained.

Suddenly there was a commotion at the ropes. "Heave!" Mr. Etheridge shouted. "Haul them all in!"

"They've lost their footing!" I cried.

Mr. Bowser grasped me by the arms. "Take over here. I'm sure you know what to do." Then he ran to help with the ropes.

My hands felt clammy and shaky, but once again the words from the books came back to steady me: "Rub the legs and arms with linseed oil until warmth returns . . ." I rummaged in the medicine chest, found the linseed oil, and poured some into my palm.

"This will warm you, sir," I said loudly enough to be heard over the wind.

Arthur nodded his bandaged head and watched nervously as I rubbed the oil into his feet and calves, then his hands and arms. He gave Mrs. Gardiner a quizzical look. "Ain't he young to be a doctor?" he asked her.

She patted his shoulder and smoothed the hair off his forehead. "He seems to know what to do, dear," she said.

"I am warming up," he said.

I lifted the lantern to look at Arthur's face and saw that his lips were no longer blue.

 STOP AND THINK

Conclusions and Generalizations Based on the events that have happened up to this point, what do you think Nathan will do for work when he grows up?

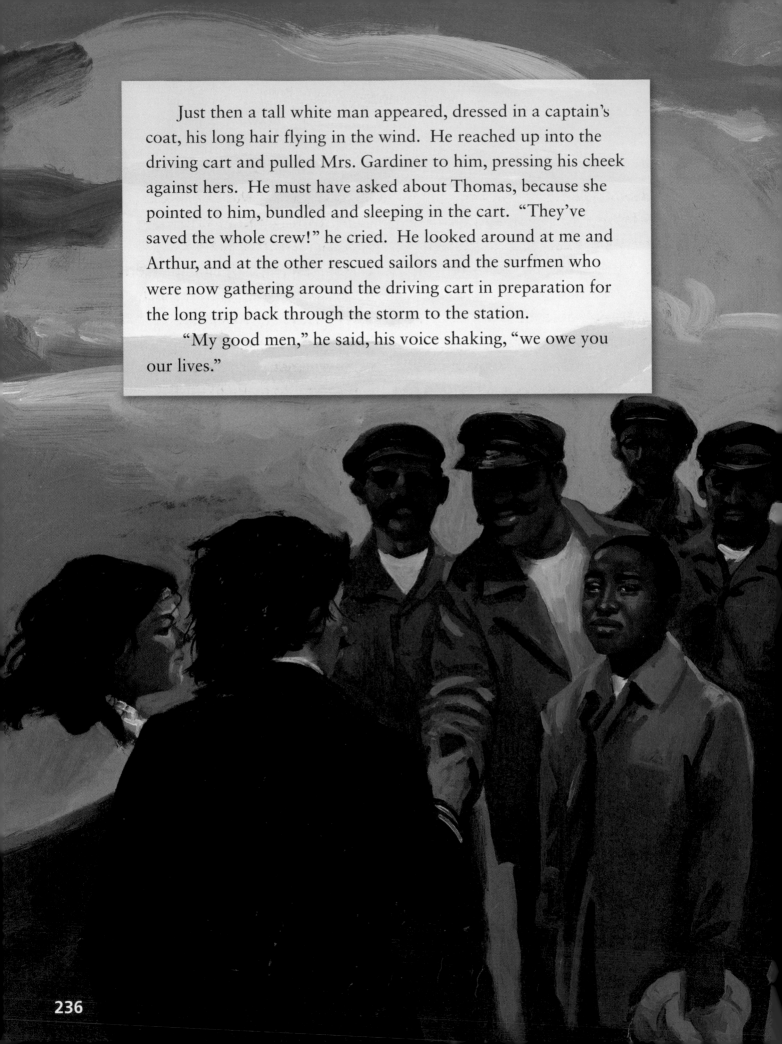

Just then a tall white man appeared, dressed in a captain's coat, his long hair flying in the wind. He reached up into the driving cart and pulled Mrs. Gardiner to him, pressing his cheek against hers. He must have asked about Thomas, because she pointed to him, bundled and sleeping in the cart. "They've saved the whole crew!" he cried. He looked around at me and Arthur, and at the other rescued sailors and the surfmen who were now gathering around the driving cart in preparation for the long trip back through the storm to the station.

"My good men," he said, his voice shaking, "we owe you our lives."

Your Turn

Everyday Knowledge

Short Response In "Storm Warriors," Nathan learns that knowledge can be as important as courage and physical strength in some situations. Write a paragraph describing important knowledge that you use every day in your life, and explain how it helps you. PERSONAL RESPONSE

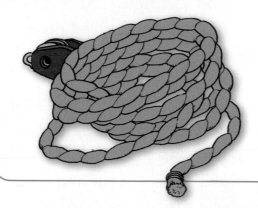

Action!

Act It Out For Nathan, helping the surfmen rescue sailors and passengers from the *E.S. Newman* was a challenge. Work with a small group to reenact the rescue. Include roles for rescued passengers, sailors, and the surfmen. Use details from the story to make the scene realistic and exciting. Rehearse the scene, and then perform it for classmates. SMALL GROUP

The Power of the Sea

Turn and Talk When Nathan runs down to the beach to help the surfmen, he sees the ship's "dark hull and white torn sails against the foaming sea." With a partner, review the story to find other details that describe the sea. Use these details to draw conclusions about the author's word choice and purpose for writing. CONCLUSIONS AND GENERALIZATIONS

Social Studies

✔ TARGET VOCABULARY

critical	annoyance
demolished	secured
elite	squalling
commotion	clammy
bundle	realization

GENRE

Informational text, such as this magazine article, gives facts and examples about a topic.

TEXT FOCUS

Primary sources are original photographs, documents, or quotes from the time period of the topic.
• The author of this selection includes photographs of Pea Island, the surfmen, and their rescue equipment. How do these primary sources help the author achieve her purpose?

Pea Island's Forgotten Heroes

by Cecelia Munzenmaier

The photograph at the museum in Beaufort, North Carolina, was small. Still, it caught Katie Burkhart's eye. Seven men in uniform stood in front of U.S. Life-Saving Service Station #17. A caption explained that these were the Pea Island surfmen. Led by Chief Richard Etheridge, they saved nine people from the *E.S. Newman* in 1896.

Fourteen-year-old Burkhart wanted to know more. She looked up information about the surfmen for an eighth-grade history project. Then she wrote a paper titled, "Forgotten Legacy: African-American Storm Warriors." It won a National Award of Merit from the American Association of State and Local Historians.

It also helped bring attention to some forgotten heroes.

Finding a Lost Story

Burkhart learned that Etheridge and his surfmen were an elite group. They were known for their skill and bravery. They were also the only African American group whose job was to save lives.

Then she came to a realization. Their bravery had never been officially recognized. "I immediately felt I had to do something about it," she says.

The eighth-grader wrote to Senator Jesse Helms and President Bill Clinton. She asked why the crew had not been given a medal. She learned that Coast Guard Officer Steve Rochon and graduate students David Zoby and David Wright were also trying to correct this wrong.

"Again and again, the crew went back through the raging sea."

The Pea Island surfmen
in about 1890

239

Reclaiming a Legacy

The researchers found Chief Etheridge's own account of what happened. He described the commotion of the hurricane that demolished the ship. "The storm was raging fearfully, the storm tide was sweeping across the beach, and the team was often brought to a standstill by the sweeping current," he wrote in the station log. Lending any help seemed impossible, yet they had to try.

Secured by a rope, two team members swam to the sinking ship. They brought back a crewman. Then a fresh team heard the squalling of the captain's baby and saved him. For six hours, they ignored their own needs. They were too busy to feel annoyance. Missed meals and clammy clothes were not important. As they saved people, they would bundle them into warm blankets at the station.

The research was critical in winning recognition for the team. One hundred years to the day after the rescue of the *E.S. Newman*, the Pea Island crew was awarded a Gold Lifesaving Medal. Katie Burkhart and several descendants of the surfmen listened with pride to the speech that described how "again and again, the Pea Island Station crew went back through the raging sea, literally carrying all nine persons from certain death to the safety of the shore."

Pea Island, 1917

Beach rescue equipment

Making Connections

 Text to Self

Design a Medal The Pea Island crewmembers were awarded a Gold Lifesaving Medal for their heroism. Design a medal for a modern-day hero whom you admire. Include an image and a message to go on the medal. Write a short speech explaining why the person deserves the medal and present your information to a partner.

 Text to Text

Compare and Contrast Themes The theme of a story is its main message. Analyzing the main character's qualities, motives, and actions can help a reader determine the story's theme. In "Storm Warriors" and "Elisa's Diary" (Lesson 5), the main characters must adjust to difficult situations. Think about the qualities, motives, and actions of Nathan and Elisa that help them overcome their challenges and what they learn about themselves. Using this information, write a paragraph comparing and contrasting the themes of "Storm Warriors" and "Elisa's Diary" using evidence from the text.

 Text to World

Research Hurricanes The Pea Island rescuers had to fight a hurricane in order to rescue the passengers and crew of the *E.S. Newman*. Work with a partner to brainstorm research questions about hurricanes or another kind of natural disaster you would like to learn more about. Then create a list of possible sources in which you could find answers to your questions.

Grammar

What Is a Complex Sentence? A **complex sentence** is a pair of sentences joined by a **subordinating conjunction** such as *because, although,* or *since.* The part of a complex sentence with the subordinating conjunction tells about the other part of the sentence. It gives information, but it cannot stand on its own as a complete sentence.

Complex Sentences
can stand on its own   **cannot stand on its own** The crew members were in danger **because** their ship had been wrecked.
cannot stand on its own   **can stand on its own** **Although** the waves were big, two surfmen swam to the ship.

Try This! **Copy each sentence onto another sheet of paper. Circle the subordinating conjunction in it. Underline the part of the sentence that cannot stand on its own.**

❶ After the men rescued the child, Nathan took care of him.

❷ When the child whimpered, Mrs. Gardiner comforted him.

❸ The child warmed up once he was wrapped in a dry blanket.

❹ As a sailor came toward the shore, he collapsed.

❺ The sailor needed treatment because he was wounded.

Sentence Fluency Good writers try to show exactly how ideas in separate sentences are related. Combining shorter sentences to form a complex sentence can show how ideas are linked or which idea is more important. Use a comma after the first part of a complex sentence if that part begins with a subordinating conjunction.

Separate Sentences

The snow was dangerously deep.

The governor declared an emergency.

Complex Sentence

Since the snow was dangerously deep, the governor declared an emergency.

Connect Grammar to Writing

As you revise your response to literature next week, look for sentences with related ideas. Try building a complex sentence by joining related sentences with a subordinating conjunction.

Write to Respond

☑ **Ideas** A **response essay** often requires that you state an opinion about a topic. After forming your opinion, write at least three reasons for it. Support your reasons with details from the story.

Josie thought about her answer to *Was Nathan a coward?* First she made notes. Then, in a chart, she restated her opinion, listed her strongest reasons, and included supporting details for them. Use the Writing Process Checklist below as you prewrite.

Writing Process Checklist

▶ **Prewrite**

☑ Did I state my opinion clearly?

☑ Did I give at least three good reasons?

☑ Did I list details from the story to support my reasons?

Draft

Revise

Edit

Publish and Share

Exploring a Topic

Opinion: Nathan is not a coward.

Reason: He wants to help.

Reason: His father doesn't want him to be a surfman.

Reason: He takes responsibility.

Reason: He helps others.

Opinion: Nathan is not a coward.

Reasons	Details
He wants to help in spite of danger.	• chooses to go help in a raging storm • helps with ropes
He takes responsibility even though he is young.	• takes care of young boy • runs to scene of injury
He uses his knowledge to help others.	• stops the bleeding • warms the sailor's limbs

When I made my chart, I strengthened my reasons by adding details from the text to support them.

Reading as a Writer

How did Josie make her reasons stronger when she made her chart? What reasons and details could be stronger in your chart?

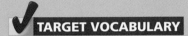

✓ **TARGET VOCABULARY**

resemble

detecting

keen

vary

unobserved

mature

particular

available

ferocious

contentment

Vocabulary Reader

Context Cards

Vocabulary in Context

1 resemble

Some house cats resemble, or look like, cougars, but cougars are much bigger.

2 detecting

Excellent eyesight and a good sense of smell help lions in finding, or detecting, their prey.

3 keen

All cats have sharp, keen night vision. It is a great aid to them when hunting.

4 vary

The color of tiger stripes can vary from black and orange to black and white.

- **Study each Context Card.**
- **Use a dictionary to determine the part of speech of each Vocabulary word.**

5 unobserved

Hiding under the rug, this kitten is unobserved, or unseen, by its owner.

6 mature

As cougars mature from cubs to adults, their eyes change from blue to greenish-yellow.

7 particular

A house cat may prefer a particular, or certain, brand of food. It will eat only that kind.

8 available

Big cats can live only where plenty of food is available, or obtainable.

9 ferocious

The savage, ferocious roar of a tiger signals that the animal is angry.

10 contentment

Like wild cats, house cats purr with contentment when they are satisfied.

Background

✔ TARGET VOCABULARY **Saving Wild Cats** Why is it important to save wild cats such as cougars and lions? After all, these animals become ferocious as they mature. Many live unobserved by humans, so why should we care about these particular creatures?

Let's look at some available facts. First of all, big cats are an important part of the ecosystem. If they died out, animals that they feed on would multiply, sending the habitat out of balance. Other animals and plants would be affected, and perhaps *they* would die out, too.

Wild cats are also beautiful. Although they vary in appearance, they resemble each other in that they are all sleek and powerful. Cougars, for example, can leap eighteen feet upward from a sitting position! They have keen eyesight for detecting prey.

Animals and humans can experience a sense of contentment when they live in harmony with nature. We need to protect wild cats.

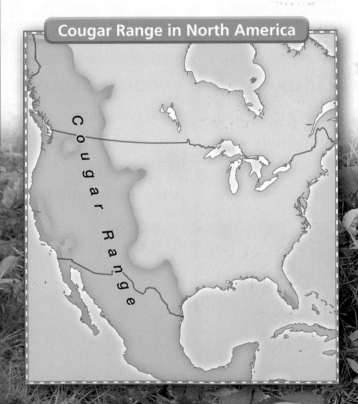

Cougar Range in North America

Cougar Range

Review the map at left. Are cougars generally found in the eastern or the western part of the United States?

Comprehension

Main Ideas and Details

As you read "Cougars," look for main ideas about these great cats and details about their lives and habitats that support each idea. A selection can have several main ideas with supporting details. Make a graphic organizer like this one to keep track of a main idea and its supporting details. Then list the supporting details in logical order.

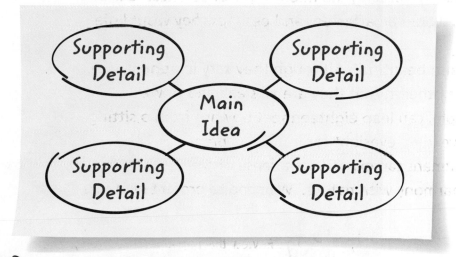

✔ **TARGET STRATEGY** **Monitor/Clarify**

Organize the main ideas and details to help you monitor, or pay attention to, what you are reading and clarify parts of the text that you do not understand.

Cougars

TARGET VOCABULARY

resemble	mature
detecting	particular
keen	available
vary	ferocious
unobserved	contentment

TARGET SKILL

Main Ideas and Details
Identify a topic's important ideas
and supporting details.

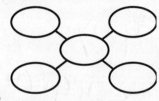

TARGET STRATEGY

Monitor/Clarify As you read,
notice what is not making sense.
Find ways to figure out the parts
that are confusing.

GENRE

Informational text gives
facts and examples about a
topic.

MEET THE AUTHOR

PATRICIA CORRIGAN

Patricia Corrigan began writing for her local
newspaper while she was still in high school.
Since then, she has been a writer for the *St.
Louis Post-Dispatch* and has published numerous
magazine articles, nonfiction books for adults,
and nature books for children. She loves to travel
and has taken trips to Argentina and Egypt.

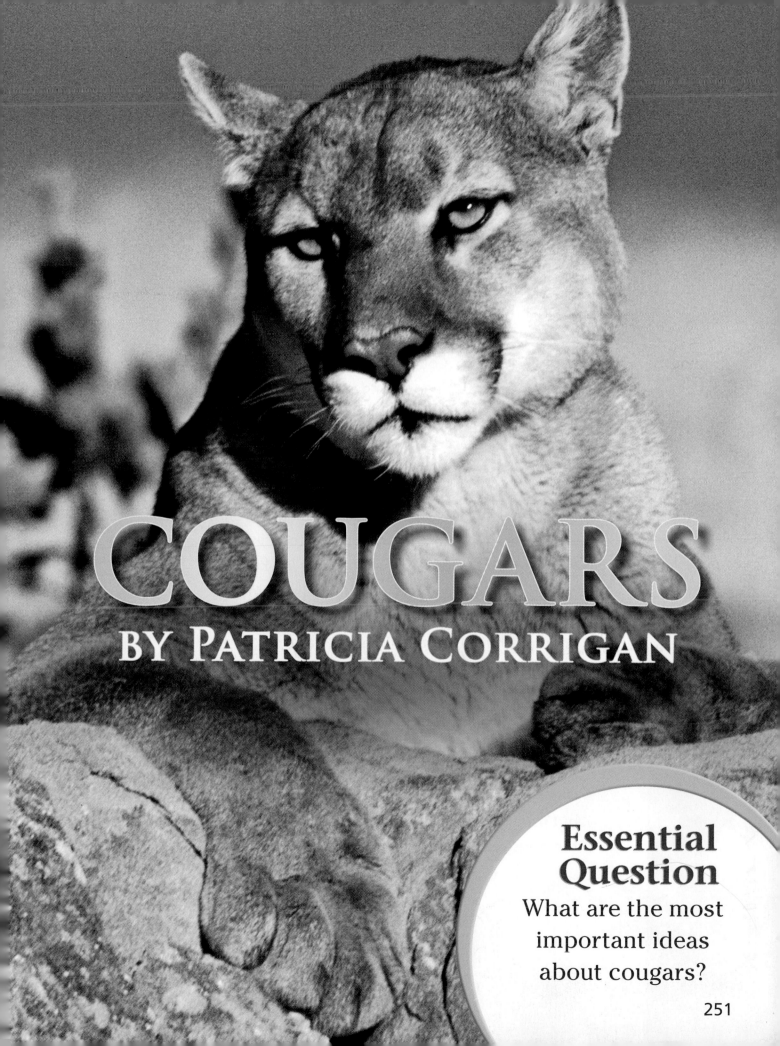

COUGARS
BY PATRICIA CORRIGAN

Essential Question

What are the most important ideas about cougars?

Cougars are seldom seen and rarely heard. In fact, they often live their entire lives unobserved by humans!

But we do know that these members of the cat family live in eleven western U.S. states. They are found from the southernmost tip of Alaska down to where the California border meets Mexico and east all the way to the edge of Texas. Their cousins, Florida panthers, live in Florida. In Canada, cougars are found in British Columbia and parts of Alberta. Cougars also live throughout Mexico, Central America, and South America.

In different areas of the world, cougars have different names. They may be called mountain lions, wildcats, pumas, painters, fire cats, swamp lions, or catamounts. In Mexico, Spanish for cougar is *el león* (leh OHN), which means "the lion." And sometimes they are known by nicknames like "ghost of the wilderness" and "ghost walker."

Fortunately, cougars are able to live in many different habitats. Over time, they have adapted, or evolved, for living in places such as snow-capped mountains, jungles thick with vegetation, cool pine forests, grassy plains, and murky swamps. For instance, cougars that live in northern mountains tend to be larger and have a thicker coat of fur than cougars that live elsewhere. They learned to climb trees. And they also can swim if necessary, but usually prefer to stay dry—like their relative, the house cat!

The average cougar measures from 3.3 to 5.3 feet long and stands about 2 feet high at the shoulder. Adult male cougars weigh up to 225 pounds, and adult females usually are slightly smaller. A cougar's tail may measure up to 32 inches, almost two-thirds the length of the animal's body.

☑ **STOP AND THINK**

Main Ideas and Details What is the topic of this selection? How do you know? Choose a paragraph on one of these pages. State its main idea. How can you tell the difference between the main idea and the details? Now list the details in logical order.

Cougars don't hunt from trees, but a high branch makes a good lookout spot.

Cougars have good balance and can easily leap over fallen trees and onto rocks without slowing down.

The cougar is one species (SPEE sees), or kind, of wild cat. Cougars are medium-sized, along with bobcats and lynxes. Tigers, lions, and leopards all are larger and heavier.

Cougars are muscular and sleek, with little fat on their bodies. Fat usually serves as excellent insulation and keeps an animal's body warm. But because cougars have little of this kind of insulation, they have another natural defense against the cold: their fur coats keep them warm.

The layer of hair closest to the skin, called the underfur, is woolly and short. The top layer is made up of longer hairs, called guard hairs. These hairs are hollow and trap the air to keep cold temperatures from reaching the animal's skin.

Unlike humans, cougars have no sweat glands, so the cougars that live in warm climates cool themselves the same way dogs do, by panting to release heat from their bodies.

STOP AND THINK

Author's Craft In nonfiction, an **author's purpose** often is to help readers understand something. The author provides a lot of detail in her description of cougars to help readers understand the unique qualities of these animals. How well do you think she achieves her purpose?

Cougars' coats are usually tawny, or orange-brown. They also may be gray, sandy brown, reddish-brown, and tan. All adult cougars have black markings on the sides of the muzzle, or snout, where the whiskers are. Some people say this area looks as if the cougar has a "mustache." If cougars were less secretive, scientists might be able to tell individual animals apart by the dark patterns on the muzzles, but few of the animals are ever seen.

The chin is white, as is the area right under the pinkish-brown nose. The tips of their tails also are black. The underside of most cougars is light, sometimes nearly white. At first glance, adult cougars resemble female lions.

Their coloring helps them blend in with their surroundings. It is good camouflage (KAM uh flahj) and helps them hide from their prey (PRAY), or the animals they hunt for food.

Cougars have good eyesight. In fact, vision is their best-developed sense. Researchers believe that they can see moving prey from long distances. The cougar's yellow eyes have large, round pupils that take in all available light. That helps the animal see at night almost as well as during the day.

A keen sense of hearing is important for cougars. They even can move their small, rounded ears to take in sounds coming from different directions. Cougars also have a strong sense of smell, which can really be useful when following prey. Still, their sense of smell is not as well developed as their senses of sight or hearing.

Like all of their cat relatives, cougars have whiskers. These sensitive hairs are also called vibrissae (vy BRIHS ee). They grow on either side of the animal's nose and mouth, above the eyes, and sometimes on the chin.

These whiskers vary in length, but most of the whiskers found on the muzzle are long enough to stretch past the side of the face and back to the edge of the ear. The cougar uses whiskers to gather information through touch. With its whiskers, a cougar can determine the height of the grass, the width of the space under a rock, and whether a bush would be easy or difficult to push through.

Cougars make a variety of sounds, or vocalizations. Their meow, which is a sign of contentment, is much louder than that of a pet cat. They also purr when they are contented. Cougars hiss first and then growl when they feel threatened. Unlike lions, cougars cannot roar.

Like all cats, cougars groom themselves. Grooming helps keep their coats clean. They use their rough tongues to remove any loose hair and to untangle any matted hair. Female cougars groom their babies constantly, and young siblings have been seen grooming one another.

Mothers pick up their kittens by the scruff of the neck to move them one at a time to a new den site.

When a cougar sees an enemy nearby, it may try to look ferocious and scare it away by showing its teeth and growling.

Cougars have very strong jaws. And they have three kinds of teeth, 24 in all. The carnassial (kar NASS ee uhl) teeth are located on both the top and bottom jaws. They are long and sharp, used for slicing or shearing. The canine (KAY nyn) teeth are thick and sharp, used for puncturing. The incisors (ihn SYZ ohrz) are small and straight, used for cutting and some chewing. But cougars don't chew their food very well. They mostly gulp down large chunks.

Most adult cougars are solitary, which means they live alone. They protect their territory from intruders, including other cougars. Each cougar needs a lot of space, an average of as much as 200 square miles for adult males and less than half that for adult females. They may walk as far as 30 miles in a day, searching for food or patrolling their territory.

Males and females look alike, but it is the female that cares for the young.

Newborn kittens have soft, fluffy-looking fur that is speckled with brown spots. This coloring helps camouflage them.

The spots disappear when the kittens are about eight months old. Kittens also have curly tails, which straighten out as they get older.

The kittens are born with blue eyes, which stay closed for about the first two weeks. Their eye color soon changes to yellow.

Kittens are totally dependent on their mother for food. They nurse for up to three months. Immediately after birth, and often in the next few weeks, the female licks the kittens to clean their fur. This helps them stay safe from enemies that might find the den site by detecting the scent of the newborn kittens.

If a female cougar thinks that her kittens are in danger in a particular spot, she often finds a new hiding place and moves them. A mother cougar will do whatever is necessary to keep the kittens away from dangerous predators, or enemies, such as wolves.

When the mother leaves to hunt for food, the kittens stay hidden and quiet at the den site. When the kittens are about two months old, their teeth have grown and they nurse less. Their mother begins to bring them food every two or three days. The mother makes no special effort to catch small prey for her small offspring. At first, the young kittens just want to play with the food, no matter what she brings. One of the first lessons the mother teaches her kittens is how to eat this new food.

By example, she shows them how to bite, how to tear meat off the bone, and how to chew. She also teaches the kittens that their rough tongues are good for cleaning the meat off bones. After about six months the kittens are good at eating this food, and they begin to explore away from the den site.

STOP AND THINK
Monitor/Clarify Name two ways mother cougars protect their young. Reread these two pages if you are not sure of the answer.

This young cougar still has some of its baby spots. It is practicing stalking its prey.

259

The kittens stay with their mother for about eighteen months. During this time, she teaches them many things about surviving in their habitat. As the kittens mature, the mother cougar takes them hunting. They learn how to find and carefully follow prey. This is called stalking.

They also learn when to pounce, or jump out suddenly, to capture the prey. They are taught how to hide their kill and protect it from other animals. With a lot of practice, they learn to hunt for themselves.

Then, the young cougars go out on their own to find a territory and a mate. If they find a good habitat with plenty of prey animals and water in the area, cougars may live about eight to ten years.

Cougar eyesight may be five times better than human eyesight.

YourTurn

A Closer Look

Short Response Cougars are sometimes known as "ghosts of the wilderness" or "ghost walkers." What details about cougars does the author provide that might help explain these nicknames? Write a paragraph about the ghost-like qualities of the cougar. Include ideas and details from the selection. MAIN IDEAS AND DETAILS

Cougar Trivia

Create a Game Work with a group to think of ten trivia questions about cougars. Write each question on a separate card, and write the answers on an answer sheet. Then join another group to play a trivia game. Mix up the cards and combine them into one stack. Have each team take turns drawing questions. Try to answer the questions without looking back at the selection. SMALL GROUP

How long is a cougar's tail?

Cat Talk

Turn and Talk With a partner, identify the most interesting ideas in "Cougars." Then discuss how the author presents these ideas and what her message to readers might be. MAIN IDEAS AND DETAILS

Poetry

✔ **TARGET VOCABULARY**

resemble	mature
detecting	particular
keen	available
vary	ferocious
unobserved	contentment

GENRE

Poetry uses the sounds and rhythms of words in a variety of forms to suggest images and express feelings.

TEXT FOCUS

Alliteration Poets often use repeating consonant sounds at the beginnings of words to create vivid images that appeal to the senses.

• As you read "Tiger," on page 262, listen for repeating initial consonant sounds the poet uses to appeal to the senses. How do the sound effects help you understand the poem's meaning?

"Purr-fection"

Have you ever wondered how a cat uses its keen eyesight and hearing for detecting mice? Have you ever wished you could be a cat, napping in perfect contentment? From ferocious tigers to timid tabbies, cats have always fascinated people. The reasons may vary from person to person and culture to culture.

There are few animals that have inspired poets as much as cats. As you read the following poems, notice how the poets have tried to capture the particular way cats move, their mysterious nature, and their entertaining antics.

Tiger

by Valerie Worth

The tiger
Has swallowed
A black sun,

In his cold
Cage he
Carries it still:

Black flames
Flicker through
His fur,

Black rays roar
From the centers
Of his eyes.

A Tomcat Is

by J. Patrick Lewis

Nightwatchman of corners
Caretaker of naps
Leg-wrestler of pillows
Depresser of laps

A master at whining
And dining on mouse
Designer of shadows
That hide in the house.

The bird-watching bandit
On needle-point claws
The chief of detectives
On marshmallow paws

A crafty yarn-spinner
A stringer high-strung
A handlebar mustache
A sandpaper tongue

The dude in the alley
The duke of the couch
Affectionate fellow
Occasional grouch

As male cats mature from kittens to tomcats, they take on different traits. The imagery in this poem describes all the different things a tomcat can resemble.

263

Disturbed, the cat
Lifts its belly
On to its back.

—Karai Senryū

Write Using Alliteration

Write a poem using alliteration. Use "Tiger" on page 262 as a model. Choose the subject of your poem and think of unusual details that are available to describe it. Create imagery that will reveal things that may go unobserved by most people. For each image, focus on a single repeating initial consonant sound. Alliteration can draw attention to unique imagery in a poem and make reading it exciting.

Making Connections

Text to Self

Respond to a Poem Rhyme is a technique used by many poets. Quietly read the poem "A Tomcat Is" to yourself a few times. What rhyming words do you hear, and where? How do the rhymes affect the way you read the poem? Do you think they enhance the poem's imagery? How might you use this technique when writing your own poems?

Text to Text

Compare and Contrast The author of "Cougars" and the poets in "Purr-fection" write about the traits and behaviors of cats. Compare and contrast the representations of cats in "Cougars" and in one of the "Purr-fection" poems. Use evidence from both selections to support your points. Pay special attention to the writers' uses of sensory details, figurative language, and sound.

Text to World

Research an Author Patricia Corrigan includes a lot of factual information in "Cougars." Choose from the text the four facts that you find most interesting. Use a research source or the Internet to verify the facts. Then select and research another wild animal that interests you. List the similarities and differences you find between your chosen animal and the cougar.

Big Idea

History is made
by individuals.

Paired Selections

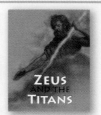

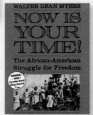

273

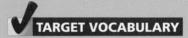

TARGET VOCABULARY

embark

surveyed

conduct

cramped

bracing

pressing

distracted

representatives

viewpoint

shattered

Vocabulary Reader   Context Cards

Vocabulary in Context

1 embark

In the 1770s, it took courage to embark, or set sail, on an ocean voyage.

2 surveyed

These soldiers surveyed the harbor, scanning for signs of the enemy navy.

3 conduct

The captain made sure that all jobs were done. He was responsible for the ship's conduct.

4 cramped

In storms, travelers were thrown about in their cramped, crowded quarters.

- **Study each Context Card.**
- **Use a dictionary or a glossary to verify the meanings of the Vocabulary words.**

5 bracing

These sailors got used to bracing, or securing, themselves when storms struck.

6 pressing

Sailing vessels served a pressing need when they delivered urgently needed trade goods.

7 distracted

The sunset distracted this sailor. She stopped working to look at the clouds.

8 representatives

Ben Franklin and other representatives of the U.S. sailed to France on diplomatic missions.

9 viewpoint

From the viewpoint of the British, their navy was best. U.S. sailors had another opinion.

10 shattered

Divers still find the shattered remains of vessels that broke up and sank long ago.

Background

TARGET VOCABULARY **The Two Presidents Adams** In the next selection, John Adams and his son, John Quincy Adams, embark on a mission to France. Many patriots held the viewpoint that John Adams should be one of the new republic's representatives. Because of his wise conduct toward the patriot cause, he served as the country's first Vice President (1789–1797) and as our second President (1797–1801). A man of great intelligence, he was not easily distracted from confronting the pressing issues of his day. John Quincy Adams grew up to become the sixth U.S. President (1825–1828). Bracing himself for more political battles, he later served in the House of Representatives, where he worked to abolish slavery. He successfully defended the African captives on the *Amistad*, who rebelled and shattered the bonds that held them in the cramped hold of a slave ship. Historians who have surveyed his life agree he was a great defender of human rights and civil liberty.

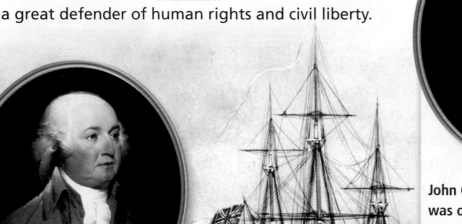

John Quincy Adams (1767–1848) was our sixth President.

John Adams (1735–1826) was our second President.

Comprehension

✔ **TARGET SKILL** **Cause and Effect**

As you read "Dangerous Crossing," look for one or more events that make something else happen. Use a graphic organizer like the one below to help you keep track of causes and effects in "Dangerous Crossing." Then explain how the Revolutionary War and related historical events in "Dangerous Crossing" affect the story's theme.

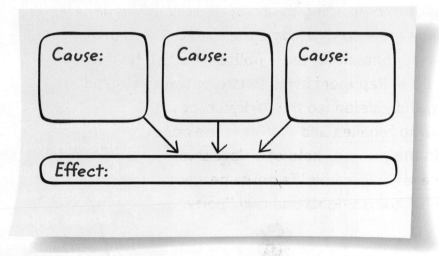

Cause:

Cause:

Cause:

Effect:

✔ **TARGET STRATEGY** **Visualize**

Understanding cause-and-effect relationships between events can help you picture, or visualize, what is happening in the selection. Visualize as you read to better understand the story's action.

Main Selection

✓ TARGET VOCABULARY

embark	pressing
surveyed	distracted
conduct	representatives
cramped	viewpoint
bracing	shattered

✓ TARGET SKILL

Cause and Effect Tell how events are related and how one event causes another.

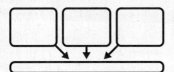

✓ TARGET STRATEGY

Visualize Use text details to form pictures in your mind of what you are reading.

GENRE

Historical fiction is a story whose characters and events are set in a real period of history.

MEET THE AUTHOR
Stephen Krensky

Stephen Krensky writes fiction, nonfiction, picture books, and novels. He writes different kinds of books because "I just happen to have a lot of different-sized ideas," he says. "Being able to try so many different kinds of books has helped me stay enthusiastic about every book I write."

MEET THE ILLUSTRATOR
Greg Harlin

Greg Harlin uses watercolors to create believable historical and scientific paintings. His art has appeared in many magazines, including *National Geographic* and *Kids Discover*. He lives with his daughter and two cats, one black and one white.

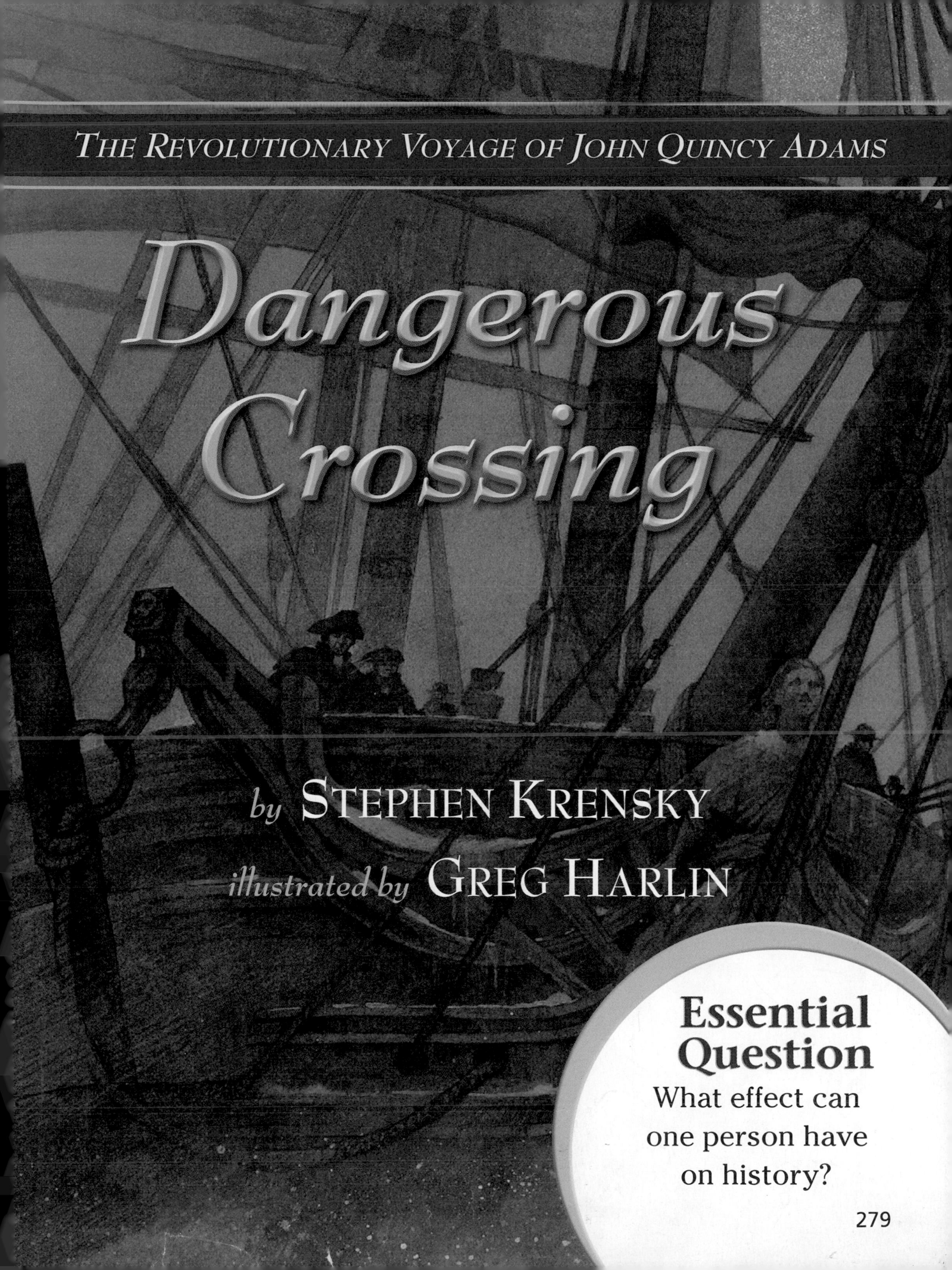

THE REVOLUTIONARY VOYAGE OF JOHN QUINCY ADAMS

Dangerous Crossing

by STEPHEN KRENSKY

illustrated by GREG HARLIN

Essential Question

What effect can one person have on history?

Young Johnny Adams could hardly believe his good fortune. On a cold February day in 1778, he stood at the ocean's edge, a few miles from home. The wind blew fiercely around him, and the blustering snow stung his cheeks like nettles.

But Johnny didn't mind. Ten years old, he had never been farther than a day's ride from home. Yet here he was, about to sail to France with his father. What did stinging cheeks matter compared to that? He could still hear the words that an elderly cousin had declared in warning.

"Mr. Adams, you are going to embark under very threatening signs. The heavens frown, the clouds roll, the hollow winds howl, the waves of the sea roar upon the beach." Johnny could not have been more pleased.

Soon the barge arrived to fetch them to the ship waiting offshore. Although they were leaving Massachusetts in a hurry and in secret, they were not going unprepared. Their baggage included two fat sheep, two hogs, one barrel of apples, five bushels of corn, some chocolate, sugar, eggs, paper, quills, ink, a double mattress, a comforter, and a pillow.

There was room for it all, and soon father and son were settled in some dry hay, bobbing up and down like corks in a bottle.

It was dangerous to cross the ocean in mid-winter, but time was pressing. The war with England, now almost three years old, was not going well. The rebel army had barely limped into their winter quarters. Many colonial soldiers lacked muskets and powder. They were also short of clothes, blankets, and shoes.

The new Americans desperately needed the support of other countries—especially France, England's greatest rival. Other representatives were in Paris already, but their progress was uncertain. It was hoped that the calm and thoughtful John Adams could do more. Captain Samuel Tucker welcomed Johnny and his father aboard just before dusk.

Captain Tucker's new twenty-four gun frigate (FRIHG uht), the *Boston*, had a deck more than a hundred feet long. Three towering masts stood guard overhead, clothed in endless furls of sail.

Down below, the view was less grand. The passageways were cramped, and everywhere was a terrible smell—of sea and sailors mingled together. Johnny and his father found their tiny cabin clean, at least, and with their blankets and pillows, it felt a little like home.

Once the *Boston* put out to sea, Johnny noticed a change. The waves looked bigger. They felt bigger, too. A strange feeling swept over him. His head was spinning, and his stomach as well. He soon took to his bed, glad that his groans were lost amid the creaking masts and the howling wind.

Though John Adams also felt ill, he distracted himself by writing in his diary. *"Seasickness,"* he wrote, *"seems to be the Effect of Agitation. . . . The smoke of Seacoal, the Smell of stagnant putrid Water, the odour of the Ship where the Sailors sleep, or any other offensive Odor"* would not trigger it alone.

No doubt this was good to know, but it did not make Johnny feel any better. The next day, a calmer sea improved everyone's mood. Johnny and his father returned to the deck, glad for a breath of fresh air.

"A ship on the weather quarter!" shouted the lookout.

STOP AND THINK

Visualize What details help you visualize what the ship looked like and what Johnny and his father experienced inside the ship?

Captain Tucker turned his glass upon the distant speck. Actually, there were three ships, and British frigates by the look of them. He was not pleased with the three-to-one odds.

But his officers protested. "We will not run from an enemy before we see him," they said. "We will not fly from danger before we know we are in it."

Besides, they were thinking, what if these were merchant ships loaded with valuable goods?

Bowing to their enthusiasm, the captain ordered the *Boston* closer.

It was soon clear, though, that his fears were well founded. These were frigates, indeed. And from their viewpoint, the odds were just right.

All three now gave chase. Two quickly fell behind, but the third kept pace. For two more days, it followed them. The sailors on watch said the frigate was closing the gap, but Johnny could not tell. His eyes were not as sharp as theirs.

"*Our Powder and balls were placed by the Guns,*" his father noted in his diary, "*and every thing ready to begin the Action.*"

Almost three years earlier, Johnny and his mother had stood on high ground, watching the Battle of Bunker Hill eight miles away. But that had been almost make-believe, little more than flashes of light and distant cries.

Here, he would be right in the thick of things. Cannons would fire and swords flash. One of the ships would be boarded. The two crews would grapple with knives and pistols and anything else that came to hand.

An officer interrupted Johnny's thoughts. He and his father should take shelter below. As if the frigate wasn't trouble enough, a storm was coming.

STOP AND THINK

Author's Craft The **flashback** the author uses on this page gives information about Johnny's experience of war before his overseas journey. How does that earlier experience help you understand what Johnny is feeling now?

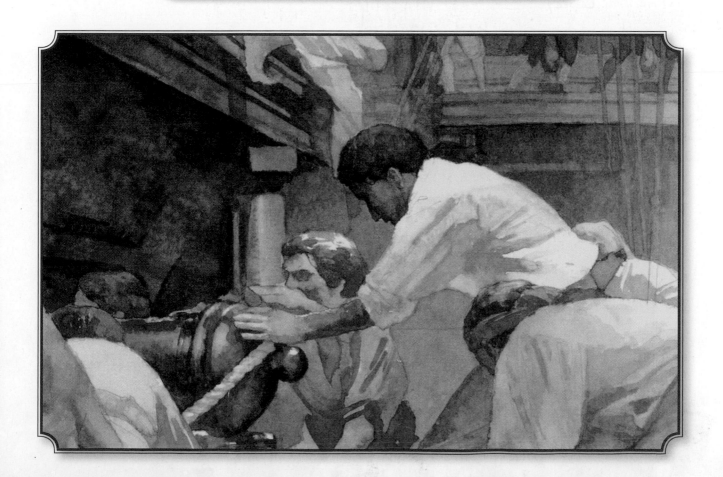

They went straight to their cabin. Soon the ship began to pitch, rocking violently back and forth. They could not sit or stand without being knocked about. "It was with the utmost difficulty," John Adams remembered, "that my little son and I could hold ourselves in bed with both our hands, and bracing ourselves against the boards, planks, and timbers with our feet."

Suddenly, there was a flash of light. *C-R-R-AAACK!* The ship shuddered from the blow. Johnny and his father shared a worried glance. Was that cannon fire? Had the British frigate overtaken them? Would the firing continue until they surrendered? Or would the *Boston* fight until it sank beneath the waves?

In truth, there were no cannons at work. "The ship has been struck by lightning!" an officer told them. The main mast was shattered, and four crew members were hurt.

For three more days and nights, the storm continued. Chests and casks were tossed about like straw, and no one could stay dry or walk steadily on deck. "The Wind blowing against the current . . . produced a tumbling Sea," Adams observed. "Vast mountains of water breaking on the ship threatened to bury us all at once in the deep."

Through it all, Johnny was proud that his father stayed calm. He was a practical man, and there was nothing to gain by making a fuss.

Finally, the skies cleared. But the pale sunlight fell on a broken ship. Sails were ripped, masts splintered. Even worse, the *Boston* had been blown hundreds of miles off course. As the captain surveyed the damage, he had only one bit of good news.

At least the British frigate was gone.

As the sailors began making repairs, Johnny took some French lessons from the ship's doctor and learned the names of the sails. "I am most satisfied with myself," Johnny had once told his father, "when I have applied part of my time to some useful employment."

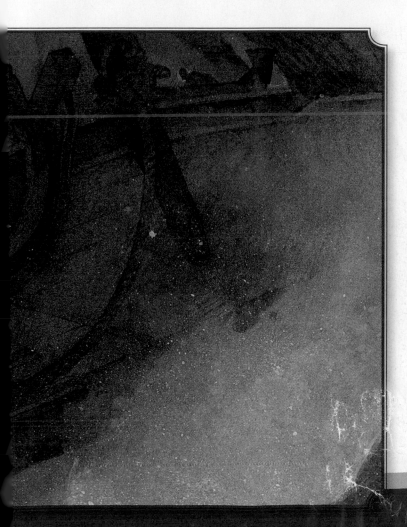

✔ STOP AND THINK
Cause and Effect What caused Johnny to think the crack he heard was cannon fire? What really caused the crack?

One day a sailor pulled up a Portuguese man-of-war in a bucket. Johnny looked on in wonder. Was this truly a fish from the sea? *"Careful,"* the sailor warned him. One touch of its twisted cords would sting like a hundred bees.

Johnny's father and the captain often spoke together of their mission and the conduct of the ship. Even from a distance, Johnny recognized his father's impatience. He spoke of a ship at sea "as a kind of prison." He was especially tired of the view. "We see nothing but Sky, Clouds, and Sea," he noted. "And then Seas, Clouds, and Sky."

After four weeks at sea, the Boston spotted another ship—a British merchantman loaded with precious goods. This was a prize worth catching. The passengers were ordered below as the *Boston* let out its sails.

But while Johnny and the rest stayed put, John Adams returned to the deck. He heard a loud boom—and then a cannonball shot over his head. The other ship had fired on them! Captain Tucker ordered the *Boston* brought about so that the merchantman could see the strength of her guns. Would the enemy captain, Adams wondered, choose to sink or surrender?

The surrender came quickly. The crew of the merchantman were taken prisoner, and their ship remanned with some of the *Boston*'s sailors. But even in victory, Captain Tucker was angry at Johnny's father for risking his life by returning to the deck.

"My dear sir, how came you here?" he asked. Had Adams forgotten his mission? Wasn't his safe arrival in France of the greatest importance to the Revolution?

John Adams stood his ground. "I ought to do my fair share of fighting," he explained simply. Johnny was not surprised. Until now, his father had been defending his country with ideas and words. But he would not shrink from any conflict if the cause was just.

On March 24, the *Boston* saw the coast of Europe at last, and soon they reached their port in France. "The Pleasure resulting from the Sight of Land, Cattle, Houses, &c. after so long and dangerous a voyage is very great," John Adams observed. He and Johnny had survived storms and seasickness, boredom and battles. They had seen firsthand that war was not all glory and games. They had seen men die and tested their own courage as well.

But the real adventure still lay ahead. Americans would need much help to achieve their freedom, and Johnny and his father were glad to be a part of it.

Your Turn

Raging Seas

Write a Description Johnny and his father survived a storm at sea that made the ship rock back and forth. Make a list of the sensory details and imagery that the author uses to help readers visualize the ordeal of Johnny and his father. Then write a paragraph vividly describing a storm you have seen or experienced. PERSONAL RESPONSE

Ahoy!

Learn Nautical Terms In "Dangerous Crossing," the author uses terms that relate to sailors, ships, and seafaring. With a small group, list ten of those terms. Write each term on a separate note card and each term's definition on another note card. Spread out the cards face-down. Then take turns flipping over two cards, trying to match each term with its definition. If you make a match, keep the cards. If not, return them to the face-down position. SMALL GROUP

> barge

> a large flat-bottomed boat for carrying loads

Presidential Wisdom

Turn and Talk What lessons did Johnny Adams learn from his father during the voyage? With a partner, discuss how these lessons may have prepared Johnny to one day become president. Do presidents and other leaders need these same skills today? CAUSE AND EFFECT

Science

Preparing for
Hurricanes

embark	pressing
surveyed	distracted
conduct	representatives
cramped	viewpoint
bracing	shattered

GENRE

Informational text, such as this brochure, gives factual information about a topic.

TEXT FOCUS

Directions A text may include a set of instructions telling how to do something, often by following a series of steps.

• After you read the brochure, review what you can do to prepare for a hurricane. Why should you clean the yard before a hurricane?

Preparing for Hurricanes

What Is a Hurricane?

A hurricane is a tropical storm with a wind speed of seventy-four miles per hour or more. Hurricanes develop each year in the Atlantic Ocean, the Caribbean Sea, and the Gulf of Mexico. A hurricane's heavy rain can cause flooding. Windows can be shattered by strong winds. High winds can also uproot trees and pull down power lines.

If a hurricane threatens your area, local representatives may call for an evacuation. If you are not evacuated, it is the viewpoint of weather experts that advance preparation can help keep you and your family safe.

An Emergency Supply Kit

Stocking an emergency supply kit is a good first step in preparing for extreme weather. You should embark on this task before hurricane season starts in June.

- Meet as a family to discuss plans.
- Decide where to store the kit.
- Tell everyone where it will be.

A prepared family can wait out a severe storm in comfort and safety.

FROM THE PAGES OF
WEEKLY READER
WR

Supply Kit Essential Items

Make a shopping list of essential items for your emergency supply kit.

☑ **Flashlights, batteries, and a battery-operated radio.** You will need them if you are without electricity.

☑ **Nonperishable food.** Buy enough dry cereal, peanut butter, and canned foods to last three days.

☑ **Bottled drinking water.** Get three gallons per person.

☑ **First aid kit.** Assemble scissors, a thermometer, sunscreen, bandages, and nonprescription medication to treat minor injuries.

☑ **Tools and supplies**. Dishes and utensils, a hammer, a screwdriver, pencil and paper, and signal flares could all come in handy.

☑ **Clothes and bedding**. Pack blankets or sleeping bags, clean clothes, shoes, and rain gear.

☑ **Board games and toys.** While waiting indoors for the storm to pass, you may feel cramped. Keep yourself distracted with games and other activities.

Right Before the Storm

Once a hurricane watch or warning is issued, the need to prepare becomes more pressing. Good conduct is essential at this time. Kids must obey all instructions. Adults may be bracing windows with plywood so the glass won't break. But kids can do important tasks.

✔ Clean the yard. Make sure you have surveyed the yard for lawn furniture, toys, or garbage cans that may blow away in high winds and cause damage.

✔ Fill bathtubs with water. Don't drink water saved this way.

✔ Unplug small electric appliances.

Hurricanes can be scary, but with planning and preparation, you and your family can be safe.

Making Connections

Text to Self

Write a Review Imagine you are a writer for a literary magazine. Write a brief review of "Dangerous Crossing." Use details about the story's conflicts and exciting events to persuade your audience to read the story. Explain how the Revolutionary War setting adds drama, affects the characters, and helps shape the story's theme.

Text to Text

Compare Points of View Both "Dangerous Crossing" and "Old Yeller" (Lesson 7) are historical fiction, but they are written using different points of view. Compare the third-person point of view in "Dangerous Crossing" to the first-person point of view in "Old Yeller." If you were writing historical fiction, which point of view would you use? Why?

Text to World

Research a Disaster Many types of weather-related disasters—such as hurricanes, blizzards, and earthquakes—occur each year. Work with a small group to research a recent natural disaster. Discuss the steps community leaders asked the affected community to take to prepare for the disaster. Ask each other questions about the effects the preparation had on human and animal safety.

Grammar

Kinds of Pronouns A **pronoun** is a word that takes the place of a noun. A **subject pronoun** takes the place of a noun used as the subject of a sentence. An **object pronoun** takes the place of a noun used after an action verb or after a word such as *to, for, with, in,* or *out.*

Academic Language

pronoun
subject pronoun
object pronoun
antecedent

Subject Pronouns		Object Pronouns	
I	we	me	us
you	you	you	you
she, he, it	they	her, him, it	them

The **antecedent** of a pronoun is the noun or nouns that the pronoun replaces. A pronoun must agree with its antecedent in number and gender.

antecedent

subject pronoun

Johnny was at the ocean. Soon he would sail to France.

Turn and Talk **Work with a partner. Find the pronouns in these sentences. Tell whether they are subject pronouns or object pronouns. Then name their antecedents.**

1 Three boats approached. They were British frigates.

2 One boat gave chase. The sailors watched it carefully.

3 Johnny remembered a battle. He and his mother had seen it.

4 Johnny's mother was at home. Johnny would not see her for a long time.

5 Johnny's father would speak with French leaders. He represented the American colonies.

Sentence Fluency To avoid using the same noun again and again in your writing, you can replace that noun with a pronoun. Do this with care! It is easy to repeat the same pronoun too many times, too. Be certain that your reader knows to which noun a pronoun refers. Remember that the pronoun must agree with its antecedent in number and gender.

Noun Overload	Improved with Pronouns
Travelers in the eighteenth century had to go by ship across an ocean full of danger. Travelers suffered many hardships. Travelers had no contact with those at home. There was no fresh food for the travelers. Travelers on today's ocean liners cruise in luxury.	Travelers in the eighteenth century had to go by ship across an ocean full of danger. They suffered many hardships. They had no contact with those at home. There was no fresh food for them. Travelers on today's ocean liners cruise in luxury.

Connect Grammar to Writing

As you revise your opinion paragraph, look for nouns that are used too many times. Replace an overused noun with a pronoun. Make sure that it is clear to which noun the pronoun refers.

Write to Persuade

In an **opinion paragraph,** you present your position on a topic. To make your writing strong and convincing, include several reasons that explain and support your feelings about the topic. As you write, think about who will be reading your paragraph.

Sonya wrote an opinion paragraph explaining why she thinks team sports build leadership skills. Later, she revised her paragraph by adding precise verbs and vivid adjectives to make her voice stronger and her opinion clearer. She also added questions to engage her audience.

Use the Writing Traits Checklist below as you revise your writing.

Writing Traits Checklist

✔ **Ideas**
Did I state a clear opinion?

✔ **Organization**
Did I connect ideas in a clear and logical way?

✔ **Sentence Fluency**
Did I use pronouns to avoid repeating nouns?

✔ **Word Choice**
Did I use words that engage the audience?

✔ **Voice**
Did I use words that make my opinion clear and convincing?

✔ **Conventions**
Did I use correct spelling, grammar, and punctuation?

Revised Draft

Do you daydream about one day being President?

Do you
~~You may~~ wonder how you can
develop leadership skills. ~~One~~ way to
the you would need? An excellent

start is by playing a team sport.
Why should you play a team sport?
~~There are several reasons for this.~~

discover
First, you'll ~~learn all about~~ your own

strengths and weaknesses.

Why Kids Should Play a Team Sport

By Sonya Sanchez

Do you daydream about one day being President? Do you wonder how you can develop the leadership skills you would need? An excellent way to start is by playing a team sport. Why should you play a team sport? First, you'll discover your own strengths and weaknesses. That is important information for any leader to have. Second, you'll learn to play by the rules. Government leaders have to follow all the laws and rules that apply to their work. Finally, when you play on a team, you'll learn how to work well with others. It takes a whole basketball team to win a game. Likewise, a good leader can get more done with strong teamwork. So if you are a fifth-grader with your eye on the White House, choose a sport you like and join a team now.

> In my final paper, I added words to make my voice stronger and my opinion more convincing. I also checked to see that I had used pronouns correctly.

Reading as a Writer

Which words did Sonya add to make her voice stronger and her opinion clearer? What words could you add or delete to make your own voice stronger?

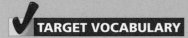

rebellious

objected

benefit

repeal

contrary

midst

temporary

advantages

previously

prohibit

Vocabulary   Context
Reader   Cards

Vocabulary in Context

1 rebellious

In April 1775, who fired first at Lexington: a rebellious patriot or a loyal British soldier?

2 objected

Colonists objected to the Stamp Act of 1765, protesting that its taxes were unfair.

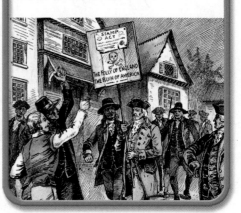

3 benefit

Sam Adams argued that it would be a help, or benefit, to be independent.

4 repeal

In 1766, Parliament voted to repeal the hated Stamp Act. The act was withdrawn.

- **Study each Context Card.**
- **Use the glossary to determine the correct pronunciation of each Vocabulary word.**

5 contrary

Willful, contrary patriots refused to obey British laws. Troops were sent to enforce the laws.

6 midst

In the Boston Massacre of 1770, five colonists died in the midst, or middle, of a riot.

7 temporary

For the Boston Tea Party, patriots wore temporary disguises, then removed them.

8 advantages

More soldiers and guns were the British army's advantages, or superior qualities.

9 previously

Many men, previously peaceful farmers, became patriot soldiers during the Revolution.

10 prohibit

The Declaration of Independence sought to prohibit, or forbid, political tyranny.

IN CONGRESS, JULY 4, 1776.

The unanimous Declaration of the thirteen united States of America.

Background

Taxation Without Representation Have you ever wondered why the colonists were so rebellious? What made them so contrary?

Britain had been in the midst of an expensive war and was short of money, so Parliament passed laws to raise money through taxes. For example, the temporary Stamp Act (Parliament would later repeal it) forced colonists to pay a tax on all printed materials. While these laws gave a benefit to Britain, they provided no advantages to the colonies. The overtaxed colonists objected because they had no voice in making the laws that governed them.

Over time, colonists who previously had been loyal to Britain became upset. What new tax would they learn of tomorrow? What would Britain prohibit next? It was time for independence!

• Read the information in the graphic below. Which British Act taxed coffee? Which British Act taxed newspapers?

Taxation Without Representation

British Act	Items Taxed
Sugar Act	In addition to sugar, this act taxed molasses, coffee, wine, and some fabrics.
Stamp Act	All legal documents, such as marriage licenses, and printed material, such as newspapers, were taxed.
Tea Act	Colonists had to pay a tax on British tea. This led to the Boston Tea Party.

Comprehension

✔ **TARGET SKILL** **Fact and Opinion**

As you read "Can't You Make Them Behave, King George?", look for facts and opinions. A fact is a statement that can be proved true. An opinion is a statement that tells what someone believes or feels. Make a graphic organizer like the one below to help you keep track of facts and opinions in the selection. Then use print or online resources to verify the facts you located.

Fact	Opinion
•	•
•	•
•	•

✔ **TARGET STRATEGY** **Question**

Use information in your graphic organizer to ask questions about events and people described in the selection. Questioning helps you decide what you think the author is saying.

rebellious	midst
objected	temporary
benefit	advantages
repeal	previously
contrary	prohibit

✔ **TARGET SKILL**

Fact and Opinion Decide whether an idea can be proved or is a feeling or belief.

✔ **TARGET STRATEGY**

Question Ask questions about a selection before you read, as you read, and after you read.

GENRE

Narrative nonfiction gives factual information by telling a true story.

MEET THE AUTHOR

Jean Fritz

Jean Fritz says it takes lots of research to learn about the subjects of her nonfiction books. She loves finding quirky details and funny facts about real people. She never makes up the things people say in her books. All the dialogue she uses comes from accounts in real letters, journals, and diaries.

MEET THE ILLUSTRATOR

Tomie dePaola

Tomie dePaola has been drawing ever since he can remember. When he was young, his parents let him work in a special space in the attic. Now he has his own studio where he paints and illustrates popular children's books such as *26 Fairmount Avenue*. He receives over 100,000 fan letters per year!

CAN'T YOU MAKE THEM BEHAVE, KING GEORGE?

by Jean Fritz

illustrated by Tomie dePaola

Essential Question

How did people's opinions lead to a revolution?

Before the American Revolution, most people who had come from England to settle in North America were English subjects loyal to King George the Third. However, some of these colonists did not like that the king made them pay money called taxes to the English government. They did not like that they had no say in the decisions made by the English government. This was the beginning of a disagreement that led to the American Revolution.

When George came to the throne, the government was costing a great deal. England had been fighting a long and expensive war, and when it was over, the question was how to pay bills. Finally, a government official suggested that one way to raise money was to tax Americans.

"What a good idea!" King George said. After all, the French and Indian part of the war had been fought on American soil for the benefit of Americans, so why shouldn't they help pay for it? The fact that Americans had also spent money and lost men in the war didn't seem important. Nor did the fact that Americans had always managed their own money up to now. They were English subjects, weren't they? Didn't English subjects have to obey the English government? So in 1765 a stamp tax was laid on certain printed items in America.

King George was amazed that Americans objected. He was flabbergasted that they claimed he had no *right* to tax them. Just because they had no say in the matter. Just because they had no representatives in the English government. What was more, Americans refused to pay. If they agreed to one tax, they said, what would come next? A window tax? A tax on fireplaces?

Now King George believed that above all a king should be firm, but the government had the vote, and in the end it voted to repeal the tax. Still, King George was pleased about one thing: The government stood firm on England's *right* to tax the colonies. And in 1767 the government tried again. This time the tax was on lead, tea, paint, and a number of items England sold to America. Part of the money from this tax was to be used to support an English army to keep order in America; part was to pay governors and judges previously under the control of the colonies. Who could object to that? King George asked.

Americans also contended that if they had been asked (instead of being forced) to raise money for England, they would have done so as they had done on previous occasions.

In King George's day the king was a "constitutional monarch." He had lost the enormous powers that a king had once had and had to abide by the vote of the government. On the other hand, unlike present kings, he took an active and leading role in the government.

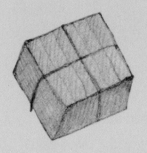

Many Americans disapproved of the Boston Tea Party. They were willing to pay for the lost tea, but when instead the king punished them so severely, they became more united against him.

The Americans did. They hated the whole business so much, especially the English soldiers stationed in their midst, that even when the other taxes were repealed and only the tea tax remained, they would not put up with it. When tea arrived in Boston, they dumped it into Boston Harbor.

When he heard this news, King George felt more like a father than he ever had in his life. A father with a family of very, very disobedient children. And of course, he must punish them. So he closed the port of Boston and took away the right of Massachusetts to govern itself.

Firm, firm, firm. From now on he would be firm. After the Battle of Lexington and the Battle of Bunker Hill, King George said he felt strong as a lion. People would soon see, he said, that Americans would back down, meek as lambs.

Instead, on July 4, 1776, Americans declared their independence. Naturally King George was annoyed. But he wasn't worried. How could children, however rebellious, succeed against a firm father? How could a few colonies hold out against a powerful empire? He'd just send a few more regiments over and then watch the Americans come around! It never occurred to George the Third that he might not be right. "I wish nothing but good," he once said, "therefore everyone who does not agree with me is a traitor or a scoundrel."

For a while King George had every reason to feel confident. The English troops captured New York, and when George heard this, he said one more battle and it would be over. When he was told that his troops had marched into Philadelphia, he ran into the queen's room. "I have beat them!" he shouted. "Beat all the Americans!"

But he hadn't beaten them. The fighting went on, and meanwhile, George the Third had to go about the business of being a king. He put his seal on official papers, gave out medals and titles, memorized the name of every ship in the navy, tasted the food sent to the troops, checked on who was spending what, and for hours on end he listened to people talk.

> **STOP AND THINK**
>
> **Author's Craft** A **common saying** is a phrase whose meaning is well known. On this page, the author uses "strong as a lion" to describe how King George feels about himself. Find the common saying that describes how the king sees the Americans. What does it mean?

Indeed, being a king, especially a good king, was often boring. He couldn't even drop a glove without half the palace, it seemed, stooping to pick it up and arguing about who should have the honor of returning it. "Never mind the honor," the king once said. "Never mind, never mind. Just give me my glove. What? what? what? Yes, you all picked it up, yes, yes, yes, all, all, all—you all picked it up." (King George had a habit of talking rapidly and repeating himself so that his talk often sounded like a gobble.)

But as king, he did have a few advantages. He was, for instance, the most prayed-for man in the empire. Naturally it was pleasant to think of the heavy traffic of prayers ascending on his behalf every Sunday morning. From every country church and every city cathedral in every corner of the kingdom. (But not in America. There the preachers gave up praying for him when the Punishment started.) The king was also the most toasted man. No party (except in America) began without all the people present raising their glasses and wishing the king a long life. (The king wished it, too.) And he had the biggest birthday celebration. Each year on June 4 all his subjects (except in America, of course) celebrated his birthday with parades and banquets and speeches and gunfire and fireworks.

All those prayers and toasts and fireworks were not to be sneezed at. Still, there were times when George wanted to forget about being a king. Fortunately he had hobbies to turn to. For one thing, he made metal buttons (he loved turning a lathe). He wrote articles on farming and signed himself "Ralph Richardson," which was the name of one of his shepherds. He played backgammon with the officers of the royal household, and he collected ship models, coins, clocks, and watches. (He had a four-sided clock that even showed the tides.) He played the flute and harpsichord, hunted, and studied the stars in his private observatory. And for the queen's special amusement, he maintained a zoo, which consisted of one elephant and one zebra.

But always in the end he had to go back to being a king. Back to the problem of America. This was the way he thought of America. A problem. King George did not really think of the Revolutionary War as a *war* until the fall of 1777, when 5,000 English soldiers surrendered to the Americans at Saratoga.

 **STOP AND THINK**
Fact and Opinion Is the first sentence on page 310 a fact or the author's opinion? What makes you think so?

In 1788 when the king was 50 years old, he became violently ill of a disease that has since been diagnosed as porphyria. One of the symptons of the disease is that one's mind is affected, but in those days people thought that the king had simply gone mad. He recovered from his first attack but in later years suffered again. For the last 10 years of his life he was a wretched-looking figure dressed in a purple bathrobe with wild white hair and a wild beard. He died in 1820 at the age of 82.

How could such a thing happen? the king asked. Hadn't he been told, even by an ex-governor of Massachusetts, that Americans would give up? That only a small number of Americans were really against him? And how could he, a peace-loving king, find himself in an honest-to-goodness war with his own colonies? He tried to console himself. He was a good king, he said. Good kings deserve to win. So this must be a temporary setback. All he had to do was to show the world that he wasn't the least bit worried. So that night after hearing about the defeat, King George went to a court party and spent the evening telling stupid jokes and laughing so uproariously that his Prime Minister, Lord North, had to take him aside and try to quiet him down.

The war dragged on. France, impressed with the victory at Saratoga, joined the war on America's side. There were people in England now who wanted to stop fighting, but not George. No, no, no. Never, never. No independence. No peace without honor. If one group of English colonies got away, what would happen to the others? What would be left of the empire?

But no matter how he showed himself in public, privately George was depressed. The world was not staying settled, everything in place, the way he liked it. Not only was America acting up, but there were difficulties in England as well. Riots even. And George's own family was misbehaving. Two of his brothers were involved in scandals, and George's son, the Prince of Wales, was so contrary he deliberately arrived for meals as much as an hour late although he *knew* that the king wanted everyone to be *exactly* on time.

STOP AND THINK

Question Ask yourself what you already know about the Revolutionary War. How does King George's knowledge of the American patriots compare to what you know about them?

On November 25, 1781, the news reached London that the English army under General Cornwallis had surrendered at Yorktown to General Washington. When Lord North heard this, he threw up his arms. "It's all over!" he said.

But the king said nothing was over. They still had ships, hadn't they? (He named them.) They still had officers. (He had learned their names, too.) They still had troops. They still had guns and gunpowder.

King George set his lips firmly and wrote a letter to the Secretary of State for America. This defeat, he said, should not make the smallest difference in their plans. Still, King George was so upset that when he dated the letter, he forgot to record the hour and the minute of the writing.

Two days later the king addressed the government. "I prohibit you from thinking of peace," he thundered.

But the government did think of peace, and eventually the government voted for it.

313

So now what? King George couldn't fight the war all by himself. He couldn't chop off the heads of all those who had voted for peace. Kings didn't do that anymore. He could, of course, abdicate—quit the king business altogether. For a time he thought seriously of this. He even drafted an announcement of his abdication, but then he put it away in his desk. He was so *used* to being a king. So when the time came for him to sign the peace proclamation, he signed. As soon as he had finished, he jumped on his horse and took a hard gallop away from the palace. When the time came to announce in public the separation of the two countries and the independence of America, he swallowed hard and announced. Afterward he asked a friend if he had spoken loudly enough.

As long as he lived, King George had nightmares about the loss of the American colonies. It certainly hadn't been his fault, he said. He hadn't done anything wrong. *He* had just wanted to teach Americans a lesson.

Your Turn

No, Your Highness

Short Response Imagine that you are an American colonist during the reign of King George the Third. Write a short newspaper article objecting to the taxes put into place by King George and the English government. Include in your article at least two facts to support your objection.

FACT AND OPINION

King for a Day

Role-play an Interview As a constitutional monarch, King George had a challenging job. Work with a partner to discuss King George's everyday activities and feelings about being a king. Prepare for a mock interview with King George by writing questions and answers about what it is like to be a king. Then act out the interview for classmates.

PARTNERS

A King's Point of View

Turn and Talk Think about King George's opinions of the colonists and his beliefs about the role of a king. With a partner, discuss the American colonists from the point of view of King George. How did his opinions contribute to the beginning of the revolution?

FACT AND OPINION

Traditional Tales

ZEUS
AND THE
TITANS

✔ TARGET VOCABULARY

rebellious	midst
objected	temporary
benefit	advantages
repeal	previously
contrary	prohibit

GENRE

A **myth** is a story that tells what a group of people believes about the world.

TEXT FOCUS

Heroes and Gods The main characters in myths are heroes and gods.

ZEUS AND THE TITANS

Retold by Matt Carroll

The ancient Greeks left behind a rich mythology. It is filled with rebellious gods whose behavior is often as contrary as that of human beings. This myth about how the world began is a good example….

Before the earth or the sky existed, there was only Chaos—a dark, endless confusion.

At last, from the midst of Chaos, came two beings: Mother Earth and Father Sky, also called Gaia (GY uh) and Uranus (YOOR uh nuhs). They fell in love. Gaia gave birth to six powerful giants called Titans. These were the first gods.

Uranus, the Titans' father, had a cruel side. He treated some of his children badly. Only the youngest Titan, Cronus, was brave enough to challenge and defeat him. As a result, Cronus became the ruler of both earth and sky. But his rule would be temporary.

In myths, events that have happened previously often happen again. Like his father, Cronus also became cruel. He learned that one of his children would one day challenge him. This child was Zeus, Cronus's youngest son. Zeus's mother, Rhea, could not prohibit Cronus from punishing their son. She sent Zeus to the island of Crete for safety.

Zeus grew quickly and returned home as a powerful god. The first thing he did was rescue his brothers and sisters from Cronus. Together, they decided to fight the Titans and repeal their rule.

The war lasted for ten years, but Zeus and his brothers, Hades and Poseidon, had advantages. Zeus could hurl thunderbolts at the Titans. Hades had a helmet that made him invisible. Poseidon had a trident, a three-pointed spear, that could shake the earth. In the end, all the Titans were defeated, except for two brothers who had fought on Zeus's side.

War had destroyed the earth. Now it needed to be created again.

With the world at peace, Zeus gave the two Titan brothers a new job—creating people and animals. Zeus told them to give their creations special gifts, such as speed and keen vision. However, one brother, Epimetheus (eh pih MEE thee uhs) used up all the gifts on the animals. What was left for people?

The other brother, Prometheus (proh MEE thee uhs) thought that humans should have the benefit of fire. He objected to Zeus's law that only the gods should possess this powerful gift. So he lit a torch from the sun and returned to earth with it. Fire has been important to people ever since.

Zeus would show his own cruel side, punishing Prometheus for going against his wishes, but that is a myth for another telling.

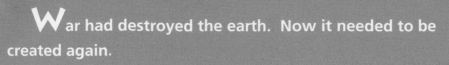

Making Connections

Text to Self

Write a Letter Imagine that King George III has asked you how he should deal with the disobedient colonists. Write a letter in which you advise him on how to calm the colonists and keep the colonies under British rule.

Text to Text

Compare Origin Myths Compare "Skywoman and Turtle" (Lesson 6) with "Zeus and the Titans." Summarize for a partner the similarities and the differences between the two myths, including the phenomena explained in each.

Text to World

Connect to Social Studies Just as the colonists did, Americans today pay taxes. The money raised by a tax has a special purpose. Use the Internet or print reference resources to research both a national and a state tax. Find out which people or government agencies are responsible for collecting the taxes and for what the collected taxes are used. Then share your information with a partner.

Grammar

What Are the Simple Verb Tenses? A verb in the **present tense** tells what is happening now, or what is happening over and over. A verb in the **past tense** tells what happened in the past. Many verbs in the past tense end with -*ed*. A verb in the **future tense** tells what will happen in the future. Verbs in the future tense use the helping verb *will*.

Academic Language

present tense

past tense

future tense

Sentence	Tense of Verb
Americans value freedom.	present tense
Long ago England ruled America.	past tense
We will celebrate our independence and freedom on July 4.	future tense

Try This! Copy these sentences onto another sheet of paper. Circle the verb in each sentence. Label it as present tense, past tense, or future tense.

1. England needed money after the French and Indian War.

2. King George III agreed on new taxes for American colonists.

3. Kings and queens expect obedience.

4. In most cases, people will protest unfair taxes.

5. Americans remember the colonists' protests with pride.

Conventions Your readers will be confused if you shift the verb tense within a paragraph that you write. Show readers whether an event is happening now, has happened in the past, or will happen in the future by choosing the best tense and sticking with it.

Shifting Tenses

When my family visited Boston last summer, we see Paul Revere's house.

We toured the house, and then we will tour the USS *Constitution*, an early American battleship.

We have a great time!

Consistent Tenses

When my family visited Boston last summer, we saw Paul Revere's house. We toured the house, and then we toured the USS *Constitution*, an early American battleship. We had a great time!

Connect Grammar to Writing

As you edit your problem-solution paragraph, make sure that your verb tenses do not shift. Using consistent verb tenses will make your writing easier to understand.

Write to Persuade

When you write a **problem-solution composition**, you describe a problem and how you think it should be solved. Discuss the problem first. Then propose your solution. You should take a strong position and give reasons you think your solution will work. Include facts and examples to support your proposal.

Noah wrote a problem-solution composition about what community leaders should do to make his local park safer. Later, he added transition words to make his points flow together more clearly. He also moved a sentence in paragraph 1 that was confusing because it did not discuss the problem.

Use the Writing Traits Checklist below as you revise your writing.

Writing Traits Checklist

☑ **Ideas**
Did I clearly explain the problem and its solution?

☑ **Organization**
Did I include transition words to make my ideas easy to follow?

☑ **Sentence Fluency**
Did I use verb tenses correctly?

☑ **Word Choice**
Did I choose words that make the problem and solution clear?

☑ **Voice**
Did I present a convincing argument?

☑ **Conventions**
Did I use correct spelling, grammar, and punctuation?

Revised Draft

My family used to enjoy Greenville
                                     However, we
Park. ~~I~~ don't go there anymore. The

playground equipment is no longer safe.
Move to ¶ 2

Community leaders need to make the

park a safe place for us to visit. Many

swings are broken, and the jungle gyms
                    Also,
are rusted. ∧The little children's sandbox

is full of leaves and scattered with

broken toys.

322

Save Greenville Park!

by Noah Friedman

My family used to enjoy Greenville Park. However, we don't go there anymore. The playground equipment is no longer safe. Many swings are broken, and the jungle gyms are rusted. Also, the little children's sandbox is full of leaves and scattered with broken toys. City records show that the equipment is more than 20 years old.

Community leaders need to make the park a safe place for us to visit. First, old and broken equipment should be replaced. Also, litter should be cleaned up and new trash bins should be installed. Finally, there should be a fenced area where dogs can run so they won't roam through the play areas. Greenville Park is located at the center of three neighborhoods. Hundreds of people will benefit from these park improvements!

In my final paper, I added transition words to make my points easy to follow. I also used past, present, and future verb tenses correctly.

Reading as a Writer

What transition words did Noah add to make the organization of his points clearer? What transition words could you use to make points in your problem-solution composition easier to follow?

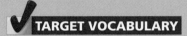

revolution

strategy

foes

legendary

formal

gushed

plunged

magnificent

retreat

shimmering

Vocabulary
Reader

Context
Cards

Vocabulary in Context

1 revolution

The goal of the American patriots in their revolution was to overthrow British rule.

2 strategy

General George Washington thought up a strategy, or plan, for the colonial army.

3 foes

Patriots sometimes fired on their British foes, or enemies, from behind rocks and trees.

4 legendary

This boy is pretending to be Paul Revere on his legendary, or famous, midnight ride.

- **Study each Context Card.**
- **Use the context of the sentences to clarify the meaning of each Vocabulary word.**

5 formal

Crispus Attucks was shot without formal, or proper, warning at the Boston Massacre.

6 gushed

As water gushed into his damaged ship, John Paul Jones vowed to keep fighting.

7 plunged

Molly Pitcher was a patriot hero even before she plunged a ramrod into a cannon.

8 magnificent

"Give me liberty or give me death," were grand, magnificent words of patriot Patrick Henry.

9 retreat

Patriot troops trained by General Steuben forced Hessians to retreat, or pull out, from battle.

10 shimmering

The signal for Paul Revere to ride was two shimmering, flickering lantern lights.

Background

The Lives of Patriot Soldiers Because they were farmers and merchants, few patriots had formal training as soldiers. The newly enlisted soldiers knew little of war strategy, and some probably didn't know the difference between an advance and a retreat. Unlike their British foes, they did not have magnificent uniforms with shimmering gold thread and brass buttons. In fact, some didn't even have shoes. When a stream gushed nearby, the soldiers probably plunged their sore feet into the soothing water. In winter, they wrapped their bare feet in rags to keep them from freezing.

Throughout the revolution, the shortages of supplies and food were legendary. The soldiers, and the women and children who traveled with them, suffered greatly. However, their dream of liberty inspired them to keep fighting and eventually to win.

• Examine the uniform of the soldier in the diagram. How might his experiences have been different from a soldier who did not have a uniform or shoes?

Patriot Soldier
The uniforms of patriot soldiers differed from state to state. Soldiers often had to provide their own uniforms.

tricorn hat

regimental coat

knapsack

waistcoat

breeches

Comprehension

✔ **TARGET SKILL** **Conclusions and Generalizations**

As you read "They Called Her Molly Pitcher," look for details that help you draw conclusions and make generalizations about a famous battle and the people who experience it. Use a graphic organizer like this one to help you record your conclusion or generalization and the text details on which you have based it.

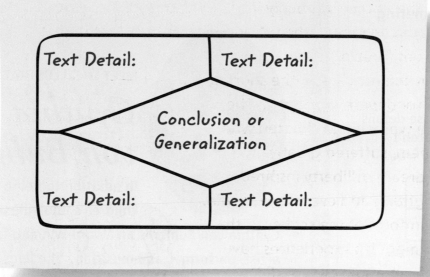

Text Detail:

Text Detail:

Conclusion or Generalization

Text Detail:

Text Detail:

✔ **TARGET STRATEGY** **Analyze/Evaluate**

Use your graphic organizer to analyze details in "They Called Her Molly Pitcher." Ask yourself questions about how the details are connected. Analyzing and interpreting parts of the text will help you evaluate the author's purpose and how well it is achieved.

Main Selection

✔ **TARGET VOCABULARY**

revolution	gushed
strategy	plunged
foes	magnificent
legendary	retreat
formal	shimmering

✔ **TARGET SKILL**

Conclusions and Generalizations Use details to explain ideas that aren't stated or are generally true.

✔ **TARGET STRATEGY**

Analyze/Evaluate Think carefully about the text and form an opinion about it.

GENRE

Narrative nonfiction gives factual information by telling a true story.

MEET THE AUTHOR

Anne Rockwell

Anne Rockwell always wanted to create art, but an injury made it difficult for her to draw, so she developed her writing talent. She tries very hard to write exciting nonfiction with "color." Her American biographies include *Only Passing Through: The Story of Sojourner Truth* and *Big George*, about George Washington.

MEET THE ILLUSTRATOR

Cynthia von Buhler

In addition to being a children's book illustrator, Cynthia von Buhler is an award-winning fine artist, performer, and musician. She lives with her many pets in a castle on Long Island in New York. She has also written and illustrated her own picture book, *The Cat Who Wouldn't Come Inside*.

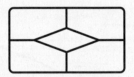

THEY CALLED HER *Molly Pitcher*

by Anne Rockwell

illustrations by
Cynthia von Buhler

Essential Question

How do individual acts of bravery shape history?

In 1777 a barber named William Hays closed up shop and joined George Washington's Continental Army in the revolution against England. He went to Valley Forge, Pennsylvania, where a Prussian general named Baron von Steuben was training the Patriot troops in the formal rules of battle that armies used in those days. Like many women of the time, Hays's wife, Mary, nicknamed Molly, went with him. Some people think that she is the legendary heroine Molly Pitcher.

General George Washington was commander in chief of the Continental Army. He and other officers, plus a bedraggled army of about 12,000 men and boys, were camped at Valley Forge just before Christmas of 1777. Snow lay deep on the ground, and Washington's troops had run out of everything they needed to keep on fighting. Washington begged the Second Continental Congress for food and supplies, but none came.

It was so cold that soldiers had to stand on their hats in the snow to keep their feet from freezing. Their shoes had holes in them from tramping over miles of rough and stony ground. They had no blankets or warm clothes. They didn't have enough to eat. Their camp was a filthy mess. Many of them were very sick. Every day, more and more soldiers deserted. Others died.

Molly and other women who'd followed husbands, sons, fathers, and brothers to Valley Forge did whatever they could to help. They cooked and cleaned, washed and mended clothes, and nursed the sick. But no matter what they did, more soldiers died each day.

Things began to look up when the Second Continental Congress finally sent supplies. General Washington began planning to go to battle again.

At the end of June, a scout brought news. A large number of British soldiers, led by Sir Henry Clinton, were gathered at Monmouth (MAHN muhth) Courthouse, near the New Jersey shore. The fight everyone had been preparing for was coming very soon.

Washington ordered General Charles Lee to lead an advance guard of 5,000 soldiers to attack the British. He'd send in a rear guard of more men soon after the fighting was under way.

William Hays was among Lee's advance guard marching to battle. As she always had, Molly followed.

✔STOP AND THINK
Conclusions and Generalizations
Based on details in the text, what can you conclude about what life was like for Washington's soldiers?

Winter at Valley Forge had been bitter cold, but June of 1778 in New Jersey was hotter than anyone could remember.

It was just after sunrise when American soldiers fired on the British near Monmouth Courthouse. Molly could see that the day was going to be a scorcher. Heat and humidity were already shimmering up from the ground. She decided what her job would be that day.

She'd spotted a green and mossy place where a spring gushed up. She ran and filled her pitcher with cold water. She raced back to the battlefield, dodging cannon and musket fire, carrying her pitcher full of water for any American soldier who needed a drink.

The Americans knew all about such hot and humid summer days. They knew they had to keep cool any way they could. They ignored what Baron von Steuben had taught them about looking neat and military at all times. They stripped off coats, belts, wigs, hats, boots, shoes, and stockings and tossed them onto the grass.

Smoke, noise, and the smell of gunpowder filled the air. Molly paid no attention. All morning, she ran back and forth from battlefield to spring, spring to battlefield, bringing water to men who'd collapsed in the heat. Over and over she heard the urgent cry of

"Molly – Pitcher!"

STOP AND THINK

Author's Craft On this page, the author reveals a lot about Molly through her actions. What conclusions can be drawn about Molly based on her willingness to go onto the battlefield in order to give water to the soldiers?

Still more British soldiers, under orders from Lord Cornwallis, marched toward Monmouth Courthouse. The men formed a line of scarlet like a winding river of blood. They were a magnificent and terrifying sight. But their fine uniforms weren't what they should have been wearing in the sun that blazed down on them.

Each man wore a tall black fur hat; a scarlet coat of thick, warm wool; a wide and shining black belt that held a sharp sword; a white waistcoat; and matching woolen pants with knee-high, brightly polished black boots. Each marched with his eyes straight ahead, a musket on his shoulder, a knapsack full of heavy lead balls of ammunition on his back. They moved to the stirring music of war. Drums were beating, fifes were playing, trumpets were sounding.

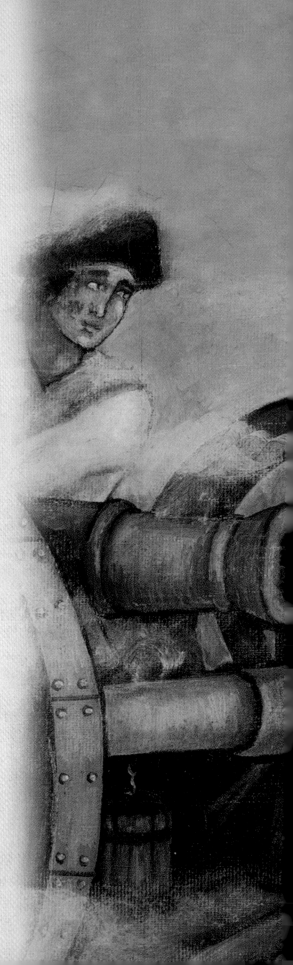

The soldiers started dropping as the sun rose higher. These Englishmen had never felt such heat in their home across the sea. It was almost a hundred degrees in New Jersey that day. Men grew faint and dizzy, and fell to the ground. But their companions went on marching. They never stopped or broke step, even when one man or more collapsed. Fifty-six British soldiers died of heat stroke that day.

That didn't stop them, though. All morning, more and more scarlet coats marched onto the field. Many American soldiers panicked at the sight of so many. General Lee couldn't maintain order. His soldiers forgot all about fighting in the disciplined ways Baron von Steuben had taught them. Instead, they ran in terror this way and that, hiding in ditches, up in apple trees, beneath hedges.

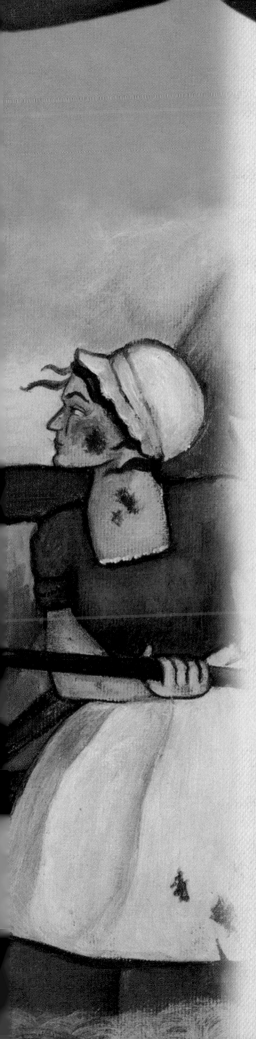

General Lee was sure there'd be a massacre of his troops before morning turned to noon. He gave the orders to retreat.

Molly saw that some of the men, including William, disobeyed the order and kept on fighting. The sun was growing hotter. As long as any member of the Continental Army needed water to drink, Molly Hays wasn't going anywhere.

On one of her trips to the spring, she stumbled over the body of an American soldier. She assumed he was dead until she heard him moan.

The British were advancing quickly, guns aimed straight at their foes. Molly knew she could run to safety, but the wounded man couldn't walk, let alone run. He lay directly in the line of fire and would surely be killed if he stayed there.

He was a good-sized fellow, but Molly wasted no time wondering how she'd do what she had to. She picked the man up, slung him over her shoulder, and ran to a clump of bushes away from the gunfire. She laid him down there on the grass in the shade.

She ran back toward the spring and passed the cannon William was firing just in time to see a ball from a British musket hit him. William fell to the ground. She examined her husband's wound and saw that he wouldn't die from it, but he couldn't fire his cannon.

Someone had to.

Molly grabbed the long ramrod, plunged it into the barrel of the cannon, and fired it off. She kept on firing.

> **STOP AND THINK**
>
> **Analyze/Evaluate**   Analyze and evaluate the author's use of detail in this scene. Which details help you picture the action? Do you think the author uses enough details? Why or why not?

A ball fired low from a British musket came whizzing straight toward Molly. She quickly spread her legs wide. The musket ball passed between them. It never touched her, but her skirt and petticoat were ripped and became a good deal shorter than they had been.

She muttered that it could have been worse and went back to work firing the cannon.

Soon General Washington galloped onto the field riding Nelson, his fine horse who never shied at the noise of guns or cannons, no matter how close they were. Washington carried the flag of commander in chief—thirteen stars in a circle on a field of blue silk. The flag fluttered and flew above the smoke of battle. It wasn't as bright as the scarlet coats the British soldiers wore, but to everyone who'd stayed on to fight, it was a cheering and glorious sight.

For the rest of that hot and steamy day, the Continental Army fought the way Baron von Steuben had taught it to. George Washington saw to that.

As he galloped over the battlefield, shouting orders and spurring his men on, he was amazed to catch a glimpse of a woman. She was blurred by the smoke that surrounded her. Her face was smudged with gunpowder and sweat. But George Washington saw her take a deep breath, then run and shove the long ramrod into the big gun with as much force as possible. The cannon boomed. The explosion shook the ground, but the woman paid no attention—she just got ready to fire the cannon again.

When the sun set, the fighting stopped. Neither side could go on in darkness. Exhausted British and American soldiers put down their guns and tended to their dead and wounded. Late that night, they sat down to eat and rest, to prepare themselves for another day of fighting.

That same night, General Washington asked some of his officers about the woman he'd seen firing a cannon. He listened to what they said about how she'd carried water through the gunfire to the soldiers all that morning.

Washington ordered that the woman be brought before him. He told her she'd been as brave in battle as any man he'd ever heard of. He decided she'd earned the rank of sergeant in the Continental Army.

As she listened to what the tall, strong general said, Molly Hays had never felt so proud in her life.

No man who heard General Washington speak to her that night doubted that Molly had earned her rank. As the news spread through the troops, no soldier sneered at the thought of a woman being a sergeant in *his* army, even though no one present had ever heard of such a thing.

That night, Sergeant Molly Hays lay down on the grass at the edge of the field beside William and the rest of the soldiers of the Continental Army. Long after the stars filled the sky, General George Washington spread his cape over the grass, tied Nelson to a tree, and lay down with his weary soldiers.

As he lay gazing up at the stars, planning his strategy for the next day's battle, fires danced on the hill across the field where the British were camped. The voices of many men carried through the night. Sentries marched back and forth, keeping their endless watch. It was very late before everything was quiet except for the chorus of frogs singing in the nearby swamp.

Molly and the other American soldiers rose before the sun. They'd had some sleep and were ready to fight again. Many believed they could win.

But they didn't fight the British that day. No scarlet-coated soldiers marched onto the field. They'd gone away.

Sir Henry Clinton and Lord Cornwallis had ordered a retreat. They didn't want their men to fight that wily old fox again this morning. They were afraid they'd lose. Washington's Continental Army didn't fight like farmers, as the British leaders had been sure they would. They fought like soldiers. And one of those soldiers was a woman.

Your Turn

Battlefield Women

Short Response Like many women of her day, Molly Hays went with her husband when he joined the Continental Army. What role did women like Molly play in the colonial military? Write a paragraph comparing and contrasting the military roles of women in the eighteenth century with the roles of women in the military today.

SOCIAL STUDIES

History in Song

Write a Song Songs often help tell a nation's story. "Yankee Doodle" was an important song about the Revolutionary War. Work with a group to write lyrics for a song about Molly Pitcher or the Battle of Monmouth. Start with a familiar tune, such as "Yankee Doodle," and add your own lyrics to the music. Perform your song for the class.

SMALL GROUP

In the Heat of Battle

Turn and Talk Think about the point in the story when General Lee orders the Continental Army to retreat, but some men continue fighting. Discuss with a partner how the actions of these men, including William Hays, shape the outcome of the Battle of Monmouth.

CONCLUSIONS AND GENERALIZATIONS

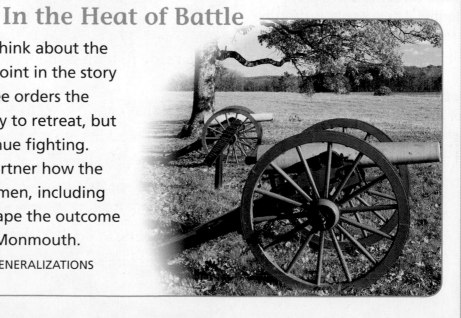

Social Studies

✔ TARGET VOCABULARY

revolution	gushed
strategy	plunged
foes	magnificent
legendary	retreat
formal	shimmering

GENRE

A **play** tells a story through the words and actions of its characters.

TEXT FOCUS

Stage directions in a play identify a time or place, describe a setting, or tell about a character's feelings or actions.

Set a Purpose Set a purpose for reading based on the genre and your background knowledge.

A Spy for Freedom

by Ann Weil

Cast of Characters
Ann Darragh (Narrator)
Lydia Darragh
General Howe
Redcoat Officer #1
Redcoat Officer #2
Thomas Craig

(The dining room of the Darragh house in Philadelphia, 1777.)

Ann Darragh (Narrator): This story is about my mother, Lydia Darragh, a legendary hero of the American Revolution. She was a housewife living in Philadelphia in 1777. She was also a Patriot spy.

(Lydia sits at a table, folding napkins. There is a knock at the door. A Redcoat officer enters.)

Redcoat Officer #1: Mrs. Darragh?

Lydia Darragh: Yes?

Redcoat Officer #1: This is a formal notice on behalf of the magnificent King George the Third of England. The British army is taking your house to use for our meetings.

Lydia Darragh: But I have young children and nowhere to go!

Ann Darragh (Narrator): Those words gushed from my mother's mouth. Her eyes were shimmering with tears. Later, General Howe let her stay in the house, as long as she let the British use one room. It was a mistake for him but lucky for the Patriots.

(Lydia sneaks in and hides in the linen closet. British officers enter and sit at a table.)

General Howe: We will attack the Americans at Whitemarsh in two days. That should end this rebellion.

Redcoat Officer #1 and Redcoat Officer #2: *(together)* Yes, sir. *(The British leave.)*

Lydia Darragh: *(stepping out of the closet)* General Washington must hear of this!

(Lydia quickly writes a note. She leaves after she has plunged it into her pocket.)

Ann Darragh (Narrator): My mother left the city to warn the American troops. On her way, she ran into my brother's friend, Thomas Craig, who was a militia soldier.

(A street in Philadelphia. Lydia enters from the left, walking quickly. Thomas is walking slowly, unaware that Lydia is approaching.)

Lydia Darragh: Thomas! Thomas Craig! Is that you?

Thomas Craig: Hello, Mrs. Darragh! How is your family?

(Lydia quickly hands Thomas the piece of paper. As Thomas reads, his eyes get wider and wider.)

Thomas Craig: Thank you for this news, Mrs. Darragh! I must warn General Washington of the British strategy.

(He runs offstage.)

Ann Darragh (Narrator): Because of my mother's information, the Americans had time to prepare. They were able to make the British forces retreat at the Battle of Whitemarsh.

(British officers meeting in Darragh's house. Lydia listens from the linen closet.)

Redcoat Officer #1: *(angry, confused)* Our foes knew we were coming, but how?

Redcoat Officer #2: *(looks around the room, shrugs)* The walls must have ears.

Ann Darragh (Narrator): The walls did not have ears, but one Patriot housewife did. Her quick action helped to bring the Americans to victory.

Making Connections

Text to Self

Write a Poem Think about the bravery displayed in this lesson's selections. Remember a time when you, someone you know, or someone you have read about did something brave. How did the act of bravery impact others? Write a poem about the event and your ideas about bravery. Use the sounds and rhythm of your words to help you decide where to break lines.

Text to Text

Role-play a Conversation Imagine a meeting between Molly Pitcher and Lydia Darragh. With a partner, review "They Called Her Molly Pitcher" and "A Spy for Freedom." Plan and role-play a conversation between the women. Have each character summarize information from the text as she describes her role in the Revolutionary War. Use the Vocabulary Words when possible.

Text to World

Connect to Social Studies Lydia Darragh was a Patriot spy during the American Revolution. Research another Patriot spy, such as Nathan Hale or James Armistead Lafayette. Use print or online resources to find out how that person's actions affected the war's outcome. Then share what you learn with a partner.

Grammar

What Is a Regular Verb? What Is an Irregular Verb? A **regular verb** adds *-ed* to its present form to show action that happened in the past. A regular verb also adds *-ed* when it is used with the helping verb *has*, *have*, or *had*. An **irregular verb** does not add *-ed* in these situations. It changes in other ways. You should memorize the spellings of irregular verbs.

Regular and Irregular Verbs	
regular verbs	The Continental Army camped at Valley Forge. General Washington had asked for supplies. His request had been ignored by the congress.
irregular verbs	The soldiers wore thin, ragged clothes. They had eaten almost all of the food. Soldiers' toes had been frozen by the frigid weather.

 **Work with a partner. Identify each underlined verb as a regular verb or an irregular verb.**

1. Molly Pitcher <u>nursed</u> the sick at Valley Forge.

2. She <u>brought</u> the troops water during a battle.

3. One American soldier had been <u>wounded</u> by a musket ball.

4. Molly Pitcher <u>won</u> fame for her work with that soldier's cannon.

Word Choice When you write, use vivid verbs to communicate action precisely. Vivid verbs help make your writing more interesting and easier to understand.

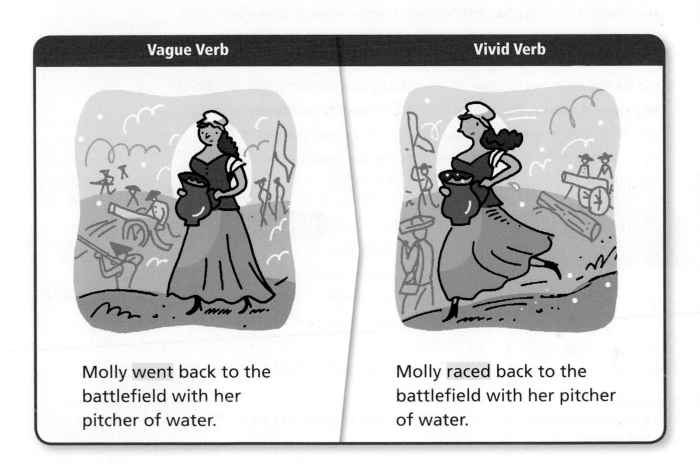

Vague Verb	Vivid Verb
Molly went back to the battlefield with her pitcher of water.	Molly raced back to the battlefield with her pitcher of water.

Connect Grammar to Writing

As you revise your persuasive letter, look for vague verbs that you can replace with vivid verbs. Use vivid verbs to create clear pictures in your writing. Make sure you are using the correct forms of both regular and irregular verbs.

Write to Persuade

☑ **Ideas** When you write a **persuasive letter,** state a goal clearly. The goal explains what you want the reader to think or do. Support your goal with at least two reasons. Give facts and examples to support your reasons. Be sure to include a date, salutation, closing, and signature.

Ed wrote a persuasive letter asking the principal of his school to honor another student who had helped raise money to build a water well in another country. As he revised his letter, Ed added details to make the support for his reasons stronger.

Writing Traits Checklist

☑ **Ideas**
Did I begin by expressing my goal clearly?

☑ **Organization**
Did I give reasons for my goal and support them with details?

☑ **Sentence Fluency**
Did I use regular and irregular verbs correctly?

☑ **Word Choice**
Did I carefully choose words that were strong and convincing?

☑ **Voice**
Did I express my interest in the subject?

☑ **Conventions**
Did I use correct spelling, grammar, and punctuation?

Revised Draft

to recognize students at Oak Ridge School Each year we have an awards night.∧

This year, we should present a special award to Molly Green. Molly led our school in the effort to raise money to build a well in another country. She organized a walk-a-thon.∧
and more than 200 kids participated

225 May Drive
Hilltop, TX 78443
January 15, 2010

Dear Mr. Ramirez,

　　Each year we have an awards night to recognize students at Oak Ridge School. This year, we should present a special award to Molly Green. Molly led our school in the effort to raise money to build a well in another country. She organized a walk-a-thon and more than 200 kids participated. We raised over $2,000! Thanks to Molly's idea, a village now has clean drinking water.

　　Through Molly's leadership, students at Oak Ridge saw that kids can make a difference. Students are already talking about other projects they might do to help people. Molly Green is a hero and deserves to be recognized.

　　　　　　　Sincerely,

　　　　　　　Ed Fung

In my final paper, I added details to support my reasons. I also changed vague verbs into more exact verbs.

Reading as a Writer

Which details did Ed add to make his ideas stronger? What details could you use to support your own ideas and generalizations?

NOW IS YOUR TIME! The African-American Struggle for Freedom
WALTER DEAN MYERS

Modern Minute Man

✓ **TARGET VOCABULARY**

provisions

dexterity

aspects

apprentice

influential

contributions

persuade

authorities

bondage

tentative

Vocabulary
Reader

Context
Cards

BATTLES at Sea

Vocabulary in Context

1 provisions
Colonial dockworkers unloaded needed goods or provisions from newly arrived ships in port.

2 dexterity
With dexterity, or skilled hands, this silversmith makes beautiful bowls.

3 aspects
Making frames and weaving fibers are aspects, or parts, of basketmaking.

4 apprentice
An apprentice to a blacksmith was trained to make horseshoes and nails.

- **Study each Context Card.**
- **Use a thesaurus to determine a synonym for each Vocabulary word.**

5 influential

Printers made books and newspapers that were influential in events before the Revolution.

6 contributions

Harvesting crops was one of many important contributions that kids made to the family farm.

7 persuade

A sign hanging above the door was used to persuade customers to enter the shoe shop.

8 authorities

Judges were the highest authorities, or officials, who could settle legal disputes.

9 bondage

Enslaved people, who were held in bondage, were often servants in the homes of the rich.

10 tentative

These merchants are shaking hands over a tentative deal. A contract will make it permanent.

Background

✔ **TARGET VOCABULARY** **Colonial African Americans** About 20 percent of colonists at the start of the Revolutionary War were of African ancestry. Most were in bondage; some were free.

Enslaved people often worked on plantations growing cotton or tobacco. Those in cities worked in homes, tending to the different aspects of domestic life, such as buying provisions, cooking, running errands, and doing housework.

Free African Americans could work at trades, often after time spent as an apprentice. Those with good manual dexterity became artisans. Others who were educated became business-people in spite of their tentative acceptance by whites. These influential African Americans made important contributions to their communities and worked to persuade authorities to end slavery and improve treatment of African Americans.

• Examine the timeline below. In which years did the construction of an early American clock and the building of a fur-trading post take place? Which event happened first?

1752 Benjamin Banneker constructs one of the first clocks in colonial America.

1773 Phillis Wheatley publishes the first book of poetry written by an African American.

1750 | **1775** | **1800**

1772 Jean-Baptiste Point Du Sable builds a fur-trading post that later becomes the city of Chicago.

1778 The 1st Rhode Island Regiment, the first all-African American military unit in the United States, is formed.

Comprehension

✔ **TARGET SKILL** **Sequence of Events**

As you read "James Forten," look for important events in the story. Notice the chronological order of these events. Use dates and signal words, such as *when* and *then,* to help you. Make a graphic organizer like this one to keep track of the sequence of events.

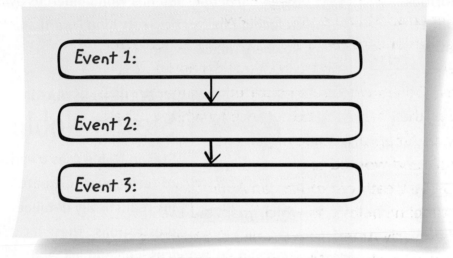

Event 1:

Event 2:

Event 3:

✔ **TARGET STRATEGY** **Summarize**

Use your graphic organizer to summarize as you read "James Forten." Then paraphrase the text. Remember that a summary should be brief. A paraphrase is a detailed retelling in your own words that is about the same length as the actual text. Summarizing and paraphrasing can help you better understand Forten's experiences.

MEET THE AUTHOR

Walter Dean Myers

Walter Dean Myers begins each new piece of writing with an outline because, he says, it "forces me to do the thinking." Then he tries to write ten pages a day until he finishes his first draft. After that he revises. Myers has written over eighty books for young people and has won numerous awards, including the Coretta Scott King Award and the Newbery Honor.

✔ TARGET VOCABULARY

provisions	contributions
dexterity	persuade
aspects	authorities
apprentice	bondage
influential	tentative

✔ TARGET SKILL

Sequence of Events
Identify the time order of events used by the author.

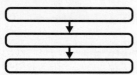

✔ TARGET STRATEGY

Summarize Briefly tell the important parts of the text in your own words.

GENRE

Biography tells about events in a person's life and is written by another person.

MEET THE ILLUSTRATOR

Steven Noble

Steven Noble uses a variety of techniques to create his realistically detailed illustrations. These include scratchboard, woodcut, pen and ink, and engraving. He lives in California.

JAMES FORTEN

from *Now Is Your Time!*

by Walter Dean Myers

selection illustrated by Steven Noble

Essential Question

What events led James Forten to fight for freedom?

James Forten was born in Philadelphia in 1766 and grew up during the American Revolution. He overcame great obstacles to become one of the most important African Americans of his time.

Thomas Forten, a free African, was employed by Robert Bridges, a sailmaker in Philadelphia. Sail making was a profitable but difficult job. Sewing the coarse cloth was brutal on the hands. The heavy thread had to be waxed and handled with dexterity. A person trying to break the thread with his hands could see it cut through his flesh like a knife. But Forten appreciated his job. It paid reasonably well and the work was steady.

Forten helped in all aspects of sail making and assisted in installing the sails on the ships the firm serviced. With the income from his work he had purchased his wife's freedom. Now, on this early Tuesday morning, a new baby was due. The baby, born later that day, was James Forten.

Young James Forten's early life was not that different from that of other poor children living in Philadelphia. He played marbles and blindman's bluff, and he raced in the streets. When he was old enough, he would go down to the docks to see the ships.

Sometimes James went to the shop where his father worked and did odd jobs. Bridges liked him and let him work as much as he could, but he also encouraged Thomas Forten to make sure that his son learned to read and write.

The Fortens sent their son to the small school that had been created for African children by a Quaker, Anthony Benezet. He believed that the only way the Africans would ever take a meaningful place in the colonies would be through education.

Thomas Forten was working on a ship when he fell to his death. James Forten was only seven at the time. His mother was devastated, but still insisted that her son continue school. He did so for two more years, after which he took a job working in a small store.

What James wanted to do was to go to sea. He was fourteen in 1781 when his mother finally relented and gave her permission. America was fighting for its freedom, and James Forten would be fighting, too.

He knew about the difficulties between the British and the American colonists. He had seen first British soldiers and then American soldiers marching through the streets of Philadelphia. Among the American soldiers were men of color.

STOP AND THINK

Author's Craft Authors sometimes use **foreshadowing**, or hints about what might happen later in the story. Where does the author use foreshadowing on this page? How can foreshadowing make a biography more interesting?

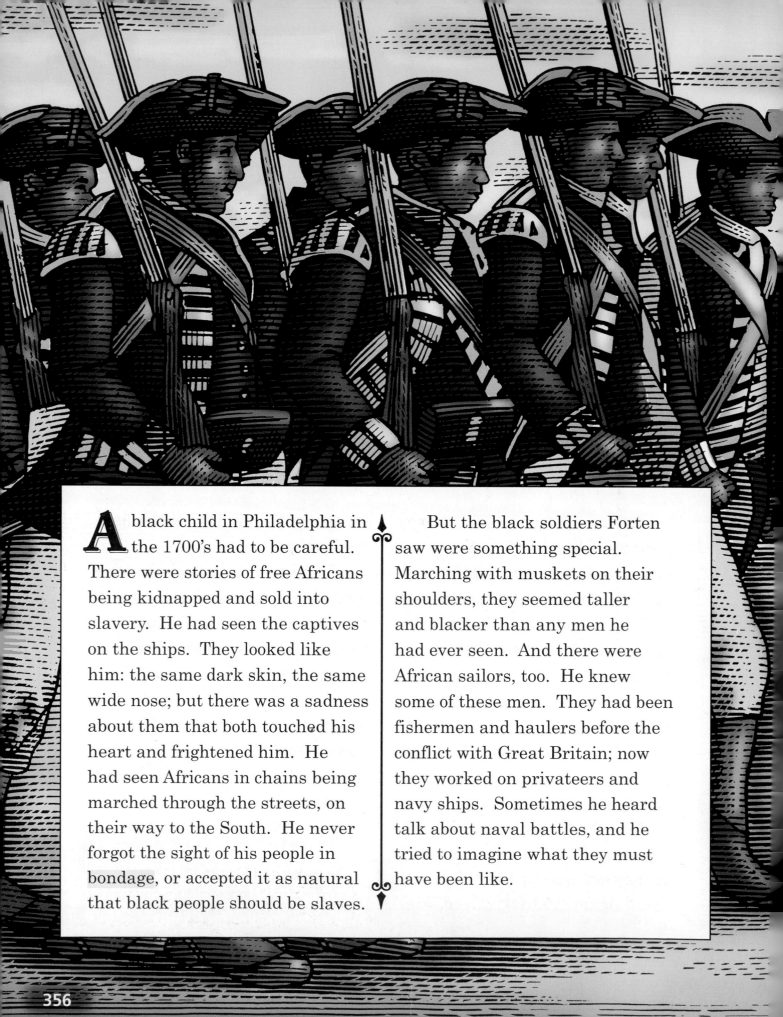

A black child in Philadelphia in the 1700's had to be careful. There were stories of free Africans being kidnapped and sold into slavery. He had seen the captives on the ships. They looked like him: the same dark skin, the same wide nose; but there was a sadness about them that both touched his heart and frightened him. He had seen Africans in chains being marched through the streets, on their way to the South. He never forgot the sight of his people in bondage, or accepted it as natural that black people should be slaves.

But the black soldiers Forten saw were something special. Marching with muskets on their shoulders, they seemed taller and blacker than any men he had ever seen. And there were African sailors, too. He knew some of these men. They had been fishermen and haulers before the conflict with Great Britain; now they worked on privateers and navy ships. Sometimes he heard talk about naval battles, and he tried to imagine what they must have been like.

In the summer of 1781, James Forten signed onto the privateer *Royal Louis*, commanded by Stephen Decatur, Sr. The colonies had few ships of their own to fight against the powerful British navy and issued "letters of marque" to private parties. These allowed the ships, under the flag of the United States, to attack British ships and to profit from the sale of any vessel captured.

The *Royal Louis* sailed out of Philadelphia in August and was quickly engaged by the British vessel *Active*, a heavy armed brig sent from England to protect its trade ships.

The *Royal Louis*'s guns were loaded with gunpowder that was tamped down by an assistant gunner. Then the cannonball was put into the barrel and pushed against the powder. Then the powder would be ignited. The powder had to be kept belowdecks in case of a hit by an enemy ship.

> ✔ **STOP AND THINK**
> **Sequence of Events** What are the important events on this page? What signal words and phrases does the author use to help you know the order of events?

Philadelphia harbor as it appeared around the time the *Royal Louis* defeated the *Active*.

Forten's job was to carry the gunpowder from below to the guns. Up and down the stairs he raced with the powder as shots from the British ship whistled overhead. There were large holes in the sails and men screaming as they were hit with grapeshot that splintered the sides of the ship. The smell of gunpowder filled the air as Captain Decatur turned his ship to keep his broadside guns trained on the *Active*. Sailors all about Forten were falling, some dying even as others cried for more powder.

Again he went belowdecks, knowing that if a shot ripped through to the powder kegs, or if any of the burning planks fell down into the hold, he would be killed instantly in the explosion. Up he came again with as much powder as he could carry.

After what must have seemed forever with the two ships tacking about each other like angry cats, the *Active* lowered its flag. It had surrendered!

Decatur brought his ship into Philadelphia, its guns still trained on the limping *Active*.

The crowd on the dock cheered wildly as they recognized the American flag on the *Royal Louis*. On board the victorious ship James Forten had mixed feelings as he saw so many of his comrades wounded, some mortally.

The *Royal Louis* turned its prisoners over to military authorities. On the twenty-seventh of September, the *Active* was sold; the proceeds were split among the owners of the *Royal Louis* and the crew.

The sailors with the worst wounds were sent off to be cared for. The others, their own wounds treated, were soon about the business of repairing the ship. Forten must have been excited. Once the fear of the battle had subsided and the wounded were taken off, it was easy to think about the dangerous encounter in terms of adventure. And they had won.

The missing crew was replaced. The ship was checked carefully by its captain and found to be in fine fighting condition. The crew carried more ammunition aboard, more powder, and fresh provisions. Once more they sailed for open waters.

On the sixteenth of October, 1781, they sighted a ship, recognized it as British, and made for it instantly. As they neared, a second ship was spotted, and then a third. Decatur turned to escape the trap, but it was already too late. The three British ships, the *Amphyon*, the *Nymph*, and the sloop *Pomona*, closed in. It was soon clear that the *Royal Louis* had two choices: to surrender or to be sunk.

The *Royal Louis* lowered its flag. It had surrendered, and its crew were now prisoners. Forten was terrified. He had heard the stories of the British sending captured Africans to the West Indies to be sold into slavery. He knew the *Pomona* had sailed back and forth from the colonies to the island of Barbados, where many Africans already languished in bondage. It was a time for dread.

The notorious British prison ship, *Jersey*, which was docked off Long Island, New York.

James was taken aboard the *Amphyon* with others from his crew. On board the British ship Captain Beasley inspected the prisoners. There were several boys among the American crew, and he separated them from the older men.

Captain Beasley's son looked over the boys who had been captured. Many of them were younger than he was. Although still prisoners, the boys were given more freedom than the men, and Beasley's son saw the Americans playing marbles. He joined in the game, and it was during this playing that he befriended Forten.

The result of this tentative friendship was that Captain Beasley did not, as he might have done, send Forten to a ship bound for the West Indies and slavery. Instead he was treated as a regular prisoner of war and sent to the prison ship the *Jersey*.

Dark and forbidding, the *Jersey* was a sixty-gunner anchored off Long Island, in New York. It had been too old to use in the war and had been refitted first as a hospital ship and then as a ship for prisoners. The portholes had been sealed and twenty-inch squares carved into her sides. Across these squares iron bars were placed.

The captain of the *Jersey* greeted the prisoners with a sneer. All were searched under the watchful eyes of British marines. The wounded were unattended, the sick ignored. The pitiful cries of other prisoners came from belowdecks. A few pale, sickly prisoners, covered with sores, were huddled around a water cask. Then came the cry that some would hear for months, others for years.

"Down, Rebels, down!"

They were rebels against the king, to be despised, perhaps to be hanged. Traitors, they were being called, not soldiers of America. James was pushed into a line on deck. The line shuffled toward the water cask, where each man could fill a canteen with a pint of water. Then they were pushed roughly belowdecks.

The hold of the ship was dark. What little light there was came from the small squares along the hull. The air was dank. Some of the prisoners were moaning. Others manned pumps to remove the water from the bottom of the boat.

Sleep was hard coming, and James wasn't sure if he wouldn't still be sold into slavery. Beasley's son had liked him, he remembered, and the boy had offered to persuade his father to take James to England. It would have been better than the hold of the *Jersey*.

In the morning the first thing the crew did was to check to see how many prisoners had died during the night. Many of the prisoners were sick with yellow fever. For these death would be just a matter of time.

Forten later claimed that the game of marbles with Beasley's son had saved him from a life of slavery in the West Indies. But on November first, two weeks after the capture of the *Royal Louis*, the news reached New York that Brigadier General Charles Cornwallis had surrendered to George Washington. Washington had strongly protested the British practice of sending prisoners to the West Indies. It was probably the news of his victory, more than the game of marbles, that saved the young sailor.

STOP AND THINK

Summarize Tell in your own words what happens to James after he boards the *Amphyon*.

Modern Minute
Man

✔ TARGET VOCABULARY

provisions	contributions
dexterity	persuade
aspects	authorities
apprentice	bondage
influential	tentative

GENRE

Informational text, such as this magazine article, gives factual information about a topic.

TEXT FOCUS

Primary sources, such as the interview in this article, give information about the topic and its time period.

• The author of this selection includes an interview with an actual person. How does this primary source help the author achieve his purpose?

Modern Minute Man

by Marcus Duren

Every year on April 19, Charles Price of Lexington, Massachusetts, is one of seventy-seven modern-day Lexington Minute Men who gather to reenact the events that took place at the Battle of Lexington in 1775. The first shot of the Revolutionary War was fired in this influential battle.

Modern Lexington Minute Men take the same oath as the original ones. Each plays a real person from history. Price plays Prince Estabrook, the only African American who fought in the battle. We asked him about different aspects of the reenactment.

How did you find information about Prince Estabrook?

It was quite difficult. For the most part, records weren't kept for slaves. There are some old documents, but some of them are in very poor condition.

How did it happen that Prince Estabrook was a militiaman?

I can only think of two reasons. One, it very well may be that his master sent him out in his place. The other reason is that maybe he felt if he fought he'd get his freedom.

The reenactment is so realistic! How do you make sure no one gets hurt?

We stress safety, safety, safety! We have many practices beforehand.

Charles Price as Prince Estabrook

It takes practice and dexterity to reenact a battle scene. Everything from the uniforms to the provisions is historically correct.

Are there kids in the reenactment?
We have kids come out to take care of the wounded soldiers. My daughter did it for about ten years.

What else should students know about the Lexington Minute Men?
These people risked everything to be out there. If they lost or were captured, they could have been hanged as traitors. I don't think people today realize how much of a chance they were taking. Every one of those people was a hero.

Freemen, Slaves, Soldiers

People of African descent made contributions to the Revolutionary War for different reasons. A freeman could often make better wages as a soldier than he could as a farmer or an apprentice. It was also common for slaves to serve in place of their owners, who chose not to fight.

Both the British and patriot armies badly needed soldiers. Authorities on both sides sometimes tried to persuade slaves to enlist by offering them freedom from bondage at the war's end. However, slaves knew that this tentative offer could be reversed if the side for which they fought lost.

Making Connections

Describe an Ordinary Hero James Forten and Prince Estabrook were ordinary people who made great contributions to history. Think of an ordinary person that you know who is making a difference in the lives of others. Write a short composition about his or her contribution. Include details and examples to make your points clear.

Compare Choices A biography uses details and examples from primary sources to tell a person's life story in sequential order. The author chooses which facts to include or emphasize and how to interpret them. Compare the way the authors of "James Forten" and "They Called Her Molly Pitcher" (Lesson 13) tell the life stories of James Forten and Molly Hays.

Learn About Reenactments "Modern Minute Man" describes a military reenactment that takes place each year in Lexington, Massachusetts. Work with a small group to research a historical reenactment in your region or state. Make a poster advertising the event. Then present your poster to another group. Discuss with each other what you learned, and ask questions about information given in each presentation.

Grammar

What Is the Active Voice? What Is the Passive Voice? A verb in the **active voice** tells what the subject does. A verb in the **passive voice** tells what was done to the subject.

Active and Passive Voice

subject   verb in active voice
American ships attacked British ships.

---

subject   verb in passive voice
British ships were attacked by American ships.

Try This! Copy each sentence onto another sheet of paper. Circle its verb. If the main verb follows any helping verbs, be sure to include them in your circle. Tell whether the verb is in the active voice or the passive voice.

1. The *Royal Louis* sailed from Philadelphia.

2. That American ship was attacked by a British vessel.

3. The *Royal Louis* returned fire.

4. The ship's guns had been filled with gunpowder by an assistant gunner.

5. The battle was won by the American ship.

Sentence Fluency When you want to make your writing livelier, you can use verbs in the active voice. Sentences with verbs in the active voice are shorter and more direct. When you want to emphasize what was done to the subject in a sentence, you can use verbs in the passive voice. By using both active and passive voice, you can add variety to your writing.

Active-Voice Verb	Passive-Voice Verb

Our captain steered the ship.	The ship was steered safely to port by our captain.

Connect Grammar to Writing

As you revise your persuasive essay next week, make sure that most of your sentences have verbs in the active voice. Look closely at sentences that have verbs in the passive voice. If they would be livelier in the active voice, rewrite them.

Write to Persuade

✔ **Organization** Good writers organize their ideas before writing a **persuasive essay.** A graphic organizer can help you identify and organize your opinion and the reasons and details that support it.

For his persuasive essay, Derek chose to write about James Forten. He did some research and took notes. Then he used an idea-support map to organize his reasons and the supporting details. Later, he revised the map to state his ideas more clearly and to arrange them in a logical order.

Use the Writing Process Checklist below as you prewrite.

Writing Process Checklist

▶ **Prewrite**

- ✔ Did I state a clear opinion?
- ✔ Did I list reasons to support my opinion?
- ✔ Did I include facts and examples to support my points?
- ✔ Did I organize my ideas in a clear and logical way?

Draft

Revise

Edit

Publish and Share

Exploring a Topic

James Forten during the Revolutionary War

—powder boy on ship

—carried gunpowder to cannons

—captured by the British

Myers, Walter Dean. Now Is Your Time! New York, NY: HarperCollins Publishers, 1992. pp. 57—62

James Forten After the War

—leader in Philadelphia

—got 2,500 African Americans to fight the British (War of 1812)

—part of abolition movement

—antislavery newspaper

Ball, Maggie. The Life and Times of James Forten. Denver, CO: Sled Dog Press, 2007. pp. 35—37

Opinion: James Forten should be recognized for his role in our nation's history.

Reason: James Forten worked on a war ship during the Revolutionary War.

Detail: He carried gunpowder to be put in the cannons.

Detail: He spent several months on a British prison ship.

Reason: James Forten was an important leader in Philadelphia after the war.

Detail: He got 2,500 African Americans to fight against the British in the War of 1812.

Detail: As part of the abolition movement, he gave money to an antislavery newspaper.

I took notes about James Forten and used them to create an idea-support map. I listed reasons to support my opinion. Then I added details to support my reasons. This helped me organize my ideas.

Reading as a Writer

How can Derek's idea-support map help him develop well-organized paragraphs? How could an idea-support map help you draft your persuasive essay?

371

Patriotic Poetry

WE WERE THERE, TOO!
YOUNG PEOPLE IN U.S. HISTORY
PHILLIP HOOSE

✓ TARGET VOCABULARY

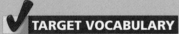

rural

tedious

lacked

personally

organize

mocking

efficient

summons

mimic

peal

Vocabulary
Reader

Context
Cards

Paul Revere
Hero on Horseback

by Carol Domblewski

Vocabulary in Context

1 rural

Many colonial children lived with their families in rural areas, on farms in the countryside.

2 tedious

These children are bored by the tedious, dreary chore of collecting firewood.

3 lacked

Colonial soldiers who lacked shoes at Valley Forge wrapped their feet in cloth.

4 personally

In wealthy homes, family members were often personally attended by servants.

- Study each Context Card.
- Use a dictionary to clarify the part of speech of each Vocabulary Word.

5 organize

Only after their chores were done could colonial children set up, or organize, games.

6 mocking

Troublesome students had to wear a dunce cap mocking their misbehavior.

7 efficient

Girls learned to be efficient when they sewed. They didn't waste scarce thread.

8 summons

This painting of a girl summons, or calls up, thoughts of childhood in colonial America.

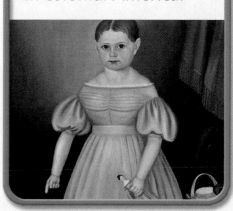

9 mimic

Colonial girls created mimic, or make-believe, situations to act out with their dolls.

10 peal

On Washington's birthday in 1846, a ring, or peal, of the Liberty Bell made it crack.

Background

✔ **TARGET VOCABULARY** **Colonial Militias** Militias are armies or fighting forces made up of ordinary people rather than professional soldiers. Often, they work their regular day-to-day jobs until their leader summons them to action.

When the American Revolution began, General Washington lacked a regular fighting force. As a result, volunteers began to organize militias. They were colonists, rural and urban, who wanted to be personally involved in the fight for freedom.

Early on, some British troops took to mocking the militias, saying that these untrained men were nothing but mimic soldiers. However, with each battle fought and each peal of gunfire, these rookie soldiers became more skilled and efficient. Though warfare was exhausting and tedious, these militias never gave up. In the end, militias, Continental troops, and their allies won America's independence from Great Britain.

This statue on the Battle Green in Lexington, Massachusetts, is of Captain John Parker, a member of a local militia known as the Minute Men.

Comprehension

Compare and Contrast

In this selection, the author compares and contrasts experiences of two individuals. Think about how each characters' situations, motives, and traits are alike and different. Then use a Venn diagram to record similarities and differences between the lives of two young patriots during the Revolutionary War.

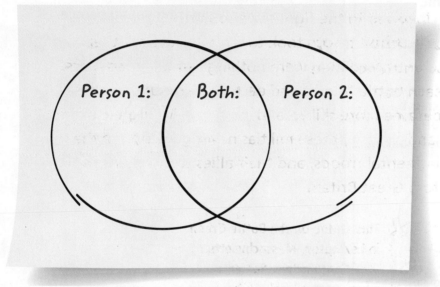

Person 1:   Both: Person 2:

✓ **TARGET STRATEGY** **Monitor/Clarify**

Monitor and clarify details about people and events in each part of the selection. Monitoring and clarifying will help you better understand the contributions Joseph Plumb Martin and Sybil Ludington made to the Revolutionary War.

JOURNEYS DIGITAL Powered by **DESTINATIONReading**
Comprehension Activities: Lesson 15

375

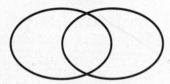

✔ **TARGET VOCABULARY**

rural	mocking
tedious	efficient
lacked	summons
personally	mimic
organize	peal

✔ **TARGET SKILL**

Compare and Contrast
Examine how the author describes two characters as alike or different.

✔ **TARGET STRATEGY**

Monitor/Clarify As you read, notice what is not making sense. Find ways to figure out the parts that are confusing.

GENRE

Biography tells about events in a person's life and is written by another person.

Set a Purpose Set a purpose for reading based on the genre and your background knowledge.

MEET THE AUTHOR
Phillip Hoose

The idea for *We Were There, Too!* came to Phillip Hoose while he was interviewing a young social activist named Sarah Rosen for his book *It's Our World, Too!* She said, "We're not taught about younger people who have made a difference. Studying history almost makes you feel like you're not a real person." Hoose decided to change that by writing about our nation's history through the stories of more than seventy amazing young people.

We Were There, Too!

by Phillip Hoose

Essential Question

How did two young people's heroic actions differ?

"The smell of war began to be pretty strong."

Joseph Plumb Martin:

"And Now I Was a Soldier"

Milford, Connecticut, 1775

Joseph Plumb Martin was a tall, strong, hardworking boy who grew up on his grandparents' farm in Connecticut. Though he never went to school, he managed to write one of the best diaries of the Revolutionary War.

Joseph Martin forced the metal plow deep down into the soil while his grandfather walked alongside, guiding the horse that pulled it. It was a fresh April morning, a perfect planting day. Suddenly the silence was broken by the sound of bells and gunshots in Milford. Joseph dropped the plow and dashed into town, his grandfather following behind as fast as he could.

A crowd was gathered in front of the tavern, where an express rider from New Haven shouted news of three days before: There had been a bloody battle in Concord, Massachusetts. Many were dead. Soldiers were needed now. A silver dollar was the reward for anyone who would enlist in the American army and march off to New York to join General Washington.

Joseph was only fourteen, a year too young to enlist. Until that day, his thoughts about soldiering had always been clear: "I felt myself to be a real coward. What—venture my carcass where bullets fly! That will never do for me. Stay at home out of harm's way, thought I."

But now friends his age and even younger were scrawling their names and grabbing up those dollars while adults cheered. Joseph was torn. He hated to stay home while his friends marched off to glory, and the thought of a whole silver dollar made "the seeds of courage begin to sprout," but he needed more time to get used to the idea. Two months later, he was ready. On June 25, 1776, Joseph slipped away from his grandparents' house and hiked into town, his mind made up to enlist for six months, the shortest term possible. When a group of boys he knew saw him coming, they began to taunt him:

"'Come, if you will enlist, I will,' says one.

"'You have long been talking about it,' says another.

"'Come, now is the time.'

REGULARS

Unlike militiamen, who volunteered to fight when men were needed, the Continentals—or "regulars"—were professional soldiers who got paid to enlist and fight in the army. Continentals and militiamen often fought together in battle. Each Continental soldier got assigned to a company of eighty-six men. Eight companies made up a regiment, also called a battalion. The Continental army had twenty-six regiments of foot soldiers, one of riflemen, and one of artillerymen.

"Thinks I to myself, I will not be laughed into it or out of it. I will act my own pleasure after all. . . . So seating myself at the table, enlisting orders were immediately presented to me. I took up the pen, loaded it with the fatal charge, made several mimic imitations of writing my name, but took especial care not to touch the paper with the pen until an unlucky [friend] who was leaning over my shoulder gave my hand a strike which caused the pen to make a woeful scratch on the paper. 'O, he has enlisted,' said he. . . . Well, thought I, I may as well go through with the business now as not. So I wrote my name fairly upon the indentures. And now I was a soldier, in name at least."

His grandparents were unhappy, but they "fit him out" with clothing, a musket, and powder. His grandmother gave him cheese and cake and stuffed it into his knapsack. He sailed to New York City to join a Connecticut company. For more than a month all they did was march in parades and practice battle drills. Joseph's biggest problem was getting used to the food—salt pork or boiled beef, hard bread, and turnips or boiled potatoes.

> **STOP AND THINK**
>
> **Monitor/Clarify** Joseph uses words and phrases that we do not use today. Reread the paragraph in which Joseph enlists. How would we describe the event differently today? It may help to use a dictionary.

A young man summons his courage and signs the enlistment roster that will make him a soldier in the Continental army.

But even as they practiced, hundreds of British warships were arriving at nearby Staten Island, unloading 32,000 redcoated soldiers. Late in August, Joseph's company was ordered to Long Island to stop British forces from taking New York City. Just before they marched off, Joseph climbed onto the roof of a house and squinted in the direction of the battlefield: "I distinctly saw the smoke of the field artillery, but the distance and the unfavorableness of the wind prevented my hearing their report, at least but faintly. The horrors of battle then presented themselves to my mind in all their hideousness. I must come to it now, thought I."

They took a ferry across the East River to Brooklyn and marched toward a field, the shots growing louder and louder with each step until they boomed like thunder. "We now began to meet the wounded men, another sight I was unacquainted with, some with broken arms, some with broken heads. The sight of these a little daunted me, and made me think of home."

And then all at once he was fighting, too. "Our officers . . . pressed forward towards a creek, where a large party of Americans and British were engaged. By the time we arrived, the enemy had driven our men into the creek . . . where such as could swim got across. Those that could not swim, and could not procure anything to buoy them up, sunk."

On the opposite bank of Gowanus Creek he could make out a long row of British soldiers—professional warriors from what was then the best army in the world. They stood straight and tall in red jackets as they fired on command at the retreating Americans. The creek was filling up with American bodies. Joseph's company shot back furiously, trying to provide cover for those still thrashing through the water.

Then they marched on to a part of Manhattan called Kip's Bay and readied themselves for another battle. One night they camped so close to a British warship that Joseph could overhear soldiers on board mocking the Americans. Early on a Sunday morning, Joseph slipped into an unlocked warehouse for a rare moment of privacy and peace. He was seated on a stool, reading some papers he'd discovered, when "all of a sudden there came such a peal of thunder from the British shipping that I thought my head would go with the sound. I made a frog's leap and lay as still as I possibly could and began to consider which part of my carcass would go first." They were soon dashing for their lives, leaping over the bodies of their friends. As Joseph put it, "fear and disorder seemed to take full possession of all and everything that day."

RECRUITING FOR THE CONTINENTAL ARMY

After the wave of enthusiasm that gripped Joseph Plumb Martin and his friends in 1775, recruiting for the army got harder each year. Part of the problem was that the Continental soldiers faced the well-equipped British forces in ragged uniforms that they had to provide for themselves. Often they fought with muskets that lacked bayonets. Food was scarce and soldiers were not always paid on time, if at all. Not that it mattered much—privates got only about seven dollars a month. Some soldiers deserted, but many more remained out of a desire for independence and a respect for General George Washington.

Joseph was still alive when October came and cool weather set in, and life got even more uncomfortable: "To have to lie, as I did almost every night on the cold and often wet ground without a blanket and with nothing but thin summer clothing was tedious . . . In the morning, the ground [often was] as white as snow with hoar frost. Or perhaps it would rain all night like a flood. All that could be done in that case was to lie down, take our musket in our arms and packe the lock between our thighs and 'weather it out'."

When Joseph was discharged from the Continental army on Christmas Day, 1776, he felt older than fifteen. A battle-tested patriot, he was proud that he had stood his ground against the British. He set off for home, fifty-two miles away, with four shillings of discharge pay in his pocket and enough stories to get him through the winter and more. He farmed for a year, got bored, and reenlisted. When the war ended six years later, he was still a soldier. And he was also a free citizen of a new nation.

WHAT HAPPENED TO
JOSEPH PLUMB MARTIN?

He moved to Maine in 1794 and began to farm. He married and became the father of five children. He loved to write, tell stories, and draw pictures of birds. When he was seventy, his Revolutionary War account was published. He died in Maine at the age of ninety.

STOP AND THINK
Author's Craft An author who writes with an **objective tone**, or attitude, reports facts without stating his or her own opinion. How can you tell the author wrote this selection with an objective tone? Why might an author need to be objective when writing a biography?

"The British are burning Danbury! Muster at Ludington's!"

Sybil Ludington:

Outdistancing Paul Revere

Fredericksburg, New York, April 26, 1777

Nearly everyone has heard of the midnight ride of Paul Revere. That's mainly because Henry Wadsworth Longfellow wrote a poem about it soon after it happened. But far fewer people know that two years later a sixteen-year-old girl rode much farther over rougher roads. Alone and unarmed, Sybil Ludington raced through the night for freedom.

Just after dark on the rainy evening of April 26, 1777, Colonel Henry Ludington, commander of a regiment of militiamen near the New York–Connecticut border, heard a rap at his door. Outside stood a saluting messenger, rain streaming from his cape. His words came fast. British soldiers had just torched the warehouse in Danbury, Connecticut. Food and guns belonging to the Continental army were being destroyed. Soldiers were burning homes, too. Could Colonel Ludington round up his men right away?

SYBIL RODE FARTHER

On April 18, 1775, Paul Revere raced from Boston to Lexington to warn American rebel leaders, "The British are coming!" He rode fourteen miles on good roads for some two hours, while Sybil Ludington rode all night—nearly forty miles over cart tracks and rutted fields in the blackness of rural farm country.

It was easier said than done. Colonel Ludington's militiamen were farmers and woodsmen whose homes were scattered throughout the countryside. Someone would have to go get them while the colonel stayed behind to organize them once they arrived. But who? Who besides he himself knew where they all lived and could cover so many miles on horseback in the dead of night? Deep in thought, he heard his daughter Sybil's voice. She was saying that she wanted to go.

For Sybil Ludington it was an unexpected chance to help the war effort. As the oldest of eight children, her days were filled with chores and responsibilities. Still, each week when her father's men drilled in their pasture, she paused from her work to watch them. She wished she could fight. People kept saying she was doing her part for liberty at home, but she wanted to do more. Suddenly, with this emergency on a rainy night, she had a chance.

The route of Sybil Ludington's night ride through the New York countryside

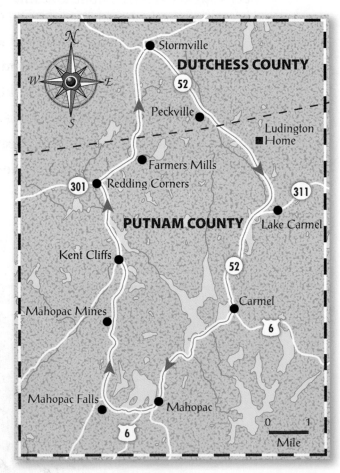

Her father looked at her. How could he let her take such a risk? The whole countryside was full of armed men. There were skinners and cowboys who stole cattle for the British, soldiers from both sides, and deserters trying to get back home under cover of darkness. But Sybil was right: She knew every soldier in her father's unit and she was a fine rider. Rebecca, her next oldest sister, could mind the children. Most of them were already asleep anyway.

Colonel Ludington walked with Sybil out to the barn and held a lantern while she threw a saddle over her yearling colt, Star. Together father and daughter went over the names of his men and where they lived. Then the colonel watched Sybil disappear into the darkness.

It was raining hard. Sybil put away thoughts of who might appear in the roadway and concentrated on the road map in her head. With no time to lose, she had to reach all the men, taking the most efficient route possible. She picked up a long stick to bang on doors. That way she wouldn't have to waste time dismounting and getting back on Star. One by one, hearing the rap of the stick, the sleepy farmers cracked their doors open, some poking muskets out into the darkness. Sybil said the same thing to all: "The British are burning Danbury! Muster at Ludington's!" Once she knew they understood, she galloped off, refusing all offers of rest and refreshment.

This bronze statue of Sybil Ludington riding Star is in Carmel, New York.

387

Sybil Ludington ✪ *Youthful Heroine*

In 1975, the U.S. Postal Service issued a Sybil Ludington stamp to mark the American Bicentennial.

It took her till dawn to get back home. She was soaked and sore, but as she rode up to her farm she could hear the sounds of drums and bugles. Many of her father's men were already there, getting ready to march. Soon her father's militia set off to join five hundred other Colonial soldiers. They missed the British at Danbury but finally fought and defeated them at Ridgefield, Connecticut, a few weeks later.

WHAT HAPPENED TO SYBIL LUDINGTON?

Word of Sybil's ride got around. George Washington thanked her personally, and Alexander Hamilton wrote her a letter of appreciation. When she was twenty-three, Sybil married her childhood sweetheart, Edmond Ogden, and became the mother of four sons and two daughters. Sybil died in New York at the age of seventy-seven. There is a bronze statue of Sybil Ludington atop Star at Lake Gleneida in Carmel, New York. In 1975, an eight-cent U.S. postage stamp was issued in her honor.

 **STOP AND THINK**

Compare and Contrast Based on what you have read, how were the responsibilities of young men and women during the Revolution alike? How were they different?

Your Turn

Heroic Times

Short Response Joseph Plumb Martin and Sybil Ludington each showed courage in support of a cause. Write a paragraph about Joseph or Sybil, comparing his or her actions with actions you might take today for a cause you believe in, such as the environment or a political vote.

COMPARE AND CONTRAST

VOTE YES

A Day's Work

Role-play a Conversation Growing up during the Revolutionary War gave Joseph Plumb Martin, Sybil Ludington, and other young people a unique experience. Role-play a conversation they might have had. Use details from the selection to discuss how the American Revolution may have affected their daily lives. SMALL GROUP

Young Patriots

Turn and Talk Joseph Plumb Martin and Sybil Ludington had different motives for becoming involved in the war. With a partner, compare and contrast the reasons why Joseph and Sybil each volunteered to help. Whose actions do you think made the bigger difference? Why?

COMPARE AND CONTRAST

✔ TARGET VOCABULARY

rural	mocking
tedious	efficient
lacked	summons
personally	mimic
organize	peal

GENRE

Poetry uses the sound and rhythm of words in a variety of forms to suggest images and express feelings.

TEXT FOCUS

Rhyme Rhyming patterns, or rhyme schemes, establish rhythm and make poems memorable.

• You can identify a poem's rhyme scheme by assigning each line a letter based on the sound of its end word. Lines that rhyme are assigned the same letter. The rhyme scheme of the first stanza of this poem, for example, is AABBA. What kind of feeling does the rhyme in the poem give you as you read?

Patriotic Poetry

On April 18, 1775, the sight of lights in a church steeple summons Paul Revere to ride from Charlestown to Lexington, warning people that the British are coming. Other patriots, such as Sybil Ludington, make similar rides at other times, but Revere becomes a huge legend. One reason is the following poem, part of which is shown here.

The Midnight Ride of Paul Revere
by Henry Wadsworth Longfellow

Listen, my children, and you shall hear
Of the midnight ride of Paul Revere,
On the eighteenth of April, in Seventy-five;
Hardly a man is now alive
Who remembers that famous day and year.

He said to his friend, "If the British march
By land or sea from the town to-night,
Hang a lantern aloft in the belfry arch
Of the North Church tower, as a signal light,—
One if by land, and two if by sea;
And I on the opposite shore will be,
Ready to ride and spread the alarm
Through every Middlesex village and farm,
For the country folk to be up and to arm."

[Therefore], his friend, through alley and street
Wanders and watches with eager ears,
Till in the silence around him he hears
The muster of men at the barrack door,
The sound of arms, and the tramp of feet,
And the measured tread of the grenadiers,
Marching down to their boats on the shore. . . .

Meanwhile, impatient to mount and ride,
Booted and spurred, with a heavy stride
On the opposite shore walked Paul Revere. . . .

Now he patted his horse's side,
Now he gazed on the landscape far and near,
Then, impetuous, stamped the earth,
And turned and tightened his saddle girth;
But mostly he watched with eager search
The belfry tower of the Old North Church,
As it rose above the graves on the hill,
Lonely and spectral and somber and still.
And lo! as he looks, on the belfry's height
A glimmer, and then a gleam of light!
He springs to the saddle, the bridle he turns,
But lingers and gazes, till full on his sight
A second lamp in the belfry burns!

Most of colonial America lacked good roads, especially in rural areas. Travel was often slow and tedious. A fast horse was the most efficient way to travel. The peal of a horse's hooves was as common then as the roar of a car engine is today.

A hurry of hoofs in a village street,
A shape in the moonlight, a bulk in the
   dark,
And beneath, from the pebbles, in
   passing, a spark
Struck out by a steed flying fearless and
   fleet;
That was all! And yet, through the
   gloom and the light,
The fate of a nation was riding that
   night;
And the spark struck out by that steed, in
   his flight,
Kindled the land into flame with its
   heat. . . .

So through the night rode Paul Revere;
And so through the night went his cry of
   alarm
To every Middlesex village and farm,—
A cry of defiance, and not of fear,
A voice in the darkness, a knock at the
   door,
And a word that shall echo forevermore!
For, borne on the night-wind of the Past,
Through all our history, to the last,
In the hour of darkness and peril and
   need,
The people will waken and listen to hear
The hurrying hoof-beats of that steed,
And the midnight-message of Paul
   Revere.

Write a Patriotic Poem

Patriotism is the love that one personally feels for one's country.
Write a patriotic poem with a rhyme scheme. First, brainstorm a list
of ideas to organize your thoughts. You may create a mimic of
Longfellow's style by beginning your poem with "Listen, and you shall
hear. . . ." Then follow with your own story. Use rhyme to establish
rhythm in your poem or to make parts of it more memorable for
readers. Try to use figurative language in your writing, and include
vocabulary words such as mocking.

Making Connections

Express Your Views Think about how the heroes Joseph Plumb Martin, Sybil Ludington, and Paul Revere are portrayed in the selections in this lesson. Imagine that you are an author. Use examples from "We Were There, Too!" and "Patriotic Poetry" to help you use literary language to write a biography about a modern-day hero you admire.

 Text to Text

Compare and Contrast Authors make decisions about the ways in which they present ideas. Analyze the choices the authors made in "We Were There, Too!" and "Patriotic Poetry." Then compare and contrast how the authors used literary devices or literary language in their writing to make it more interesting.

 Text to World

Learn About Places As you read "Patriotic Poetry," write down the names of unfamiliar places that are mentioned. Research these places to help you clarify the action in the poem. Then use a map of the United States to find each location.

393

Grammar

Easily Confused Verbs Some pairs of verbs have such closely related meanings that they are easily confused. Most of these verbs are **irregular verbs**. A few are **helping verbs**. By studying the meanings of both verbs, you can avoid using the wrong one in your speaking and writing.

Easily Confused Verbs			
can	"is able to do"	**may**	"is allowed to do by someone" or "is fairly likely to do"
sit	"to lower yourself onto a seat"	**set**	"to place an item onto something"
teach	"to give instruction to someone"	**learn**	"to receive instruction from someone"
lie	"to recline on something"	**lay**	"to put an item carefully on top of something"
rise	"to get up" or "to stand up"	**raise**	"to lift something up"

 **Work with a partner. Tell which sentences have verbs that are used incorrectly. Say each of these sentences, replacing the incorrect verb with the correct one.**

1 The young recruit sets in a chair.

2 "We will learn you how to march," the soldier says.

3 "I can march already," the recruit replies.

4 The recruit signs the papers and lies the pen on the table.

5 The soldier raises from his seat and shakes the recruit's hand.

Conventions You know that some pairs of verbs have meanings that are related but different. These verbs are easily confused with each other. When you proofread your writing, it is important to pay special attention to these verbs.

Incorrect Verbs	Correct Verbs
I sit my diary on the table. I lay on my bed but am unable to sleep. When I rise my head from the pillow, I hear the sounds of battle.	I set my diary on the table. I lie on my bed but am unable to sleep. When I raise my head from the pillow, I hear the sounds of battle.

Connect Grammar to Writing

As you edit your persuasive essay, look closely at each sentence for mistakes with easily confused verbs, such as those above. Using verbs correctly is an essential part of good writing.

Reading-Writing Workshop: **Revise**

Write to Persuade

☑ **Word Choice**   In a **persuasive essay,** you state a clear opinion, or position, about what you want your audience to think or do. Include strong reasons to support your opinion, and support those reasons with facts and examples. To avoid plagiarizing, write the facts in your own words.

   Derek wrote a first draft of his persuasive essay about James Forten, using his idea-support map. Then he revised his draft by replacing weak or vague words with strong, specific words to make his ideas clearer and more convincing.

   Use the Writing Process Checklist below as you revise your writing.

Writing Process Checklist

Prewrite

Draft

▶ **Revise**

☑ Did I state my opinion clearly?

☑ Did I support it with reasons and details?

☑ Did I use strong, specific words to make my points convincing?

☑ Did I use easily confused words correctly?

Edit

Publish and Share

Revised Draft

Every student studying the American Revolution will ~~teach~~ learn about John Adams, George Washington, and Thomas Jefferson. The name James Forten ~~can~~ may be less ~~known~~ familiar, but he, too, played an important ~~part~~ role in the ~~forming~~ founding of our nation.

   James Forten was a free African whose parents had been enslaved. During his youth, James ~~was~~ worked as a powder boy on a Revolutionary War ship.

396

Why We Should Remember James Forten

by Derek Johnson

Every student studying the American Revolution will learn about John Adams, George Washington, and Thomas Jefferson. The name James Forten may be less familiar, but he, too, played an important role in the founding of our nation.

James Forten was a free African whose parents had been enslaved. During his youth, James worked as a powder boy on a Revolutionary War ship. His job was to haul gunpowder from belowdecks so that it could be loaded into the cannons. It was a very dangerous job, and he did it well. When James Forten's ship was captured, he spent several months on a British prison ship. James did not become a war hero, but he served his country like thousands of other men and women. Without people like him, the war would not have been won.

In my final paper, I replaced weak and vague words with stronger, more specific words. I also made sure I used easily confused words correctly.

Reading as a Writer

Which words did Derek replace to make his writing stronger? What words could you replace in your own writing to make it sound more confident?

Read the next selection. Think about the cause-and-effect relationships in the tale.

Davy Crockett Gets a Pet

David "Davy" Crockett was a real person. He was born in Tennessee in 1786. He grew up on the frontier, hunting and clearing land. He went into politics and served in the United States Congress. Davy Crockett was famous for his sense of humor and his bear-hunting skills. For these reasons, he became a folk hero. After his death in 1836, stories about his life were exaggerated and became tall tales.

Long ago in Tennessee, a comet shot across the sky. People watched in amazement as it hit the top of the tallest mountain. The sky lit up like fireworks. When the smoke cleared, there was a baby on that mountaintop. This was the birth of Davy Crockett.

People took one look at this newborn baby and knew that he was special. As he grew, his remarkable differences became unquestionable. He shot up like a sapling. He ate huge amounts of bear meat and drank gallons of buffalo milk. As a result, Davy weighed more than 200 pounds by the time he was six years old! He was often seen carrying thunder in one hand and throwing lightning with the other. He boasted, "I can outrun, outfight, and outyell anyone!"

As Davy grew up, he seemed to have both human and animal qualities. He ran as fast as a cheetah. He swam as easily as a fish. He was as strong as an ox. He bragged about all the animals he had fought, including wildcats and bears.

Bragging can sometimes cause trouble, however. That is exactly what happened to Davy. One day he was walking home through a thick forest. Dark clouds rolled in, and the sky grew as black as night. The wind gusted and thunder rumbled above. Davy had been walking for a long time. He was tired. He was famished, too. As sheets of rain began to fall, Davy knew that he had to find something to eat.

Davy saw two eyes shining from behind a group of trees. "Aha!" said Davy. "Here is a chance for a meal!" He said to the animal hiding behind the trees, "My name is Davy Crockett. I'm very hungry. That's bad news for you because I am going to eat you!"

At that moment, lightning lit up the forest. Davy saw what was behind the tree. It was not a small, helpless creature. It was a huge, strong cougar! Davy quickly changed his tune. "Excuse me," he said. "I made a mistake. I wasn't talking to you."

The cougar didn't listen to Davy. Instead, it crept slowly from behind the tree. It crouched low, ready to pounce. It began growling and baring its teeth.

Davy tried a little humor. He laughed and said, "You want to sing, do you? How about we try a duet?" Still, the cougar kept inching toward him. Davy said to the cat, "I guess it's time to get serious. I've fought wildcats before. I can fight you, too."

Davy started to growl. He bared his teeth. Soon he sounded as fierce as the cougar. Davy crouched low. He moved toward the cougar. Then the two were upon each other. They began to wrestle.

The fight was vicious. It went on and on. Finally, Davy picked up the cougar by the tail. He swung him around and around like a lasso. The cougar yowled in pain. "Okay," said Davy to the wildcat. "I'll stop." He put the cougar back on the ground, but he did not loosen his grasp on the cat's tail. "You are coming home with me. I'm going to teach you some manners!"

Davy took the wildcat back to his cabin. He taught that cat to rake leaves with its huge claws. The wildcat learned to sing in a choir. It used its keen eyesight to lead Davy home in the dark. Over time, Davy and the wildcat became the best of companions. They were often heard singing duets together.

Unit 3 Wrap-Up

The Big Idea

Look at Both Sides King George III felt the English government had the right to tax the colonists, but the American patriots thought differently. Think of an issue on which people in your community or school disagree. Find out what people on each side of the debate believe. Then design two bumper stickers, one in support of each side.

Listening and Speaking

Patriotic Symbols Molly Hays's pitcher became a symbol of her bravery. Research a symbol of the United States or a symbol of your state, such as its quarter or an important landmark. Find or draw a picture of your chosen symbol to show to a classmate. Discuss its history and meaning.

What's Your Story?

unit 4

Big Idea

Everyone has a
story to tell.

Paired Selections

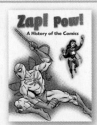

 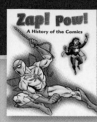

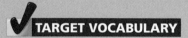
TARGET VOCABULARY

feature

record

assuming

mental

launch

thumbed

developed

incredibly

episodes

villains

Vocabulary Reader	Context Cards

Vocabulary in Context

1 feature

Storytellers often feature, or focus on, tales from their own cultural tradition.

2 record

One of these tiny volumes could claim the record as the world's smallest book.

3 assuming

Mimes can tell stories without words, assuming viewers follow their motions.

4 mental

Exact words help readers create mental pictures of a story's characters and setting.

- **Study each Context Card.**
- **Use a dictionary or a glossary to verify the meaning of each Vocabulary word.**

5 launch
After the launch, or initial printing, of his book, this author signs a copy of it at a store.

6 thumbed
At the library, this student thumbed through books to find a story to read later.

7 developed
An artist developed, or planned, this character from pencil sketch to final color drawing.

8 incredibly
Roman heroes like Hercules are often incredibly, or unbelievably, strong.

9 episodes
A story told in several episodes, or parts, is sometimes called a series.

10 villains
In old movies most villains had evil grins, wore black clothes, and battled the heroes.

Background

☑ **TARGET VOCABULARY** **Making a Comic Book** You have probably thumbed through a lot of comic books in your time. Before the launch of any comic book, writers and authors must do a lot of work.

The writers don't try to set a speed record when writing the story. The plot must be carefully developed to capture readers' interest. Writers decide where to split the story into episodes. They try to feature strong characters, both good guys and villains, who may be incredibly strong or fast.

Before the artist starts to draw, he or she must form a mental image of the characters. Assuming that everyone has done their job, a new superhero adventure is born.

Behind every successful comic book is a team of talented writers and artists.

Comprehension

Author's Purpose

The author of "Lunch Money" provides details from which you can infer his viewpoint. As you read, think about how a character's thoughts and actions help you figure out the author's viewpoint, even when it is not directly stated. Use a graphic organizer like this one to help you understand the author's purpose.

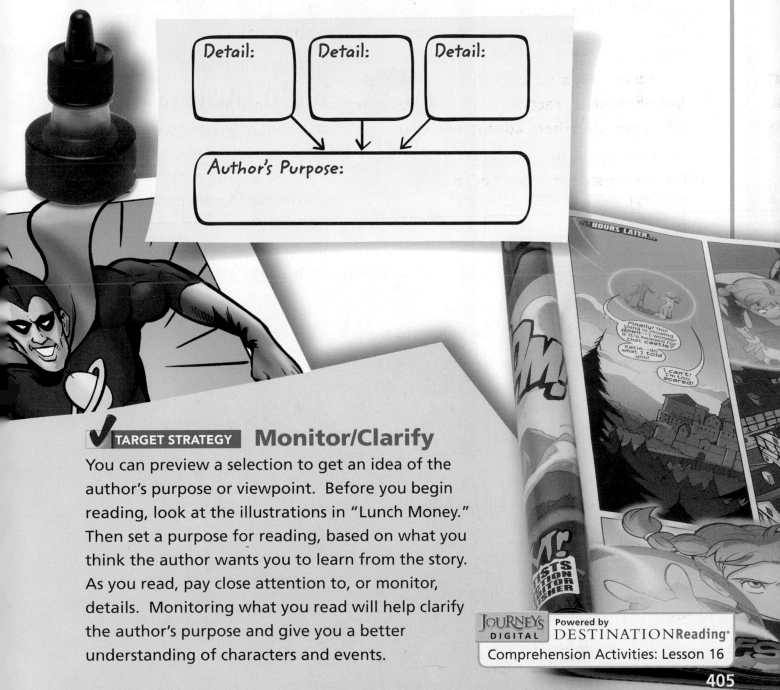

Detail: Detail: Detail:

Author's Purpose:

✓ TARGET STRATEGY **Monitor/Clarify**

You can preview a selection to get an idea of the author's purpose or viewpoint. Before you begin reading, look at the illustrations in "Lunch Money." Then set a purpose for reading, based on what you think the author wants you to learn from the story. As you read, pay close attention to, or monitor, details. Monitoring what you read will help clarify the author's purpose and give you a better understanding of characters and events.

JOURNEYS DIGITAL   Powered by DESTINATIONReading®
Comprehension Activities: Lesson 16

TARGET VOCABULARY

feature	thumbed
record	developed
assuming	incredibly
mental	episodes
launch	villains

TARGET SKILL

Author's Purpose Use text details to figure out the author's viewpoint and reasons for writing.

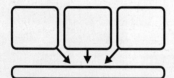

TARGET STRATEGY

Monitor/Clarify As you read, notice what is not making sense. Find ways to figure out the parts that are confusing.

GENRE

Realistic fiction is a present-day story with events that could take place in real life.

Set a Purpose Set a purpose for reading based on the genre and what the author wants you to know.

MEET THE AUTHOR

Andrew Clements

Andrew Clements says, "I mostly write realistic fiction, novels that feel a lot like real life." Like his character Greg, Clements works hard at his writing. To avoid distractions, he writes in his backyard shed with no phone, no television, and no Internet!

MEET THE ILLUSTRATOR

Adam Gustavson

Adam Gustavson wanted to be a cowboy, but he was allergic to horses. Then he wanted to be a crocodile farmer, but there weren't any crocodiles in New Jersey where he lived. He finally settled on art. He has illustrated several books for young people.

LUNCH MONEY

by Andrew Clements
selection illustrated by
Adam Gustavson

Essential Question

Why does an author want to tell a story?

Standing in the cafeteria line, Greg opened his red plastic pencil case. He counted once, and then he counted again, just to be sure. Then he grinned. There were thirteen left.

Sweet! That means I sold seventeen units.

That's what Greg called the comic books he'd been selling—units. And selling seventeen units before lunch was a new sales record.

Greg's comic books weren't the kind for sale at stores. Regular comic books were sort of tall. Also a little floppy. Not Greg's.

Greg's comic books were about the size of a credit card, and they could stand up on one end all by themselves. They were only sixteen pages long, and he could fit about fifty of them into his pencil case. These comic books were short and sturdy. And that's why they were called Chunky Comics.

Greg loved that name. He had chosen it himself. He got to pick the name because he was the author of all the Chunky Comics stories. He had drawn all the pictures too. And he was also the designer, the printer, and the binder. Plus he was the marketing manager, the advertising director, and the entire sales force. Chunky Comics was a one-kid operation, and that one kid was Greg Kenton.

Greg snapped the pencil case shut and grabbed a tray. He took a grilled cheese sandwich, a cup of carrot sticks, and then looked over the fruit cocktail bowls until he found one with three chunks of cherry. He got a chocolate milk from the cooler, and as he walked toward his seat, Greg did some mental math.

Monday, the first day Chunky Comics had gone on sale, he had sold twelve units; Tuesday, fifteen units; Wednesday, eighteen units; and today, Thursday, he had already sold seventeen units—before lunch. So that was . . . sixty-two units since Monday morning, and each little book sold for $.25. So the up-to-the-minute sales total for September 12 was . . . $15.50.

Greg knew why sales were increasing: word of mouth. Kids had been telling other kids about his comic book. The cover illustration was powerful, the inside pictures were strong, and the story was loaded with action. The title was *Creon: Return of the Hunter*, and it was volume 1, number 1, the very first of the Chunky Comics. So that made it a collector's item.

Greg sat down at his regular lunch table, next to Ted Kendall. Ted nodded and said, "Hi," but Greg didn't hear him. Greg picked up his sandwich and took a big bite. He chewed the warm bread and the soft cheese, but he didn't taste a thing. Greg was still thinking about sales.

Fifteen fifty in three and a half days—not so hot.

Greg had set a sales goal for the first week: twenty-five dollars—which meant that he had to sell one hundred units. It looked like he was going to fall short.

STOP AND THINK

Monitor/Clarify To clarify why Greg needs to sell one hundred units to make twenty-five dollars, reread the previous page. What happens when you multiply the price of one unit times one hundred?

The idea of making and selling comic books had hit Greg like a  KRAK over the head from Superman himself. It made perfect sense. Candy and gum were against school rules, and tiny toys were boring—and also against the rules. But how could he go wrong selling little books? School was all about books and reading. True, reading a comic book wasn't exactly the same as reading a regular book, but still, there was a rack of comics right in the kids' section at the public library downtown, and some new graphic novels, too.

Comic books had been part of Greg's life forever, mostly because of his dad's collection. His dad's collection filled three shelves in the family room—and it was worth over ten thousand dollars. Once Greg had shown he knew how to take care of the comic books, he had been allowed to read and look at them all he wanted. Greg had even bought a few collectible comics of his own, mostly newer ones that weren't very expensive.

It was his love of comic books that had first gotten Greg interested in drawing. Comics had led Greg to books like *How to Draw Comic Book Villains*, *You Can Draw Superheroes*, *Make Your Own Comic-Book Art*, and *Draw the Monsters We Love to Hate*. Back in third grade Greg had used his own money to buy india ink, dip pens, brushes, and paper at the art supply store. And drawing new comic-book characters was one of his favorite things to do—when he wasn't earning money.

That whole summer before sixth grade Greg had worked toward the launch of Chunky Comics. From the start he had felt pretty sure he could come up with a story idea, and he knew he would be able to do the drawings.

But first he'd had to deal with a lot of *hows*: How does a whole comic book get put together? How big should each be? How was he going to print them? How much would it cost him to make each one? And finally, how much money should he charge for his finished comic books—assuming he could actually make some?

But one by one, Greg had found the answers. An encyclopedia article about printing books had helped a lot. It showed how pages of a book start as one large sheet of paper that gets folded in half several times. Each time the sheet is folded, the number of pages is doubled. So Greg took a piece of regular letter-size paper, and folded it in half three times the way it showed in the encyclopedia. That one piece of paper turned into a chunky little sixteen-page book—Chunky Comics. It was so simple.

STOP AND THINK

Author's Craft Authors often use **repetition**, repeating a word or phrase, to bring extra attention to something. Why do you think the author repeats the word *how* so many times in the third paragraph on this page?

But not really. Greg figured out that making little comic books was a ten-step process.

1. Write a story that can be told on twelve to fourteen mini-comic book pages.

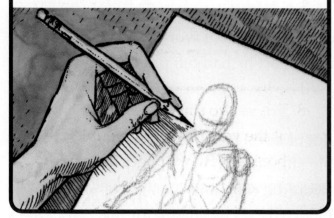

2. Sketch, draw, ink, and then letter all sixteen minipages—which include the front and back covers.

3. Paste eight of the minipage drawings into their correct positions on a piece of paper to make "master copy one"—a sheet that can be copied again and again.

4. Paste up the other eight minipages to make "master copy two."

5. Using a copier, print the images from "master copy one" onto one side of a "press sheet"—a piece of regular letter-size paper.

6. Print "master copy two" onto the flip side of the press sheet—making eight page images on the front, and eight on the back.

7. Carefully fold the press sheet with the sixteen copied minipages on it.

8. Put in two staples along the crease at the very center of the little book—between pages 8 and 9.

9. Trim the three unstapled edges—and that makes one finished mini-comic book.

10. Repeat.

And each of the ten steps had to be done perfectly, or no one would ever want to spend money on his little comics.

After all the *hows* had been settled, then came the writing. But Greg hadn't written just one story. He had developed a master publishing plan. Volume 1 was going to be about Creon, an incredibly intelligent Stone Age hero who helped his tribe deal with ancient dangers, like prehistoric beasts and Cro-Magnon marauders. Greg figured there could be seven or eight issues about Creon.

Chunky Comics volume 2 would feature the future, where a superhero named Eeon tried to protect a small colony of humans living in a world of melting ice caps and mutant life-forms that were part human, part toxic sludge, and part recycled trucks and airplanes. Again, there would be seven or eight issues featuring Eeon.

> **STOP AND THINK**
> **Author's Purpose** Why do you think the author explains how Greg makes comic books in such detail?

CREON!

EEON!

414

Then Chunky Comics volume 3 would feature Leon, a fairly normal modern-age technodude who suddenly finds himself energized when his digital atomic watch overheats and burns its circuits into the nerves on his wrist. Leon learns that the watch can be set for the future or the past. The six or seven time-travel adventures of volume 3 would follow Leon to the past, where he would team up with Creon, and then to the future, where he would offer his services to the amazing Eeon. And eventually, all three characters would have some final episodes together: Creon, Leon, and Eeon—past, present, and future.

Once the master plan was set, writing the first Creon story, *Return of the Hunter*, had been pretty easy for Greg. But the drawing was more difficult than he'd thought it would be. It had taken a long time to get each small page looking just the way he wanted. It wasn't like doodling or sketching. These pictures had to be good— good enough to sell.

When both covers and the fourteen inside pages had been drawn and inked and pasted in place to make the two master copies, Greg tackled his first printing.

The copier he used was his dad's, and it was actually part of the printer that was hooked up to the computer in the family room. It was an ink-jet printer, plus a scanner, plus a copier—one of those "all-in-one" machines. It made copies in either black and white or color.

Greg had stuffed about forty ruined sheets of paper into the recycling bin before he had figured out how to get all sixteen page images copied correctly onto the front and back of one sheet of paper.

But finally, he had folded his first perfectly printed sheet, stapled it twice, and trimmed the top, front, and bottom edges. And then, one hot night in the middle of July, Greg stood there in his family room and thumbed through the very first volume of Chunky Comics. It had been a proud moment.

THE END.

Your Turn

A Proud Moment

Short Response One hot night in July, Greg thumbed through the first volume of his comic book series. It was a proud moment for him. Have you, or has someone you know, worked so hard to create something that the resulting feelings of pride and accomplishment were as strong as Greg's? Write a paragraph explaining what happened. Be sure to include vivid details. PERSONAL RESPONSE

Buy Chunky Comics!

Create a Poster Work with a partner to design and create a promotional poster for a bookstore or library that can help Greg advertise his comic books. Use details from the selection to make the comic books come alive. PARTNERS

Past, Present, Future

Turn and Talk Do you think Creon, Leon, and Eeon will be good characters for a series of comic books? Do you think Greg will be successful? Discuss with a partner what makes comic books popular and fun to read. Then discuss why the author might have included Greg's detailed plans for his Chunky Comics series. AUTHOR'S PURPOSE

✔ **TARGET VOCABULARY**

feature	thumbed
record	developed
assuming	incredibly
mental	episodes
launch	villains

GENRE

Informational text gives facts and examples about a topic.

TEXT FOCUS

A **timeline** marks the sequence of important events in a period of history or other span of time.

• Preview the timeline on pages 418–419. How do the facts and dates relate to the title of the selection?

Zap! Pow!

A History of the Comics

by Linda Cave

Do you read the funnies in the paper? They have been popular for more than one hundred years. They tell stories with words and pictures, and new episodes appear each day. Assuming you read comics, you know they can be funny. Sometimes they feature adventures or political issues. Some comics are in books, too.

Development of Comics

1907: Daily comics

1896: *Yellow Kid*

1934: *Flash Gordon*

1900

1920

1933: First comic books

1897: Speech balloons; story panels

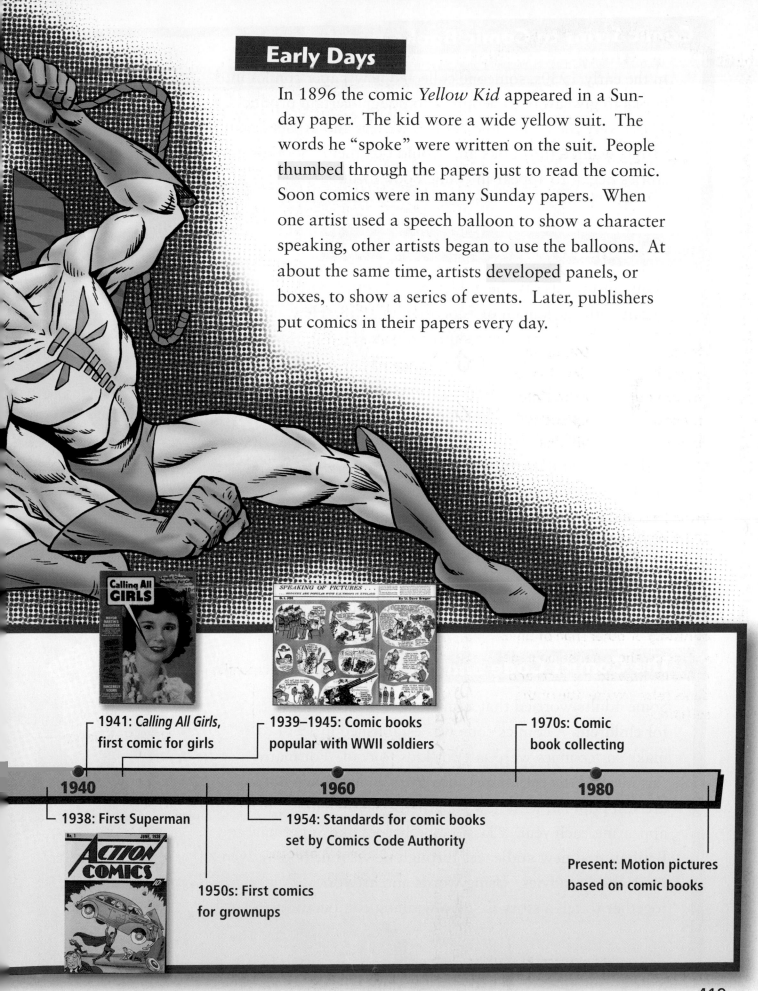

Early Days

In 1896 the comic *Yellow Kid* appeared in a Sunday paper. The kid wore a wide yellow suit. The words he "spoke" were written on the suit. People thumbed through the papers just to read the comic. Soon comics were in many Sunday papers. When one artist used a speech balloon to show a character speaking, other artists began to use the balloons. At about the same time, artists developed panels, or boxes, to show a series of events. Later, publishers put comics in their papers every day.

1941: *Calling All Girls,* first comic for girls

1939–1945: Comic books popular with WWII soldiers

1970s: Comic book collecting

1940

1960

1980

1938: First Superman

1954: Standards for comic books set by Comics Code Authority

1950s: First comics for grownups

Present: Motion pictures based on comic books

Comic Strips to Comic Books

In the early 1930s, someone collected newspaper comics into books to give away to people who bought certain products. These were the first comic books. Writers and artists saw that people wanted the books and would buy them. Soon original stories began to appear in comic book form.

The Golden Age of Comic Books

Many historians say the golden age of comic books began with the launch of Superman in 1938. He was the first character to have super powers. His comic books were incredibly popular. They set a new sales record, with over one million copies sold per issue. Noticing the new superhero's popularity, other comic book artists created Batman, The Flash, the Green Lantern, Captain America, and Wonder Woman. They all fought villains. Some used amazing tools or had super physical and mental powers.

The Comics Code and After

Some adults worried that comic books were bad for children. A comics code was established in 1954 to make sure comics were safe for kids to read. For many, this marked the end of a golden age. Today comic books are still popular, with new superheroes and villains appearing each year. Classic superheroes like Superman and Batman find new audiences through new comic book adventures and in movies. Using words and artwork together to tell a story is still a winning combination.

Making Connections

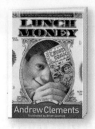 

 Text to Self

Write a Letter to a Hero You do not have to be a superhero to do incredible things. Write a letter to someone you know who has done something special or out of the ordinary. In your letter, explain why you think what that person did is special.

 Text to Text

Create a Comic In "Lunch Money," Greg creates three comic book characters—Creon, Eeon, and Leon. Create a comic about an adventure one of these characters has. Use one of the comic book formats described in "Zap! Pow! A History of the Comics" to write your comic.

 Text to World

Expand a Timeline Work with a partner to add to the timeline in "Zap! Pow! A History of the Comics." Begin by studying the captions and illustrations on the timeline on pages 418–419. Use print sources or the Internet to find additional information to include on the timeline. Then add to the timeline three other important events in the history of comics. Review the new timeline. How has the audience for comics changed over the years?

Grammar

What Is an Adjective? An **adjective** is a word that gives information about a noun, such as *how many* and *what kind*. An adjective that tells *what kind* is called a **descriptive adjective**. One special type of descriptive adjective tells the origin of the person, place, or thing being described. These adjectives are formed from names of places, so they are capitalized.

Academic Language

adjective

descriptive adjective

descriptive adjective	Suzette likes comics with dynamic artwork.
descriptive adjective giving origin	She especially likes the Japanese comics called manga.

Turn and Talk **Work with a partner. Find the descriptive adjectives in these sentences. Tell which identify the origin of a person, place, or thing.**

❶ Her favorite adventures take place in Asian cities.

❷ Modern buildings make a great background for intense action.

❸ Korean costumes from ancient times add appeal.

❹ Phil has a comic with Chinese warriors in it!

❺ A capable superhero knows karate, jiujitsu, and kickboxing.

Word Choice When you write, use precise descriptive adjectives to create clear images for your readers. Using precise descriptive adjectives will help make your writing more interesting.

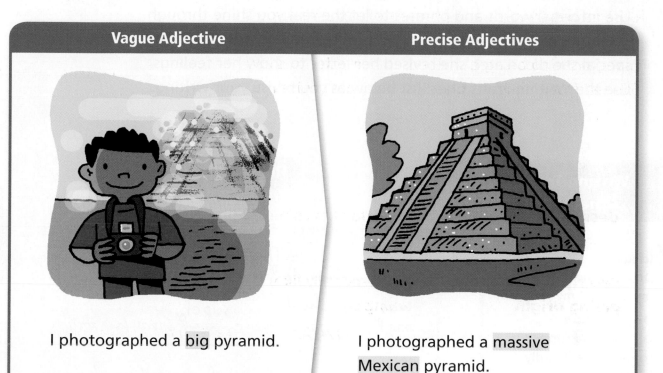

Vague Adjective	Precise Adjectives
I photographed a big pyramid.	I photographed a massive Mexican pyramid.

Connect Grammar to Writing

As you revise your friendly letter, look for opportunities to replace vague adjectives with precise descriptive adjectives. Using descriptive adjectives will help readers visualize what you are writing about.

Write to Narrate

☑ **Voice** In "Lunch Money," Greg's feelings show clearly when he thinks, "Sweet! That means I sold seventeen units." A well-written **friendly letter** also shows your feelings and really sounds like you. Use informal words and phrases to let the real you shine through.

Nicole drafted a letter to her cousin telling him about something special she did. Later, she revised her letter to show her feelings. Use the Writing Traits Checklist below as you revise your writing.

Writing Traits Checklist

☑ **Ideas**
Do all of the details in my letter fit my purpose?

☑ **Organization**
Did I use the correct format for a friendly letter?

☑ **Sentence Fluency**
Did I vary my sentence types?

☑ **Word Choice**
Did I use informal words and expressions?

☑ **Voice**
Do my feelings and personality come through?

☑ **Conventions**
Did I use correct spelling, grammar, and punctuation?

Revised Draft

Dear Jerome,

~~I liked the~~ The comic book you made for me was awesome! It gave me a ~~good~~ super idea for my school project, too. I started reading about Colonial life. ~~Then~~ After I learned what the Pilgrims really ate, ~~Then I~~ made some drawings of their food and ~~Then I~~ wrote funny captions for the drawings.

555 East Central Street
Rockford, IL 61102
March 25, 2009

Dear Jerome,

The comic book you made for me was awesome! It gave me a super idea for my school project, too. I started reading about Colonial life. After I learned what the Pilgrims really ate, I made some drawings of their food and wrote funny captions for the drawings. Suddenly I realized that this could be my social studies project! I made a 12-page comic book about cooking in Colonial times.

My project was a total success! My teacher wants her own copy of the book, and so does the principal. I'll make a copy for you, too.

Your very best cousin,
Nicole

In my final letter, I changed some words to show my feelings more clearly. I also replaced the overused adverb *then* and used precise adjectives.

Reading as a Writer

What words and expressions tell you how Nicole feels? Where can you show your feelings more clearly in your own letter?

impressed

collected

produced

destination

original

concentrate

suspense

admitted

compliment

rumor

Vocabulary Reader   Context Cards

Vocabulary in Context

1 impressed
This judge was impressed and awed by a young writer's remarkable talent.

2 collected
Chess players must remain calm and collected as they plot their next move.

3 produced
Amazing structures were produced, or created, at this sand castle contest.

4 destination
This marathoner's goal is to be the first to reach the finish line, his destination.

- **Study each Context Card.**
- **Use a glossary to determine the pronunciation of each Vocabulary word.**

5 original
Olympia, Greece, is the original, or first, place where Olympic Games were held.

6 concentrate
This tennis player has to concentrate on the ball in order to hit it back to her opponent.

7 suspense
These fans are in suspense, wondering who will win the big game.

8 admitted
This spelling bee contestant admitted, or confessed, how nervous he was.

9 compliment
A first-place trophy is a compliment praising the dog and its handler.

10 rumor
Sometimes a rumor, or unproved news, can spread about who won a contest.

427

Background

Imagining the Future   At one time or another, we have all admitted that we are curious about the future. If the suspense of waiting to see what's in store is too much, you can always read science fiction. Even the earliest, or original, science fiction authors, such as H.G. Wells, produced stories about time travel. The stories often concentrate on new inventions and changes in society that impressed the fictional time travelers. There are often cool and collected scientists and brave adventurers who select another time for their destination. However, time travel is only a rumor. It could never really happen. It is a compliment to the skill of science fiction writers that they can make us believe in their imaginary futures.

Some science fiction stories feature mechanical devices that send characters forward or backward in time.

Comprehension

✔ **TARGET SKILL** **Story Structure**

As you read "LAFFF," identify a character's problem or conflict
and the events in the story that resolve the conflict, or lead to a
solution. Think about the character's role in what happens, when it
happens, and why. Use a story map like the one below to help you
understand how a story unfolds. Remember to list story events in
sequential order.

Setting: Characters:

Problem(Conflict):
Events:
Solution(Resolution):

✔ **TARGET STRATEGY** **Infer/Predict**

When a character has a conflict or a problem, think about the way
the story unfolds to bring about a resolution. Look to the events in
a story to predict what will happen next. Making predictions and
finding out if they come true can make reading fun.

✔ TARGET VOCABULARY

impressed	concentrate
collected	suspense
produced	admitted
destination	compliment
original	rumor

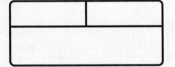

✔ TARGET SKILL

Story Structure Examine details about characters, setting, and plot.

✔ TARGET STRATEGY

Infer/Predict Use text clues to figure out what the author means or what might happen in the future.

GENRE

Science fiction is a fantasy story whose plot often depends on scientific ideas.

MEET THE AUTHOR
Lensey Namioka

Lensey Namioka was nine when she moved to the United States from China. Although she loved stories, learning English was difficult. Math was easier for her, so she became a math teacher. However, she never stopped reading, and eventually her love of stories led her to become a writer.

MEET THE ILLUSTRATOR
Hiromitsu Yokota

Hiromitsu Yokota has created illustrations for numerous books, magazines, and calendars. He uses digital technology to create his illustrations because it allows him to play with color and light in the pictures.

LAFFF

from *Best Shorts*

by Lensey Namioka

selection illustrated by Hiromitsu Yokota

Essential Question

What problem does the character face?

431

In movies, geniuses have frizzy white hair, right? They wear thick glasses and have names like Dr. Zweistein.

Peter Lu didn't have frizzy white hair. He had straight hair, as black as licorice. He didn't wear thick glasses, either, since his vision was normal.

Peter's family, like ours, had immigrated from China, but they had settled here first. When we moved into a house just two doors down from the Lus, they gave us some good advice on how to get along in America.

I went to the same school as Peter, and we walked to the school bus together every morning. Like many Chinese parents, mine made sure that I worked very hard in school.

In spite of all I could do, my grades were nothing compared to Peter's. He was at the top in all his classes. We walked to the school bus without talking because I was a little scared of him. Besides, he was always deep in thought.

Peter didn't have any friends. Most of the kids thought he was a nerd because they saw his head always buried in books. I didn't think he even tried to join the rest of us or cared what the others thought of him.

Then he surprised us all. As I went down the block trick-or-treating, dressed as a zucchini in my green sweats, I heard a strange, deep voice behind me say, "How do you do."

I yelped and turned around. Peter was wearing a long, black Chinese gown with slits in the sides. On his head he had a little round cap, and down each side of his mouth drooped a thin, long mustache.

"I am Dr. Lu Manchu, the mad scientist," he announced, putting his hands in his sleeves and bowing.

He smiled when he saw me staring at his costume. It was a scary smile, somehow.

Some of the other kids came up, and when they saw Peter, they were impressed. "Hey, neat!" said one boy.

I hadn't expected Peter to put on a costume and go trick-or-treating like a normal kid. So maybe he did want to join the others after all—at least some of the time. After that night he wasn't a nerd anymore. He was Dr. Lu Manchu. Even some of the teachers began to call him that.

When we became too old for trick-or-treating, Peter was still Dr. Lu Manchu. The rumor was that he was working on a fantastic machine in his parents' garage. But nobody had any idea what it was.

One evening, as I was coming home from a baby-sitting job, I cut across the Lus' backyard. Passing their garage, I saw through a little window that the light was on. My curiosity got the better of me, and I peeked in.

STOP AND THINK

Infer/Predict Think about what you know about Peter and the narrator. What might Peter's "fantastic machine" be, and how might it affect the plot? As you read, think about your prediction and adjust it as you learn new details.

I saw a booth that looked like a shower stall. A stool stood in the middle of the stall, and hanging over the stool was something that looked like a great big shower head.

Suddenly a deep voice behind me said, "Good evening, Angela." Peter bowed and smiled his scary smile. He didn't have his costume on and he didn't have the long, droopy mustache. But he was Dr. Lu Manchu.

"What are you doing?" I squeaked.

Still in his strange, deep voice, Peter said, "What are *you* doing? After all, this is my garage."

"I was just cutting across your yard to get home. Your parents never complained before."

"I thought you were spying on me," said Peter. "I thought you wanted to know about my machine." He hissed when he said the word *machine*.

Honestly, he was beginning to frighten me. "What machine?" I demanded. "You mean this shower-stall thing?"

He drew himself up and narrowed his eyes, making them into thin slits. "This is my time machine!"

I goggled at him. "You mean . . . you mean . . . this machine can send you forward and backward in time?"

"Well, actually, I can only send things forward in time," admitted Peter, speaking in his normal voice again. "That's why I'm calling the machine LAFFF. It stands for Lu's Artifact For Fast Forward."

Of course Peter always won first prize at the annual statewide science fair. But that's a long way from making a time machine. Minus his mustache and long Chinese gown, he was just Peter Lu.

"I don't believe it!" I said. "I bet LAFFF is only good for a laugh."

"Okay, Angela. I'll show you!" hissed Peter.

He sat down on the stool and twisted a dial. I heard some *bleeps, cheeps*, and *gurgles*. Peter disappeared.

He must have done it with mirrors. I looked around the garage. I peeked under the tool bench. There was no sign of him.

"Okay, I give up," I told him. "It's a good trick, Peter. You can come out now."

Bleep, cheep, and *gurgle* went the machine, and there was Peter sitting on the stool. He held a red rose in his hand. "What do you think of that?"

I blinked. "So you produced a flower. Maybe you had it under the stool."

"Roses bloom in June, right?" he demanded.

That was true. And this was December.

"I sent myself forward in time to June when the flowers were blooming," said Peter. "And I picked the rose from our yard. Convinced, Angela?"

It was too hard to swallow. "You said you couldn't send things back in time," I objected. "So how did you bring the rose back?"

But even as I spoke I saw that his hands were empty. The rose was gone.

"That's one of the problems with the machine," said Peter. "When I send myself forward, I can't seem to stay there for long. I snap back to my own time after only a minute. Anything I bring with me snaps back to its own time, too. So my rose has gone back to this June."

435

I was finally convinced, and I began to see possibilities. "Wow, just think: If I don't want to do the dishes, I can send myself forward to the time when the dishes are already done."

"That won't do you much good," said Peter. "You'd soon pop back to the time when the dishes were still dirty."

Too bad. "There must be something your machine is good for," I said. Then I had another idea. "Hey, you can bring me back a piece of fudge from the future, and I can eat it twice: once now, and again in the future."

"Yes, but the fudge wouldn't stay in your stomach," said Peter. "It would go back to the future."

"That's even better!" I said. "I can enjoy eating the fudge over and over again without getting fat!"

It was late, and I had to go home before my parents started to worry. Before I left, Peter said, "Look, Angela, there's still a lot of work to do on LAFFF. Please don't tell anybody about the machine until I've got it right."

A few days later I asked him how he was doing.

"I can stay in the future time a bit longer now," he said. "Once I got it up to four minutes."

"Is that enough time to bring me back some fudge from the future?" I asked.

"We don't keep many sweets around the house," he said. "But I'll see what I can do."

A few minutes later, he came back with a spring roll for me. "My mother was frying these in the kitchen, and I snatched one while she wasn't looking."

I bit into the hot, crunchy spring roll, but before I finished chewing, it disappeared. The taste of soy sauce, green onions, and bean sprouts stayed a little longer in my mouth, though.

It was fun to play around with LAFFF, but it wasn't really useful. I didn't know what a great help it would turn out to be.

Every year our school held a writing contest, and the winning story for each grade got printed in our school magazine. I wanted desperately to win. I worked awfully hard in school, but my parents still thought I could do better.

Winning the writing contest would show my parents that I was really good in something. I love writing stories, and I have lots of ideas. But when I actually write them down, my stories never turn out as good as I thought. I just can't seem to find the right words, because English isn't my first language.

I got an honorable mention last year, but it wasn't the same as winning and showing my parents my name, Angela Tang, printed in the school magazine.

The deadline for the contest was getting close, and I had a pile of stories written, but none of them looked like a winner.

Then, the day before the deadline, *boing*, a brilliant idea hit me.

I thought of Peter and his LAFFF machine.

I rushed over to the Lus' garage and, just as I had hoped, Peter was there, tinkering with his machine.

STOP AND THINK

Author's Craft When authors use words, such as *buzz* or *clang*, that sound like the noises they describe, it is called **onomatopoeia**. Where has the author used onomatopoeia on this page and how does it help the story?

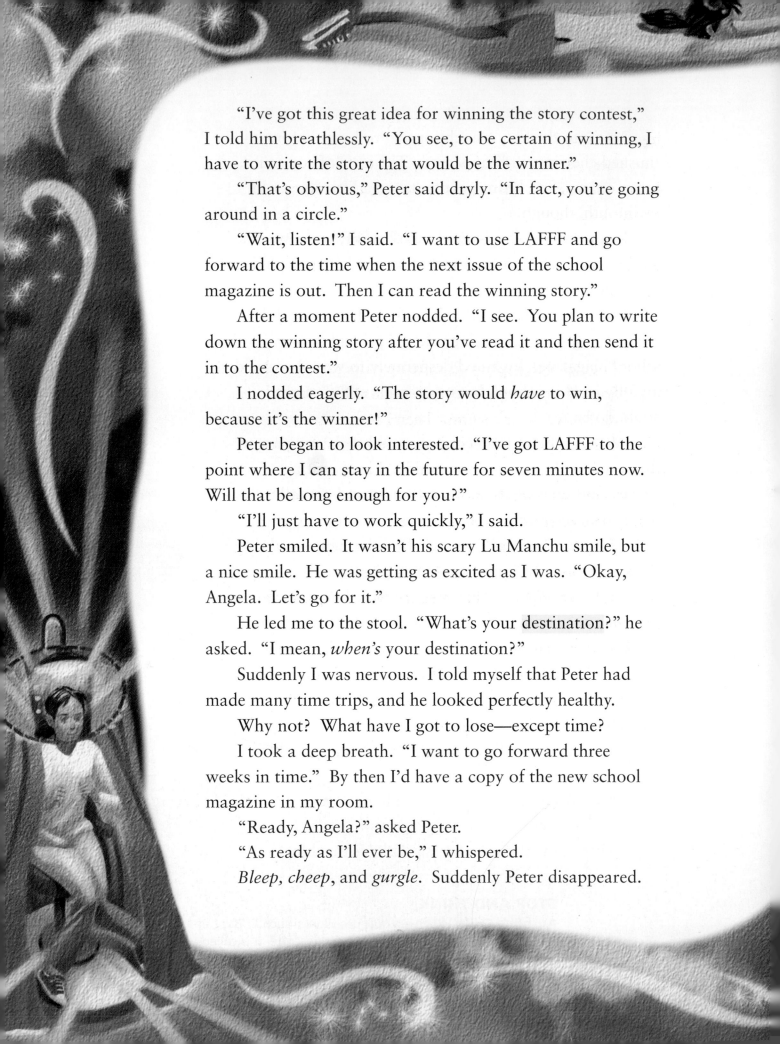

"I've got this great idea for winning the story contest," I told him breathlessly. "You see, to be certain of winning, I have to write the story that would be the winner."

"That's obvious," Peter said dryly. "In fact, you're going around in a circle."

"Wait, listen!" I said. "I want to use LAFFF and go forward to the time when the next issue of the school magazine is out. Then I can read the winning story."

After a moment Peter nodded. "I see. You plan to write down the winning story after you've read it and then send it in to the contest."

I nodded eagerly. "The story would *have* to win, because it's the winner!"

Peter began to look interested. "I've got LAFFF to the point where I can stay in the future for seven minutes now. Will that be long enough for you?"

"I'll just have to work quickly," I said.

Peter smiled. It wasn't his scary Lu Manchu smile, but a nice smile. He was getting as excited as I was. "Okay, Angela. Let's go for it."

He led me to the stool. "What's your destination?" he asked. "I mean, *when's* your destination?"

Suddenly I was nervous. I told myself that Peter had made many time trips, and he looked perfectly healthy.

Why not? What have I got to lose—except time?

I took a deep breath. "I want to go forward three weeks in time." By then I'd have a copy of the new school magazine in my room.

"Ready, Angela?" asked Peter.

"As ready as I'll ever be," I whispered.

Bleep, cheep, and *gurgle*. Suddenly Peter disappeared.

What went wrong? Did Peter get sent by mistake, instead of me?

Then I realized what had happened. Three weeks later in time Peter might be somewhere else. No wonder I couldn't see him.

There was no time to be lost. Rushing out of Peter's garage, I ran over to our house and entered through the back door.

Mother was in the kitchen. When she saw me, she stared.

"Angela! I thought you were upstairs taking a shower!"

"Sorry!" I panted. "No time to talk!"

I dashed up to my room. Then I suddenly had a strange idea. What if I met *myself* in my room? Argh! It was a spooky thought.

There was nobody in my room. Where was I? I mean, where was the I of three weeks later?

Wait. Mother had just said she thought I was taking a shower. Down the hall, I could hear the water running in the bathroom. Okay. That meant I wouldn't run into me for a while.

I went to the shelf above my desk and frantically pawed through the junk piled there. I found it! I found the latest issue of the school magazine, the one with the winning stories printed in it.

How much time had passed? Better hurry.

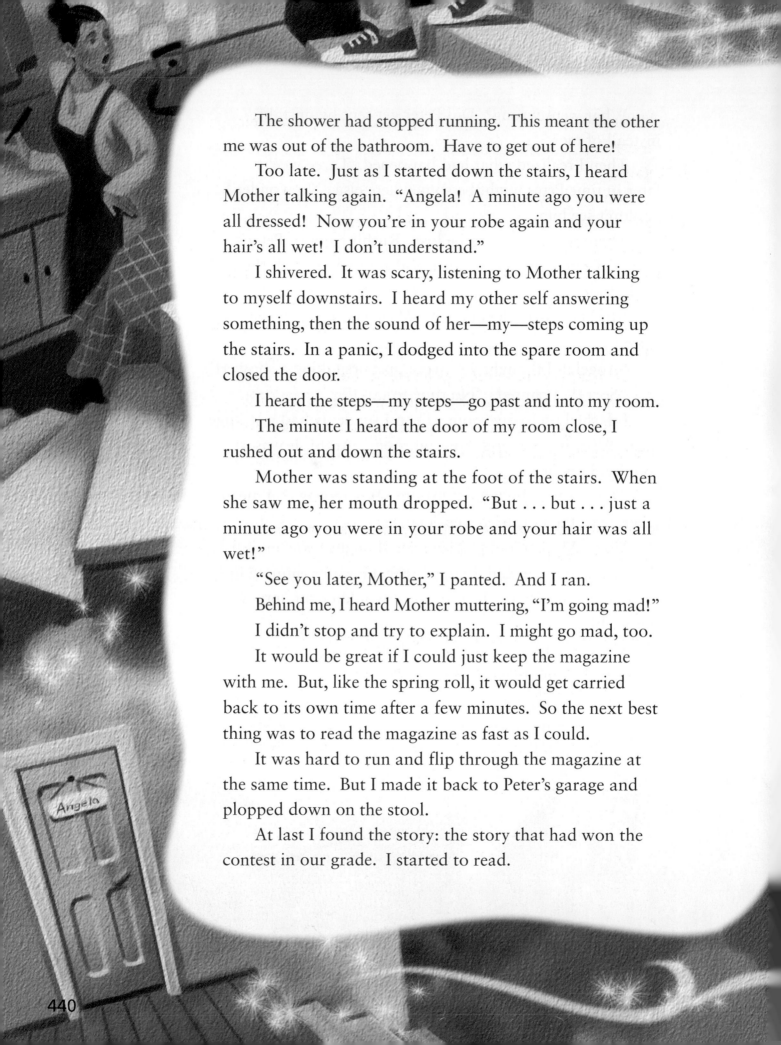

The shower had stopped running. This meant the other me was out of the bathroom. Have to get out of here!

Too late. Just as I started down the stairs, I heard Mother talking again. "Angela! A minute ago you were all dressed! Now you're in your robe again and your hair's all wet! I don't understand."

I shivered. It was scary, listening to Mother talking to myself downstairs. I heard my other self answering something, then the sound of her—my—steps coming up the stairs. In a panic, I dodged into the spare room and closed the door.

I heard the steps—my steps—go past and into my room.

The minute I heard the door of my room close, I rushed out and down the stairs.

Mother was standing at the foot of the stairs. When she saw me, her mouth dropped. "But . . . but . . . just a minute ago you were in your robe and your hair was all wet!"

"See you later, Mother," I panted. And I ran.

Behind me, I heard Mother muttering, "I'm going mad!"

I didn't stop and try to explain. I might go mad, too.

It would be great if I could just keep the magazine with me. But, like the spring roll, it would get carried back to its own time after a few minutes. So the next best thing was to read the magazine as fast as I could.

It was hard to run and flip through the magazine at the same time. But I made it back to Peter's garage and plopped down on the stool.

At last I found the story: the story that had won the contest in our grade. I started to read.

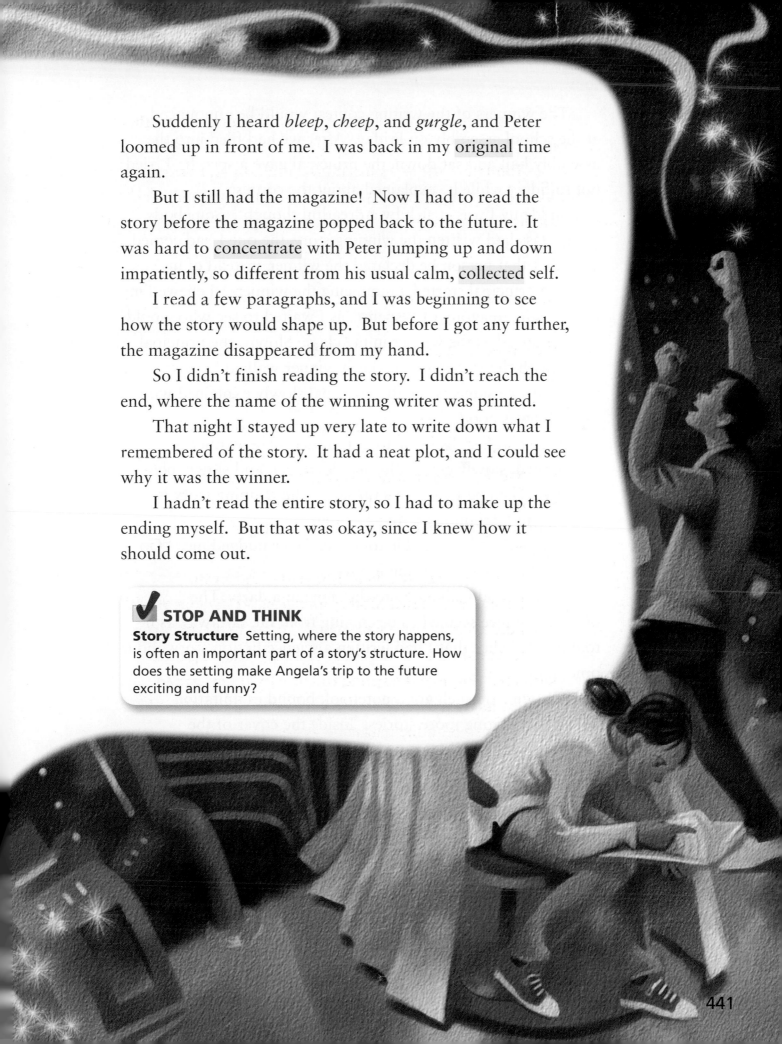

Suddenly I heard *bleep*, *cheep*, and *gurgle*, and Peter loomed up in front of me. I was back in my original time again.

But I still had the magazine! Now I had to read the story before the magazine popped back to the future. It was hard to concentrate with Peter jumping up and down impatiently, so different from his usual calm, collected self.

I read a few paragraphs, and I was beginning to see how the story would shape up. But before I got any further, the magazine disappeared from my hand.

So I didn't finish reading the story. I didn't reach the end, where the name of the winning writer was printed.

That night I stayed up very late to write down what I remembered of the story. It had a neat plot, and I could see why it was the winner.

I hadn't read the entire story, so I had to make up the ending myself. But that was okay, since I knew how it should come out.

✔️ **STOP AND THINK**

Story Structure Setting, where the story happens, is often an important part of a story's structure. How does the setting make Angela's trip to the future exciting and funny?

The winners of the writing contest would be announced at the school assembly on Friday. After we had filed into the assembly hall and sat down, the principal gave a speech. I tried not to fidget while he explained about the contest.

Suddenly I was struck by a dreadful thought. Somebody in my class had written the winning story, the one I had copied. Wouldn't that person be declared the winner, instead of me?

The principal started announcing the winners. I chewed my knuckles in an agony of suspense, as I waited to see who would be announced as the winner in my class. Slowly, the principal began with the lowest grade. Each winner walked in slow motion to the stage, while the principal slowly explained why the story was good.

At last, at last, he came to our grade. "The winner is . . ." He stopped, slowly got out his handkerchief, and slowly blew his nose. Then he cleared his throat. "The winning story is 'Around and Around,' by Angela Tang."

I sat like a stone, unable to move. Peter nudged me. "Go on, Angela! They're waiting for you."

I got up and walked up to the stage in a daze. The principal's voice seemed to be coming from far, far away as he told the audience that I had written a science fiction story about time travel.

The winners each got a notebook bound in imitation leather for writing more stories. Inside the cover of the notebook was a ballpoint pen. But the best prize was having my story in the school magazine with my name printed at the end.

Then why didn't I feel good about winning?

After assembly, the kids in our class crowded around to congratulate me. Peter formally shook my hand. "Good work, Angela," he said and winked at me.

That didn't make me feel any better. I hadn't won the contest fairly. Instead of writing the story myself, I had copied it from the school magazine.

That meant someone in our class—one of the kids here—had actually written the story. Who was it?

My heart was knocking against my ribs as I stood there and waited for someone to complain that I had stolen his story.

Nobody did.

As we were riding the school bus home, Peter looked at me. "You don't seem very happy about winning the contest, Angela."

"No, I'm not," I mumbled. "I feel just awful."

"Tell you what," suggested Peter. "Come over to my house and we'll discuss it."

"What is there to discuss?" I asked glumly. "I won the contest because I cheated."

"Come on over, anyway. My mother bought a fresh package of humbow in Chinatown."

I couldn't turn down that invitation. Humbow, a roll stuffed with barbecued pork, is my favorite snack.

Peter's mother came into the kitchen while we were munching, and he told her about the contest.

Mrs. Lu looked pleased. "I'm very glad, Angela. You have a terrific imagination, and you deserve to win."

"I like Angela's stories," said Peter. "They're original."

It was the first compliment he had ever paid me, and I felt my face turning red.

After Mrs. Lu left us, Peter and I each had another humbow. But I was still miserable. "I wish I had never started this. I feel like such a jerk."

Peter looked at me, and I swear he was enjoying himself. "If you stole another student's story, why didn't that person complain?"

"I don't know!" I wailed.

443

"Think!" said Peter. "You're smart, Angela. Come on, figure it out."

Me, smart? I was so overcome to hear myself called smart by a genius like Peter that I just stared at him.

He had to repeat himself. "Figure it out, Angela!"

I tried to concentrate. Why was Peter looking so amused?

The light finally dawned. "Got it," I said slowly. "*I'm* the one who wrote the story."

"The winning story is your own, Angela, because that's the one that won."

My head began to go around and around. "But where did the original idea for the story come from?"

"What made the plot so good?" asked Peter. His voice sounded unsteady.

"Well, in my story, my character used a time machine to go forward in time . . ."

"Okay, whose idea was it to use a time machine?"

"It was mine," I said slowly. I remembered the moment when the idea had hit me with a *boing*.

"So you s-stole f-from yourself!" sputtered Peter. He started to roar with laughter. I had never seen him break down like that. At this rate, he might wind up being human.

When he could talk again, he asked me to read my story to him.

I began. "'In movies, geniuses have frizzy white hair, right? They wear thick glasses and have names like Dr. Zweistein . . . .'"

Your Turn

Future Plans

Short Response Angela uses Peter's time machine to read the story that won the writing contest. What if you were able to travel into the future? Think about your goal and purpose. Write a paragraph that describes how far forward in time you would choose to go and what you would do when you got there. PERSONAL RESPONSE

Imagine the Future

Drawing Tomorrow Imagine what your classroom might look like in 100 years. How do you think important subjects such as reading, math, science, and social studies might be taught? With a partner, illustrate and label the classroom setting, showing changes in technology and other features that would make learning fun and exciting. PARTNERS

Time Travel

Turn and Talk Think about how the plot of the story unfolds after Angela uses Peter's time machine to travel three weeks into the future. Discuss with a partner how the time machine affects Peter's and Angela's lives. STORY STRUCTURE

✔ **TARGET VOCABULARY**

impressed	concentrate
collected	suspense
produced	admitted
destination	compliment
original	rumor

GENRE

Informational text like this magazine article gives facts and examples about a topic.

TEXT FOCUS

Photographs and illustrations are used in both fiction and nonfiction selections to show story elements or important details.

from Dreams to Reality

Sci Fi Authors Predict the Future

Long ago, computers, fax machines, and satellites seemed impossible. There was not a hint or a rumor that they could ever be a part of our lives. Yet now we use them every day. They were first dreamed up not by engineers, but by science fiction writers. Jules Verne was a writer who could concentrate on amazing ideas. In 1863, he published an early science fiction book, *Five Weeks in a Balloon*. Since then, people have been impressed by how the genre can predict the future. Many predictions, like time travel, are not possible in the real world. But sometimes machines first dreamed up by writers *do* become real.

In this drawing from Verne's *From the Earth to the Moon,* a crowd watches in suspense as the space capsule is prepared to take off.

Manned Flight to the Moon

Verne was a master at predicting what lay ahead. In 1864, he wrote *From the Earth to the Moon*. The book tells about a flight to the moon. This was 105 years before the first manned mission to the moon reached its destination.

Verne's mission has a three-man team. That's the same number used in real moon landings. His space travelers are sent from Florida. NASA sends astronauts into space from there, too. The size of Verne's space capsule is also very close to that of the real Apollo spacecraft.

Not all the ideas that Verne produced are true. His space capsule is shot from a cannon. Today, rocket engines propel modern spacecraft.

A *Saturn V* rocket blasts off for the moon. On July 20, 1969, the world watched *Apollo 11* astronaut Neil Armstrong step onto the moon's surface. They heard him say in a collected voice, "That's one small step for a man, one giant leap for mankind."

447

Robots

The word *robot* first entered our language through a play, not a laboratory. Czech writer Karel Čapek used the word in his 1921 play, *R.U.R.: Rossum's Universal Robots*. In the play, robots look like humans and are used for cheap labor. Fifty years later real labor-saving robots would be putting together manufactured goods in factories.

Not everyone is a fan of science fiction. But most people have admitted that these writers seem to see the future. It is a compliment to the power of imagination that so many sci-fi dreams do become true. The next time you read science fiction, remember, you *may* be reading about your future.

Karel Čapek's imaginary robots looked like humans.

Making Connections

 Text to Self

Describe a Talent In "LAFFF," Angela has a talent for writing. Think of something you are good at. Write a paragraph describing a time when you got to show off that talent to others. Describe how you felt as you displayed your talent.

 Text to Text

Compare and Contrast Science Fiction In "Lunch Money," Greg plans to write a comic book set in the future. Compare Greg's science fiction ideas to those in Lensey Namioka's story "LAFFF." How are they alike? How are they different? Use examples from both texts to support your response.

 Text to World

Research Technology With a partner, review the photographs, illustrations, and captions in "From Dreams to Reality." Use print sources or the Internet to find three additional facts about the United States space program or the car-making industry discussed in the captions. Create a timeline using all your information.

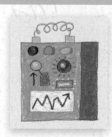

Grammar

Academic Language

adverb
adverb of frequency
adverb of intensity

What Is an Adverb? A word that describes a verb is an **adverb**. Adverbs tell *how*, *when*, or *where* an action happens. Many adverbs end with *–ly*.

How	The time machine buzzed loudly.
When	Soon its door opened.
Where	I took a deep breath and stepped inside.

An **adverb of frequency** tells *how often* something happens. **Adverbs of intensity** often tell *how much* about a verb.

Adverb of Frequency: I sometimes feel cramped in small spaces.

Adverb of Intensity: When the time machine door closed,

I almost screamed!

Turn and Talk **Identify the adverb that describes each underlined verb. Explain to a partner whether the adverb tells *how*, *when*, *where*, *how often*, or *how much*.**

❶ Karl <u>stared</u> intently at the blank screen.

❷ He usually <u>found</u> himself with no inspiration.

❸ He <u>closed</u> his eyes again and thought of story ideas.

❹ Karl imagined a future world in which time machines <u>worked</u> everywhere.

❺ He typed the story at top speed and almost <u>sprained</u> his fingers.

Word Choice   To make your descriptions more vivid, try using precise adverbs. By doing this, you can make your writing more lively and create details that help readers visualize images clearly.

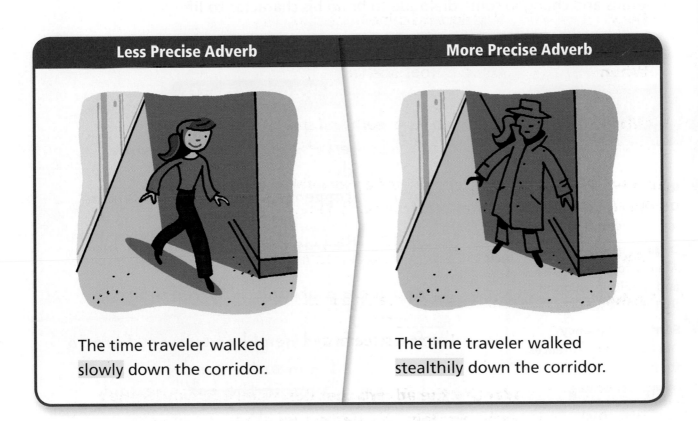

Less Precise Adverb	More Precise Adverb
The time traveler walked slowly down the corridor.	The time traveler walked stealthily down the corridor.

Connect Grammar to Writing

As you revise your character description, look for opportunities to use precise adverbs. These adverbs will help readers visualize your descriptions, and they will make your writing interesting.

Write to Narrate

A good **character description** uses exact words, vivid details, and dialogue to show what a character is like. You can almost see Angela's expression in "LAFFF" when she says, "I feel like such a jerk." When you write a descriptive paragraph, use words that will help your readers imagine your subject.

Theo drafted a description of his friend James. Later, he added details and changed some dialogue to bring his character to life.

Writing Traits Checklist

✔ **Ideas**
Do my details show what my character is like?

✔ **Organization**
Are my topic sentences and details in an order that makes sense?

✔ **Sentence Fluency**
Did I combine sentences for better flow?

✔ **Word Choice**
Did I use exact words, vivid details, and dialogue?

✔ **Voice**
Do my words reveal my feelings or attitude about my character?

✔ **Conventions**
Did I use correct spelling, grammar, and punctuation?

Revised Draft

"Come with me!" shouted James
                                    quickly
as he ∧ disappeared down the basement

stairs. ~~He was quick.~~ I followed him

and looked around. My red-haired,

freckle-faced neighbor was nowhere to
                    I'm in outer space!
be seen. "~~I am in the box~~," he said.
              ∧   ∧

in a loud whisper. The sound was coming
from a big box

My Friend James

by *Theo Pothoulakis*

"Come with me!" shouted James as he quickly disappeared down the basement stairs. I followed him and looked around. My red-haired, freckle-faced neighbor was nowhere to be seen. "I'm in outer space!" he said in a loud whisper. The sound was coming from a big box.

That was my introduction to James McGinnis and his fabulous imagination. His box could be a submarine, an intergalactic transporter, or a time machine. Later, when we were in third grade, James discovered the Time Warp Trio books, and we excitedly read the whole series together.

Last summer, James moved away. "What we need now is a distance-warp machine," he says. I agree!

> In my final paper, I made the dialogue sound more natural. I also used precise adverbs to create clear images for readers.

Reading as a Writer

What details did Theo use to make his description of James vivid? How can you make your own description more vivid?

453

✓ **TARGET VOCABULARY**

career

publication

background

household

insights

required

uneventful

edition

formula

destruction

Vocabulary   Context
Reader   Cards

Vocabulary in Context

1 career

The career, or chosen work, of a journalist involves carefully gathering the facts.

2 publication

A news publication might take the form of a newspaper, news magazine, or website.

3 background

Years of experience as reporters often give TV newscasters their needed background.

4 household

This boy delivers newspapers to nearly every household in his neighborhood.

Study each Context Card.

Break each Vocabulary word into syllables. Use a dictionary to verify your answers.

5 insights

During interviews, reporters hear the insights and opinions of other people.

6 required

TV cameras are often required, or needed, to record all the action at a sports event.

7 uneventful

This meteorologist predicts an uneventful week. The weather won't change much.

8 edition

A special edition, or version, of a newspaper might be published after a huge news event.

9 formula

Use this formula, or rule, in all news articles: tell *who*, *what*, *when*, *where*, *why*, and *how*.

10 destruction

Papers reported that the destruction caused by the hurricane left some people homeless.

455

Background

What's in a Newspaper? If you like to write, a newspaper career may be for you. No day is uneventful, so there is always interesting news to gather. Reporters are required to record events accurately.

Here is some background on this type of publication. A newspaper usually has its own formula for choosing articles. Usually, each edition contains the same sections. The front page of each section presents major stories, perhaps of courage or of destruction. Editorial pages offer insights into the editors' opinions. Other sections—sports, business, comics, and entertainment—appeal to different people in a household. Working on one of these sections might appeal to you.

• Analyze the graph below. How much greater was the percentage of people reading newspapers in 1994 than the percentage in 2002?

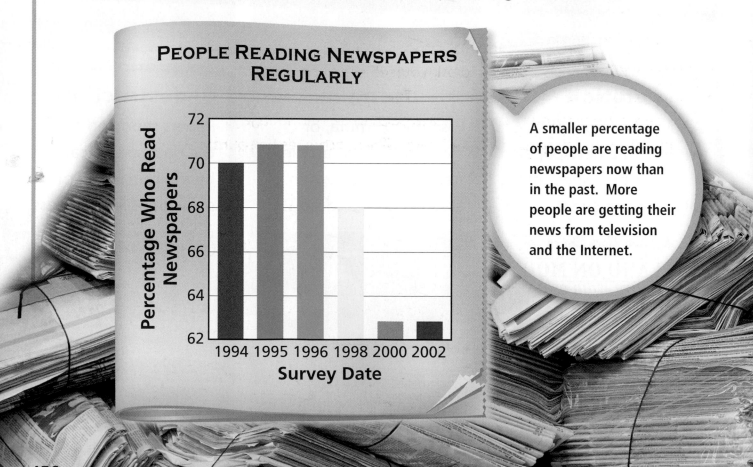

PEOPLE READING NEWSPAPERS REGULARLY

Percentage Who Read Newspapers (y-axis: 62, 64, 66, 68, 70, 72)

Survey Date (x-axis: 1994 1995 1996 1998 2000 2002)

A smaller percentage of people are reading newspapers now than in the past. More people are getting their news from television and the Internet.

Comprehension

As you read "The Dog Newspaper," watch for true information, or facts, and for statements that are the author's opinion. Use a graphic organizer like this one to keep track of facts and opinions. If you are unsure if a statement is a fact or an opinion, use a reliable source to help you determine if the statement is a fact.

Facts	Opinions
•	•
•	•
•	•

Use your graphic organizer to ask yourself questions about information the author presents in "The Dog Newspaper." Analyzing the author's reasons for including certain facts and opinions can help you evaluate how well she achieves her purpose.

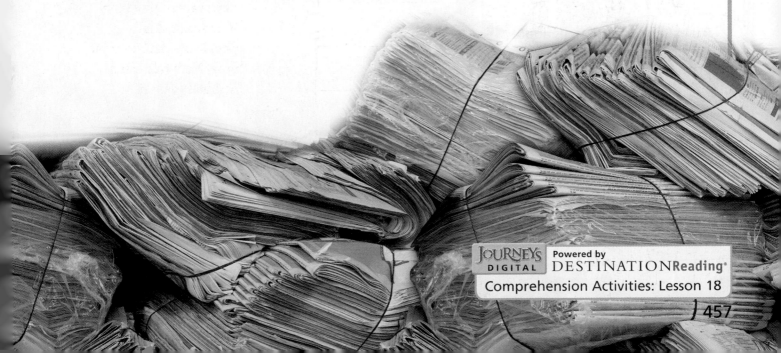

career	required
publication	uneventful
background	edition
household	formula
insights	destruction

✔ **TARGET SKILL**

Fact and Opinion Decide whether an idea can be proved or is a feeling or belief.

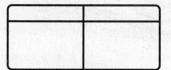

✔ **TARGET STRATEGY**

Analyze/Evaluate Think carefully about the text and form an opinion about it.

GENRE

Autobiography tells about events in a person's own life, written by that person.

Set Purpose Set a purpose for reading based on the genre and your background knowledge.

MEET THE AUTHOR

Peg Kehret

B.J. may have been the first animal to inspire Peg Kehret's writing, but he certainly was not the last. The author loves animals and lives with several adopted pets. She has written both fiction and nonfiction, including *Shelter Dogs: Amazing Stories of Adopted Strays*.

MEET THE ILLUSTRATOR

Tim Jessell

Tim Jessell calls his digital illustration style realistic "with a twist." He used to be a drummer for a rock band, but now he spends most of his time either with his three children or practicing the sport of falconry with his bird, Spike.

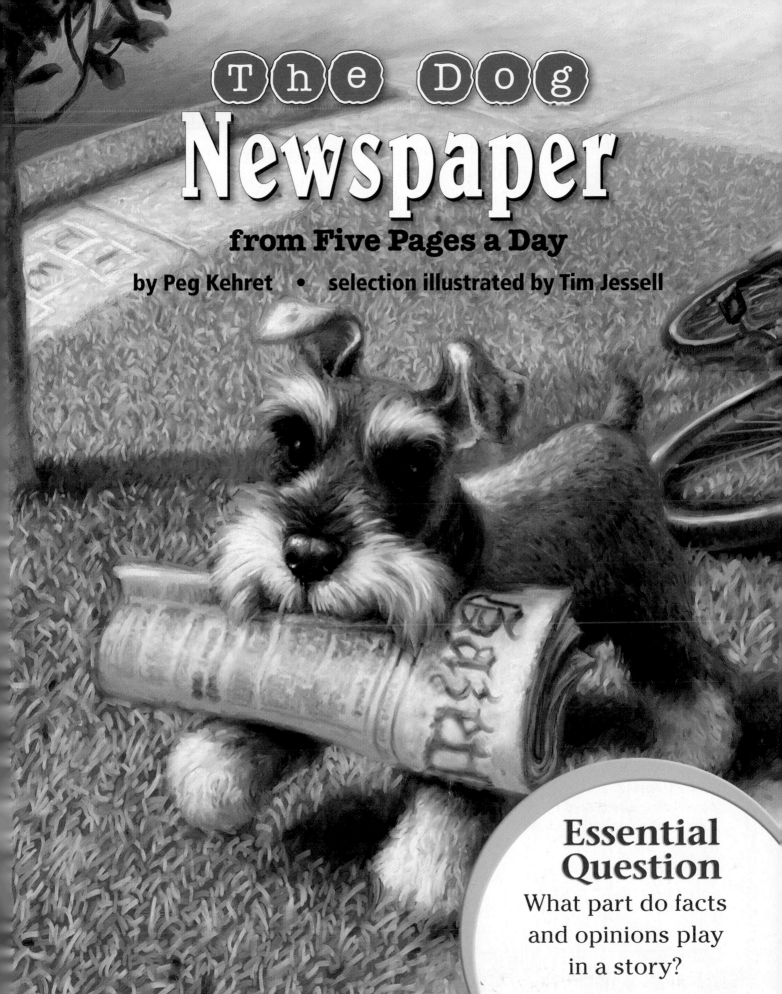

The Dog
Newspaper

from Five Pages a Day

by Peg Kehret • selection illustrated by Tim Jessell

Essential Question

What part do facts and opinions play in a story?

I began my writing career at the age of ten when I wrote and sold the *Dog Newspaper*. This weekly publication, which cost five cents a copy, reported on the local dogs.

I interviewed every neighbor who had a dog. "What exciting thing has your dog done?" I asked.

People responded, "All Fluffy does is eat, sleep, and bark at the mailman." Or, "Max's only excitement is his daily walk on the leash." Such answers did not lead to important news stories.

I didn't give up. "If your dog could talk," I asked, "what do you think he would say?"

"Feed me," was the most common answer, followed by, "Let's play."

What could a writer do with such boring material? The solution sat at my feet, wagging his tail.

The first issue of the *Dog Newspaper* featured my dog, B.J., on the entire front page. Although his life at that time was as uneventful as the lives of the other neighborhood dogs, B.J. had a unique background.

Uncle Bill, my mother's younger brother, was a soldier in the U.S. Army during World War II. While in Germany, his unit went into a town that had recently been bombed. As they searched for survivors in a destroyed building, they came across a mother dog and her litter of puppies. The mother dog was dead. So were all the puppies except one.

The soldiers, who had seen far too much of death and destruction, carefully lifted that little brown dog from his littermates. One soldier tucked the puppy inside his jacket to keep him warm. The men fed him from their own food supplies, shared water from their canteens, and decided to keep him as the company mascot.

From then on, wherever Uncle Bill and his comrades went, the dog went, too. They named him B.J. because he was a Big Job to take care of, especially when they were fighting a war.

B.J. grew bigger and stronger as he traveled with the soldiers, tagging along on every mission and somehow surviving even when the men were too busy to pay attention to him.

As the soldiers fought to protect the free world, B.J. did his duty, too. He slept with them in foxholes; he trudged long miles across burned and barren land; he helped search rubble for signs of life. Most of all, he offered love and laughter to a group of lonely, weary men who were far from home.

When the war ended, the soldiers rejoiced. Soon they would be going home to their loved ones. But what about B.J.? They knew they could not leave him in Germany. The German people were faced with the task of rebuilding their cities and their lives; no one wanted to bother with a dog, especially a dog who belonged to the Americans.

The men decided to chip in enough money to fly B.J. back to the United States. Then they had a drawing to see who got to keep him. Each soldier wrote his name on a slip of paper and put the paper in a helmet. The winning name was drawn: Bill Showers! My uncle.

Uncle Bill lived with my family, so B.J. was flown from Germany to Minneapolis, where my parents picked him up at the airport and drove him to our home in Austin, Minnesota.

I was nine years old and delighted by the addition of this wire-haired schnauzer (at least, we thought he might be a schnauzer) to our household.

According to Uncle Bill, B.J. understood many commands in both English and German. Since none of us spoke German, we had no way to prove this claim.

B.J. quickly became my dog. Although B.J. was overjoyed when my uncle arrived home after his discharge, Uncle Bill did not stay in Austin long. He got married and headed to the University of Minnesota, where dogs were not allowed in student housing. B.J. stayed with my family.

I showered him with loving attention. I brushed him, tied ribbons on his collar, took him for walks, and read aloud to him. B.J. seemed especially fond of the Raggedy Ann and Andy stories, which were favorites of mine as well.

STOP AND THINK

Author's Craft The author uses a **flashback**, a scene that shows earlier events, to tell about B.J.'s life before he came to live with her. Why is this information important to the story? Why is a flashback a good way to present information?

B.J. had lived with us for a year when I launched the *Dog Newspaper*. He was a fascinating front-page subject, and the first edition of the *Dog Newspaper* sold twelve copies.

Even though my lead story required little research, this sixty cents was not easy money. All those interviews about the neighbor dogs took time. Also, I grew up before there were copy machines, so I couldn't just go to the local copy center and run off twelve copies of the paper. Using a pencil, I wrote every word twelve times. Then I delivered my newspapers and collected my pay.

B.J. and I became famous on our block. Neighbors were enthralled by the story, and I gobbled up congratulations on my writing the way B.J. ate his dinner. All of my customers agreed to purchase the next issue of the *Dog Newspaper*.

Giddy with success, I immediately began writing the second issue. The neighborhood dogs were still every bit as boring as they had been a week earlier, so I decided to repeat my winning formula and use B.J. as the main article again. Since I had already told the only unusual thing about my dog, this time I wrote a story called "B.J.'s Gingerbread House."

Our new washing machine had arrived in a large cardboard box. I kept the box to create a special house for B.J., who slept in the basement every night.

I spent hours decorating the box, copying a picture of a gingerbread house that was in one of my books. I colored curlicues; I blistered my hands cutting designs in the cardboard; I painted flowers on the sides. The gingerbread house was absolutely breathtaking.

At bedtime that night, I took B.J. down to the basement and put his blanket in the beautiful gingerbread house. I petted him and kissed him and told him I knew he would sleep well.

The next morning, I couldn't believe my eyes. B.J. had licked the glue from the cardboard, creating a sticky mess in his beard, and had chewed the house into dozens of pieces. He pranced toward me through the wreckage that littered the floor.

This story was quite a bit shorter than the story of B.J.'s rescue from a bombed-out house in Germany—and far less interesting. I filled the rest of issue number two of the *Dog Newspaper* with stirring reports such as "Rusty Knocks over Garbage Can" and "Cleo Chases Cat." After I delivered my papers, I eagerly waited for more compliments on my exciting journalism. None came. The next issue was even worse. Since B.J. still had done nothing newsworthy, I used the front page to describe what a beautiful and great dog he was. The other dogs, as always, got brief mention on the back page. Desperate to fill the space, I even wrote a story titled "Skippy Gets a Bath."

Issue number three was a publishing disaster. Few people read it, and the only person who purchased issue number four was my grandpa. Less than one month after its launch, the *Dog Newspaper* went out of business.

 **STOP AND THINK**

Fact and Opinion Why is the author's statement above, "Less than one month after its launch, the *Dog Newspaper* went out of business," a fact? What are some other facts on this page?

465

I believed my writing career was over. My mistake, I thought then, was always putting my own dog on the front page. Now I realize that having dull material was an even bigger error. Would the *Dog Newspaper* have succeeded if I had featured Rusty or Fluffy or Cleo? Probably not, because Rusty, Fluffy, Cleo, and all the other neighborhood dogs hadn't done anything special.

If Fluffy had gotten lost and been returned home in a police car, or if Cleo had won a prize in a dog show, or if Rusty had given birth to puppies, then perhaps the neighbors would have wanted to read my articles.

Now I know that if I want people to read what I write, I must write something that they find interesting. I need exciting plots, unique information, and fresh insights.

When I wrote the *Dog Newspaper*, I was so caught up in the fun of creating a newspaper and getting paid for my work that I lost sight of my audience. What was in it for them? Except for the first issue, not much.

B.J. took one more plane ride, from Minneapolis to Fresno, California, where my parents moved shortly after I got married. He loved the California sunshine and spent his old age sleeping on the patio. He lived to be sixteen, a good long life for an orphaned puppy who entered the world during a wartime bombing.

No one bothered to save any issues of the *Dog Newspaper*. I can't imagine why.

STOP AND THINK

Analyze/Evaluate What lesson does the author try to teach? How does this story help to teach that lesson?

Your Turn

True Tales

Short Response The most popular issue of the *Dog Newspaper* included the true story of how the soldiers found B.J. in Germany. Have you, or has someone you know, had an unusual adventure with a pet that you think others might find interesting? Write a paragraph describing that adventure.

PERSONAL RESPONSE

Publish It!

Plan a Newspaper The failure of her first newspaper teaches the author a lot about how to be a successful writer. If you were to start a newspaper of your own, what would you do to make it successful? Work with a small group to plan an edition of a school or community newspaper. Decide what kinds of articles, photographs, editorial features, and advertisements or comics you would include. Then share your ideas with the class.

SMALL GROUP

In Your Opinion

Turn and Talk Think about the facts and opinions the author includes in the story. With a partner, analyze the author's reasons for including various facts and her own opinions about her newspaper. Discuss what the information reveals about the author's outlook and how it has changed since the time in which the story's events took place. FACT AND OPINION

Poetry

✔ **TARGET VOCABULARY**

career	required
publication	uneventful
background	edition
household	formula
insights	destruction

GENRE

Poetry uses the sounds and rhythm of words in a variety of forms to suggest images and express feelings.

TEXT FOCUS

Form Poets may use different line shapes, line lengths, and groupings of lines called *stanzas*. Poets use the different line shapes, lengths and groupings to create rhythm, to focus a reader's attention on certain images, or to reinforce meaning.

Set a Purpose Set a purpose for reading based on the genre and your background knowledge.

Poetry About Poetry

Poetry lovers agree that a really great poem can turn an uneventful afternoon into an exciting one for the reader. The poets on these pages write about their love of poetry or about poetry itself. Think about what you like most about poetry. Is it the rhythm of the language, the images it creates, or the way it makes you feel?

To Write Poetry/ Para escribir poesía

by Francisco X. Alarcón

To Write Poetry
we must
first touch
smell and taste
every word

Para escribir poesía
debemos
primero tocar
oler y saborear
cada palabra

Genius

by Nikki Grimes

"Sis! Wake up!" I whisper
in the middle of the night.

　　Urgently, I shake her
　　till she switches on the light.

The spiral notebook in my hand
provides her quick relief.

　　It tells her there's no danger
　　of a break-in by a thief.

"Okay," she says, then props herself
up vertically in bed.

　　She nods for me to read my work.
　　I cough, then forge ahead.

The last verse of my poem leaves
her silent as a mouse.

　　I worry till she says, "We have
　　a genius in the house."

Nikki Grimes

How would you feel if you suddenly discovered your sister or brother was a poet? Nikki Grimes writes about this in her poem "Genius." In it, she uses insights from her own background.

Grimes had always wanted a career as a poet and writer. Her first poem was accepted for publication while she was in high school and was printed in an edition of a poetry journal. She was always close to members of her household, especially her sister. As you read "Genius," think about how Grimes shows the sisters' feelings for each other.

A Seeing Poem
by Robert Froman

A SEEING POEM HAPPENS WHEN WORDS TAKE A SHAPE THAT HELPS THEM TO ON A LIGHT IN SOMEONE'S MIND TURN

Write a Concrete Poem

Write your own concrete, or seeing, poem. There is no exact formula for writing one. The only element required is that the words you use create the shape of the object or action your poem describes. For instance, how could you create a concrete poem to show the destruction B.J. caused to Peg's gingerbread house in "The Dog Newspaper?"

Making Connections

Text to Self

Write About Yourself Think about how the author of "The Dog Newspaper" tells the story of her creation of the first issue of her neighborhood paper. What language and devices does she use to help readers relate to her experience? Write a short paragraph about an interesting project you have worked on. Present your information in ways that will help readers relate to you and your experience.

Text to Text

Analyze Poetry Reread Nikki Grimes's poem "Genius," and Jane Yolen's poem "Karate Kid" from Lesson 4. Look for examples of imagery in each selection. Pay special attention to sound effects, such as rhyme and repetition, used by the poets. Then compare the two pieces of poetry and tell how they are alike and different. How does each poet convey a certain feeling about the activity featured in her poem?

Text to World

Research Rescue Dogs Revisit Peg Kehret's flashback about B.J. on page 461. Think about how B.J.'s rescue and experiences with the soldiers helped him survive his time in Germany. Then work with a group to find information, either in print or online, about rescue dogs. Discuss with your group whether you think B.J. would have made a good rescue dog. Take time to consider each person's point of view.

Grammar

What Is a Preposition? **Prepositions** are words that show relationships between other words in a sentence. Prepositions convey location, time, or direction. **Prepositional phrases** begin with a preposition and end with a noun or pronoun. They add meaning and details to sentences. Some common prepositions are *above*, *after*, *at*, *during*, *for*, *through*, *in*, *of*, *to*, and *with*.

Prepositions and Prepositional Phrases	
Direction	A dog walker was moving toward the east.
Time	She had been walking three dogs for an hour.
Location	She stopped at the smallest dog's home.
Additional Details	A woman with red hair happily patted her dog.

Try This! **Copy these sentences onto a sheet of paper. Circle each preposition. Then underline each prepositional phrase and tell whether it conveys location, time, or direction, or provides details.**

1. I am the dog walker for our family's dog.

2. We always walk to the south.

3. We visit the park on Seventh Street.

4. We play fetch the stick until five o'clock.

5. I write entries in my dog walker's diary.

Sentence Fluency In your writing, you can combine two short sentences by moving a prepositional phrase. If two sentences tell about one subject, you can combine them by moving a prepositional phrase from one sentence to the other.

Short Sentences

Our dog Growler chased a cat.

Growler ran <u>into Mr. Hernandez's garden</u>.

Combined Sentence

Our dog Growler chased a cat <u>into Mr. Hernandez's garden</u>.

Connect Grammar to Writing

As you revise your personal narrative paragraph, look for short sentences that you can combine by moving a prepositional phrase from one sentence to the other. Using a variety of sentence lengths will make your writing more interesting to read.

Write to Narrate

☑ **Voice** The author of "The Dog Newspaper" tells her feelings when she says she was "giddy with success." When you revise a **personal narrative,** add words that express your own thoughts and feelings, and include details that help your readers picture what happened.

Amanda drafted a personal narrative about a puppy party she planned. Later, she revised it to show her feelings more clearly.

Writing Traits Checklist

☑ **Ideas**
Did I include only important events?

☑ **Organization**
Will my beginning grab my readers' attention?

☑ **Sentence Fluency**
Did I combine sentences for better flow?

☑ **Word Choice**
Did I use words that sound like me?

☑ **Voice**
Does my narrative reveal my inner thoughts and feelings?

☑ **Conventions**
Did I use correct spelling, grammar, and punctuation?

Revised Draft

My friend Ana and I ~~have a lot in~~ are both dog crazy. ~~common.~~ Last summer, the best thing happened! Both of our families got puppies! Ana and I love walking our puppies. ~~There's~~ to a local dog park. There they wrestle and play and ~~chase each other.~~ make us laugh

The Puppy Party
by Amanda West

My friend Ana and I are both dog crazy. Last summer, the best thing happened! Both of our families got puppies! Ana and I love walking our puppies to a local dog park. There they wrestle and play and make us laugh.

One rainy day, when we were stuck indoors, I had a brilliant idea. I invited Ana and her puppy over for a puppy party. I put out little doggy toys and treats, but as soon as Ana arrived, the puppies started chasing each other around the house. A lamp crashed to the floor. A potted plant spilled out all over the rug. The pups grabbed a sock and played tug-of-war until it was ruined. The house was a mess, and I was in big trouble. That's the day I learned rule number one for puppy parties: Keep them outdoors!

In my final paper, I added some words to show my feelings. I also used prepositional phrases to combine sentences.

Reading as a Writer

What thoughts or feelings does Amanda express in this narrative? How can you make your thoughts and feelings clear in your narrative?

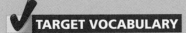

urge

minimum

effective

deteriorating

dependent

violations

granted

issue

ordinance

exception

Vocabulary Reader	Context Cards

Vocabulary in Context

1 urge

Teachers can urge, or coax, students to get involved in helping their community.

2 minimum

The food collected by students exceeded the minimum, or least, amount needed.

3 effective

Picking up litter can be effective in keeping parks and beaches clean. It gets results.

4 deteriorating

Many deteriorating buildings will only get worse if volunteers don't help repair them.

- Study each Context Card.
- Use a thesaurus to find an alternate word for each Vocabulary word.

5 dependent

A literacy group may be dependent on volunteers. It needs them as reading tutors.

6 violations

If they pollute too much, companies can be fined for violations of clean air laws.

7 granted

The principal granted, or gave, these students and teacher permission to hold a car wash.

8 issue

Providing better care for senior citizens is an issue, or concern. You can help in many ways.

9 ordinance

An ordinance, or city law, can create volunteer community service groups.

10 exception

With the exception of rainy days, this class works in the school garden every day.

Background

✓ **TARGET VOCABULARY** **Town Meetings**   Have you ever been to a town or city council meeting? If not, many would urge you to go to one. At a minimum, you'll learn a lot about your local government.

The representatives to a town meeting are elected, so they're dependent on voters to choose them. These officials have been granted many powers. One issue they can decide is how much to tax people so the town has money. Another task is to vote on each local ordinance, or rule. When violations of town rules occur, town meeting members decide how to punish the rule breakers. Finally, they vote on how to spend the town's money. For example, they may decide to repair a deteriorating town building or to give a town department more money to make it more effective. Without exception, the decisions made at town meetings affect our lives.

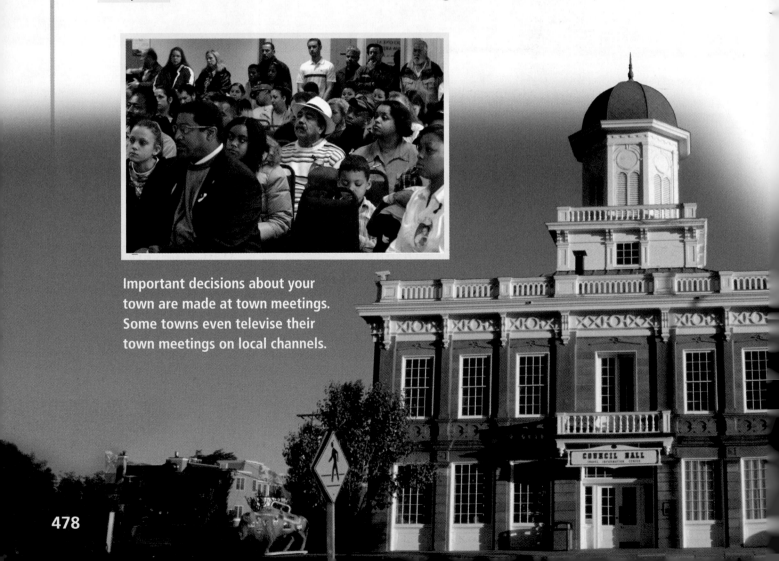

Important decisions about your town are made at town meetings. Some towns even televise their town meetings on local channels.

478

Comprehension

✓ **TARGET SKILL** **Persuasion**

In "Darnell Rock Reporting," Darnell uses persuasion in an article to gain support for a garden for the homeless. Look for words and facts that Darnell uses to influence people's opinions. Make a graphic organizer like this one to show a persuasive argument.

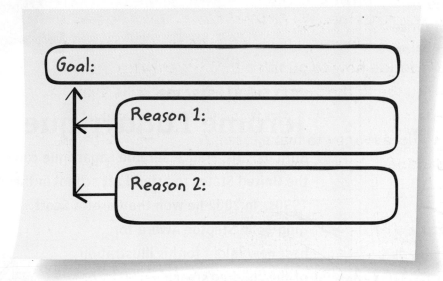

Goal:

Reason 1:

Reason 2:

✓ **TARGET STRATEGY** **Summarize**

Summarizing and paraphrasing as you read can help you understand Darnell's reasons for writing his article. Use your graphic organizer to summarize and paraphrase his article. Remember, paraphrasing is a detailed retelling or explanation. Putting the article into your own words will help you analyze his argument.

Main Selection

✔ **TARGET VOCABULARY**

urge	violations
minimum	granted
effective	issue
deteriorating	ordinance
dependent	exception

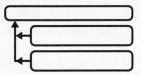

✔ **TARGET SKILL**

Persuasion Examine how an author tries to convince readers to support an idea.

✔ **TARGET STRATEGY**

Summarize Briefly tell the important parts of the text in your own words.

GENRE

Realistic fiction is a present-day story with events that could take place in real life.

Set a Purpose Before reading, set a purpose based on your background knowledge and what you know about the genre.

MEET THE AUTHOR

Walter Dean Myers

Like Darnell Rock, Walter Dean Myers was nervous about speaking in public when he was young. But when his fifth-grade teacher invited students to read aloud their own writing, Myers found that he was able to relax. He began to write more and hasn't stopped since!

MEET THE ILLUSTRATOR

Jérôme Lagarrigue

Born in Paris, France, Jérôme Lagarrigue came to the United States to attend art school in the 1990s. In 2002 he won the Coretta Scott King–John Steptoe Award for best new talent for his illustration of the children's book *Freedom Summer*.

DARNELL ROCK REPORTING

by Walter Dean Myers

selection illustrated by Jérôme Lagarrigue

Essential Question
How do you persuade people to support your ideas?

Darnell Rock feels that his teachers only notice him, his friends, and his sister Tamika, when they get into trouble. Then a homeless man, Sweeby Jones, inspires Darnell to write an article in his school newspaper about turning a deteriorating basketball court into a garden to feed the homeless. Soon editor Peter Miller publishes Darnell's article in the town newspaper. Not everyone agrees with him, though, including student Linda Gold and teacher Miss Joyner. A city council meeting will decide what to do with the basketball court. Darnell is nervous about presenting his opinion, but his parents, and teachers like Mr. Baker and Miss Seldes, all support him. Before the meeting, everyone at school has read Darnell's article (pictured below) and an opposing article written by Linda that ran in the school newspaper (shown on page 483).

"Nobody wants to be homeless," Sweeby Jones said. He is a homeless man who lives in our city of Oakdale. It is for him and people like him that I think we should build a garden where the basketball courts were, near the school. That way the homeless people can help themselves by raising food.

"You see a man or woman that's hungry and you don't feed them, or help them feed themselves, then you got to say you don't mind people being hungry," Mr. Jones said. "And if you don't mind people being hungry, then there is something wrong with you."

This is what Mr. Sweeby Jones said when I spoke to him. I don't want to be the kind of person who says it's all right for some people to be hungry. I want to do something about it. But I think there is another reason to have the garden.

Things can happen to people that they don't plan. You can get sick, and not know why, or even homeless. But sometimes there are things you can do to change your life or make it good. If you don't do anything to make your life good, it will probably not be good.

"I was born poor and will probably be poor all my life," Mr. Sweeby Jones said.

I think maybe it is not how you were born that makes the most difference, but what you do with your life. The garden is a chance for some people to help their own lives.

_____

Darnell Rock is a seventh-grader at South Oakdale Middle School. The school board has proposed that the site that Mr. Rock wants to make into a garden be used as a parking lot for teachers. The City Council will decide the issue tomorrow evening.

Teaching is a difficult profession. Teachers need as much support as they can possibly get. After all, we are dependent on them for our future. Education is the key to a good and secure future, and teachers help us to get that education. We must give them all the support we can. This is why I am supporting the idea of building a parking lot near the school.

There are some people in our school who think it is a good idea to build a garden so that the homeless can use it. Use it for what? Homeless people don't have experience farming and could not use the land anyway. This is just a bad idea that will help nobody and will hurt the teachers. The teachers give us good examples of how we should live and how we should conduct ourselves. The homeless people, even though it is no fault of theirs, don't give us good examples.

On Friday evening at 7:00 p.m., the City Council will meet to make a final decision. I urge them to support the teachers, support education, and support the students at South Oakdale.

"You see anybody from the school?" Larry looked over the large crowd at the Oakdale Court building.

"There goes Mr. Derby *and* Mr. Baker." Tamika pointed toward the front of the building.

Darnell felt a lump in the pit of his stomach. There were at least a hundred people at the City Council meeting.

Tamika led them through the crowd to where she had spotted Mr. Derby and South Oakdale's principal. The large, high-ceilinged room had rows of benches that faced the low platform for the City Council. Linda Gold was already sitting in the front row. Darnell saw that her parents were with her.

He had brought a copy of the *Journal* with him and saw that a few other people, grown-ups, also had copies of the paper.

The nine members of the City Council arrived, and the meeting was called to order. The city clerk said that there were five items on the agenda, and read them off. The first three items were about Building Code violations. Then came something about funding the city's library.

"The last item will be the use of the basketball courts as a parking lot at South Oakdale Middle School," the clerk said. "We have three speakers scheduled."

Linda turned and smiled at Darnell.

Darnell didn't know what Building Code violations were but watched as building owners showed diagrams explaining why there were violations. The first two weren't that interesting, but the third one was. A company had built a five-story building that was supposed to be a minimum of twenty feet from the curb, but it was only fifteen feet.

"You mean to tell me that your engineers only had fifteen-foot rulers?" one councilman asked.

"Well, er, we measured it right the first time"—the builder shifted from one foot to the other—"but then we made some changes in the design and somehow we sort of forgot about the er . . . you know . . . the other five feet."

To Darnell the builder sounded like a kid in his homeroom trying to make an excuse for not having his homework.

"Can you just slide the building back five or six feet?" the Councilman asked.

Everybody laughed and the builder actually smiled, but Darnell could tell he didn't think it was funny.

Somebody touched Darnell on his shoulder, and he turned and saw his parents.

"We have this ordinance for a reason," a woman on the Council was saying. "I don't think we should lightly dismiss this violation. An exception granted here is just going to encourage others to break the law."

"This is going to ruin me," the builder said. "I've been in Oakdale all of my life and I think I've made a contribution."

"Let's have a vote." The head of the Council spoke sharply.

STOP AND THINK
Author's Craft Authors try to make **dialogue,** or conversation, reflect the way people speak. What does the author do in the third paragraph on this page that makes the builder's speech seem realistic?

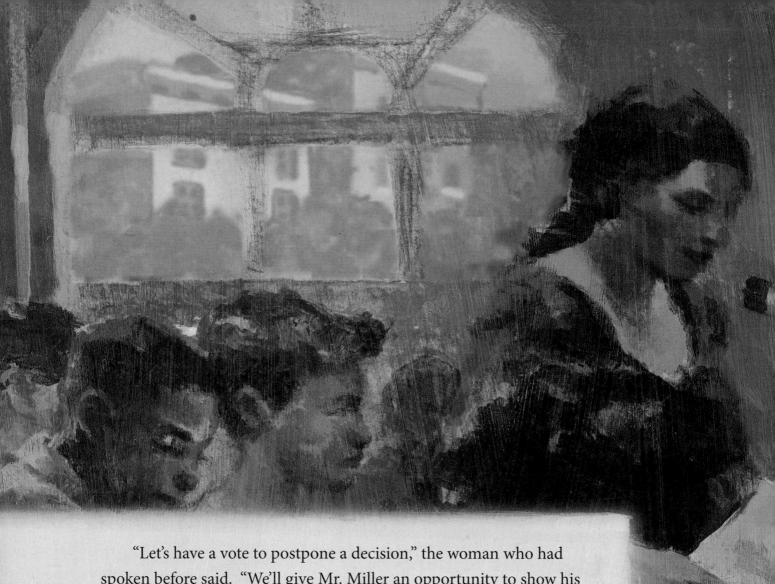

"Let's have a vote to postpone a decision," the woman who had spoken before said. "We'll give Mr. Miller an opportunity to show his good faith."

"What do you want me to do?" the builder asked.

"That's up to you," the woman said.

"Next time you'd better get it right!" Tamika called out.

"She's right," the councilwoman said.

There was a vote, and the decision was postponed. The builder gave Tamika a dirty look as he pushed his papers into his briefcase.

The city library funding was next, and eight people, including Miss Seldes, spoke for the library, but the Council said it didn't have any more money. There was some booing, including some from Tamika and Larry. Darnell knew that if he didn't have to speak he would have enjoyed the meeting.

"The issue at South Oakdale is should the old basketball courts be used as a parking lot, or should they be used as a community garden?"

"Who's going to pay for paving the lot?" a councilman asked. "Does it have to be paved?"

"It's my understanding that it doesn't have to be paved," the head of the Council answered. "Am I right on that?"

"Yes, you are," Miss Joyner spoke up from the audience.

"We have two young people from the school to speak," the councilwoman said. "The first is a Miss Gold."

Linda went into the middle aisle, where there was a microphone. She began reading her article in the snootiest voice that Darnell had ever heard. He felt a knot in his stomach. He turned to look at his mother, and she was smiling. On the stage some of the councilmen were looking at some papers.

"I hope I don't mess up," he whispered to Tamika.

"You won't," Tamika said.

Linda finished reading her article and then turned toward Darnell.

"Although everybody would like to help the homeless," she said, "schools are supposed to be for kids, and for those who teach kids! Thank you."

There was applause for Linda, and Miss Joyner stood up and nodded toward her. Darnell felt his hands shaking.

Darnell's name was called, and he made the long trip to the microphone.

"When I first thought about having a garden instead of a parking lot, I thought it was just a good idea," Darnell said. "Then, when the *Journal* asked me to send them a copy of my interview with Mr. Jones, I was thinking that it was mainly a good idea to have a garden to help out the homeless people. But now I think it might be a good idea to have the garden to help out the kids—some of the kids—in the school.

"Sometimes, when people go through their life they don't do the things that can make them a good life. I don't know why they don't do the right thing, or maybe even if they know what the right thing is sometimes.

"But I see the same thing in my school, South Oakdale. Some of the kids always do okay, but some of us don't. Maybe their parents are telling them something, or maybe they know something special. But if you're a kid who isn't doing so good, people start off telling you what you should be doing, and you know it, but sometimes you still don't get it done and mess up some more. Then people start expecting you to mess up, and then *you* start expecting to mess up. Teachers get mad at you, or the principal, or your parents, and they act like you're messing up on purpose. Like you want to get bad marks and stuff like that. Then you don't want people getting on your case all the time so you don't do much because the less you do the less they're going to be on your case. Only that doesn't help anything, and everybody knows it, but that's the way it goes."

"You seem to be doing all right, young man," the head of the City Council said.

"I wasn't doing too hot before," Darnell said, taking a quick look over to where Mr. Baker sat. "But when I got on the paper and the *Journal* printed my article, then everybody started treating me different. People came up to me and started explaining their points of view instead of just telling me what to do. And you people are listening to me. The kids I hung out with, they called us the Corner Crew, are mostly good kids, but you wouldn't listen to them unless they got into trouble.

"In South Oakdale some kids have bad things happen to them—like they get sick   and I don't know why that happens, but all they can do is to go to the hospital. And some kids just get left out of the good things and can't find a way of getting back into them. People get mad at them the same way they get mad at the homeless people or people who beg on the street. Maybe the garden will be a way for the homeless people to get back into some good things, and maybe seeing the homeless people getting back into a better life will be a way for some of the kids to think about what's happening to them. Thank you."

STOP AND THINK

Persuasion What is Darnell's argument in favor of the community garden?

There was some applause as Darnell turned to go back to his seat.

"Just a minute, young man," one of the councilmen called to him. "The girl said that these people don't know anything about raising a garden. Is that true?"

"It doesn't matter," someone said from the audience. "I'm from the college, and we can help with technical advice."

"I didn't ask you," the councilman said.

"I'm telling you anyway," the man said.

"I don't know how effective a community garden would be," the councilman said. "You can't feed people from a garden."

"You could sell what you grow," Darnell heard himself saying.

"I think bringing people who are . . . nonschool people into that close a contact with children might not be that good an idea," the councilman said. "Who's the last speaker?"

"A Mr. Jones," the clerk said. Sweeby came into the middle aisle, and a lot of people began to talk among themselves. There were a lot of things they were interested in, and most of them were not interested in the school parking lot.

"I just wanted to ask you why you don't want to listen to this boy," Sweeby asked.

"You have four minutes to speak," the councilman said. He seemed angry. "We don't have to answer your questions."

"You don't have to answer my questions," Sweeby said. "And you don't have to have the garden. You don't have to think about us—what did you call us?—nonschool people?

"But it's a shame you don't want to listen to this boy. I wish he had been my friend when I was his age. Maybe I would be sitting in one of your seats instead of being over here."

"Is there anything more?" the councilman asked.

"No, you can just forget about the whole thing now," Sweeby said. "Go on back to your papers."

"I think we can vote on this issue now," the councilman said. "I think Mr."—the councilman looked at the agenda to find Darnell's name—"Mr. Darnell Rock had some good points, but it's still a tough issue. Let's get on with the vote."

The vote went quickly. Three councilpeople decided not to vote, five voted against the garden, and only one voted for it.

Darnell took a deep breath and let it out slowly. Tamika patted him on his hand. When he looked at her she had tears in her eyes.

Darnell felt he had let Sweeby down. His father patted him on his back, and Miss Seldes came over.

"You did a good job," she said. "Really good."

"I lost," Darnell said.

"Sometimes you lose," Miss Seldes said. "But you still did a good job."

STOP AND THINK

Summarize Summarize the main events that happen on pages 490–491. Remember to include only the most important details.

491

Sweeby and some of his friends were waiting outside the Council meeting, and they shook hands with Darnell. Sweeby was telling him how the members of the Council didn't really care about people when Darnell saw Linda through the crowd. She waved and he waved back. She was smiling.

Larry's mother came over and asked his father for a lift home, and they were waiting for Larry when Peter Miller from the *Journal* came over.

"Hey, you want to write another article for the paper?" he said. "There's a guy who wants to donate a couple of lots for a garden in another location. My boss wants to run it as a human interest piece."

"Yeah, sure," Darnell said. "You want a long article or a short one?"

"I don't know. Call the paper tomorrow and ask for the city desk," the reporter said. "My editor will give you the word count."

"Okay!" Darnell said.

Your Turn

Speak Your Mind

Short Response Darnell Rock spoke his mind even though others disagreed with him. Write a paragraph describing a time when you spoke up even though you knew others might disagree with you. Explain what you learned from the experience.

PERSONAL RESPONSE

Use and Reuse

Make a Proposal Imagine that your school has an unused space like the one at South Oakdale Middle School. With a partner, think of three ways the space might be used. Choose your favorite one, and write a speech you might present to the community in order to convince them to support your idea. Then rehearse your speech, and deliver it to the class. PARTNERS

Powers of Persuasion

Turn and Talk Think about the speeches that Linda and Darnell give at the City Council meeting. With a partner, discuss how the two students use persuasion to gain support for their ideas. Then evaluate which student is more convincing and why. PERSUASION

Social Studies

✓ TARGET VOCABULARY

urge	violations
minimum	granted
effective	issue
deteriorating	ordinance
dependent	exception

GENRE

Persuasive text, like this speech, seeks to persuade the reader to think or act a certain way.

TEXT FOCUS

Persuasive techniques may be used in a speech to persuade the reader to think or act a certain way.

DE ZAVALA: A VOICE FOR TEXAS

In February 1836, people living in the part of Mexico called Texas faced a big decision. The Mexican leader, General Santa Anna, was a cruel dictator who would not share power. Many Texans wanted to separate from Mexico. A year before, at a meeting, or "Consultation," they had voted to stay in Mexico but form their own government. One of the delegates to the Consultation was a respected Mexican statesman named Lorenzo de Zavala. He and others would meet again in March to vote on independence. We can imagine de Zavala giving a speech like this one to a crowd in Harrisburg, Texas, the town he represented.

My good friends, independence is an issue that affects all of us. I know that many of you were unhappy with the Consultation of 1835. I beg you to be patient. Our fight continues, and the solution is nearer than ever before.

I have fought for democracy since I was a young man. I went to prison for my beliefs. While I was there, I resolved to help people the best way I could. I thought I would become a doctor. Instead I became a politician. Today it is Texas that needs to be healed.

I know you work hard and love this land. You do not deserve to have your rights reduced to a minimum. You do not need another ordinance from leaders you did not elect. I tell you that we will have no justice as long as we are under Santa Anna's rule. Just as Mexico once declared its independence from Spain, today Texas has no choice but to declare its independence from Mexico!

For a time, I believed in our leaders. But times have changed, and I have changed, too. Our freedom is deteriorating. There have been violations of the law that I cannot ignore. Our leaders do not respect the Mexican constitution, and I can no longer work for them. There are others who feel the same way. We plan to write a new constitution for an independent Texas.

When we do, we will remember the rights of all Texans. We will never make an exception for the rich over the poor. The leaders of Texas are dependent on the trust of the people. They must be elected fairly and democratically.

My friends, we are being granted a chance to make an example of our republic. I urge you to give us your support, and in return we will give you the most effective government possible.

From March to October of 1836, Lorenzo de Zavala served as the first vice-president of the Republic of Texas. He died of pneumonia in November 1836. Nine years later, Texas joined the United States as the twenty-eighth state.

Making Connections

 Text to Self

Evaluate a Speech Imagine you are a reporter in the crowd in Harrisburg, Texas, listening to De Zavala's speech. Write a short paragraph in which you summarize De Zavala's viewpoint and main ideas for your newspaper readers. Note any parts of the speech that you think are exaggerated. Then evaluate which parts of the speech are most effective. Describe the atmosphere and the mood of the crowd so readers will feel as if they are there, too.

 Text to Text

Compare Character Perspectives Lorenzo de Zavala was a respected Mexican statesman and a talented public speaker. If De Zavala could speak to Darnell Rock about his speech at the City Council meeting, what do you think he would say? What kinds of tips might he be able to give Darnell? What kinds of questions might Darnell ask De Zavala?

 Text to World

Discuss Media Techniques Darnell Rock writes a newspaper article to present to the public his thoughts on a community issue. Work with a small group to think of a community or national issue that has been covered in various media. Make a list of where you have seen information about the issue, such as in newspaper articles, magazine advertisements, television commercials, and documentaries. Then discuss how the different kinds of media present the issue. Consider how written text, sound effects, images, video, narration, and other techniques contribute to an overall message.

Grammar

More Kinds of Pronouns A **pronoun** is a word that takes the place of a noun. There are several kinds of pronouns. Words like *someone* and *something* refer to a person or thing that is not identified. These pronouns are called **indefinite pronouns**. Pronouns that replace possessive nouns are called **possessive pronouns**. Words such as *who*, *what*, and *which* can be used to begin questions. These pronouns are called **interrogative pronouns**.

Academic Language

indefinite pronouns
possessive pronouns
interrogative pronouns

Pronouns	Examples
indefinite pronoun	Anyone can become a gardener here.
possessive pronoun	Mr. Mogannum never had his own yard.
interrogative pronoun	What is that orange vegetable in the garden?

 **Try This!** **Copy each sentence below onto a sheet of paper. Underline each indefinite pronoun. Circle each possessive pronoun. Draw a box around each interrogative pronoun.**

❶ Who is the woman in the purple bonnet?

❷ Everyone in the garden asks that woman for advice!

❸ Her tomatoes are the biggest and reddest!

❹ Which is Mr. Jackson's garden plot?

❺ The plot with the sunflowers is his plot.

Sentence Fluency Possessive pronouns can help you avoid repeating proper nouns in your writing. When you use possessive pronouns, be sure that your readers will be able to understand to whom each possessive pronoun refers.

Poor Use of Possessive Pronouns

Carla will present Carla's proposal at the council meeting tonight. Carla's mother and aunt will attend the meeting, along with Carla's cousin. Carla has used their ideas in Carla's proposal.

Better Use of Possessive Pronouns

Carla will present her proposal at the council meeting tonight. Her mother and aunt will attend the meeting, and Carla's cousin will be there, too. Carla has used her mother's and aunt's ideas in her proposal.

Connect Grammar to Writing

As you revise your personal narrative next week, make sure you have used possessive pronouns effectively. Check to see that readers will understand to whom each possessive pronoun refers.

Write to Narrate

✔️ **Ideas** Good writers explore their ideas before they draft. You can collect your ideas for a **personal narrative** on an events chart. List the main events in the order they happened, and then add interesting details about each event.

Rama decided to write about his Warm Coat Project. First, he jotted down the notes below. Then he organized them in a chart.

Writing Process Checklist

▶ **Prewrite**

✔️ Did I think about my audience and purpose?

✔️ Did I choose a topic that I am eager to write about?

✔️ Did I explore my topic to remember important events and interesting details?

✔️ Did I list the events in the order in which they happened?

Draft

Revise

Edit

Publish and Share

Exploring a Topic

Topic: my warm coat project

What? coat wouldn't fit in closet

Why? too many coats

other people need coats

How? persuaded family members

did research on Internet

Where? took coats to an agency

Event: Tried to hang my coat in the closet.
Details: The closet was too full. Left my coat on the floor. Mom told me to pick it up.

↓

Event: Saw how many coats we don't wear. Got an idea. Give some to needy people.
Details: I put the coats in piles. Mom wasn't happy about the mess.

↓

Event: Talked my family into giving coats to those who can't afford to buy them.
Details: First, I told Mom my idea. She loved it! Family agreed to choose coats to give away.

In my events chart, I organized my ideas into main events and details. I added a new event and some details.

↓

Event: Found an agency on the Internet that gives away coats.
Details: We delivered the coats. We learned that many more were needed.

↓

Event: Started a coat drive.
Details: Friends and relatives agreed to help out. Next year, will get help from my whole school.

Reading as a Writer

How did Rama organize his events chart? Which parts of your chart can you organize more clearly?

quests

transformed

plagued

faithful

noble

pierced

ignorance

thrust

exploits

antique

Vocabulary Reader

Context Cards

Vocabulary in Context

1 quests
In the Middle Ages, lords sent their knights on quests, journeys to help others.

2 transformed
A ceremony changed, or transformed, squires into knights after years of training.

3 plagued
Knights may have been plagued, or bothered, by the weight of their armor.

4 faithful
A faithful horse was a knight's loyal companion in battle.

- **Study each Context Card.**

- **Use the context of the sentence to clarify the meaning of the Vocabulary word.**

5 **noble**

Knights needed courage, generosity, and honor to perform noble deeds.

6 **pierced**

Tournament weapons were blunted to prevent knights' armor from being pierced.

7 **ignorance**

Medieval royalty, nobility, and clergy were educated. Others lived in ignorance.

8 **thrust**

In swordplay, a thrust is a lunge with the sword held straight out.

9 **exploits**

The fictional exploits, or great deeds, of heroes include stories about slaying dragons.

10 **antique**

Many museums display antique armor. It was made hundreds of years ago.

Background

Cervantes Spain's Miguel de Cervantes Saavedra (1547–1616) published *Don Quixote de la Mancha* in 1605. This famed tale follows the exploits of Don Quixote, a poor but noble man who thinks he is a knight. In the next selection, you'll see why Don Quixote pierced a windmill with a thrust of his antique lance.

Cervantes was unlucky in his personal quests. He lost the use of his left hand in a war. Later, pirates sold him into slavery in Algeria. Plagued by five years of bondage and four failed escape attempts, he gained freedom only when his faithful family and friends paid a ransom.

Cervantes then transformed himself into a writer. Unable to make a living by writing, he took government jobs. Sadly, he was thrown into prison because of his ignorance of record keeping. Some say that Cervantes began *Don Quixote* while in prison.

By the time he died, Cervantes was a well-known writer. His masterpiece, *Don Quixote*, was published in two parts, in 1605 and in 1615.

504

Comprehension

✔ **TARGET SKILL** **Understanding Characters**

As you read "Don Quixote and the Windmills," look for thoughts, actions, and words that tell you about a character's feelings and motives. Use a graphic organizer like the one below to help you determine Don Quixote's motives from his thoughts, actions and words.

Thoughts	Actions	Words
•	•	•
•	•	•
•	•	•

✔ **TARGET STRATEGY** **Question**

Asking questions about why a character does or says something can help you infer his or her motives and feelings when they are not directly stated. As you read, ask questions in order to make more sense of the characters and plot of a story. It will allow you to see the humor when the answers are not what you expect!

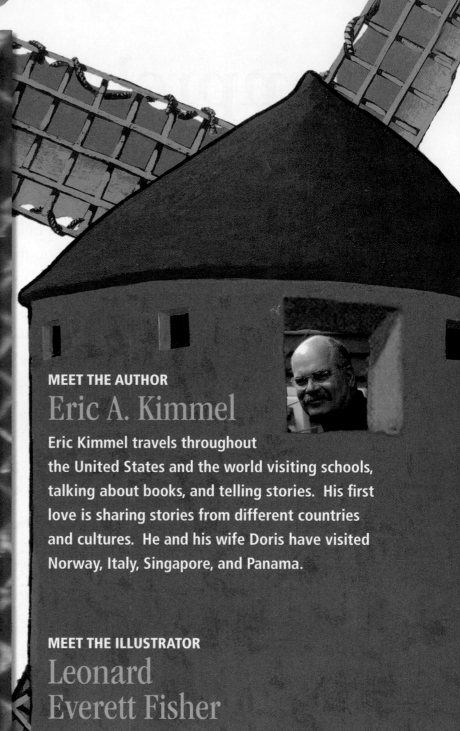

✔ **TARGET VOCABULARY**

quests	pierced
transformed	ignorance
plagued	thrust
faithful	exploits
noble	antique

✔ **TARGET SKILL**

Understanding Characters
Use text details to explain why characters act, speak, and think as they do.

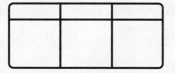

✔ **TARGET STRATEGY**

Question Ask questions about a selection before you read, as you read, and after you read.

GENRE

Humorous fiction is a story that is written to make the reader laugh.

MEET THE AUTHOR

Eric A. Kimmel

Eric Kimmel travels throughout the United States and the world visiting schools, talking about books, and telling stories. His first love is sharing stories from different countries and cultures. He and his wife Doris have visited Norway, Italy, Singapore, and Panama.

MEET THE ILLUSTRATOR

Leonard Everett Fisher

Leonard Everett Fisher has published over two hundred children's books since 1954. He has also been a teacher, produced public murals such as one for the Washington Monument, and designed postage stamps for the United States Postal Service.

DON QUIXOTE
AND THE
WINDMILLS

BY ERIC A. KIMMEL   ILLUSTRATED BY LEONARD EVERETT FISHER

Essential Question

How do the beliefs of a character affect a story?

Are you one who loves old stories? Does your heart beat faster when you hear tales of knights in armor? Of castles and dragons? Of ogres, giants, and damsels in distress? Beware! Those tales can drive you mad. It happened to a certain Spanish gentleman who lived four centuries ago in the province of La Mancha (lah MAHN chah).

Señor Quexada (sehn YOHR keh HAH dah) was his name. He had a tall, lean figure and wore a woeful expression on his face, as if his heart held some secret sorrow.

Indeed, it did. Señor Quexada longed to live in days gone by, when gallant knights battled for the honor of ladies fair. Books of their adventures filled his library. *Amadis of Gaul, The Mirror of Chivalry,* and *The Exploits of Esplandián* were but a few of the volumes that tumbled from his shelves.

Señor Quexada buried himself in these books. He read all day and far into the night, until his mind snapped. "Señor Quexada is no more," he announced to his astonished household. "I am the renowned knight and champion Don Quixote (kee HOH teh) de la Mancha."

In the attic he found a rusty suit of armor, his grandfather's sword, a round leather shield, and an antique lance. His helmet was a foot soldier's steel cap that lacked a visor. Don Quixote made one out of paperboard and tied it on with ribbons. It would serve until he won himself a proper helmet on the field of battle.

A knight must have a noble steed. Don Quixote owned a nag as tall and bony as himself. He named the horse Rocinante (ROH sihn AHN teh), which means "Nag No More."

A knight must also have a squire, a faithful companion to share his quests. Don Quixote invited Sancho Panza (SAHN choh PAHN sah), a short, fat farmer from the neighborhood, to accompany him. "Come with me, Sancho," Don Quixote said. "Within a week I will conquer an island and make you king of it."

"That will be no bad thing," Sancho replied. "If I were king of an island, my wife would be queen, and all my children princes and princesses." So Sancho agreed to come along. Although he was not as crackbrained as Don Quixote, he certainly saw no harm in seeing a bit of the world.

Finally, a knight must have a fair lady to whom he has pledged his loyalty and his life. "A knight without a lady is like a tree without leaves or fruit, a body without a soul," Don Quixote explained to Sancho. After considering all the damsels in the district, he chose a pretty farm girl—Aldonza Lorenzo— from the village of Toboso.

Don Quixote rechristened his lady as he had rechristened his horse. He called her "Dulcinea," (dool see NEH ah) meaning "Sweetness." The very word breathed music and enchantment.

"Dulcinea of Toboso . . . Dulcinea . . . Dulcinea . . ." The knight's heart overflowed with devotion as he whispered the sacred name.

STOP AND THINK
Question Ask yourself what you have learned about knights in shining armor. How does Don Quixote compare to these knights?

One moonless night, while everyone in town lay asleep, Don Quixote and Sancho set forth. By dawn they were miles away. Don Quixote rode ahead, scanning the plain for ogres and giants. Sancho followed on his little donkey, munching his breakfast of bread and cheese.

Don Quixote halted. "Fortune has favored our quest, good Sancho. Can you see what lies yonder? There stand the monstrous giants who have plagued this countryside long enough. I intend to strike them down and claim their wealth as our just reward."

Sancho squinted into the distance. "Giants, Master? What are you talking about? I see no giants."

"There they are. Straight ahead. Can't you see them? They have four arms, each one more than six miles long."

"Oh, Master, you are mistaken. Those aren't giants. They're windmills. What you call arms are really sails to catch the wind. The wind turns the sails and makes the millstones go round and round."

"It is plain you know nothing at all," Don Quixote replied. "I say those are giants, whether or not you recognize them as such. I intend to slay them. If you are frightened, you may hide yourself away and say your prayers while I challenge them to mortal combat."

Having said this, Don Quixote lowered his visor and put his spurs to Rocinante. He galloped across the plain to do battle with the windmills.

"Take to your heels, cowardly giants! Know that it is I, the noble Don Quixote, Knight of La Mancha, who am attacking you!"

"Master! They are only windmills!" Sancho called after him.

The wind picked up. The sails billowed. The great arms of the windmills began to turn.

Don Quixote laughed with scorn. "Do you think to frighten me? Though you have more arms than the giant Briarcus, I will still make an end of you!" He lifted his eyes toward heaven. "Beautiful damsel, Dulcinea of Toboso, in your honor do I claim the victory. If I am to die, let it be with your sweet name upon my lips."

Shouting defiance, he charged at the nearest windmill.

> ✔ **STOP AND THINK**
> **Understanding Characters** What have you learned about Don Quixote so far that explains why he attacks the windmills?

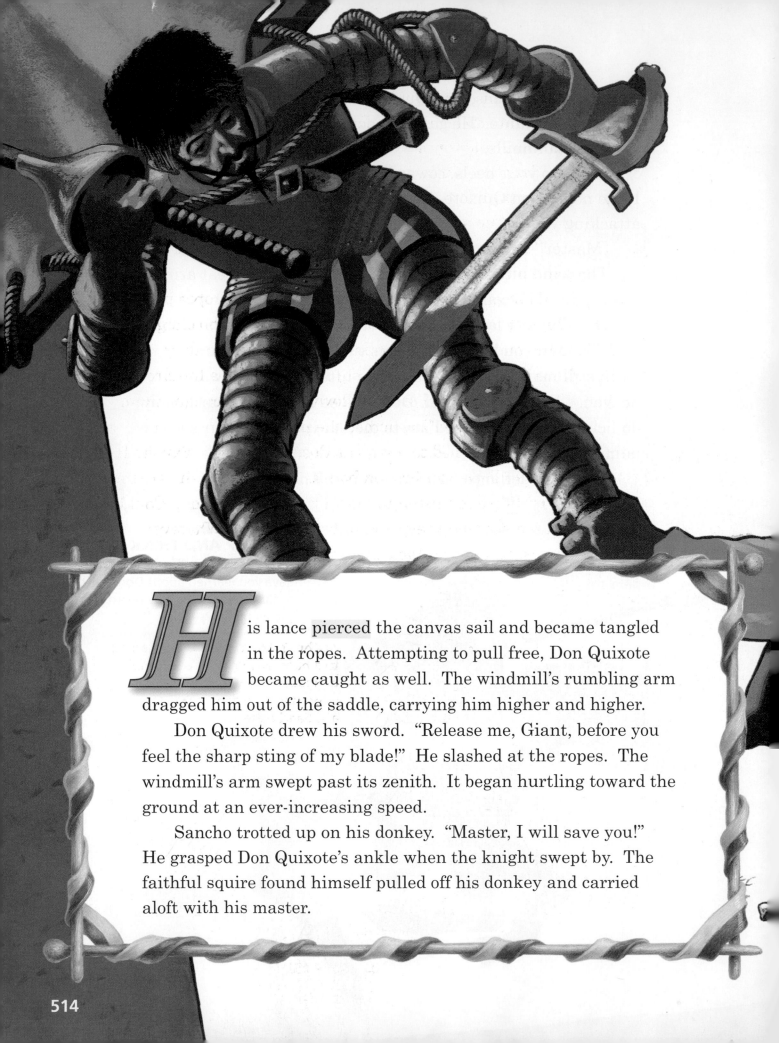

His lance pierced the canvas sail and became tangled in the ropes. Attempting to pull free, Don Quixote became caught as well. The windmill's rumbling arm dragged him out of the saddle, carrying him higher and higher.

Don Quixote drew his sword. "Release me, Giant, before you feel the sharp sting of my blade!" He slashed at the ropes. The windmill's arm swept past its zenith. It began hurtling toward the ground at an ever-increasing speed.

Sancho trotted up on his donkey. "Master, I will save you!" He grasped Don Quixote's ankle when the knight swept by. The faithful squire found himself pulled off his donkey and carried aloft with his master.

"Do not fear, good Sancho. I feel the giant weakening. I will soon make an end of this villain." Don Quixote hacked at the ropes with renewed vigor.

Sancho saw the cords begin to fray. "Master! Spare the poor giant a few moments of life. At least until he brings us closer to the ground."

"Giant, in the name of my lady, Dulcinea of Toboso, I command you to yield or die."

Don Quixote made one last thrust. The ropes parted. The sail blew away. Don Quixote, with Sancho clinging to his ankle, plunged straight down. Together they would have perished, knight and squire, dashed to a hundred pieces, had the sail of the following arm not caught them and sent them rolling across the plain.

They tumbled to a stop at Rocinante's feet. Sancho felt himself all over for broken bones. "Ay, Master!" he groaned. "Why didn't you listen to me? I tried to warn you. Could you not see that they were only windmills? Whatever possessed you to attack them?"

STOP AND THINK

Author's Craft The phrase "dashed to a hundred pieces" is an example of imagery. How does it help you understand the danger Don Quixote and Sancho are in?

Social Studies

✓ TARGET VOCABULARY

quests	transformed
plagued	faithful
noble	pierced
ignorance	thrust
exploits	antique

GENRE

A **play**, like this dramatic adaptation, tells a story through the words and actions of its characters.

TEXT FOCUS

Characters In a play, characters are often listed first. Each character is named before his or her lines of dialogue so readers know who is speaking.

LitBeat: Live from La Mancha

Retold by Rob Hale

Cast of Characters

Reed Daley, Anchor

Paige Turner, Reporter

Don Quixote

Sancho Panza

Miller

Reed Daley: This is LitBeat, bringing you breaking news from the world of literature. We go now to reporter Paige Turner, who is following a story outside of Toboso, Spain. Paige?

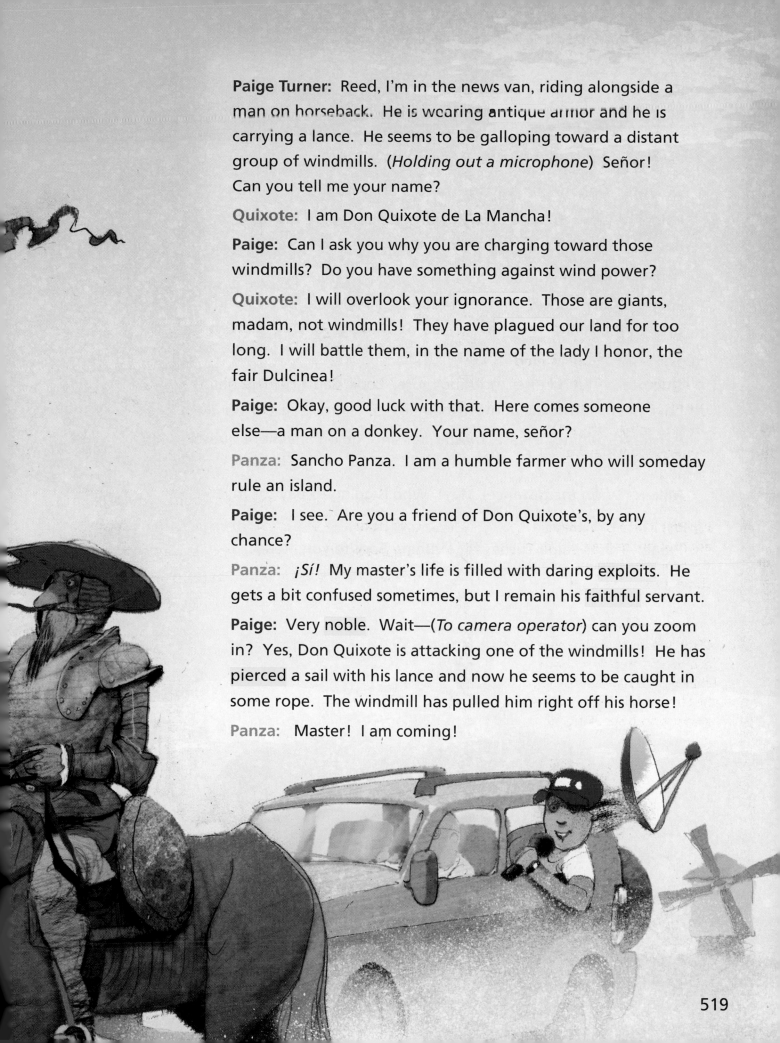

Paige Turner: Reed, I'm in the news van, riding alongside a man on horseback. He is wearing antique armor and he is carrying a lance. He seems to be galloping toward a distant group of windmills. (*Holding out a microphone*) Señor! Can you tell me your name?

Quixote: I am Don Quixote de La Mancha!

Paige: Can I ask you why you are charging toward those windmills? Do you have something against wind power?

Quixote: I will overlook your ignorance. Those are giants, madam, not windmills! They have plagued our land for too long. I will battle them, in the name of the lady I honor, the fair Dulcinea!

Paige: Okay, good luck with that. Here comes someone else—a man on a donkey. Your name, señor?

Panza: Sancho Panza. I am a humble farmer who will someday rule an island.

Paige: I see. Are you a friend of Don Quixote's, by any chance?

Panza: *¡Sí!* My master's life is filled with daring exploits. He gets a bit confused sometimes, but I remain his faithful servant.

Paige: Very noble. Wait—(*To camera operator*) can you zoom in? Yes, Don Quixote is attacking one of the windmills! He has pierced a sail with his lance and now he seems to be caught in some rope. The windmill has pulled him right off his horse!

Panza: Master! I am coming!

Paige: Sancho Panza is trying to pull him back down, but—Oh, no, this is terrible! Both men are caught in the ropes. Those giant sails are pulling them up…up…like a Ferris wheel!

Quixote: Unhand me, villain! Take that! And that!

Paige: With each thrust of his sword, the ropes are giving way, Reed, but the men are too far up! They're going to fall!

Panza: Help!!!

Paige: Wait! Luckily another windmill sail has caught them and broken their fall! They have rolled onto the ground…(*She runs over.*) Señor Quixote, are you all right?

Quixote: A few bruises, nothing more. Look, Sancho! The giants have been transformed into windmills.

Panza: (*Groaning*) Please, master, let's not go on any more quests for a while.

Miller: (*Off in the distance*) Hey! Who is going to pay for my broken windmill?

Paige: This is Paige Turner for LitBeat. Back to you, Reed!

Making Connections

Text to Self

Write a Story If you could be a hero for one day, what good deeds would you do? Write an imaginative story about the adventures you might have during your day as a hero. Include in your story a believable setting and an interesting plot. When you are finished, read your story to a small group.

Text to Text

Compare Literary Forms "LitBeat: Live from La Mancha" is a play based on the characters and events in the story "Don Quixote and the Windmills." Compare and contrast the ways in which these two selections tell about Don Quixote's adventure. How are the story and the play similar? How are they different?

Text to World

Research Windmills Today, many people are interested in wind as a source of renewable energy to produce electricity. Use print and electronic resources to research how windmills work. Then write a paragraph explaining your findings. Brainstorm and discuss with a small group other possible ways to use wind power as a renewable energy source. Take notes as you listen to others speak. Use your notes to write a short summary of your group's ideas.

Grammar

What Is a Contraction? A **contraction** is a word formed by joining two words into one shorter word. An **apostrophe** (') takes the place of the letter or letters that are dropped in making the shorter word. You can combine some verbs with the **negative** word *not* to make contractions. You can also combine personal pronouns with verbs such as *is, are, have, had*, and *will* to make contractions.

Examples of Contractions Made with Verbs Plus *Not*			
do not	don't	were not	weren't
does not	doesn't	will not	won't
is not	isn't	has not	hasn't

Examples of Contractions Made with Pronouns Plus Verbs			
I am	I'm	I have	I've
he is	he's	he has	he's
you are	you're	you have	you've
they are	they're	they have	they've
you will	you'll	you had	you'd

Try This! **Rewrite each sentence below on another sheet of paper. Replace each pair of boldfaced words with a contraction.**

❶ You **are not** going to believe this tale.

❷ **It is** about a knight on a quest.

❸ **He is** determined to slay dragons.

❹ **They are** nowhere to be found.

❺ You **will not** guess what he attacks instead!

Conventions When using a contraction, make sure you put the apostrophe in the correct place. In a contraction with a pronoun and a verb, make sure the verb agrees in number with the pronoun. When using a contraction with *not*, avoid including another "no" word and creating a double negative. Finally, avoid using the contraction *ain't*.

Incorrect	Correct
He does'nt like giants.	He doesn't like giants.
They's watching the battle.	They're watching the battle.
He doesn't fear nobody.	He doesn't fear anybody.
Once again, he ain't the winner.	Once again, he isn't the winner.

Connect Grammar to Writing

As you edit your personal narrative, make sure you have used and written contractions correctly. Be sure to correct any contraction errors you find.

Write to Narrate

☑ **Voice** A good **personal narrative** tells about an important or interesting event in your life in ways that only you can express. When you revise your narrative, add words and ideas that let the reader "hear" your own voice.

Rama used his events chart to draft a narrative about his Warm Coat Project. Later, he added a new opening to grab his readers' attention.

Writing Process Checklist

Prewrite

Draft

▶ **Revise**

☑ Did I begin with an attention-grabber?

☑ Did I include only important events and tell them in order?

☑ Did I use vivid details and dialogue?

☑ Do my feelings come through?

☑ Are my sentences smooth and varied?

☑ Does my ending show how the events worked out?

Edit

Publish and Share

Revised Draft

"What is this jacket doing on the floor?" demanded my mother.

"No room in the closet, that's what," I replied. ~~My mother~~ She told me to hang up ~~my~~ it anyway, of course. ~~coat.~~

As I was trying to squeeze my fat winter jacket into our overstuffed hall closet, I had a brainstorm. "What's causing this closet to be crowded?" I thought. "There are only four of us Ramdevs."

My Warm Coat Project

by Rama Ramdev

"What is this jacket doing on the floor?" demanded my mother.

"No room in the closet, that's what," I replied. She told me to hang it up anyway, of course.

As I was trying to squeeze my fat winter jacket into our overstuffed hall closet, I had a brainstorm. "What's causing this closet to be crowded?" I thought. "There are only four of us Ramdevs."

Right then, I started pulling everything out. I put the coats in piles and saw that every member of the family had at least one coat they didn't use anymore.

When my mother saw the mess I'd made, she wasn't too pleased. I quickly explained my idea. I said, "Think about all the people in this city who can't afford to buy a warm coat! Why don't we give them our extras?"

> In my final paper, I added dialogue to grab readers' attention. I also used contractions to make my writing sound more natural.

Reading as a Writer

How does Rama's opening capture his readers' interest? In your story, where could you add dialogue or interesting details?

Skateboarding Through the Decades

Skateboarding has been around for more than fifty years. It all began in the 1950s. When the waves were flat and real surfing wasn't an option, surfers still wanted to have some fun. Maybe they could "surf the sidewalks"! Someone attached roller skate wheels to the bottom of a wooden board. Skateboarding was born.

In the early 1960s, companies manufactured huge numbers of skateboards. More than 50 million of them were sold in three years! There were skateboarding contests. A famous music group sang "Sidewalk Surfing" while riding a skateboard across the stage. Then, in the late 1960s, skateboarding's popularity crashed. It seemed that the fad was over.

Things picked up again in the 1970s. That's when urethane skateboard wheels were invented. Wheels made from this tough material gave a smooth and stable ride. Other improvements were made, too. Now skateboarders had better control. They could do new tricks, such as the "ollie." In this trick, skaters kick the tail of the board down while jumping, making the board pop into the air. During the 1970s, concrete skate parks sprang up—but closed when insurance rates skyrocketed.

During the 1980s, skaters took to the streets. Any place that offered a ramp, a wall, or a set of steps would do. People built wooden skate ramps in backyards and empty lots.

In 1995, ESPN's Extreme Games showed skateboarding events. Skateboarding stars appeared in commercials. Skateboarding clothing became a fashion style.

As the new century rolled around, so did the wheels of millions of skateboards. Cities built new skate parks. There were skateboarding camps. In 2004, a new holiday was created. Every year on June 21st, skateboarders around the globe take part in Go Skateboarding Day.

Extreme Sports Journal

The Best Place to Skateboard

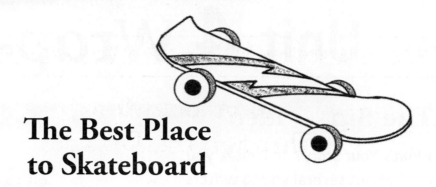

Sam, Marco, and Jade stood in front of the sign, staring in disbelief. "Construction zone. Do not enter!" Sam read.

"Unbelievable!" said Jade. "That was the perfect place to skateboard. Where are we supposed to skateboard now?"

Glumly, Marco spun the urethane wheels on his board. "The nearest skate park is too far away," he said.

Sam looked thoughtful. "I have some work to do in the library," he said.

For the rest of the week, Sam went to the library every day after school. Marco and Jade hardly saw him.

Finally, Jade said to Sam, "You don't have to give up skateboarding just because we don't have a good place to practice! Why are you always at the library?" Sam just said that he was working on something. Marco and Jade didn't see him after school the next week, either.

On Saturday, Sam showed up at Marco's house. Marco and Jade were in the driveway on their skateboards. "Ask your parents if you can walk with me to the warehouse where my mom works," Sam said. "Bring your boards and your gear. I want to show you something."

The three friends walked to the warehouse. Sam led the way to an area behind the building.

"Look at those ramps!" said Jade.

"Where did you get the money to buy them?" asked Marco.

"I didn't buy them," answered Sam. "I built them. I researched the plans in the library. Then I got the wood from the warehouse. It was left over from a job. My mom's boss said I could use the wood to build the ramps. He even said that we could skate here on the weekends!"

"Way to go, Sam!" said Marco. "Now, let's practice some ollies!"

Unit **4** Wrap-Up

The Big 💡 Idea

What's Your Story? In Unit 4, you read about several young writers and their creations. Write a short story that *you* would like to tell. Draw a picture that captures the setting of your story. Then write a caption that tells about the picture.

Listening and Speaking

Worth 1,000 Words Take another look at the illustrations in the selections you read in Unit 4. Choose the three you like best. Then tell a partner why you think they are the best, and explain how the illustrations add to the selection.

Under Western Skies

Unit 5

Big 💡 Idea

Our country
is always
changing.

Paired Selections

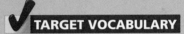

TARGET VOCABULARY

pace

undoubtedly

seep

evident

factor

vain

mirages

shuffled

salvation

stunted

Vocabulary Reader   Context Cards

Vocabulary in Context

1 pace

Pony Express riders rode at a fast pace in order to deliver mail as quickly as possible.

2 undoubtedly

Westbound travelers were undoubtedly glad to make it across the mountains alive.

3 seep

If a storm lasted awhile, rain could seep through protective clothes and hats.

4 evident

When it is evident, or obvious, that a wagon wheel is broken, it is repaired or replaced.

- Study each Context Card.
- Make up a new context sentence that uses two Vocabulary words.

5 factor

The weather was just one factor, or element, that determined the speed of a journey.

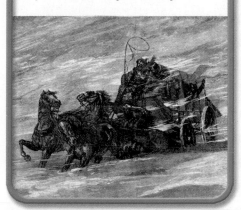

6 vain

These pioneers made a vain, or fruitless, attempt to cross the river. It was too deep.

7 mirages

Travelers could be fooled by mirages. It was a blow to learn these visions were false.

8 shuffled

The journey was tiring. Many walkers shuffled slowly along the trail after a few weeks.

9 salvation

A freshwater spring could be the salvation of thirsty travelers, saving their lives.

10 stunted

Only small, stunted trees can grow in the harsh desert conditions of the Southwest.

Background

A Dangerous Trip Travel was undoubtedly difficult for the thousands of people who journeyed to the American West by wagon train in the mid-1800s. Travelers encountered pouring rain, howling wind, and cold that seemed to seep into their bones. As they shuffled along under a blistering sun, some saw mirages of water or food that raised vain hopes for relief. In reality, the water found along the trail barely supported stunted trees and often carried diseases such as cholera. In this time, before modern medicine, illness spread quickly and many of the sick died.

Meeting people along the trail was another unknown factor in the journey. When travelers met Native Americans, it was not evident whether the encounter would be friendly or fierce. Other strangers could be thieves intent on robbing wagon trains. These hardships and other difficulties slowed the travelers' pace. Finally reaching their destinations must have seemed like salvation.

• Review the information in the graphic below. In which year did the fewest number of pioneers move west? In which year did the most pioneers move west?

Despite the many dangers, thousands of people moved west by wagon train after the discovery of gold in California in 1848. Thousands more traveled by sea.

Number of Pioneers Who Moved West by Wagon Train

Year	Estimated Number of Travelers
1848	4,000
1849	40,000
1850	65,000
1851	10,000
1852	70,000
1853	35,000
1854	20,000
1855	7,000

Comprehension

✔ **TARGET SKILL** **Sequence of Events**

As you read "Tucket's Travels," notice the sequence, or order, in which events take place. Look for clue words that show time, such as *coming*, *last night*, and *by now*. Make a graphic organizer like the one below to show the sequence of events in "Tucket's Travels."

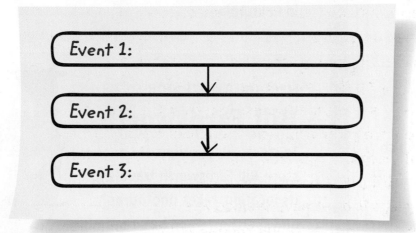

Event 1:

↓

Event 2:

↓

Event 3:

✔ **TARGET STRATEGY** **Visualize**

Use sequence of events and details from "Tucket's Travels" to help you visualize the action in the story. Creating mental pictures of what is happening makes the story more vivid and interesting.

JOURNEYS DIGITAL Powered by DESTINATIONReading®
Comprehension Activities: Lesson 21

✔ **TARGET VOCABULARY**

pace	vain
undoubtedly	mirages
seep	shuffled
evident	salvation
factor	stunted

✔ **TARGET SKILL**

Sequence of Events
Identify the time order in which events take place.

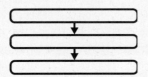

✔ **TARGET STRATEGY**

Visualize Use text details to form pictures in your mind of what you are reading.

GENRE

Historical fiction is a story whose characters and events are set in a real period of history.

MEET THE AUTHOR

Gary Paulsen

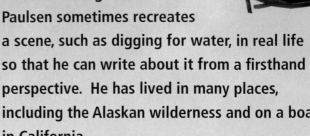

Gary Paulsen's characters often rely on wilderness survival skills to survive tough situations. Paulsen sometimes recreates a scene, such as digging for water, in real life so that he can write about it from a firsthand perspective. He has lived in many places, including the Alaskan wilderness and on a boat in California.

MEET THE ILLUSTRATOR

Bill Farnsworth

To create illustrations for a story, Bill Farnsworth travels to its location, takes photographs, and sketches. Then he's ready to paint. He says, "My goal is to give the viewer a sense of what the main character in the story is feeling, so you can imagine yourself actually there!"

TUCKET'S TRAVELS

by Gary Paulsen

selection illustrated by Bill Farnsworth

Essential Question

What events take the children across a changing land?

If there was one thing Francis Tucket knew with certainty it was that death was close to taking them.

Dawn was coming and here he was, a fifteen-year-old boy in charge of two children, walking across a sunbeaten, airless plain that seemed to be endless. Francis, Lottie and Billy had no food or water or any immediate hope of getting any, and at any moment a dozen or two of the dirt-meanest men Francis had ever seen in a world *full* of mean men could come riding up on them and . . .

He didn't finish the thought. There was no need. Besides, in surviving Indian fights, blizzards, battles and thieves, he had learned the primary rule about danger. It would come if it would come. You could try to be ready for it, you could plan on it, you could even expect it, but it would come when it wanted to come.

Lottie and Billy understood this rule too. He had found them sitting in a wagon on the prairie all alone. Their father had died of cholera (KAHL ur uh) and their wagon train had abandoned the family, afraid of disease. Lottie had been nine then, Billy six. Francis hadn't thought he and the children would stay together long—after all, he had to keep searching for his own family. He'd been separated from them a year before, when Pawnees had kidnapped him from the wagon train on the Oregon Trail. But Francis and Lottie and Billy—well, they were used to each other. They stuck together. Unlike Francis and Jason Grimes, the one-armed mountain man.

Jason Grimes had rescued Francis from the Pawnees and taught him how to survive in the West on his own. Then they'd parted ways.

Until last night. Last night when Grimes had helped them to escape from the Comancheros (koh mahn CHEH rohs). The Comancheros were an outlaw band, ruthless, terrifying, inhumanly tough. To escape, Grimes had had to take the packhorses Francis and Lottie and Billy had been riding and lead them off empty, hoping the Comancheros would follow his tracks westward while the three children headed north on foot in the dark of night.

It was a decent plan—it was their *only* plan—and it seemed to be working. As Francis and the two children had moved north in the dark, they had seen the Comancheros ride past them after Mr. Grimes, tracking the horses. The Comancheros had missed the footprints of the children, partly because it was hard to see them and partly because Francis made Lottie and Billy walk in each other's footprints. He came last, brushing out the trail with a piece of mesquite behind him.

But luck was the major factor in the plan. If the Comancheros caught Grimes or even got within sight of him they'd know that Francis and the children weren't with him. They'd turn and come back for the children. Children meant real money because they could be sold or traded into slavery.

Francis knew that brushing out the tracks would only work in the pitch dark of night. In daylight the brush marks themselves would be easy to follow.

"I'm tired." Billy stopped suddenly. "I think we've gone far enough."

Francis frowned. When Francis had first met Billy, the boy wouldn't say a word. And now he'd gone from never talking at all to complaining.

"If they catch us they'll skin you," warned Lottie. "Now keep walking. If we don't keep moving they'll be on us like dogs, won't they, Francis? On us just like dogs . . ."

Lottie loved to talk, would talk all the time if she had the chance, seemed to have been talking since Francis had found her in that wagon. Lottie would explain every little detail of every little part of every little thing she was talking about so that not a single aspect of it was missed, and she sometimes drove Francis over the edge. Now, as Billy started moving again, Francis picked up the pace, pushed them as hard as they could stand it and then harder, and Lottie didn't have breath left to speak.

Dawn brought the sun and the sun brought heat. Francis and the children were bareheaded and the sun quickly went to work on them. Billy wanted to complain, especially as the morning progressed and there was no water and the sun rose higher and became hotter, but Francis drove them until Billy began to weave. Then Francis picked Billy up and carried him piggyback, mile after mile, then yard after yard, and finally, step after step.

✔ **STOP AND THINK**

Sequence of Events What steps do Tucket and the children take to escape the Comancheros during the night? What is happening now that it is day?

Lottie saw it first.

"There," she said. "See the spot?"

Francis was near dead with exhaustion. He had hardly slept at all for the two nights before and had been used roughly by the Comancheros in the bargain. He was close to the breaking point as he said, "What spot?"

"There. No, more to the right. On the horizon. It's trees. I'm sure of it. A stand of trees."

They had seen many mirages—images of trees and water that were not there. But Francis looked where she was pointing and saw it instantly. He stopped and set Billy down. The boy was asleep, and he collapsed in a heap, still sleeping. "You're right! Trees. And trees mean water."

He turned and studied the horizon. He hadn't been able to look up when carrying Billy and he was shocked now to see a plume of dust off to the west and south. It was at least fifteen miles away, against some hills in the distance. It was so far away that it seemed tiny, but Francis knew it was probably caused by riders, many riders.

Lottie saw him staring.

"Could it be buffalo?" She watched the dust. "A small herd?"

Not here, Francis thought. Not here in this dust and heat with no grass and no water. Buffalo wouldn't be that stupid. "Sure. It's buffalo."

"You're lying." She sighed. "I can tell when you're lying to me, Francis Tucket. It's them, isn't it?"

Francis said nothing but his mind was racing. So the riders were heading back eastward. But why would they be coming back so soon? Had they caught Grimes already? If so they'd be looking for the children. Or had they given up the chase or just seen Grimes and found that he was alone and turned back, still looking for the children? They might miss the tracks . . .

He knew this was a vain hope. There hadn't been a breath of wind to blow the dust over the brush marks he'd left, and undoubtedly they had men who were good trackers, men who were alive because they could track mice over rocks. So the Comancheros would find them and then . . . and then . . .

They reached the trees just as the edge of the clouds caught up with them.

"Ten more feet and I would have died," Lottie whispered, and sank to the ground.

Francis dropped Billy like a stone—the boy fell without awakening—and studied their location. It was a meandering dry streambed with a row of stunted but leafy cottonwoods on each side. There were also stands of salt cedar, thick and green, and while no water was evident the streambed seemed moist. Francis knew there was water beneath the surface or the trees would have been dead.

"Lottie, scoop a hole there, at the base of that rock."

"You want to start digging, why don't you just go ahead? I have more important things to do than scrape at the old ground."

"Water." Francis was so dry he croaked. "Dig down and let it seep in."

"Oh. Well, why didn't you say so?" Lottie knelt by the rock and started digging in the loose sand with her hands. When she was down two feet, she yelped.

"Here it is! Just like you said, coming in from the sides. Oh, Francis, it's so clear, come see." She scooped some up and drank it. "Sweet as sugar. Come, try it."

Francis knelt and cupped his hand and drank and thought he had never tasted anything so good. But he stopped before he was full.

The wind was picking up now, blowing hard enough to lift dust and even sand, and he could no longer see the dust from the riders. The wind was blowing at the coming thunderheads and he smiled because even if it didn't rain there was a good chance the wind would fill in and destroy their tracks.

By now the thunderhead was over them, dark, so huge it covered the whole sky, and the wind had increased to a scream.

> **STOP AND THINK**
> **Author's Craft** A **metaphor** is a description that compares one thing to another thing without using *like* or *as*. Metaphors make descriptions more vivid. What metaphor does the author use on this page to describe the sound of the wind?

"Over here!" Francis yelled to Lottie. "Beneath this ledge." Incredibly, Billy was still asleep. Francis grabbed the boy and shook him until his eyes opened. "Get over by that rock ledge. Everything is going to break loose—"

A bolt of lightning hit so close Francis felt it ripple his hair, so close the thunder seemed to happen in the same split instant, and with it the sky opened and water fell on them so hard it almost drove Francis to his knees. He had never seen such rain. There seemed to be no space between the drops; it roared down, poured down in sheets, in buckets. Francis couldn't yell, couldn't think, couldn't breathe. He held Billy by the shirt and dragged him in beneath the ledge that formed the edge of the streambed, away from the trees and out of the wind.

Lottie was there already and they huddled under the overhang just as the clouds cracked again and hail the size of Francis's fist pounded down. One hailstone glanced off the side of his head and nearly knocked him out.

"Move in more," he yelled over the roar of the storm. "Farther back—move!"

He pushed against Billy, who slammed into Lottie. They were already up against the clay bank beneath the ledge and could not go farther in. Francis's legs and rear were still out in the hail and took a fearful beating. He doubled his legs up but even so the pain was excruciating and though the large hailstones quickly gave way to smaller ones, his legs were immediately stiff and sore.

The streambed filled in the heavy downpour. Luckily they were near the upstream portion of the storm and so avoided the possibility of a flash flood—which would have gouged them out of the overhang and taken them downstream to drown. As it was, the water came into the pocket beneath them and turned the dirt to mud and soon they were sitting in a waist-deep hole of thick mud and water. And just as soon, in minutes, the rain had stopped, the clouds had scudded away and the sun was out, cooking the mud dry.

Aching, Francis pulled himself into the sun. The children crawled after. Water still ran in the stream but was receding quickly. The hot sun felt good, and Francis wanted to take his buckskin shirt off to hang. But he knew that if he didn't keep wearing it the shirt would dry as stiff as a board.

He straightened slowly, working the pain out of his legs. He looked to the west and smiled.

There would be no tracks after *that*.

Your Turn

A Big Responsibility

Short Response Francis realizes that he'll need to use all of his survival skills and instincts if he, Lottie, and Billy are to escape the Comancheros. What personal qualities help Francis on the difficult walk across the desert? Write a paragraph describing the personal qualities you possess that would help you in a similar situation.

PERSONAL RESPONSE

Breaking News

Francis, Lottie, and Billy reach the trees right before the storm. With a small group, create a script for a news broadcast in which the three young people are interviewed about their experience during the rainstorm. Choose roles, including the role of the interviewing reporter. Use details from the story to make the report realistic and exciting. Rehearse the broadcast, and then perform it for classmates. SMALL GROUP

Where's the Water?

Turn and Talk As Francis, Lottie, and Billy walk across the desert, the sun makes the dry land hotter and hotter. With a partner, list and discuss the events that bring them water and the role each person plays in finding it. SEQUENCE OF EVENTS

✔ **TARGET VOCABULARY**

pace	vain
undoubtedly	mirages
seep	shuffled
evident	salvation
factor	stunted

GENRE

Informational text, such as this science text, gives facts and examples about a topic.

TEXT FOCUS

Graphic Sources
Informational text may include charts or tables, which organize related information about a topic.

DESERT SURVIVAL
Adapting to Extremes

Summer temperatures in the Mojave, Sonoran, and Chihuahuan deserts can soar as high as 120°F. Undoubtedly, any plant or animal must be specially suited to survive such extremes. Temperature extremes are only one challenge. Another factor that makes desert survival difficult is lack of water. Some deserts receive less than ten inches of rain a year. Others get more rain, but the moisture evaporates more quickly than it falls. Despite these harsh conditions, the desert is home to a variety of plant and animal life.

Desert Plant Adaptations

Desert plants have developed many ways to collect and store water. Water is often deep in the ground, and it will rarely seep to the surface. Mesquite tree roots can reach water eighty feet underground. The barrel cactus holds so much water that desert wanderers have found salvation from thirst by chewing the moist pulp from its woody stem.

Plants in arid regions are also good at conserving water. Their leaves are small and thick-skinned to hold in moisture. Many grow close to the ground in the shade of stunted trees.

Some plants are adapted to the desert's short rainy season. The desert lily becomes inactive during the dry season but blooms when it rains. The seeds of some plants do not germinate until it rains. The plants then grow and flower at a rapid pace. They create new seeds that will lie dormant until the next rain.

Average Annual Rainfall in Desert and Temperate Locations, in inches, 2001–2006

City	2001	2002	2003	2004	2005	2006
Las Vegas, NV	3.94	1.44	6.86	7.76	7.37	1.70
El Paso, TX	4.29	6.89	4.21	12.09	12.87	17.51
Albuquerque, NM	6.50	6.39	6.35	11.80	11.42	13.06
Phoenix, AZ	6.72	2.82	6.82	7.98	7.04	5.45
Atlanta, GA	38.39	47.82	52.91	53.60	56.43	48.46
New York City, NY	35.65	45.20	58.42	51.93	55.97	59.89
Seattle, WA	37.56	31.36	41.78	31.10	35.44	48.42

Analyze the information listed above. The first four cities are all located in desert areas. Compare the average yearly rainfall in these locations to the average rainfall in cities in other areas. Which city had the most rainfall in 2003? Which had the least rainfall in 2003?

Source: NOAA

Desert Wildlife Adaptations

In a desert, mirages give the appearance of water, but your search for drinking water would be a vain one. To survive in this harsh climate, desert animals have adapted to the dry climate. For example, desert toads get all their moisture from food. Others, such as the Gila (HEE lah) monster, store water in their bodies.

To avoid the heat, many desert animals are inactive during the day. Some are inactive longer. After it has shuffled to a safe location, the desert tortoise sleeps through the heat of summer. Another desert dweller, the sidewinder snake, moves sideways so that only two small parts of its body touch the hot sand at the same time.

Desert animals often use more than one survival strategy. Kangaroo rats, for example, stay in sealed burrows during the day. They get moisture from their recycled breath and the dry seeds they eat.

A desert environment may be extreme, but it is evident that plants and animals can adapt to its challenges.

Gila monsters are poisonous lizards well adapted to living in the desert.

Making Connections

 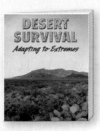

 Text to Self

Write About Weather The selections you read described environments with extreme weather conditions. Think of a time when you experienced extreme weather, such as a storm or a heat wave. Describe in a few paragraphs the weather and how it affected you or others around you. Explain what you or others did to adapt to the conditions. Be sure to use vivid details that will interest the reader.

 Text to Text

Connect to Science People, plants, and wildlife living in desert climates do some surprising things to survive extreme heat and lack of water. Use details from both selections to compare and contrast how each kind of living thing can avoid moisture loss in the desert.

 Text to World

Present Information With a partner, use a combination of resources to research the Mojave, Sonoran, or Chihuahuan desert. Create a chart or table of some animals and plants that live there. Next to each living thing, list one or more adaptations it has made to survive in a harsh climate. Then compile your information and present it to another group. Be sure to make eye contact and speak loudly enough for everyone to hear you.

Grammar

Correct Uses of the Verbs *be* and *have* The verbs *be* and *have* can be used as **main verbs** or **helping verbs**. As you have learned, a verb and its subject must agree in number. *Be* and *have* are **irregular verbs.** You must change the forms of the verbs *be* and *have* in special ways to achieve **subject-verb agreement.**

Subject	Form of *be*		Form of *have*	
	Present	**Past**	**Present**	**Past**
Singular Subjects:				
I	am	was	have	had
You	are	were	have	had
He, She, It (or singular noun)	is	was	has	had
Plural Subjects:				
We	are	were	have	had
You	are	were	have	had
They (or plural noun)	are	were	have	had

Try This! **Rewrite each sentence below on another sheet of paper. Use the correct form of *be* or *have* shown in parentheses.**

1. Francis (is, are) a skilled tracker.

2. He (has, have) survived battles and blizzards.

3. (Are, Is) you familiar with his story?

4. Lottie and Billy (is, are) the children in his care.

5. They (has, have) no one else to look out for them.

Conventions Remember to use the correct forms of *be* and *have*. When you write, make sure you keep the verb tenses consistent so your paragraphs make sense.

Shifting Tenses	Consistent Tenses
The thunderstorm has frightened the children, and they took shelter.	The thunderstorm has frightened the children, and they have taken shelter.

Connect Grammar to Writing

As you edit your procedural paragraph, pay special attention to the verbs in your sentences. Make sure the verb tenses are consistent.

Write to Inform

In a **procedural paragraph,** you describe a process, or series of events or steps. You should begin by introducing the topic. Then explain each event in the order in which it happens or should happen. Using transition words, such as *first, next, then,* and *finally,* will make the order of events more clear to readers.

   Dan wrote a procedural paragraph explaining how a pioneer family prepared to journey westward. Later, he reordered events and added transition words to make his ideas more organized. Use the Writing Traits Checklist below as you revise your writing.

Writing Traits Checklist

☑ **Ideas**
Did I describe the steps in a process?

☑ **Organization**
Did I explain events in order and use transitions to make that order clear?

☑ **Sentence Fluency**
Did I use the verbs *be* and *have* correctly?

☑ **Word Choice**
Did I use specific nouns and strong verbs?

☑ **Voice**
Did I express my ideas in a clear and interesting way?

☑ **Conventions**
Did I use correct spelling, grammar, and punctuation?

Revised Draft

Traveling to the West was a long, dangerous journey for a pioneer family. They had to prepare carefully for their trip. Next, They had to gather and pack supplies they would need on their trip such as tools, bedding, and cooking utensils. They also took dry goods such as flour, sugar, and rice. First, They had to get a strong wagon and a team of oxen to pull it.

How a Pioneer Family Planned a Trip West

by Dan Morse

Traveling to the West was a long, dangerous journey for a pioneer family. They had to prepare carefully for their trip. First, they had to get a strong wagon and a team of oxen to pull it. Next, they had to gather and pack supplies they would need on their trip such as tools, bedding, and cooking utensils. They also took dry goods such as flour, sugar, and rice. Once their wagon was packed, they usually joined up with other families. The families would then either join a longer wagon train or hire their own guide. The guide was a person who had already made the trip to the West and knew the best routes to take. Even after all this careful planning, the families would face many challenges along the way to their new home.

> In my final paper, I reordered steps in the process and added transitions to make the sequence of events clearer. I also checked to see that I had used *be* and *have* correctly.

Reading as a Writer

Which steps did Dan reorder? Which transitions did he add? What changes can you make to your procedural paragraph to clarify the sequence of events in the process?

astonished

nerve

bared

banish

reasoned

envy

spared

margins

deserted

upright

Vocabulary Reader

Context Cards

Vocabulary in Context

1 astonished

People may be astonished at seeing wild animals. The sight can be amazing.

2 nerve

He was scared, but this boy worked up the nerve, or courage, to handle the snake.

3 bared

This lion opened its mouth and bared its teeth. Everyone could see its fangs.

4 banish

The leader of a wolf pack will banish a defeated challenger. The loser must leave.

- **Study each Context Card.**
- **Use a thesaurus to determine a synonym for each Vocabulary word.**

5 reasoned

Scientists reasoned, or logically figured out, how to assemble these fossil bones.

6 envy

People may watch seals with envy. They are jealous of the seals' swimming ability.

7 spared

This cat played with the mouse but spared its life and did not harm it.

8 margins

You can sometimes see deer standing in fields at the margins, or edges, of the woods.

9 deserted

A baby bird that is all alone may seem deserted, but its mother may be nearby.

10 upright

Meerkats stand upright, or straight up, to keep a lookout for nearby predators.

Background

The Ojibwe People The Ojibwe lived around the margins of the Great Lakes. Their homes, called wigwams, were held upright by a frame of saplings and covered in birchbark. In summer they lived in large groups, harvesting plants and berries. In winter they left their large camps deserted and headed for smaller ones. They reasoned that small groups could hunt game more easily. It took a lot of nerve for an Ojibwe hunter to face down an angry black bear as it bared its teeth. If their harvesting and hunting were successful, the Ojibwe were spared from hunger. In the 1600s, the Ojibwe began trading beaver furs to the French for other goods and were astonished at their success. Other native peoples in the region felt envy. They battled with the Ojibwe over hunting grounds. Then settlers moving westward tried to banish the Ojibwe from the area.

The Ojibwe often decorated their clothing with beautiful beadwork.

Comprehension

Theme

All stories have a theme, or message, that runs through them. You can determine a story's theme by looking at a main character's qualities, motives, and actions. How the character responds to conflict can also provide clues to the theme. As you read, use a graphic organizer to record details about the main character to help you determine the theme.

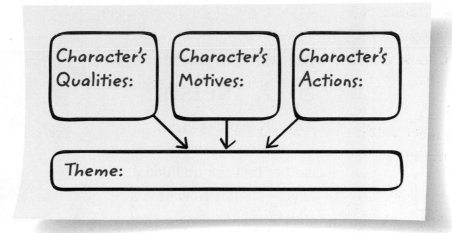

Character's Qualities:

Character's Motives:

Character's Actions:

Theme:

✔ **TARGET STRATEGY** **Infer/Predict**

To determine the theme of a text, sometimes you must infer a character's qualities and motives because they are not directly stated. Inferring can help you better understand a story's characters, predict what they might do, and determine how those actions affect the theme of the story.

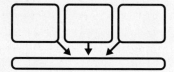

astonished	envy
nerve	spared
bared	margins
banish	deserted
reasoned	upright

✔ **TARGET SKILL**

Theme Examine the main character's qualities, motives, and actions to recognize the theme of the story.

✔ **TARGET STRATEGY**

Infer/Predict Use text clues to figure out what the author means or what might happen in the future.

GENRE

Historical fiction is a story whose characters and events are set in a real period of history.

MEET THE AUTHOR

Louise Erdrich

Louise Erdrich is a member of the Turtle Mountain Band of Ojibwe. While she was growing up in North Dakota, her father often recited memorized poetry to her and her six siblings. She was inspired to write *The Birchbark House* while she and her mother were researching their own family history.

MEET THE ILLUSTRATOR

S.D. Nelson

When he was young, S. D. Nelson's Lakota/Sioux mother told him traditional Coyote stories. Now he is a storyteller. He is the author-illustrator of many books for young readers, including *Coyote Christmas, Gift Horse, Quiet Hero,* and *The Star People,* winner of the Western Writers of America Spur Award.

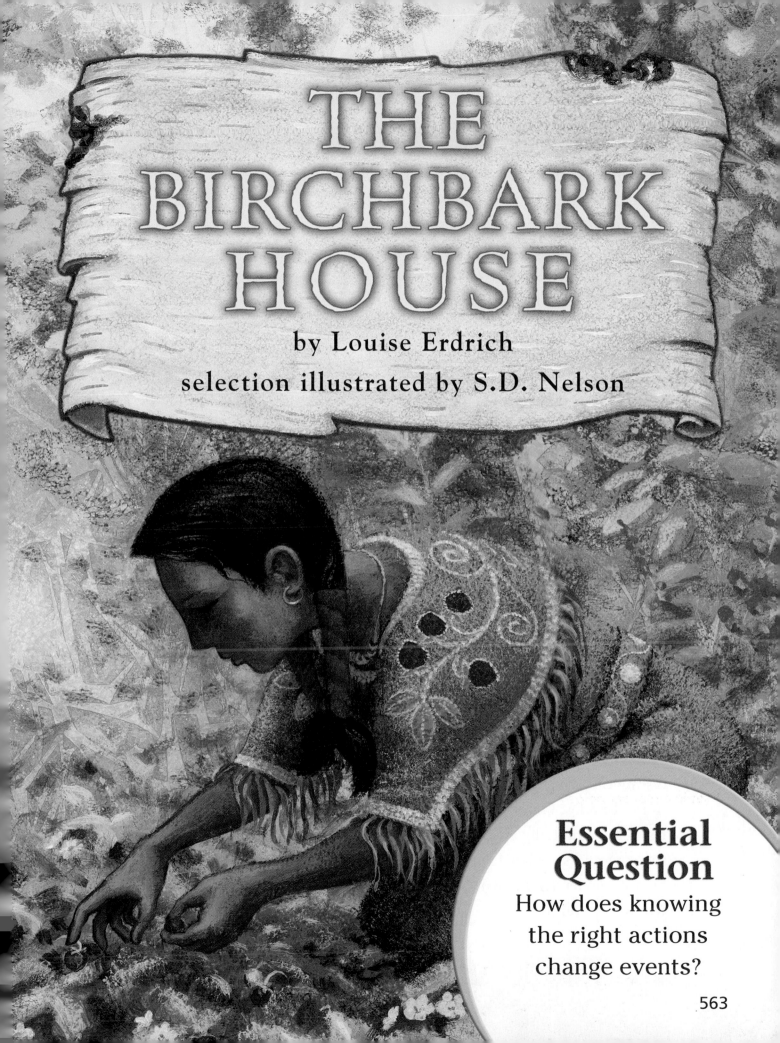

THE BIRCHBARK HOUSE

by Louise Erdrich

selection illustrated by S.D. Nelson

Essential Question

How does knowing the right actions change events?

Omakayas (oh MAHK ay ahs) is returning home from an errand. She carries scissors for her mother and a lump of sweet maple candy for herself. Both the scissors and the candy are rare and valued items in her Ojibwe village in 1847. She is not eager to return home to the chore of tanning a moose hide and to her older sister, Angeline, who made fun of her earlier in the day. Her feelings are hurt, and she wants nothing but to be respected by Angeline.

Before she went back on the trail, Omakayas rinsed off the old candy lump in the lake. It came out beautifully, creamy-golden, translucent and grainy-dark. And sweet. She started walking, her treasure now wrapped in a leaf. As she walked, Omakayas thought. There was no way to share such a tough nut of sweetness. How would she divide it? Omakayas decided she did not want to cause trouble at home. Furthermore, it suddenly made sense to her that at least one person in the family should get the full effect of the maple sugar. She would pop the whole thing into her mouth. All at once! This would save problems. Aaaaah. The lump was delicious, tasting of spring sweetness and the inside of trees. Besides, Omakayas reasoned, as she walked contentedly along, the taste of the sugar would save her from eating every one of the berries she was sure she would find on the path.

Omakayas's feet moved slower and even slower yet. For one thing, the moose hide waited. For another, she was still angry with her older sister, and didn't want to see Angeline. She could still feel that sister foot pressing hateful on her back. If only there were some way to impress Angeline, cause her envy, make her say, "Can I have some of those berries, please, please, please?" You can be sure, Omakayas thought, her face taking on a faraway, haughty expression, she would be slow in answering! Yet the worst of it was this: her sister was usually on her side, helping her plan tricks on the other children in the village or gathering new ferns or snaring rabbits, visiting the grave houses looking for sugar or food left for the spirits, tossing off her clothes to swim with her. And to have her older sister laugh at her hurt Omakayas so much inside that she both wanted Angeline to smile in surprise, to be proud, to envy her, and to feel rotten and be sorry forever. So Omakayas took the slow way back looking for odaemin (oh DAY mihn), little red heartberries, in the sunny margins of the woods near the ground.

She carefully removed the hard lump of sweetness from her mouth, stuck it back in its leaf just inside the pocket of her dress. Just as the taste of maple sugar faded along her tongue, she bent over, pushed back delicate leaves, and found masses of plump red little berries. Ah! One, two, three. She'd eaten a huge handful. Another. She grinned, thinking that she'd allow her sister to return with her to plunder them, but only if Angeline changed her ways.

STOP AND THINK

Theme How might Omakayas's feelings about her sister have affected her decision not to share the maple candy?

All of a sudden, a rustle and then a thump in a bush ahead made Omakayas freeze. A long moment passed as she stared through the dark leaves. Suddenly, *crash!* Two bear cubs burst from the bush and rushed pell-mell, tumbling head over heels straight for her. They came on in such a hurry that they didn't see Omakayas until they were nearly in her lap, and then, with comical looks of shock, they tried to stop themselves. One flew flat on its face, bumping its nose and squealing. The other twisted in midair and landed in a heap on the ground, shaking its head in confusion at Omakayas.

The bear boys looked at her. Slowly, she put out her open hand filled with heartberries. Curious, the cubs jumped forward, lost their nerve. They scampered backward, and then crept forward shyly again. The smaller cub seemed slightly bolder and sniffed at Omakayas's hand.

The bear cub took one berry, then jumped away in seeming fright at its own bold act. But the taste of the berry seemed to banish fear. The two now tumbled at her, growling, mock-ferocious. Their long pink tongues touched up every berry from her hands, eagerly flicking them from her fingers as fast as she could pick. They seemed to like the game. It could have gone on for hours, that is, until she stood upright. Then they tumbled backward in alarm. Their chubby bottoms rolled them over like playing balls, and she laughed out loud. She realized they had thought Omakayas was their own size. They were astonished the same way Omakayas had been the first time she saw the trader Cadotte unfold a seeing glass, something he called a telescope, a long shiny tube that grew in his hands.

She bent down again.

"Ahneen, little brothers," she said to them kindly, and they came forward.

She looked around. No mother bear. Omakayas was well aware that she shouldn't stay so close to these cubs, but after all, they seemed deserted. She looked around again. They were orphans! Perhaps the mother bear's skin was now draped across old Tallow's bed, although she hadn't heard about a recent kill. But still, no mother bear in sight. And these little ones so hungry. Wouldn't her big sister be thrilled when Omakayas returned with these two new brothers! Eagerly, Omakayas began to plan out her triumphant walk back to the house. She would enter the little clearing with the cubs, one at her heels and one before her. Everyone would make way, impressed. She would lead the bear cubs around the fire four times before she presented one of them to Angeline, who would look at her with new respect.

There was no warning. One moment Omakayas was wiggling a leafy stick, making it move on the ground so the cubs would jump on it, biting fiercely. Then next moment, she found herself flipped over on her back and pinned underneath a huge, powerful, heavy thing that sent down a horrible stink. It was the sow bear, the mother. Breathing on her a stale breath of decayed old deer-hides and skunk cabbages and dead mushrooms. Owah! The surprising thing was, Omakayas realized later, that although she had no memory of doing so, she had the scissors out of their case and open, the sharp ends pointing at the bear's heart. But she didn't use them as a knife. She knew for certain that *she should not move*. If the bear began to bite and claw, she would have to plunge the tip of the scissors straight in between the bear's strong ribs, use all of her strength, sink the blade all the way in to the rounded hilt and then jump clear, if she could, while the bear went through its death agony. If she couldn't get clear, Omakayas knew she would have to roll up in a ball and endure the bear's fury. She would probably be clawed from head to foot, bitten to pieces, scattered all over the ground.

Until the mother bear made the first move, Omakayas knew she should stay still, or as still as possible, given the terrified jumping of her heart.

STOP AND THINK

Infer/Predict Why do you think the bear attacks Omakayas? Use what you know about bears from your own knowledge and from the selection to understand the bear's behavior.

569

For long moments, the bear tested her with every sense, staring down with her weak eyes, listening, and most of all smelling her. The bear smelled the morning's moose meat stew Omakayas had eaten, the wild onion seasoning and the dusty bit of maple sugar from old Tallow stuck to the inside of her pocket. How she hoped the bear did not smell the bear-killing dogs or the bear claw that swung on a silver hoop from Old Tallow's earlobe. Perhaps the bear smelled the kind touch of Grandma and Mama's bone-and-sprucewood comb, her baby brother's cuddling body, the skins and mats she had slept in, and Little Pinch, who had whined and sobbed the night before. The bear smelled on Omakayas's skin the smell of its own cousin's bear grease used to ward off mosquitoes. Fish from the night before last night. The berries she was eating. The bear smelled all.

Omakayas couldn't help but smell her back. Bears eat anything and this one had just eaten something ancient and foul. Hiyn! (HY n) Omakayas took shallow breaths. Perhaps it was to take her mind off the scent of dead things on the bear's breath that she accidentally closed the scissors, shearing off a tiny clip of bear fur, and then to cover her horror at this mistake, started to talk.

> **STOP AND THINK**
>
> **Author's Craft** Authors use **sensory details** that make readers feel what is happening in a story. Which details of the bear encounter make you feel Omakayas's fear?

"Nokomis," she said to the bear, calling her grandmother. "I didn't mean any harm. I was only playing with your children. Gaween onjidah (gah WEEN ohn jee dah). Please forgive me."

The bear cuffed at Omakayas, but in a warning manner, not savagely, to hurt. Then the bear leaned back, nose working, as though she could scent the meaning of the human words. Encouraged, Omakayas continued.

"I fed them some berries. I wanted to bring them home, to adopt them, have them live with me at my house as my little brothers. But now that you're here, Grandmother, I will leave quietly. These scissors in my hands are not for killing, just for sewing. They are nothing compared to your teeth and claws."

And indeed, Omakayas's voice trembled slightly as the bear made a gurgling sound deep in her throat and bared her long, curved yellowish teeth, so good at ripping and tearing. But having totaled up all of the smells and sifted them for information, the bear seemed to have decided that Omakayas was no threat. She sat back on her haunches like a huge dog. Swinging her head around, she gave a short, quick slap at one of the cubs that sent it reeling away from Omakayas. It was as though she were telling them they had done wrong to approach this human animal, and should now stay away from her. Omakayas's heart squeezed painfully. Even though it was clear her life was to be spared, she felt the loss of her new brothers.

"I wouldn't ever hurt them," she said again.

The little cubs piled against their mother, clung to her. For a long moment the great bear sat calmly with them, deciding where to go. Then, in no hurry, they rose in one piece of dark fur. One bear boy broke away, again tried to get near Omakayas. The other looked longingly at her, but the big bear mother abruptly nosed them down the trail.

Your Turn

Beware of Bears

Short Response Omakayas knows that she should not get close to the bear cubs in the woods. However, she goes against her better judgment, feeding and playing with the cubs. Think about real-life wild animal encounters you have heard or read about. Then write a paragraph explaining whether you would have handled the situation differently and why.

PERSONAL RESPONSE

Sibling Rivalry

Predict a Reaction Do you think Omakayas will gain Angeline's respect when she tells her about what happened in the woods? Use story details to predict Angeline's reaction to Omakayas's story. Then work with a partner to write a script for a conversation in which the two sisters discuss Omakayas's bear encounter. Choose roles. Rehearse your conversation, and perform it for the class. PARTNERS

Knowing the Right Actions

Turn and Talk When Omakayas finds herself pinned under the huge, powerful mother bear, she is able to stay calm. Discuss with a partner how Omakayas's respect for and knowledge of wild animals seems to help her escape harm. Then discuss how this scene reinforces the story's theme. THEME

Four Seasons of Food

by Joyce Mallery

Think about what your life would be like if you had to grow and find everything that you ate. That is exactly what the Ojibwe people did for centuries.

Between 1817 and 1854, most Ojibwe moved to, or were forced to move to, reservations. Before that, they lived in an area extending from the shores of the Great Lakes to the plains of North Dakota. The Ojibwe who lived along the margins of the Great Lakes gathered wild rice, made maple syrup, and hunted game to eat. However, the seasons of the year dictated what they hunted and gathered.

Spring The Ojibwe gathered roots and ate plants such as leeks and fiddleheads. By late spring, they began tapping maple trees. The sap was boiled to make sugar, syrup, and candy.

Summer The Ojibwe gathered berries and grew vegetables such as squash and beans. The women and girls began storing food for the winter. They reasoned that they would need extra food in the cold months ahead.

Fall The Ojibwe harvested wild rice from nearby lakes. Typically, the men steered a canoe through the upright reeds. Then the women knocked the grains of rice from the plants into the canoe.

An Ojibwe woman collects maple sap from a tapped tree.

An Ojibwe woman uses one long stick to bend the rice plants and the other stick to knock the grains into the canoe.

Making Ojibwe Wild Rice Breakfast

This recipe combines several traditional Ojibwe ingredients. You will be astonished by how good this sweet and nutty breakfast dish tastes.

Ingredients:

Wild rice

Raisins, blueberries, or raspberries

Maple syrup

Milk (optional)

Directions:

Ask an adult to cook the rice.

Add the fruit and maple syrup to the rice.

Add milk if you want.

NOTE: If you want to eat the dish cold, cook the rice the night before.

Make enough for everyone. Anyone left out will surely feel envy when they see you eating this delicious treat.

• Reread the recipe for Ojibwe Wild Rice Breakfast. Do you think you must include milk? Why or why not?

Winter Summer camps were deserted in winter. New hunting spots were sought. Imagine the nerve that men needed to hunt deer and moose with just a bow and arrows. A hunter had to banish fear if a wolf bared its teeth and attacked. His life depended on it.

Almost no part of an animal was spared. The women dried the meat, made clothes from hides, and made tools from bones.

All parts of an animal hunted for food were used. Here, an Ojibwe woman scrapes a hide, preparing it to be made into clothing.

Making Connections

 Text to Self

Imagine the Past If you lived in an Ojibwe village in the 1800s, what modern conveniences would you miss the most? What aspects of life during that time would appeal to you? Explain your ideas in a short essay.

 Text to Text

Compare Themes "The Birchbark House" and "Storm Warriors," from Lesson 9, both describe encounters that people have with nature. With a partner, review "Storm Warriors" and use details from both selections to compare and contrast the themes. What lessons about people's relationship to nature do you think readers learn from the two selections?

 Text to World

Compare the Media Message The photo essay "Four Seasons of Food" gives facts and examples showing what life was like for the Ojibwe, who grew or gathered their food. Imagine a documentary film on the same topic. Compare how the photo essay and the documentary film would use words, images, graphics, or sound differently to present their message.

Grammar

What Are the Perfect Tenses? You have already learned the simple verb tenses: past, present, and future. English has another group of tenses called the **perfect tenses.** All perfect-tense verbs include *has, have,* or *had* as a helping verb. A verb in the **past perfect tense** includes *had* as a helping verb. A verb in the **present perfect tense** includes *has* or *have* as a helping verb. A verb in the **future perfect tense** includes *will have* as a helping verb.

Academic Language

perfect tenses
past perfect tense
present perfect tense
future perfect tense

Sentence	Tense of Verb
Two bears have tumbled into the berry patch.	present perfect tense
Omakayas had picked some berries minutes earlier.	past perfect tense
Soon the mother bear will have found her cubs.	future perfect tense

Try This! **Copy these sentences onto a sheet of paper. Circle each verb. Then label the verbs as present perfect, past perfect, or future perfect tense.**

1. Now the mother bear has captured Omakayas.

2. That huge, smelly bear had surprised Omakayas.

3. Apparently the bear had eaten something foul earlier.

4. Omakayas has kept calm somehow.

5. In a few minutes the mother bear and her cubs will have left the area.

Conventions You know that regular verbs add *-ed* when used with *has*, *have*, or *had*. You must add a special ending to irregular verbs used with *has*, *have*, or *had*. Use the correct forms of regular and irregular verbs when you write sentences in the perfect tenses.

Incorrect	Correct
A baby bear has ate some berries.	A baby bear has eaten some berries.
Omakayas had share them with the cub.	Omakayas had shared them with the cub.
By tonight, Omakayas will have telled her story many times.	By tonight, Omakayas will have told her story many times.

Connect Grammar to Writing

As you revise your paragraphs, look for incorrect verb forms in perfect-tense verbs. Correct these errors so that your writing makes sense.

Write to Inform

✔ **Ideas** The author of "The Birchbark House" reveals characters through their thoughts and actions. The bear cubs "crept forward shyly." Omakayas spoke to them "kindly." You can use details like these to compare and contrast characters.

Carleasa drafted some **compare-contrast paragraphs** to explain how Omakayas and Angeline are alike and different. Later, she added specific details to support her ideas. Use the Writing Traits Checklist below as you revise your writing.

Writing Traits Checklist

✔ **Ideas**
> Did I explain how the characters are alike and different?

✔ **Organization**
Did I support my ideas with specific examples?

✔ **Sentence Fluency**
Did I use verbs and verb phrases effectively?

✔ **Word Choice**
Did I use vivid expressions and details?

✔ **Voice**
Is my writing clear and informative?

✔ **Conventions**
Did I use correct spelling, grammar, and punctuation?

Revised Draft

In "The Birchbark House," Omakayas is upset because Angeline her older sister has made fun of her. Usually Angeline is on Omakayas's side. She helps her plan tricks on other children. ~~She helps her~~ gather new ferns and ~~She helps her~~ snare rabbits. The sisters do many things together.

She even helps her visit grave houses to steal food left for the spirits.

Omakayas and Angeline
by Carleasa Dutton

In "The Birchbark House," Omakayas is upset because her older sister Angeline has made fun of her. Usually Angeline is on Omakayas's side. She helps her plan tricks on other children, gather new ferns, and snare rabbits. She even helps her visit grave houses to steal food left for the spirits. The sisters do many things together.

The biggest difference between the sisters is their age. Omakayas desperately wants her older sister's respect, but Angeline doesn't worry about impressing Omakayas. When Omakayas meets the bear cubs, she imagines how she could use the cubs to impress Angeline. Omakayas wishes she could make Angeline envy her and also feel sorry for making fun of her. That's the way a young girl feels when an older sister puts her down.

> In my final paper, I added specific examples to support my ideas. I also combined sentences and used a perfect-tense verb.

Reading as a Writer

Which examples made the sisters' similarities and differences clear? Where in your writing can you make similarities and differences clearer?

dominated

extending

sprawling

hostile

acknowledged

flourished

residents

prospered

acquainted

decline

Vocabulary Reader

Context Cards

Vocabulary in Context

1 **dominated**
Herds of cattle once dominated the plains. They were often the biggest thing in sight.

2 **extending**
This cowgirl wears chaps extending, or reaching, from the hips to the ankles.

3 **sprawling**
This cowboy rides his horse over the vast and sprawling range.

4 **hostile**
A farmer who is hostile, or unfriendly, to cattle ranchers can use fences to stop cattle drives.

- **Study each Context Card.**
- **Use a dictionary or a glossary to verify the meaning of each Vocabulary word.**

5 acknowledged

This rodeo cowboy acknowledged, or recognized, his fans with a smile.

6 flourished

Cattle were driven to towns near rail lines. These towns flourished and grew rich.

7 residents

When cowboys were not living on the trail, they were residents in the ranch bunkhouse.

8 prospered

A cowboy who has prospered, or succeeded, may buy fancy boots and a hat.

9 acquainted

Cowboys get to know one another on cattle drives. They become well acquainted.

10 decline

Because there has been a decline in cattle drives, there are fewer cowboys today.

Background

✓ TARGET VOCABULARY **The Spanish West** For centuries Spain dominated many parts of the West. California, Texas, and other regions were part of Spanish territory extending south through Mexico. Spanish explorers were acquainted with the California coast as early as 1542. Starting in 1769, Spanish priests built missions on sprawling tracts of this land. Fearing that the region's native residents were hostile, the Spanish enslaved them. When the missionaries left in the early 1800s, missions prospered as private cattle ranches.

Then Spanish power began a decline. In 1821, Mexico became independent from Spain. In 1836, Texas, a part of Mexico at the time, declared its independence. Texas, which was then acknowledged as a republic, joined the U.S. in 1845. In 1848, after the Mexican-American War, Mexico gave up territory that became California, Arizona, and other states. The Spanish influence has flourished in these areas up to the present.

- Examine the map below. Use the scale to determine the distance between the northernmost point of New Spain and the southernmost point.

New Spain Before 1821

NORTH AMERICA

ATLANTIC OCEAN

PACIFIC OCEAN

San Diego • Santa Fe

El Paso •

St. Augustine

San Antonio •

Gulf of Mexico

Mexico City •

LEGEND
New Spain
Present-day border

km 0   300   600
mi 0   300   600

Spain held vast territory in the New World before 1821 (see map above). Mission Santa Barbara (right), founded in 1786, is one of 21 missions established between 1769 and 1823.

584

Comprehension

✔ **TARGET SKILL** **Main Ideas and Details**

As you read "Vaqueros: America's First Cowboys," look for the author's main ideas about the vaqueros and their way of life. Find details that support each main idea. Remember that a text can have more than one main idea. Use a graphic organizer like the one below to keep track of each main idea and its supporting details in the selection.

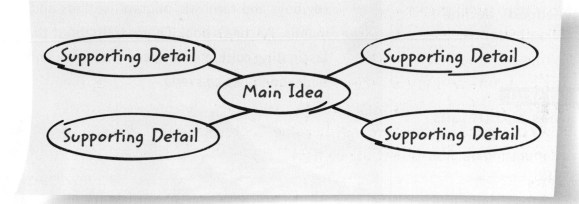

✔ **TARGET STRATEGY** **Summarize**

Use your graphic organizer to help you summarize and paraphrase "Vaqueros: America's First Cowboys." Summarizing is briefly restating the main ideas. Paraphrasing is retelling an author's ideas in your own words. Summarizing and paraphrasing will help you better understand and remember what you read.

VAQUEROS

dominated	flourished
extending	residents
sprawling	prospered
hostile	acquainted
acknowledged	decline

✓ **TARGET SKILL**

Main Ideas and Details
Identify the topic's important ideas and supporting details.

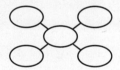

✓ **TARGET STRATEGY**

Summarize Briefly tell the important parts of the text in your own words.

GENRE

Informational Text gives facts and examples about a topic.

Set a Purpose Set a purpose for reading based on genre and your background knowledge.

MEET THE AUTHOR AND PHOTOGRAPHER

George Ancona

George Ancona grew up in Coney Island, New York, where his father practiced photography as a hobby. Ancona says that "as a photographer, I can participate in other people's lives…producing something that can be shared and has a life of its own." He has created books about horses and helicopters, cowboys and carnivals, migrant workers and murals. Ancona's book *Charro* tells about the fascinating culture of Mexican horsemen and their rodeo-like *charrería*.

VAQUEROS

America's First Cowboys

by George Ancona

Essential Question

Which ideas about vaqueros show how America changed?

Imagine: five hundred years ago there were no cows or horses in North and South America. Thousands of years earlier there had been horses, but they disappeared. Since there were no cows, there were no cowboys. Of course, today there are cowboys. It is all because of Christopher Columbus.

The Journeys

After his voyage to the Americas in 1492, Christopher Columbus returned to Spain. He told the Spanish king and queen of the riches to be found in the paradise he discovered. He described the native people who lived there. The royal couple agreed to more voyages. They needed gold to help pay for their expanding empire.

The following year, Columbus returned to the West Indies. He brought seventeen ships loaded with over a thousand settlers, horses and cattle. The ships dropped anchor at an island they named Hispaniola (ees pah NYOH lah). Today the island is shared by Haiti and the Dominican Republic.

For the next twenty-five years Spanish ships sailed in and out of Hispaniola. The Spaniards explored and conquered the nearby islands. The native islanders were enslaved. Thousands died of smallpox, a terrible disease for which they had no resistance. As the islanders disappeared, they were replaced by the settlers and their animals.

Christopher Columbus landing on the island of Hispaniola, 1493

Hernán Cortés brought horses back to the mainland of North America.

In 1503, Hernán Cortés (ayr NAHN kor TEHS), a Spanish adventurer, arrived in the West Indies. He spent several years helping to conquer Cuba. Then in 1518, Cortés set out with a fleet of six ships to explore the nearby coast to the west. On board were five hundred men and sixteen horses strong enough to carry a man in full armor.

The ships dropped anchor near where the port of Veracruz, Mexico, is today. The Totonac people who lived there welcomed Cortés. They offered to help him conquer the hostile Aztec empire that had long dominated them. Cortés did so in two years. He claimed all the lands in the name of the Spanish king. He called the land New Spain.

It wasn't long before the Spanish conquerors brought more livestock to the colonies. The animals were allowed to graze on the open grasslands. Many took off into the wilderness, forming large herds of wild horses and cattle.

 **STOP AND THINK**

Main Ideas and Details Summarize this section of the text. What is the main idea? How do the details the author includes about Columbus and Cortés support the main idea?

589

The Expanding Colony

The Spanish king rewarded Cortés and his soldiers with gifts of land. Throughout New Spain they built ranches called *haciendas* (ah SYEHN dahs) and prospered.

Accompanying the soldiers and settlers were Catholic missionaries. They had come to convert the native people. They moved north, building missions and churches along the California coast, extending the lands of New Spain.

In 1540, Francisco Vázquez de Coronado (VAHS kehs day koh roh NAH doh) organized an expedition into the northern territories. Coronado was searching for the legendary Golden Cities of Cíbola (SEE boh lah). Along with the men and supplies he brought five hundred longhorn cattle to supply meat and hides.

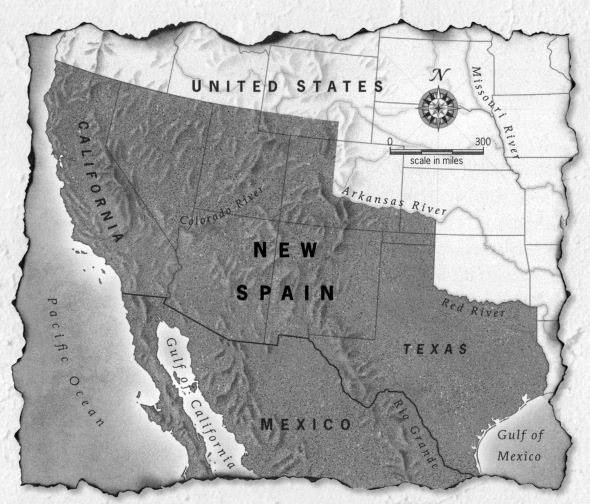

Review the map. What water sources run through the area known as New Spain?

An early vaquero lassoes a steer.

The expedition never found the city of gold. However, it did introduce the first longhorns to what is now the American Southwest. From those first five hundred longhorns, ten million had spread across the Texas plains by the 1800s.

The soldiers and priests of New Spain were already acquainted with raising cattle in Spain. Many were skilled horsemen. Even so, they needed help in rounding up the livestock on their sprawling lands.

At that time it was against the law for any native person to ride a horse. But the ranchers and priests needed help. They taught the native converts to ride and use the *lazo* (LAH soh), or lasso, a looped rope. These men who worked with horses and cattle were called *vaqueros* (vah KAY rohs). In Spanish, the word means "cow-men." With the vaqueros, a new culture took root in the west. It lives on today.

Coronado introduced the longhorn.

A herd of mustangs

A Way of Life

The vaquero's job was to keep tabs on cattle in the wild and round them up. It took many vaqueros to surround a herd so that it could be moved to the hacienda. These roundups are called *rodeos* (roh DEH ohs) in Spanish. Rodeo comes from a verb that means "to go around."

The vaqueros were also needed to capture the wild horses that flourished on the prairies and valleys of the large haciendas. The vaqueros called the horses *mesteños* (mehs TAY nyohs), a word that would become "mustangs."

Vaqueros spent most of their lives in the saddle, riding hard, in all kinds of weather. At night they sat around the fire where they cooked their meals. They told stories and sang songs about their lives. Then they rolled up into their ponchos to sleep. From California to Texas, native vaqueros were acknowledged to be the best horsemen in the world.

An early vaquero with his lariat

Doing the Job

A vaquero had to cope with a rough landscape and harsh weather. He needed the right tools to do his job.

Vaqueros wore wide-brimmed hats called *sombreros* (sohm BRAY rohs). *Sombra* (SOHM brah) means "shade" in Spanish. The sombrero protected vaqueros from the burning sun.

A vaquero also wore *chaparreras* (chah pah REH rahs) or chaps. These were leather leggings, worn over trousers. They protected the vaquero from cactus, thickets of wild brush, and rope burns.

A modern saddle

The horses belonged to the owner of the hacienda. The vaquero, however, owned the saddle that he put on the horse. The saddle had to be comfortable for both horse and rider. The vaquero's feet slid into two wooden stirrups that hung from the saddle.

A vaquero's most trusted tool was his lasso, also known as the lariat. Often a vaquero would have to gallop after a runaway steer. He would toss the loop of the lariat around the steer's horns, neck, or foot. Then he would wrap the rope around his saddle horn and rein in his horse. This would hold the steer or bring it to the ground.

Once the herds were together they calmed down and began to graze. Mounted vaqueros would separate the calves from their mothers to brand them with the hacienda's mark.

The Vaquero Legend

In 1821 Mexico won its war of independence from Spain. All of New Spain became the independent nation of Mexico. The northern lands of Mexico, however, were difficult to govern. Many American immigrants crossed into the territory that would one day become Texas. Soon there was a large population of Americans in Texas. In fact, they outnumbered the Mexican residents who lived there for generations.

With the Americans came changes in the culture of the vaquero. Even the word changed. When the Americans tried to say *vaqueros* it came out "bukera." Later the word became *buckaroo*. It was only after 1860 that men who worked with cattle were called cowboys.

Cowboys continued the culture of the vaquero.

In 1836 Texas declared itself independent from Mexico. Nine years later it joined the United States. Then, in 1847, Mexico lost a war with the U.S. As a result, it lost its northern lands. They would become the states of California, Nevada, Utah and parts of Arizona, New Mexico, Colorado and Wyoming.

After the end of the Civil War, the vaqueros were joined by freed slaves and young men from the east. These newcomers wanted a new life in the wide-open spaces. They had to learn what the vaqueros had been doing for centuries.

The large ranches needed many men to manage the huge herds of cattle on the vast prairies. Cattle drives would take weeks to travel from ranches to railroads. From there, the cattle traveled to the markets in eastern and western cities.

The invention of barbed wire made it possible to build fences to keep cattle in pastures. The vaquero was not needed to ride the wide-open spaces. Long cattle drives became unnecessary. The decline of the vaquero began.

Yet the vaquero's traditions did not fade from the American imagination. At the turn of the century the cowboy became the hero of the west. Books, magazine stories, and the early movies featured the brave exploits of the American cowboy.

HIS FIRST TALKING PICTURE!

CARL LAEMMLE presents Tom MIX AND HIS WONDER HORSE "TONY" in "DESTRY RIDES AGAIN"

with CLAUDIA DELL, ZASU PITTS, ANDY DEVINE, EARLE FOXE, FRANCIS FORD, STANLEY FIELDS.

Cowboy movies were among the first movies made.

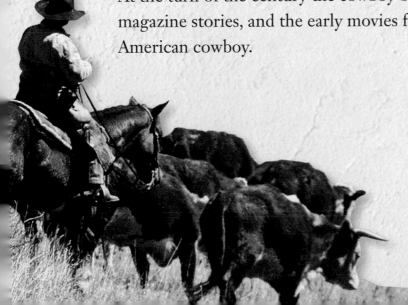

STOP AND THINK
Summarize Summarize the information on these two pages. Then paraphrase what caused the culture of the vaquero to change.

Celebrating Traditions

Today the arts and skills of the vaquero can be seen in two countries. They appear in the *charrerías* (chah ray REE ahs) of Mexico and the rodeos of the United States. Both vaqueros and cowboys pride themselves in their skills. They keep alive the traditions and cultures of their past.

On September 14th, Mexicans celebrate *El dia del charro*. It is a holiday of parades, church services, music and *charrerías*. The charrería is a rodeo where vaqueros can exhibit their skills. They perform with *charros* (CHAH rohs) and *charras* (CHAH rahs), gentlemen and women riders. The men dress in their elegant silver-buttoned outfits and large sombreros. The women wear the traditional dress of the *China Poblana* (CHEE nah poh BLAH nah).

Many of the events performed in rodeos and charrerías are similar. Both may include riding a bucking horse or bull and getting thrown off, for example. But like the first vaqueros, the riders are ready. There is an old saying in the corrals. It goes: "There's never been a horse that can't be rode. There's never been a cowman who hasn't been throwed."

The grammar may not be right, but the idea is pure cowboy.

STOP AND THINK

Author's Craft The author uses an **adage**, or a traditional saying, in the third paragraph on this page. Why do you think he chooses to end the selection in this way? What do you think the author means when he says "the idea is pure cowboy"?

A horse rears, throwing its rodeo rider.

Your Turn

Cowboy Culture

Short Response Even though the need for vaqueros declined as ranchers built fences for cattle pastures, interest in their skills and traditions remains strong. Write a paragraph explaining why you think vaqueros are still so popular today. Include details from "Vaqueros: America's First Cowboys" to support your conclusions. PERSONAL RESPONSE

Cowboys at Work

Design a Tool Vaqueros needed special equipment and clothing to do their jobs on the range. Work with a small group to brainstorm another device that vaqueros might have found useful. Create a drawing or diagram of your invention that shows how it works or how its parts go together. Label the invention, and write a caption that explains how it would be used. SMALL GROUP

All Things Change

Turn and Talk Vaqueros, trained by mission ranchers to round up cattle on their land, established a new culture in the West. With a partner, discuss how the lives of the vaqueros changed over time, and explain what these details reveal about how America was changing. MAIN IDEAS AND DETAILS

✓ TARGET VOCABULARY

dominated	flourished
extending	residents
sprawling	prospered
hostile	acquainted
acknowledged	decline

GENRE

Poetry uses the sound and rhythm of words in a variety of forms to suggest images and express feelings.

TEXT FOCUS

Imagery Poets create vivid descriptions in their poems by using words and phrases that appeal to the senses.

• In "The Cowboy's Life" on page 598, how does the poet's use of vivid sound words help you better relate to the life of a cowboy?

RHYME ON THE RANGE

Cowboy poetry flourished in the 1800s when ranches and farms dominated the American West. These poems, which were sometimes sung, cover subjects like the sprawling landscape, hostile weather, and the loneliness of cowboy life.

The Cowboy's Life

Poet unknown, from *Songs of the Cowboys*

The bawl of a steer
To a cowboy's ear
Is music of sweetest strain;
And the yelping notes
Of the gray coyotes
To *him* are a glad refrain.

For a kingly crown
In the noisy town
His saddle he wouldn't change;
No life so free
As the life we see
Way out on the Yaso range.

The winds may blow
And the thunder growl
Or the breeze may safely moan;
A cowboy's life
Is a royal life,
His saddle his kingly throne.

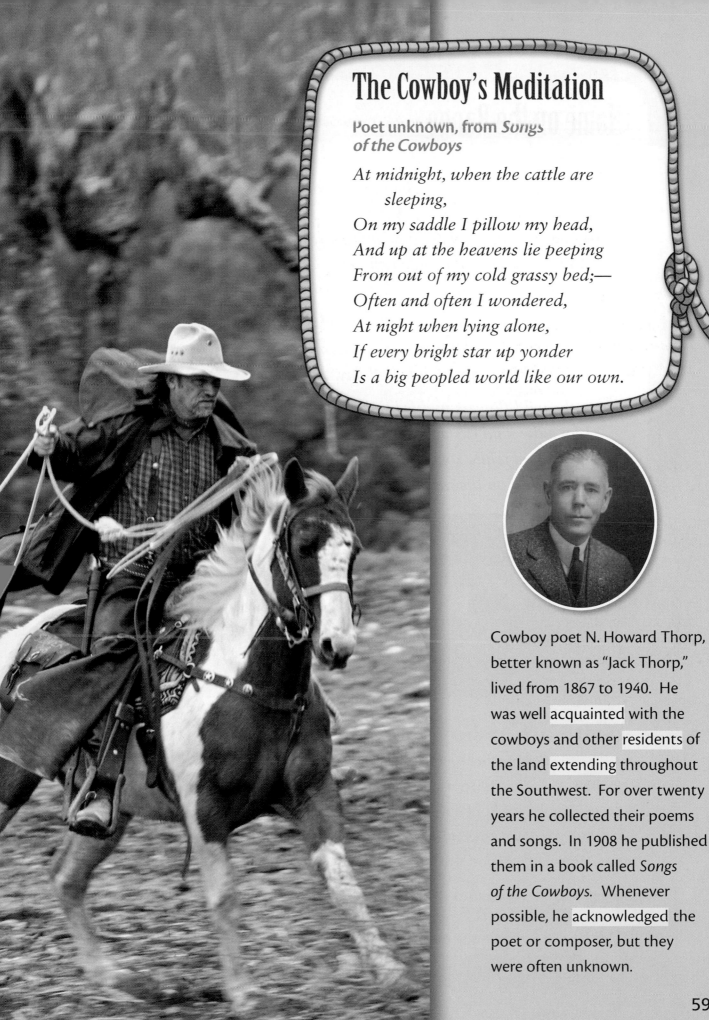

The Cowboy's Meditation

Poet unknown, from *Songs of the Cowboys*

At midnight, when the cattle are
   sleeping,
On my saddle I pillow my head,
And up at the heavens lie peeping
From out of my cold grassy bed;—
Often and often I wondered,
At night when lying alone,
If every bright star up yonder
Is a big peopled world like our own.

Cowboy poet N. Howard Thorp, better known as "Jack Thorp," lived from 1867 to 1940. He was well acquainted with the cowboys and other residents of the land extending throughout the Southwest. For over twenty years he collected their poems and songs. In 1908 he published them in a book called *Songs of the Cowboys*. Whenever possible, he acknowledged the poet or composer, but they were often unknown.

Home on the Range

by Brewster Higley

Oh, give me a home where the Buffalo roam
    Where the Deer and the Antelope play;
Where never is heard a discouraging word,
    And the sky is not clouded all day.

Home, home on the Range
    Where the Deer and the Antelope play,
Where never is heard a discouraging word,
    And the sky is not clouded all day.

I love the wild flowers in this bright land of ours,
    I love the wild curlew's shrill scream;
The bluffs and white rocks, and antelope flocks
    That graze on the mountains so green.

Write a Cowboy Poem

The cowboy lifestyle eventually went into a decline, but cowboy poetry has still prospered. Today, Cowboy Poetry Week is celebrated every April during National Poetry Month.

Write your own cowboy poem or song. Review the poets' uses of imagery. As you write, try to use imagery in similar ways.

Making Connections

Text to Self

Imagine Being a Vaquero Would you have enjoyed being a cowboy or cowgirl in the 1800s? What aspects of life during that time would you have liked or disliked? Explain your ideas in a short composition. Support your opinions with facts and details from "Vaqueros: America's First Cowboys."

Text to Text

Compare Poems Each of the poems in "Rhyme on the Range" uses sound effects such as alliteration, onomatopoeia, or rhyme. Choose two of the poems and compare the sound effects used. How do the sound effects support the meanings of the poems? How do they affect your enjoyment of the poems? Discuss your responses with a partner.

Text to World

Connect to Social Studies "Vaqueros: America's First Cowboys" gives some information about cattle ranching. Work with a partner to research the impact that cattle ranching had on the history of the western United States. Discuss the effects cattle ranching had on western settlers, the environment, and the land. Include details from the selection or from other research sources. Practice presenting a brief report with your partner.

Grammar

What Are Transitions? **Transitions** connect sentences and ideas, and help readers make sense of what they read. Some **transition words**, such as *first*, *next*, *then*, *later*, and *finally*, can indicate time order in a sequence of events. Others, such as *also*, can link two things that happen at the same time. The transition *therefore* and **transitional phrases** such as *to sum up* and *as a result* can begin the conclusion of an article, speech, or essay.

Academic Language

transitions
transition words
transitional phrases

Transition Words and Phrases

After Mexico won its independence in 1821, many American immigrants settled in its northern lands. Mexican forces battled the legions of settlers, but in time, the settlers won independence for themselves. They then declared their lands to be the Republic of Texas. Later, in 1845, Texas joined the United States, and the United States and Mexico went to war. Once again, Mexico lost. As a result, the United States gained land that would become the states of California, Nevada, and Utah, and parts of Arizona, New Mexico, Colorado, and Wyoming.

Turn and Talk **Work with a partner. Identify the transitions in the sentences below. Tell which ones indicate time order and which one indicates a conclusion.**

1. First, cattle had to be rounded up by vaqueros.

2. Next, the vaqueros drove the cattle north to a railroad town.

3. Then, the cattle were loaded into railroad cars.

4. After that, the cattle were brought to cities.

5. To sum up, bringing cattle from the open range to the city dweller's table was a long process.

Ideas You can use transitions in your own writing to make clear the connections between ideas. You also can use transitions to clarify the order in which events happen.

Unclear	Clear
Changes came to the Plains. Long cattle drives were no longer necessary. The open-range vaquero was out of a job. Railroads extended their tracks into cattle country. Ranchers began using barbed wire to keep cattle in pastures.	In time, changes came to the Plains. Ranchers began using barbed wire to keep cattle in pastures. Also, railroads extended their tracks into cattle country. As a result of these developments, roundups and long cattle drives were no longer necessary, and the open-range vaquero was out of a job.

Connect Grammar to Writing

As you draft and revise your writing, look for sentences with related ideas. When you can, use transition words to make the relationships between the ideas clearer.

Write to Inform

Organization The author of "Vaqueros: America's First Cowboys" uses specific facts to explain why cattle ranching in the West changed over time. When you revise your **cause-and-effect paragraph**, make sure your supporting details are specific.

Sara drafted a paragraph on the effects that the discovery of gold at Sutter's Mill had on cattle ranching. Later, she made her supporting details more precise.

Writing Traits Checklist

☑ **Ideas**
Did I support my ideas with details from the text?

☑ **Organization**
Did I make the relationship between causes and effects clear?

☑ **Sentence Fluency**
Did I use transitions effectively in my sentences?

☑ **Word Choice**
Did I use words that signal cause and effect?

☑ **Voice**
Is my writing clear and informative?

☑ **Conventions**
Did I use correct spelling, grammar, and punctuation?

Revised Draft

The first great cattle drives in the American West were a result of the California Gold Rush. After the discovery of gold at Sutter's Mill, ~~many~~ hordes of miners rushed to the gold fields around Sacramento in ~~northern California.~~ ~~The miners were hungry.~~ In order to provide food for the hungry miners in southern California, ranchers began driving their cattle north.

Cattle Drives in California

by Sara Luna

The first great cattle drives in the American West were a result of the California Gold Rush. After the discovery of gold at Sutter's Mill, hordes of miners rushed to the gold fields around Sacramento. In order to provide food for the hungry miners, ranchers in southern California began driving their cattle north. Indian vaqueros herded thousands of cattle through California's rugged, wild country during the 1850s. The end of the Gold Rush brought an end to the California cattle drives. Cattle raising in California began a slow decline as ranches gave way to farms.

In my final paper, I made my supporting details more precise. I also used transitions to connect ideas.

Reading as a Writer

How do precise details make the causes and effects clearer? Where can you add precise details in your cause-and-effect paragraph?

mishap

rustling

lectured

beacon

torment

surged

disadvantage

balked

quaking

fared

Vocabulary
Reader

Context
Cards

Vocabulary in Context

1 mishap

These hikers took a wrong turn by accident. They were lost due to the mishap.

2 rustling

A rustling in nearby brush can worry you. Look for the sound's cause, and stay calm.

3 lectured

This ranger lectured, or explained, about the importance of staying on the trail.

4 beacon

A tall object in the distance can serve as a beacon to guide you to a familiar area.

- **Study each Context Card.**
- **Use a dictionary or a glossary to help you pronounce each Vocabulary word.**

5 torment

This girl suffered torment, or distress, because she couldn't find her homework.

6 surged

After this river surged, or swelled, over its banks, hikers had to find a new trail.

7 disadvantage

Losing the trail was a disadvantage, or handicap, to finding camp before dark.

8 balked

This woman balked, or refused to move, after realizing she was lost.

9 quaking

You may start quaking, or trembling, when you're lost. Your body expresses fear that way.

10 fared

Once he was rescued, this boy slept and ate. He fared, or progressed, better after that.

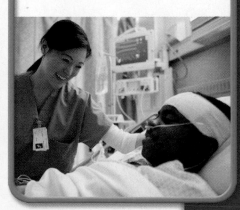

Background

✔ TARGET VOCABULARY **Journals as History** In journals, people record everyday events as well as thoughts that they might have balked at telling others. When these private accounts survive through time, historians use them as a beacon to shine on daily life in the past. The disadvantage of other historical records is they can't show us what life was like for an average person. Reading a boy's journal, we might learn how he fared in school. A farmer might describe his joy at the rustling of corn in his own field. A mother might record the torment of having a sick child. Someone else might quote what a famous man said when he lectured. A survivor of a mishap might note an act of bravery. An account of a river that surged and flooded a town might include descriptions of lost buildings. A pioneer could describe the quaking of the ground during a buffalo stampede. If only these writers were still available to answer our questions!

A journal entry can reveal many details about where and when a writer lived.

Comprehension

✔ **TARGET SKILL** **Cause and Effect**

As you read "Rachel's Journal," look for related events that happen during Rachel's journey. Which events are the results of characters' decisions? Which result from multiple causes? Think about how westward expansion in the 1800s affects the story's theme. Use a graphic organizer like this one to help you identify causes and effects.

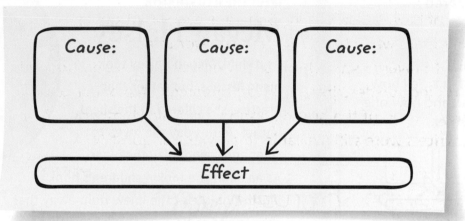

✔ **TARGET STRATEGY** **Analyze/Evaluate**

Use your graphic organizer to analyze the causes and effects in "Rachel's Journal." Ask questions about how causes work together to influence events. Analyzing and evaluating these relationships will give you a deeper understanding of the story.

✔ TARGET VOCABULARY

mishap	surged
rustling	disadvantage
lectured	balked
beacon	quaking
torment	fared

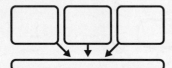
✔ TARGET SKILL

Cause and Effect Tell how events are related and how one event causes another.

✔ TARGET STRATEGY

Analyze/Evaluate Think about the text, ask questions, and form an opinion about it.

GENRE

Historical fiction is a story whose characters and events are set in a real period of history.

Set Purpose Set a purpose for reading based on the genre and your background knowledge.

MEET THE AUTHOR
Marissa Moss

Marissa Moss "always kept a notebook as a girl and loved to read those of others." To try to make Rachel's voice sound real, she relied on her own childhood memories and read "firsthand accounts written by pioneers at this time—mostly women and children."

MEET THE ILLUSTRATOR
Megan Halsey

As a child, Megan Halsey took piano lessons, but rather than practice, she colored in the sheet music! To this day she loves to color and cannot play the piano. As an adult she took a children's book illustration class. She knew right away that she wanted to be a children's book illustrator. Since then, she has illustrated more than forty children's books.

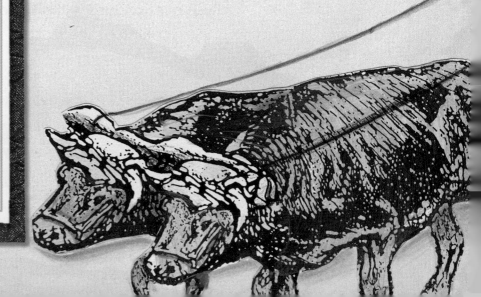

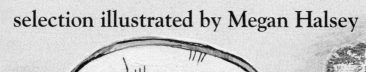

Rachel's Journal

THE STORY OF A PIONEER GIRL

by Marissa Moss

selection illustrated by Megan Halsey

Essential Question

Why does a pioneer traveler record events in a journal?

It has been two months since Rachel's family left Illinois in a wagon train bound for good farmland in California. During the long ride, Rachel spends time with her brothers Ben and Will, as well as Frank and Prudence, children from other families in the wagon train. She writes about their adventures in her journal.

May 10, 1850

Pa says we are taking the Oregon Trail until it splits and we veer south for California. Now we are following the Platte River. The sight of the broad river and the bluffs is restful, but the dust kicked up by all the stock is not. Especially when our wagons are in the rear—then it is so thick, I can barely see past our own teams. But I found a way to escape the heat and dirt of the main road. All along the trail there are narrow cut-off paths. Pa says they were made and used by Indians and hunters. These cut-offs run diagonally to the road and are often by shady creeks, so they are pleasant to walk along. Since they always lead back to the trail, there is no need to fret about getting lost. The boys have to drive the stock, so they have no choice but to eat dust, but I take the younger children with me, and we have great fun, picking berries and wildflowers and wading in the creeks.

May 16, 1850

Today I had my first adventure. We had been walking on the cut-off for 2—3 hours, traveling upstream into a deep canyon. The trail was not only out of sight, but out of earshot as well. I liked feeling alone, but Emma fretted that we were lost and the twins were tired, whining that a jouncing wagon ride would be better than tramping on. I tried to cheer everyone by singing "Turkey in the Straw" when we heard a rustling in the bushes. Something much larger than a turkey—Indians! Frank pulled out his little knife, all fierceness, but I hushed him and went to look for myself. (All quaking inside, I admit, but I could not let _them_ see that!) And what should I see when I parted the bushes with trembling hand? The moist snout of a very content ox, chomping on leaves. Somebody must have lost him. If it _had_ been an Indian, Frank declared, he would have protected us. I hope we have no such need.

That was just the beginning of our adventure. When the cut-off reached the trail, there was no sign of our train, either ahead or behind. There was nothing for it but to continue on the cut-off in the hopes of coming out ahead of our wagons soon. On and on we walked. Frank and Emma never complained, nor did little Caroline, but those twins whined worse than the mosquitoes. Still we found no wagons. The sun set, the buffalo wolves started in to howl, and it was too dark to see the trail before us. I would have sat down in the darkness and cried, but I had to take care of the others. Then I recalled what Ben had said about looking for a high view point if you get lost, so I urged everyone up a hill before us. It was not very high, but we were rewarded with the sight of 3 campfires. Since our train is not large, we headed for the smallest one, going straight across country. We barged through brambles and sloshed through creeks, but we always kept that light in view, like the beacon of a lighthouse.

At last I was greeted with the welcome sight of Prudence nibbling bacon. I could not help but embrace her, though she did not appreciate my smudged arms and dress. In fact, she was so startled by our abrupt appearance, she screamed as if we were ghosts or Indians.

Mrs. Arabella Sunshine, Mrs. Elias, and Mother were first joyous, then mad. In between hugging me and scrubbing my face, Mother scolded. Now I cannot take cut-offs after the noon break. That means swallowing dust in the hottest part of the day. At least we still have the mornings.

The bacon and coffee smelled wonderful!

May 23, 1850

Now we are not permitted ever to walk along the cut-offs! Not that we got lost today—something much more exciting happened. Once again we were out of sight of the train, singing as we strolled, when an Indian brave came riding straight at us. I was so amazed to see a true Indian, I forgot to be frightened. We all stood staring at him (though Frank once again reached for his knife—I hissed at him to leave it be, no sense <u>asking</u> for trouble). The twins hid behind my skirt, and the others huddled around me when the brave rode up to us and leapt off his pony. You could have heard a pin drop! He stepped toward me and said something, then held his hand straight out. I did not know what else to do, but shake it, so I did. And that was exactly what he wanted! He offered his hand to each child. Even Frank shook it, grinning so broadly his mouth looked like he had swallowed an ear of corn whole.

The brave knew some English, and he clearly thought we were lost. He asked if I knew where our wagon was. I nodded yes. Satisfied that we were not in trouble, he got back on his pony, waved good-bye, and rode off. It was all over in two shakes of a lamb's tail. After all the horrible stories we had heard about Indians, we had a story of our own to tell and a pretty funny one at that. Only somehow when the adults heard of our meeting, they were not amused. Instead they lectured us on all the awful things that <u>might</u> have happened. And so the cut-offs are forbidden from now on.

STOP AND THINK

Author's Craft Authors sometimes use **hyperbole**, or exaggeration, to make a point or to describe something. For example, Rachel says, "You could have heard a pin drop." What does this tell you about how quiet it was when the brave approached the children?

615

My shoes are so caked with mud, they are more mud pie than footwear.

It's hard keeping this journal dry— I do my best.

Sunbonnets are definitely <u>not</u> meant for rain, unless you find a sopping curtain before your face desirable—I do not!

May 30, 1850

It has rained for days, which has the benefit of keeping down the dust but the disadvantage of turning the trail into an enormous puddle. Despite our cover claiming to be watertight, everything is soaked through. The Platte is swollen and wild. I am relieved we do not have to ford it. Pa says we will reach the government ferry tomorrow.

> **STOP AND THINK**
>
> **Analyze/Evaluate** Ask yourself if you do or do not think this story seems like a real journal written by a girl in 1850. Consider the language Rachel uses and the events she tells about.

The prairie is so low and the sky so close that in a storm you feel the clouds pressing down on you.

June 7, 1850

Yesterday was the first time I truly felt scared. Getting lost, howling wolves, Indians—nothing compares to the fury of this river! We arrived at the ferry only to discover that it had broken loose of its moorings when the rains started. Some men finally retrieved it, but it took so long that an enormous line of wagons waited ahead of us to take the ferry. The man said it would be 3 <u>weeks</u> before our turn came. Mr. Elias warned that we were already behind schedule and such a long delay would surely mean crossing the Sierra Nevada Mountains in the snow. No one wants to suffer the fate of the Donner Party, frozen and starving in the mountains. Mr. Elias determined that we should take the wagons off their wheel beds and raft them over the river. The current was swift and the banks like quicksand, but there was no other way. Both Sunshine families balked at the danger and refused to go first. Mr. Elias offered to cross, but he has young children, so Pa suggested we go. Mother's face was drawn tight, but she nodded. Ben and Will stayed behind to drive the stock over, so Pa, Mother, and I each took a pole to make our way across. The waves were high and it was hard to keep from tipping. Twice I almost fell in. The second time I lost my pole and clung on to the wagon hoops, not much help to anyone after that. Somehow we landed. My knuckles were white from holding so tightly to the hoops, but Mother's face was even paler. What a relief to be on land again!

The worst part was trying to avoid the sandy islands in the middle of the broad river. I could not steer worth a bean.

617

The others followed with no mishap. (And Frank declared that he was not scared, not a bit. I do not credit that!) Only the stock still had to be driven over. Ben and Will, along with Samuel, John, Daniel, and Jesse, rounded up all 115 head of cattle and drove them to the river, but they refused to go in. They had no idea of the dangers of the Sierras, but they could plainly see the dangers of the Platte. Three times the boys gathered the cattle together only to have them split and stampede at the water's edge. It was getting dark, and it looked like we would have to camp on opposite shores when Will decided he had stood enough, he would <u>make</u> those cattle cross. He rode next to Bo, the lead herd ox, and just as the stubborn animal reached the banks, Will leapt from his horse onto Bo's back, clung to his horns, and, kicking and screaming, drove that ox into the river. And it worked! Bo started swimming across and all the stock followed. Safe on the other side, Will jumped off Bo and looked back to see his own horse foundering in the water. His foreleg had gotten tangled up in the loose reins. Will rushed into the water to free his horse just as a clap of thunder split the sky open. Lightning flashed with an eerie brightness followed by pitch black and the deafening roll of thunder.

In the dark we could not see Will, but his horse clambered safely onto shore. When the next lightning flashed, Pa cried out that Will had made it to a sandbar in the river. Whether he was dead or alive, no one could say, and while the storm raged, no one dared swim out to rescue him.

✔ **STOP AND THINK**

Cause and Effect There are several factors that cause Will to become stuck on the sandbar in the river. What are they?

618

That was a miserable and awful night! It was total confusion—thunder booming, oxen bellowing, children crying, men shouting, as light as day one minute, as dark as a cave the next. Add to that the torment of not knowing how poor Will fared and feeling utterly helpless to do anything for him. All we could do was huddle together, a pile of drenched human rags, as the men worked blindly to control the stock.

At dawn the storm quieted, and Pa rushed into the churning river and brought back Will's limp body. He was so pale and still, I thought sure he was dead. Pa started rubbing him down. When at last he opened his eyes, the whole company cheered. He was alive! I have never been so proud—nor so scared.

I never thought I would be so happy to see the sun rise.

June 15, 1850

We took some days' rest to wash everything and dry it out, to put the wagons back together and repair them, to coddle Will and return him to his usual good health. We are fortunate no one drowned in that crossing. There are several new graves of men who died that way, and we heard that in a wagon train near ours, a woman was killed by lightning. Will has always claimed to live a charmed life, and now I believe him.

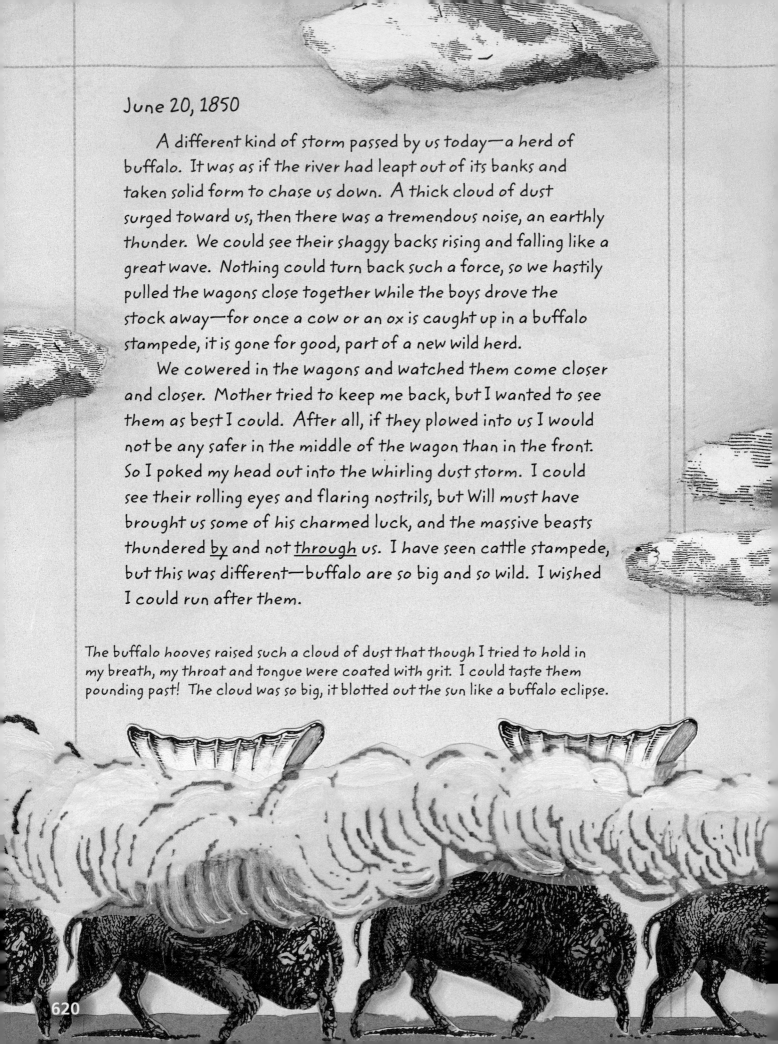

June 20, 1850

A different kind of storm passed by us today—a herd of buffalo. It was as if the river had leapt out of its banks and taken solid form to chase us down. A thick cloud of dust surged toward us, then there was a tremendous noise, an earthly thunder. We could see their shaggy backs rising and falling like a great wave. Nothing could turn back such a force, so we hastily pulled the wagons close together while the boys drove the stock away—for once a cow or an ox is caught up in a buffalo stampede, it is gone for good, part of a new wild herd.

We cowered in the wagons and watched them come closer and closer. Mother tried to keep me back, but I wanted to see them as best I could. After all, if they plowed into us I would not be any safer in the middle of the wagon than in the front. So I poked my head out into the whirling dust storm. I could see their rolling eyes and flaring nostrils, but Will must have brought us some of his charmed luck, and the massive beasts thundered <u>by</u> and not <u>through</u> us. I have seen cattle stampede, but this was different—buffalo are so big and so wild. I wished I could run after them.

The buffalo hooves raised such a cloud of dust that though I tried to hold in my breath, my throat and tongue were coated with grit. I could taste them pounding past! The cloud was so big, it blotted out the sun like a buffalo eclipse.

Your Turn

A Look at the Past

Short Response Rachel keeps a journal as her family travels west in the wagon train. What features of the journal make it an interesting and informative way of telling Rachel's story? Write a paragraph explaining how the text and illustrations work together to help readers understand what life was like for Rachel and her family. SOCIAL STUDIES

In On the Action

Rewrite a Scene Rachel's journal includes several unexpected challenges and adventures. Imagine that you and a partner are along for the ride, keeping your own journal while traveling in the wagon train. Rewrite one of the scenes in Rachel's journal from your perspective. Include a caption and a date for your journal entry. Add illustrations that show how things look to the two of you. Then share your journal entry with the class. PARTNERS

Telling a Good Tale

Turn and Talk Think about the first and last sentences in Rachel's journal entry for June 7, 1850. With a partner, discuss how the events that occur in this entry lead to Rachel's feelings of fear and pride. Then discuss how causes and effects in other journal entries shape Rachel's understanding of how to survive in the wagon train. CAUSE AND EFFECT

Social Studies

WESTWARD TO
FREEDOM

✔ **TARGET VOCABULARY**

mishap	rustling
lectured	beacon
torment	surged
disadvantage	balked
quaking	fared

GENRE

Informational text, such as this social studies text, gives facts and examples about a topic.

TEXT FOCUS

A **timeline** identifies the sequence of important events in a period of history or other span of time.

• Preview the timeline on pages 622–623. How do the facts and dates relate to the title of the selection?

WESTWARD to FREEDOM

by Tracy Moncure

To many African Americans in the 1800s, the West meant freedom, independence, adventure, and the good life. For those who wanted to leave behind memories of slavery, the West offered a chance to start a new life. The trip west was not easy. Travelers risked danger and mishap. Every rustling of the brush might signal a threat. After the torment of slavery, however, African American pioneers were up to the challenge.

MILESTONES IN THE WESTWARD MOVEMENT OF AFRICAN AMERICANS

1835	1850
1848 Southwest and California are acquired.	**1849–1852** Up to 4,000 African Americans join the California Gold Rush.

From Mountain Men to Settlers

African Americans were part of United States westward expansion from the start. York, William Clark's "manservant," was a valued member of the Lewis and Clark expedition in 1803. Mountain men such as James Beckwourth (1798–1866) were early settlers of the Wild West. Some historians believe that as many as one in four cowboys was African American.

Other African Americans built homes, started cities, or upheld the law. In 1889, the Indian Territory opened to settlers. African Americans surged over the tall grasses of the Oklahoma plains. They built more all-black towns in Oklahoma than in all the rest of the country. Bass Reeves (1838–1910) was a U.S. Marshal in the Indian Territory. People thought of him as being tough but fair. Outlaws must have started quaking in their boots when they heard his name.

1863 Emancipation Proclamation frees slaves in the Confederacy.

1877-1879 Benjamin "Pap" Singleton helps African Americans settle in Kansas.

1889 African Americans join the Indian Territory land rush.

1865   **1880**   **1895**

1861-1865 Civil War

1868 Fourteenth Amendment grants citizenship to African Americans.

623

Helping Others on the Path to Freedom

Many African American pioneers became successful in business. They often used their wealth to help others find better lives.

Biddy Mason (1818–1891) traveled with her owner to California in 1847. Her owner balked at giving her freedom. So a judge lectured him, saying that California was a free territory. Later, she owned land in Los Angeles. She became the city's richest citizen. She used her wealth to help those in need.

Clara Brown (1800–1885) also began her life enslaved. After some time, she overcame this disadvantage and fared well. She gained freedom and became the first African American woman to settle in the Colorado gold fields. She started a laundry business. She invested in mines, too. A beacon of hope to freed slaves, she helped many people move to the West.

A regiment of African American cavalry, known as "Buffalo Soldiers," stand next to their horses.

Making Connections

Text to Self

Evaluate Figurative Language The author of "Rachel's Journal" uses hyperbole, or exaggeration, to help describe the children's encounter with an Indian brave. With a partner, find two examples of metaphor on page 616 of "Rachel's Journal." Ask each other questions about how the author's uses of metaphor help you understand more about Rachel's experience.

Text to Text

Write About History In the 1800s, people traveled west for many reasons. Compare the experiences of the characters described in "Rachel's Journal" to the experiences of the African American pioneers in "Westward to Freedom." Use information from both selections to write a paragraph explaining what was happening in the United States during the time in which these two selections are set.

Text to World

Connect to Social Studies "Rachel's Journal" is a story set in a real period in history. Think of what you know about the Oregon Trail, prairie life, or westward migration in the 1800s. Then think about the theme of "Rachel's Journal." Discuss with a group how the historical period and events surrounding it affect the story's theme. Consider the reasons people decided to move west and the hardships they might have faced.

Grammar

Comparative and Superlative Forms A **comparative adjective** compares two people, places, or things. Add *-er* to a short adjective, or use *more* before a long one, to make its comparative form. A **superlative adjective** compares more than two persons, places, or things. Add *-est* to a short adjective, or use *most* before a long one, to make its superlative form. The adjectives *good* and *bad* have special comparative and superlative forms.

Academic Language

comparative adjective
superlative adjective
comparative adverb
superlative adverb

Adjective	Comparative	Superlative
young (short adjective)	younger	youngest
restful (long adjective)	more restful	most restful
good	better	best
bad	worse	worst

Many adverbs have comparative and superlative forms. Use the word *more* in front of an adverb to make a **comparative adverb**. Use *most* in front of an adverb to make a **superlative adverb**.

Adverb	Comparative	Superlative
cheerfully	more cheerfully	most cheerfully

Work with a partner. Identify each comparative and superlative adjective and adverb.

1. Wolf howls made the night seem eerier.

2. The lead ox behaved the most stubbornly of any animal.

3. was more afraid of the thunder than of the lightning.

4. That river crossing was the worst situation ever.

5. Will acted more bravely than anyone else.

Ideas You can sometimes make comparisons, sentences, or ideas in your writing clearer by using comparative and superlative forms of adjectives and adverbs.

Less Clear	Clearer
I am eight years old. I have a sister and a brother.	I am eight years old. I have an older brother and an older sister. My sister is the oldest of us all.

Grammar in Writing

As you revise your research report next week, look for opportunities to make your ideas clearer by using comparative and superlative forms. Make sure you use the correct forms when writing comparative or superlative adjectives or adverbs.

Write to Inform

☑ **Organization**   To plan a **research report**, find good sources to answer your questions on your topic. Record facts on note cards. Then organize your notes into an outline. Each main topic in your outline will become a paragraph in your report.

Kira researched the exploration of the Colorado River. For her outline, she grouped her notes into three main topics.

Writing Process Checklist

▶ **Prewrite**

☑ Did I choose a topic that will interest my audience and me?

☑ Did I ask questions to focus my research?

☑ Did I gather facts from a variety of good sources?

☑ Did I organize facts into an outline with main topics and subtopics?

Draft

Revise

Edit

Publish and Share

Exploring a Topic

What problems did the explorers face?
—Rapids, waterfalls made travel difficult.
—Boats broke, supplies were lost.
—Men exhausted
Wyman, Jed. Explorers of the American West. Chicago, IL: Bower Books, 2007. p. 86

Why was this exploration important?
—Colorado R. serves many purposes for Americans.
—Dams create lakes to make water available for people to use.
"Colorado River." Globe Encyclopedia. 2004. Globe Encyclopedia Online. 4 May 2010. www.globeencyclopedia.com/article-85948.

Outline

I. Powell's difficult 1869 expedition
    A. Purpose: to map Colorado R. and canyons
    B. Rapids and waterfalls made journey harder—boats broke, lost supplies
    C. Discovered Grand Canyon
    D. Men exhausted, journey ended in 3 months

II. Powell's second expedition
    A. Was better prepared for journey
    B. Brought back photos, maps, info on land, plants, animals

III. The importance of Powell's exploration
    A. Powell was first American "to recognize the significance of the Colorado for the future of the West"
    B. Dams along river make water available
    C. Lake formed from dam

In my outline, I organized facts into main topics and subtopics. I listed subtopics in time order.

Reading as a Writer

Is Kira's outline well organized? Why do you think so? What parts of your outline can you organize better or make more complete?

expedition

tributaries

trek

barrier

despite

fulfilled

range

techniques

resumed

edible

Vocabulary Reader   Context Cards

Vocabulary in Context

1   **expedition**

Adventurer Edmund Hillary led an expedition to climb Mount Everest.

2   **tributaries**

This creek is one of the tributaries, or small branches, of a larger river.

3   **trek**

These hikers are on a week-long trek through a national park.

4   **barrier**

Thick vegetation forms a barrier in the jungle. Explorers must cut through the obstacle.

- **Study each Context Card.**

- **Use a thesaurus to find a word to replace each of the Vocabulary words.**

5 despite

Despite the blazing heat, these pioneers crossed the prairie.

6 fulfilled

This astronaut fulfilled his lifelong dream of going to the moon.

7 range

Jim Bridger explored the mountain chain known as the Rocky Mountain range.

8 techniques

This hiker knows different techniques, or methods, for starting a campfire.

9 resumed

After resting, this boy resumed his bike ride. He felt ready to ride again.

10 edible

Hikers need to know which berries are edible and which ones they must not eat.

Background

TARGET VOCABULARY **Exploring the West** In 1803, President Thomas Jefferson bought from France the vast territory of Louisiana. It stretched west from the Mississippi River to the Rocky Mountains. Jefferson sent a team of explorers on an expedition across the land he had gained in the Louisiana Purchase. Despite many hardships, the explorers fulfilled Jefferson's orders. They traveled up the mighty Missouri River, which split into smaller tributaries. They crossed the barrier of the Rocky Mountain range.

One member of the expedition was a Native American woman named Sacagawea (sak uh juh WEE uh). She taught the explorers techniques for surviving in the wilderness, such as identifying edible wild plants.

The explorers continued on and reached the Pacific Ocean in 1805. They spent the winter near the coast of present-day Oregon. The following spring, they resumed their trek, heading back east. They concluded their long journey in September of 1806.

• Examine the map below. Use the scale to determine, in miles, the length and width of the Louisiana Purchase.

The Louisiana Purchase

0   500 Mi
0   500 Km

BRITISH TERRITORY

OREGON COUNTRY

LOUISIANA PURCHASE

UNITED STATES

Atlantic Ocean

N

SPANISH TERRITORY

Pacific Ocean

Gulf of Mexico

The Louisiana Purchase cost the United States about $11 million and doubled the country's size. Which country do you think benefited more, France or the United States? Tell why.

632

Comprehension

✔ TARGET SKILL **Author's Purpose**

As you read "Lewis and Clark," note details that suggest the author's purpose for writing. Also identify examples that help you infer his viewpoint about the people who took part in this historic expedition. Use a graphic organizer like the one below to list the text evidence that leads you to infer the author's viewpoint. Then ask yourself how well the author's purpose was achieved.

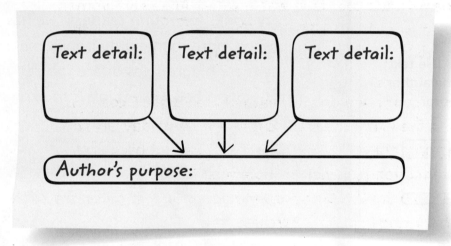

Text detail: Text detail: Text detail:

Author's purpose:

✔ TARGET STRATEGY **Monitor/Clarify**

Monitor and clarify details the author provides in the selection to present and describe the Corps of Discovery and its expedition. Note his choice of words and the examples he uses. Understanding how the facts are presented helps you determine the author's viewpoint.

expedition	fulfilled
tributaries	range
trek	techniques
barrier	resumed
despite	edible

✓ **TARGET SKILL**

Author's Purpose Use text details to figure out the author's viewpoint and reasons for writing the selection.

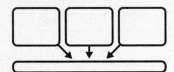

✓ **TARGET STRATEGY**

Monitor/Clarify As you read, notice what is not making sense. Find ways to figure out the parts that are confusing.

GENRE

Narrative nonfiction gives factual information by telling a true story.

Set a Purpose Set a purpose based on the genre and what the author wants you to know.

MEET THE AUTHOR

R. Conrad Stein

R. Conrad Stein knew from the time he was twelve years old that he wanted to be a writer. After serving as a Marine, he studied history at the University of Illinois. A few years after he graduated, his background in history helped him get assignments writing history books for young readers. He has published more than eighty books; many of them are biographies or are focused on history. Stein believes his job is to express the drama of historical events.

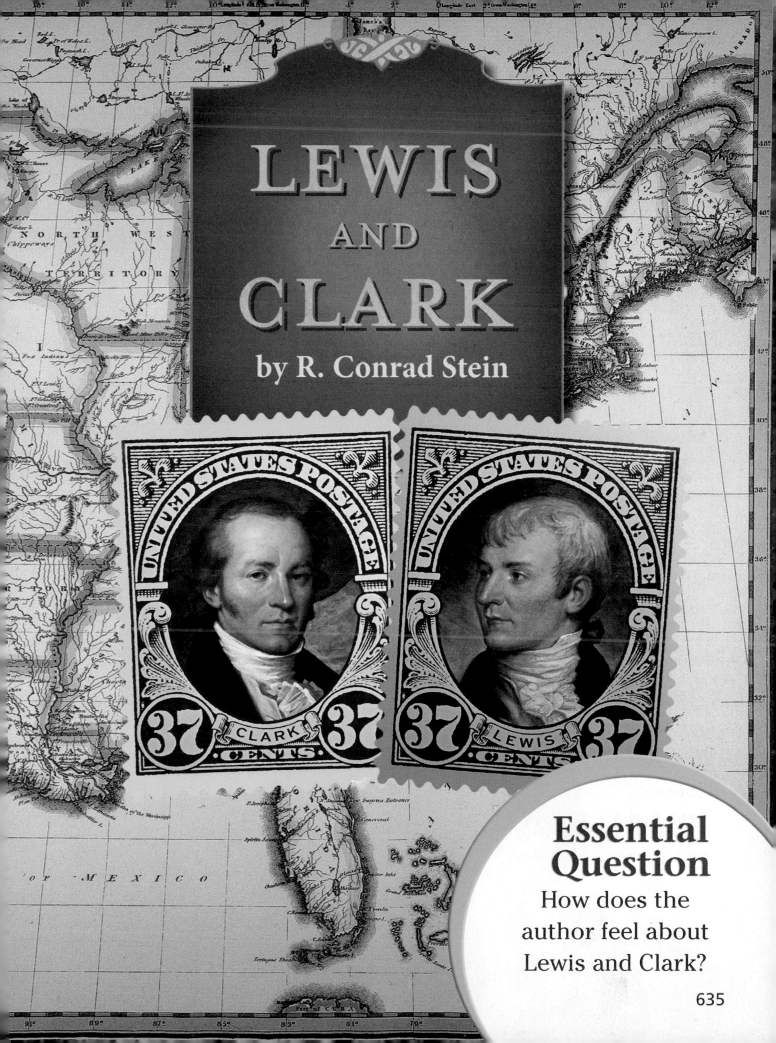

LEWIS
AND
CLARK

by R. Conrad Stein

UNITED STATES POSTAGE
37 · CLARK · 37 CENTS

UNITED STATES POSTAGE
37 · LEWIS · 37 CENTS

Essential Question

How does the author feel about Lewis and Clark?

In 1803, President Thomas Jefferson doubled the size of the United States after completing an agreement with France called the Louisiana Purchase. He had acquired the vast Louisiana Territory west of the Mississippi River. Jefferson decided to form an expedition through the unexplored Territory to the Pacific Ocean. He asked Meriwether Lewis to lead a group called the Corps of Discovery. Lewis chose William Clark to help him as co-leader. In 1804, Lewis and Clark began their journey from St. Louis, Missouri. They traveled through the Great Plains and then stopped for the winter season. A trader and his wife, a Native American named Sacagawea (sak uh juh WEE uh), joined the expedition when it resumed its journey in April 1805.

Lewis considered the Mandan (MAN duhn) Indians' stories about huge bears to be fanciful tales until one of the explorers was chased by a grizzly bear.

The Great Falls of the Missouri River were a beautiful sight, but also were difficult to travel around.

William Clark had perhaps the best eyesight of any crew member. On May 26, he saw the outline of a great mountain range to the west. In the next few days, all of the explorers could see the snow-covered Rocky Mountains on the horizon. The sight was inspiring as well as troubling. The explorers knew that they would have to find a way to cross the incredible barrier.

Before they could cross the Rockies, the Corps of Discovery faced the Great Falls of the Missouri River in present-day Montana. Here the river tumbled down a bluff that was as high as a modern six-story building. The roar of the water was deafening. Lewis called it, "the grandest sight I ever beheld." But the waterfall meant that the explorers had to carry their boats and supplies up steep cliffs before they could set out again on quieter waters upstream. Traveling around the falls took the party twenty-four days, and left everyone exhausted.

Sacagawea quickly proved to be a valuable asset to the expedition.

Carrying her baby boy on her back, Sacagawea won the admiration of the crew. She carefully scanned the riverbank to find edible roots and fruit. These foods provided a welcome relief from the customary diet of meat and water. And in the mountain country, the Missouri River became a crooked stream that split into many small tributaries. Sacagawea pointed out landmarks that she remembered from a journey as a slave child, and she helped the captains choose the correct river branches on which to travel.

Soon the members of the party began to wonder why they had not yet seen any Shoshone (shoh SHOH nee) or other American Indians. They had seen signs of Indian settlement—hunters' trails and abandoned campsites—but since they left the Mandan and Hidatsa (hee DAHT suh) villages, the Corps of Discovery had not encountered any other people at all.

STOP AND THINK

Monitor/Clarify How does Sacagawea win the crew's admiration? How might their experiences during the expedition have been different without her?

In mid-August, Meriwether Lewis, hiking ahead of the party with a few other explorers, came upon three Shoshone women and several children. Lewis had carried an American flag in his pack for just such a meeting.

He waved the banner and walked slowly toward the group. One of the children fled. The women sat very still as if frozen with fear. Lewis explained that he was an explorer, and the women led him to their village.

The Shoshone were a small tribe who were almost always at war with their powerful neighbors, the Blackfeet. They had never seen white people, but constant warfare made the Shoshone suspicious of all outsiders. Lewis hoped to buy horses from the tribe. Now that the rivers had all but disappeared, he needed horses to cross the peaks of the Rocky Mountains. But the chief, Cameahwait (kuh MEE uh wayt), would not part with any of the animals. Lewis did persuade Cameahwait to send a few Shoshone to find Clark and the rest of the party and bring them to the village.

At first, the Shoshone were cautious of Lewis and Clark, but the explorers soon realized that they were fortunate to encounter the Indians.

The next morning, Clark and the others arrived at the village, and a meeting was held with Chief Cameahwait. Sacagawea prepared to serve as the translator. When the meeting began, Sacagawea stared intently at the chief. Then she broke into tears of joy. Lewis wrote, "She jumped up, ran, and embraced him, and threw her blanket over him, and cried profusely." Sacagawea recognized Cameahwait as her brother, whom she had not seen in six years. Cheers and laughter rose from the village. The Shoshone hailed Sacagawea as a lost daughter who had come home.

On September 1, 1805, the Corps of Discovery left the Shoshone territory. Chief Cameahwait not only provided the party with horses, he also gave them a guide to show them the best route through the mountains. Crossing the Rockies proved to be a difficult ordeal. The trails were too rugged to ride on, so the party walked and used the horses as pack animals.

The expedition crossed the Rockies on foot, using the horses to carry their equipment and supplies.

STOP AND THINK

Author's Craft The author uses a **primary source**, a direct quote from Lewis's writing, in the first paragraph. What can you conclude about Lewis from his words?

Upon reaching the Clearwater River Valley, the expedition built new canoes to continue their journey west.

In mid-September, a blinding snowstorm struck. Even the Shoshone guide got lost. Worst of all, the once-abundant wild game could not be found on the high mountain peaks. The explorers were forced to kill some of their pack animals for meat. The explorers' journals report that the men laughed out loud when they finally crossed the mountains and reached grasslands on level terrain.

The Lewis and Clark expedition emerged from the Rocky Mountains into the lovely valley of the Clearwater River in present-day Idaho. The waters were so clear that the river bottom and schools of fish were visible despite the river's depth. In the Clearwater country, Lewis and Clark abandoned their pack horses and built new canoes. They reasoned that the streams on this side of the Rockies would all eventually flow into the Columbia River, the major river of the Pacific Northwest. American Indians called the Columbia River the *Ouragon* or *Origan*. The land around it was later called the Oregon Territory.

Traveling the rivers, the voyagers met the Nez Perce (NEZ PURS) Indians, who taught them valuable techniques for building and sailing log canoes. Less friendly were the Chinook (shih NOOK), who drove hard bargains when trading for goods. But encountering the Chinook meant that the Pacific Ocean was not far away. One of the Chinook wore a black navy coat that he may have bought from a North American or European sailor.

A dismal rain pelted the travelers in early November as they sailed down the Columbia River. They made a camp near an Indian village and spent a restless night. On the morning of November 7, 1805, the rain stopped and the fog cleared. A chorus of shouts suddenly went up from the camp. William Clark scribbled in his notes, "Ocean in view! O! the joy." On the horizon, still many miles to the west, lay the great Pacific Ocean. Upon seeing the ocean, some of the explorers wept, and others said prayers of thanksgiving.

The explorers experienced some difficulty in dealing with the Chinook Indians, but their encounter brought signs that the Pacific Ocean was near.

The explorers saw the Pacific Ocean for the first time near present-day Astoria, Oregon.

But arriving at the Pacific Ocean did not end the Lewis and Clark expedition. The party still had to return home to St. Louis. President Jefferson had provided Meriwether Lewis with a letter of credit guaranteeing payment to any ship captain who would take the explorers to the eastern coast. The party made a winter camp at the mouth of the Columbia River near present-day Astoria, Oregon, and kept a watch for ships. No vessels were spotted. Finally, on March 23, 1806, the crew broke camp and began the long trek east toward St. Louis.

To the explorers, the six-month return journey seemed to be easier than their first journey because they knew what to expect in the river and mountain country. When the crew reached the Mandan village, they said good-bye to Sacagawea and her husband and continued back to St. Louis.

On September 23, 1806, the Lewis and Clark expedition arrived safely back in St. Louis, Missouri, where their journey had begun more than two years earlier. The travelers had gone a distance of just less than 4,000 miles (6,400 km) from St. Louis to the mouth of the Columbia River and back. But the twisting rivers and mountain trails meant that the Corps of Discovery had actually covered about 8,000 miles (13,000 km) on the history-making trip. Throughout the explorers' travels, they encountered more than fifty American-Indian tribes.

The journals kept by Captains Lewis, Clark, and several members of their expedition have been compiled into many published accounts since the journey ended in 1806.

The expedition returned with numerous samples of plant and animal life that had never before been seen by American scientists. Before the expedition, President Jefferson had hoped that the explorers would find a broad river that ships could use to sail directly to the Pacific Ocean. Lewis and Clark failed to find such a river, and the expedition was final proof that an inland waterway in North America did not exist.

From St. Louis, Lewis and Clark traveled to Washington, D.C. Almost every town they passed through brought out bands to welcome them as heroes. In Washington, D.C., the explorers delighted President Jefferson with tales of grizzly bears and high mountain passes. The president said, "Lewis and Clark have entirely fulfilled my expectations....

The world will find that those travelers have well earned its favor."

To Meriwether Lewis and William Clark, the mission itself was their greatest reward. Traveling through virtually unexplored lands was an exhilarating experience that they would cherish for the rest of their lives. Although they faced many dangers, the thrill—not the peril—of the expedition bursts from the pages of the journals they kept. As Lewis wrote the day he left the Indian village to enter the Western wilderness, "I could but esteem this moment of my departure as among the most happy of my life."

 **STOP AND THINK**

Author's Purpose Do you think including President Jefferson's reaction to Lewis and Clark helps the author achieve his purpose for writing? Why or why not?

Your Turn

One of a Kind

Short Response As a Native American and a woman, Sacagawea stood out from everyone else on the expedition. Her unique background provided knowledge and talents that contributed greatly to the expedition's success. Think of another person in early United States history who you think is remarkable. Write a paragraph describing that person and the contributions he or she made.

SOCIAL STUDIES

Exploring the West

Create a Map Lewis and Clark's expedition crossed unexplored territory from St. Louis, Missouri, to the Pacific coast of what is now Oregon. Work with a group to create a timeline showing important events that happened on the journey. Use the dates in the text and on several of the primary sources to guide you. Include illustrations of key people, places, and events. Then share your timeline with another group. SMALL GROUP

What's Your Purpose?

Turn and Talk Think about the words, descriptions, and examples the author uses when he refers to the explorers Meriwether Lewis and William Clark. Find and list some of these details. Then discuss with a partner how these details are presented and what they help you understand about Lewis and Clark. What do the details help you infer about the author's feelings toward the two explorers? AUTHOR'S PURPOSE

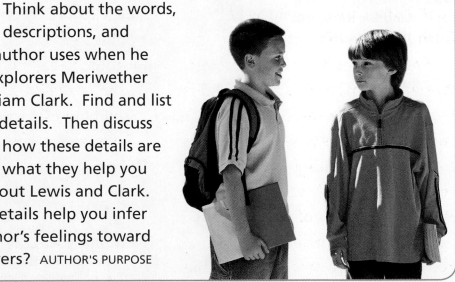

✔ **TARGET VOCABULARY**

expedition	fulfilled
tributaries	range
trek	techniques
barrier	resumed
despite	edible

GENRE

A **play**, like this dramatic adaptation, tells a story through the words and actions of its characters.

TEXT FOCUS

Dialogue is lines of text in a play that stand for the words spoken by the characters.

A SURPRISE REUNION

By Byron Cahill

Cast of Characters

Narrator
Chief Cameahwait
Captain Meriwether Lewis
Captain William Clark
Sacagawea
Shoshone Scout

Narrator: It is August of 1805 in the camp of the Shoshone. The main party of the Lewis and Clark Expedition is making its way back to Captain Lewis's group. While Shoshone scouts are out searching for them, Lewis is asking the chief, Cameahwait, for help.

Lewis: Chief Cameahwait, won't you please reconsider parting with a few of your horses? They would be a great help to us in crossing the western mountain range.

Cameahwait: (*Firmly*) No, stranger. You could be allies of the Blackfoot.

Lewis: We simply seek passage to the other side of these mountains.

Cameahwait: So you say, but despite your words, you are intruders in my lands.

Lewis: I give you my word. We mean the Shoshone no harm.

Cameahwait: We Shoshone judge others by their actions, not by words alone. We have lost much in war. I myself lost a sister years ago.

Shoshone Scout: (*Entering with Clark and Sacagawea*) Cameahwait, we have brought the strangers to you. We found them camped near one of the tributaries of the river.

Lewis: (*Relieved*) Captain Clark! Sacagawea! It is good to see you safe.

Clark: Everyone is in good health, Meriwether, thanks to the edible plants Sacagawea found and her excellent techniques for preparing them.

Lewis: Good! Sacagawea, perhaps you can convince Cameahwait that our journey can be resumed much sooner if he agrees to trade with us.

Clark: Sacagawea? What is wrong? You are shaking!

Narrator: Sacagawea does not answer. She gazes at Cameahwait, then rushes into his arms and throws her blanket around his shoulders, weeping loudly.

Sacagawea: (*Through her tears*) Brother! It is you, is it not?

Cameahwait: It is not possible! You were taken. Are these men your captors?

Sacagawea: No! I am a free woman. I am helping them on their journey. My husband and child are outside with the rest of the group.

Cameahwait: (*Surprised*) Husband? Child?

Sacagawea: Yes, Brother! You are an uncle! These men are friends!

Cameahwait: Then let distrust no longer be a barrier between us, Captain Lewis. I promise you horses for your journey, and one of my best guides. My promise will be fulfilled after we celebrate my sister's return to her tribe!

Narrator: With the help of Cameahwait, the Lewis and Clark Expedition safely completed its trek through the dangerous terrain of the Rocky Mountains. They arrived at the shores of the Pacific Ocean just three months later.

Making Connections

 Text to Self

Write a Story Write a short story about a key event that happened during the Lewis and Clark Expedition after the explorers left North Dakota. Include sensory details and dialogue in your story. Read your story aloud to a small group. Use different voices, facial expressions, and gestures to add interest to your presentation.

 Text to Text

Compare Texts Compare "Lewis and Clark" to the play "A Surprise Reunion." Find similarities and differences between the original story and the dramatic adaptation. Then discuss your ideas with a partner. Provide evidence from both texts to support how the two selections are the same and how they are different.

 Text to World

Connect to Social Studies Use print or online sources to research the Louisiana Purchase. Take notes on the new facts you learn about this historic land purchase. Then discuss those facts with a partner.

Grammar

What Are the Mechanics of Writing Titles? You have learned to capitalize proper nouns and important words in titles of various kinds. In handwritten work, you should **underline** titles of longer works, such as books, movies, and plays. In word-processed papers, you should write these types of titles in **italics**. Place titles of shorter works, such as stories, poems, and songs, inside quotation marks in both written and word-processed work.

Academic Language

underline

italics

> Have you read <u>Sarah, Plain and Tall</u>, by Patricia MacLachlan?
>
> Have you read *Sarah, Plain and Tall*, by Patricia MacLachlan?
>
> Let's sing "Home on the Range."

You can also use underlining and italics for emphasis.

> I <u>love</u> books and songs about America's early years.
>
> I *love* books and songs about America's early years.

Try This! **Write each sentence on another sheet of paper. Capitalize proper nouns and important words in titles. Underline titles of longer works. Place titles of shorter works in quotation marks.**

❶ The book By the Great Horn Spoon! describes California pioneer life.

❷ Can you sing Yankee doodle to us?

❸ The movie The sound of Music is still a favorite.

❹ I've written a short story called Trouble on the trail.

Conventions Your readers will have an easier time reading and understanding what you write if you check your work carefully to eliminate errors in capitalization, punctuation, and mechanics of titles.

Sentences with Titles

Incorrect	Correct
The book "The virginian" was one of the first novels about cowboys, and the song Buffalo gals was a popular song about Pioneer life!	The book *The Virginian* was one of the first novels about cowboys, and the song "Buffalo Gals" was a popular song about pioneer life.

Connect Grammar to Writing

As you edit your research report, correct any errors you find in capitalization, punctuation, or mechanics of titles. Pay special attention to titles and proper nouns. Remember that you can use italics and underlining for emphasis.

Write to Inform

☑ Word Choice In a **research report**, good writers are careful not to copy sentences or phrases from their sources. As you revise your report, use synonyms—different words with the same meaning—to help you express the facts in your own way.

Kira drafted her report on the exploration of the Colorado River. Later, she reworded a sentence that she had accidentally copied. She made other changes as well.

Writing Process Checklist

Prewrite

Draft

▶ **Revise**

☑ Does my first paragraph introduce the main ideas in an interesting way?

☑ Did I write at least one paragraph for each main topic?

☑ Did I show how my ideas are connected?

☑ Did I use my own words?

☑ Does my conclusion sum up my main ideas?

☑ Did I include an accurate list of sources?

Edit

Publish and Share

Revised Draft

In 1869, many Americans had settled in the big territories of the West, but the region of the Colorado River was still a 500-mile empty space on the map. ∧ ~~This~~ Although Native Americans had lived there for thousands of years, no one ~~extraordinary area had been inhabited~~ from the United States had completely ~~by Native Americans for centuries, but~~ explored this amazing place yet. ~~no explorers from the United States had~~ ~~thoroughly traveled its land and water.~~

Exploring the Mighty Colorado River

by Kira Delaney

In 1869, many Americans had settled in the big territories of the West, but the region of the Colorado River was still a 500-mile empty space on the map. Although Native Americans had lived there for thousands of years, no one from the United States had completely explored this amazing place yet. John Wesley Powell decided to change that.

Powell set out with four boats, nine men, and supplies to last ten months. Soon, the river made his plan for a slow, careful journey impossible. Every day, the men had to move their heavily loaded boats around or over dangerous rapids and waterfalls. One boat broke apart, and the supplies in it were lost.

> In my final report, I made sure to use my own words. I also capitalized proper nouns and used correct punctuation.

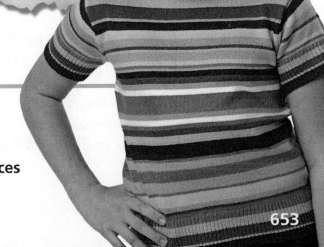

Reading as a Writer

In what other ways could Kira have reworded the sentence she copied? How can you reword any copied sentences in your report?

In Honor of Grandmother

Julie felt jealous as she watched her older sister work. Minna's skillful hands wove the thread and bundles of pine needles into tidy coils to form a basket. As it took shape, the basket was beginning to look like the baskets their grandmother had made.

Julie picked up a photograph of her grandmother. It was one of Julie's favorites, taken in the last year of Grandmother's life. In this picture, Grandmother was holding a beautiful pine needle basket that she had made. The picture reminded Julie of how much she missed her grandmother.

The girls' school was holding a fair at which students could share special family customs. Julie and Minna wanted to share something from their Cherokee background. The pine needle baskets seemed like the perfect thing. Baskets had an important role in Cherokee culture. The Cherokee used them for gathering food and storing things.

By the following week, Minna had completed her basket, but Julie had barely begun to weave hers. She was not skilled enough to make even a single basket in time for the fair.

"Minna, what am I going to do?" Julie cried. "I won't have anything to share!"

Minna always stayed calm when Julie got upset. "Maybe you can think of something else. Look through some of Grandmother's things. Maybe you'll get another idea."

Julie went to Grandmother's old room. It was easy to remember Grandmother here. Julie opened a dresser and quietly went through a drawer that held Grandmother's special things. Julie set aside some beautiful woven belts and small baskets. She picked up a folder and leafed through it. "Minna!" she cried. "I've found the perfect thing! Grandmother left directions for using ribbon and pine needles to make a picture frame. I know I can do this!"

Minna smiled encouragingly. Julie worked on her frame, carefully threading the ribbon and pine needles. She used green and blue ribbons because those had been Grandmother's favorite colors. When she was finished, she put the photograph of her grandmother in the frame. Julie knew Grandmother would have been proud.

Welcoming Grandfather

"Edgar, you need to move the rest of your things into Hector's room today," Mrs. Valdez reminded her oldest son.

"But Mom, that room isn't big enough for both of us," Edgar complained for the twentieth time.

Mrs. Valdez sighed. She had explained it many times to her three children. Their grandfather, almost eighty years old, needed help with a few things now. Since Grandmother had passed away a year ago, Mrs. Valdez had been caring for him. Together they had decided that it would be easier for everyone if Grandfather moved in. Grandfather would help the family by being home with the children after school. Mrs. Valdez and the children would also be there for Grandfather if he needed help.

Lupita and Hector, the younger Valdez children, were excited about having Grandfather come to live with them. Only Edgar was unhappy. He liked things the way they were. He didn't want to share a room with his brother.

On Friday, Grandfather moved in. That night during dinner, Edgar hardly said a word, but Grandfather did not seem to notice. He entertained everyone with stories about how things were when he was young. If Edgar hadn't been so grumpy, he would have enjoyed the stories.

"When I was growing up, we always sat down together for an evening meal," Grandfather said. "We would talk about what we did that day. I would like to do that here, if everyone agrees."

"I think that's a lovely idea," said Mrs. Valdez.

"I'd like to start," Grandfather continued, "by thanking each of you for allowing me to move into your home. I would especially like to thank you, Edgar, for giving up your room for me. I know this is a big change for you." Edgar felt his face turning red. He felt bad about the fuss he had made over his room.

After dinner, Grandfather offered to do the dishes. Edgar wanted to make Grandfather feel welcome. "Let me help you," he said.

Unit 5 Wrap-Up

The Big Idea

Way Out West In Unit 5, you read about dangers and hardships people faced in the Old West. Draw a comic strip that shows an event you read about. Share your comic strip with a classmate, and discuss which details would be different today.

Listening and Speaking

Time Travel What if Francis Tucket, Meriwether Lewis, or Omakayas suddenly appeared at your school? What would you want to ask that person? What do you think he or she would want to ask you? Work with a partner to create a dialogue between a student in your school and a person from one of the selections in this unit. Perform your dialogue for the class or a small group.

Glossary

This glossary contains meanings and pronunciations for some of the words in this book. The Full Pronunciation Key shows how to pronounce each consonant and vowel in a special spelling. At the bottom of the glossary pages is a shortened form of the full key.

Full Pronunciation Key

Consonant Sounds

b	**b**i**b**, ca**bb**age	kw	**ch**oir, **qu**ick	t	**t**igh**t**, stopp**ed**
ch	**ch**ur**ch**, sti**tch**	l	**l**id, need**le**, ta**ll**	th	ba**th**, **th**in
d	**d**ee**d**, mail**ed**, pu**dd**le	m	a**m**, **m**an, du**mb**	*th*	ba**th**e, **th**is
f	**f**ast, **f**i**f**e, o**ff**, **ph**rase, rou**gh**	n	**n**o, sudd**en**	v	ca**v**e, val**v**e, **v**ine
		ng	thi**ng**, i**nk**	w	**w**ith, **w**olf
g	**g**a**g**, **g**et, fin**g**er	p	**p**o**p**, ha**pp**y	y	**y**es, **y**olk, on**i**on
h	**h**at, **wh**o	r	**r**oar, **rh**yme	z	ro**s**e, si**z**e, **x**ylophone, **z**ebra
hw	**wh**ich, **wh**ere	s	mi**ss**, **s**au**c**e, **sc**ene, **s**ee	zh	gara**g**e, plea**s**ure, vi**s**ion
j	**j**u**dg**e, **g**em	sh	di**sh**, **sh**ip, **s**ugar, ti**ss**ue		
k	**c**at, **k**i**ck**, s**ch**ool				

Vowel Sounds

ă	p**a**t, l**au**gh	ŏ	h**o**rrible, p**o**t	ŭ	c**u**t, fl**oo**d, r**ou**gh, s**o**me
ā	**a**pe, **ai**d, p**ay**	ō	g**o**, r**ow**, t**oe**, th**ough**	û	c**i**rcle, f**u**r, h**ear**d, t**er**m, t**ur**n, **ur**ge, w**or**d
â	**ai**r, c**a**re, w**ea**r	ô	**a**ll, c**au**ght, f**or**, p**aw**		
ä	f**a**ther, k**o**ala, y**a**rd	oi	b**oy**, n**oi**se, **oi**l		
ĕ	p**e**t, pl**ea**sure, **a**ny	ou	c**ow**, **ou**t	yo͞o	c**u**re
ē	b**e**, b**ee**, **ea**sy, p**ia**no	o͝o	f**u**ll, b**oo**k, w**o**lf	yo͞o	ab**u**se, **u**se
ĭ	**i**f, p**i**t, b**u**sy	o͞o	b**oo**t, r**u**de, fr**ui**t, fl**ew**	ə	**a**go, sil**e**nt, penc**i**l, lem**o**n, circ**u**s
ī	r**i**de, b**y**, p**ie**, h**igh**				
î	d**ea**r, d**ee**r, f**ie**rce, m**e**re				

Stress Marks

Primary Stress ´: bi·ol·o·gy [bī **ŏl**´ ə jē]

Secondary Stress ´: bi·o·log·i·cal [bī´ ə **lŏj**´ ĭ kəl]

Pronunciation key and definitions copyright © 2007 by Houghton Mifflin Harcourt Publishing Company. Reproduced by permission from *The American Heritage Children's Dictionary* and *The American Heritage Student Dictionary*.

A

aspect

Aspect comes from the Latin prefix *ad-* ("at") and the Latin word root *specere,* which means "to look." A *spectator,* which comes from the same word root, is a watcher. A *prospect,* which is something that is looked forward to, comes from the prefix *pro-*, "in front of" or "before," and *specere.*

attract

Attract comes from the Latin prefix *ad-* ("toward") and the Latin word root *trahere,* "to pull or to draw." The English word *tractor,* a vehicle that pulls another vehicle or object, also comes from *trahere.* *Contract,* an agreement between two or more parties, comes from the Latin prefix *com-* ("together") and *trahere.* *Retract,* which means "to take back," comes from the Latin prefix *re-* ("again") and *trahere.*

ac·knowl·edge (ăk **nŏl´** ĭj) *v.* To recognize: *They were **acknowledged** as experts in science.*

ac·quaint·ed (ə **kwānt´** ĭd) *adj.* Familiar or informed: *People **acquainted** through mutual friends develop meaningful relationships.*

a·cute (ə **kyoot´**) *adj.* Keen; perceptive: *The cat has an **acute** sense of hearing.*

a·dapt·ed (ə **dăp´** tĭd) *adj.* Fitted or suitable, especially for a specific purpose: *A dog's claws are **adapted** for digging.*

ad·just (əd **jŭst´**) *v.* To change, set, or regulate in order to improve or make regular: *I **adjusted** the seatbelts in the car to fit the child.*

ad·mit (ăd **mĭt´**) *v.* To acknowledge or confess to be true or real: *He **admitted** that I was right.*

ad·van·tage (ăd **văn´** tĭj) *n.* A beneficial factor or feature: *Museums and libraries are some of the **advantages** of city life.*

an·a·lyze (**ăn´** ə līz´) *v.* To break up into parts to learn what the parts are: *After **analyzing** the test results, doctors know how to help patients.*

an·noy·ance (ə **noi´** əns) *n.*
1. Something causing trouble or irritation; a nuisance: *His tummy ache was a minor **annoyance**.*
2. Irritation or displeasure: *He swatted at the mosquito in **annoyance**.*

an·tique (ăn **tēk´**) *adj.* Belonging to, made in, or typical of an earlier period: *The castle was full of **antique** furniture.*

ap·pren·tice (ə **prĕn´** tĭs) *n.* A person who works for another without pay in return for instruction in a craft or trade: *The blacksmith's **apprentice** was trained to make horseshoes.*

as·pect (**ăs´** pĕkt) *n.* A way in which something can be viewed by the mind; an element or facet: *The doctor reviewed all **aspects** of the patient's history.*

as·sum·ing (ə **soo mĭng**) *conj.* If; supposing: ***Assuming** our guests arrive on time, we'll have dinner at 6:00.*

as·ton·ish (ə **stŏn´** ĭsh) *v.* To surprise greatly; amaze: *It **astonished** me that we finished our project on time.*

at·tract (ə **trăkt´**) *v.* To cause to draw near; direct to oneself or itself by some quality or action: *Crowds were **attracted** to the beautiful beach.*

ă rat / ā **pay** / â **care** / ä **father** / ĕ **pet** / ē **be** / ĭ **pit** / ī **pie** / î **fierce** / ŏ **pot** / ō **go** /
ô **paw**, **for** / oi **oil** / ōō **book**

au·thor·i·ty (ə thôr´ ĭ tē) *n.* A person or an organization having power to enforce laws, command obedience, determine, or judge: *City authorities closed the street for repairs.*

a·vail·a·ble (ə vā´ lə bəl) *adj.* Capable of being obtained: *Tickets are available at the box office.*

ax·is (ăk´ sĭs) *n.* A straight line around which an object rotates or can be imagined to rotate: *The axis of the earth passes through both of its poles.*

B

back·ground (băk´ ground´) *n.* A person's experience, training, and education: *Math knowledge is a perfect background for jobs in science.*

balk (bôk) *v.* To stop short and refuse to go on: *My pony balked at the gate and would not jump.*

ban·ish (băn´ ĭsh) *v.* To drive out or away; expel: *Banish such thoughts from your mind.*

bare (bâr) *v.* To open up to view; uncover: *The bear opened its mouth and bared its teeth at the wolf.*

bar·ri·er (băr´ ē ər) *n.* Something that blocks movement or passage: *Cows crossing the road are a barrier to traffic.*

bask (băsk) *v.* To rest in and enjoy a pleasant warmth: *The snake has been basking in the spring sunshine for an hour.*

bea·con (bē´ kən) *n.* A light or fire used as a warning or guide: *The flashing beacon on the lighthouse warned the ship that it was nearing the coast.*

beck·on (bĕk´ ən) *v.* To signal (a person), as by nodding or waving: *The principal beckoned us to her office.*

ben·e·fit (bĕn´ ə fĭt) *n.* Something that is of help; an advantage: *The field trip was of great benefit to the students.*

bon·dage (bŏn´ dĭj) *n.* The condition of being held as a slave or serf; slavery or servitude: *The slaves were held in bondage.*

bound (bound) *v.* To leap, jump, or spring: *The deer was bounding into the woods.*

brace (brās) *v.* To give support to; make firm; strengthen: *The camper is bracing a tent with poles.*

bru·tal (broōt´ l) *adj.* Cruel; ruthless: *The enemy launched a brutal attack.*

bun·dle (bŭn´ dl) *v.* To dress (a person) warmly: *She made sure to bundle up before heading out in the snow.*

beacon

ōo b**oo**t / ou **ou**t / ŭ c**u**t / û f**u**r / hw **wh**ich / th **th**in / *th* **th**is / zh vi**si**on / ə **a**go, sil**e**nt, penc**i**l, lem**o**n, circ**u**s

C

call·ing (kô′ lĭng) *n.* Job, occupation, profession, or career: *She always felt that nursing was her* **calling.**

ca·reer (kə rîr′) *n.* A profession or occupation: *She is considering a* **career** *in medicine.*

check (chĕk) *v.* To stop or hold back: *The defenders were in charge of* **checking** *the opposing offense during the soccer match.*

clam·my (klăm′ ē) *adj.* Unpleasantly damp, sticky, and usually cold: *My feet feel* **clammy** *in wet boots.*

col·lapse (kə lăps′) *v.* To fall down or inward suddenly; cave in: *Part of the roof* **collapsed** *after the fire.*

col·lect·ed (kə lĕk′ tĭd) *adj.* In full control of oneself; composed; calm: *He did his best to stay cool and* **collected** *when making his speech.*

com·mo·tion (kə mō′ shən) *n.* A disturbance or tumult: *The argument created a* **commotion** *in the hall.*

com·pe·ti·tion (kŏm pĭ tĭsh′ ən) *n.* A test of skill or ability; a contest: *The soccer match was a* **competition** *between two talented teams.*

com·pli·ment (kŏm′ plə mənt) *n.* An expression of praise, admiration, or congratulation: *She gave me a* **compliment.**

con·cen·trate (kŏn′ sən trāt′) *v.* To keep or direct one's thoughts, attention, or efforts: *It's hard to* **concentrate** *on my homework when the television is on.*

con·duct (kŏn′ dŭkt) *n.* The act of directing; management: *The coach was responsible for the team's* **conduct.**

con·serve (kən sûrv′) *v.* To protect from loss or harm; preserve: **Conserving** *energy is important.*

con·tent·ment (kən tĕnt′ mənt) *n.* The condition of being content; satisfaction: *Cats purr with* **contentment** *when they are satisfied.*

con·trar·y (kŏn′ trĕr′ ē) *adj.* Stubbornly opposed to others; willful: *Little children often become* **contrary** *when they need a nap.*

competition

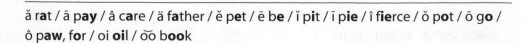

ă rat / ā pay / â care / ä father / ĕ pet / ē be / ĭ pit / ī pie / î fierce / ŏ pot / ō go / ô paw, for / oi oil / o͝o book

G4

con·tri·bu·tion (kŏn′ trĭ **byoo**′ shən) *n.* Something that is given: *We made **contributions** of food to the poor.*

cramped (krămpt) *adj.* Confined and limited in space: *A family of four lived in a **cramped** little apartment.*

crit·i·cal (**krĭt**′ ĭ kəl) *adj.* Extremely important or decisive: *The surgeon performed a **critical** surgery.*

D

de·bate (dĭ **bāt**′) *n.* A discussion or consideration of the arguments for and against something: *The class held a **debate** to discuss the fairness of the school dress code.*

de·cline (dĭ **klīn**′) *n.* The process or result of going down in number or quality: *Some people think the neighborhood is in **decline**.*

dec·o·rate (**dĕk**′ ər āt′) *v.* To furnish with something attractive, beautiful, or striking; adorn: *The students **decorated** the auditorium with flowers for graduation.*

del·i·cate (**dĕl**′ ĭ kĭt) *adj.* Easily broken or damaged; fragile: *Don't drop a **delicate** china cup.*

de·mol·ish (dĭ **mŏl**′ ĭsh) *v.* To tear down completely; level: *They **demolished** the old building.*

de·pend·ent (dĭ **pĕn**′ dənt) *adj.* Relying on or needing the help of another for support: *Plants are **dependent** upon sunlight.*

de·sert·ed (dĕ **zûrt**′ ĭd) *adj.* Left alone; abandoned: *The girl felt **deserted** when her friends walked away from her.*

de·spite (dĭ **spīt**′) *prep.* In spite of: *Lewis and Clark traveled to the Pacific **despite** the unknown land.*

des·ti·na·tion (dĕs′ tə **nā**′ shən) *n.* The place to which a person or thing is going or is sent: *The **destination** of that package is written on the label.*

de·struc·tion (dĭ **strŭk**′ shən) *n.* The condition of having been destroyed: *The tornado caused great **destruction**.*

de·tect (dĭ **tĕkt**′) *v.* To discover or determine the existence, presence, or fact of: ***Detecting** the smell of smoke could save your life.*

de·te·ri·o·rate (dĭ **tîr**′ ē ə rāt) *v.* To make or become inferior in quality, character, or value; worsen: *The moisture is **deteriorating** the cover of the old book.*

de·vel·op (dĭ **vĕl**′ əp) *v.* To bring into being: *The author **developed** the book's plot gradually.*

dex·ter·i·ty (dĕks **tĕr**′ ĭ tē) *n.* Skill or grace in using the hands, body, or mind: *A silversmith with **dexterity** can make beautiful pots.*

destruction
Destruction comes from the Latin prefix *de-* ("off" or "down") and the Latin word root *struere*, which means "to construct." Related words are *structure*, "something that is constructed," and *instruct*, "to teach," which come from the same Latin word root.

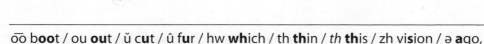

oo b**oo**t / ou **ou**t / ŭ **cu**t / û f**u**r / hw **wh**ich / th **th**in / *th* **th**is / zh vi**si**on / ə **a**go, sil**e**nt, penc**i**l, lem**o**n, circ**u**s

dis·ad·van·tage (dĭs´ əd văn´ tĭj) *n.* A circumstance or condition that makes it harder to do something or to be successful: *A disadvantage of river transportation is its slowness.*

dis·tract (dĭs trăkt´) *v.* To draw (the attention, for example) away from something: *The noise distracted the students in the library.*

dis·turb (dĭs tûrb´) *v.* To intrude upon; bother: *The visitors were disturbing the musician's practice.*

dom·i·nate (dŏm´ ə nāt´) *v.* To have controlling power or occupy a commanding position over: *The mayor dominated the town hall meeting.*

E

ed·i·ble (ĕd´ ə bəl) *adj.* Safe to eat: *James was surprised to learn that some flowers are edible.*

e·di·tion (ĭ dĭsh´ ən) *n.* The entire number of copies of a book or newspaper printed at one time and having the same content: *Today's edition of the paper is sold out.*

ef·fec·tive (ĭ fĕk´ tĭv) *adj.* Having an intended or expected effect: *The vaccine is effective against the flu.*

ef·fi·cient (ĭ fĭsh´ ənt) *adj.* Acting or producing effectively with a minimum of waste, expense, or unnecessary effort: *High gas mileage makes this car an efficient vehicle.*

el·e·ment (ĕl´ ə mənt) *n.* A part of a whole, especially a fundamental or essential part: *The novel is a detective story with one element of a science fiction story.*

e·lite (ĭ lēt´) or (ā lēt´) *adj.* Relating to a small and privileged group: *The athletes were the elite stars of the sports world.*

em·bar·rass (ĕm băr´ əs) *v.* To cause to feel self-conscious or ill at ease; disconcert: *Not knowing the answer to the question embarrassed me.*

em·bark (ĕm bärk´) *v.* To set out on an adventure; begin: *The sailors embark on an ocean voyage.*

en·dan·gered (ĕn dān´ jərd) *adj.* Nearly extinct: *The endangered animals were put in a preserve.*

en·vy (ĕn´ vē) *n.* A feeling of discontent at the advantages or successes enjoyed by another, together with a strong desire to have them for oneself: *I was filled with envy when I saw their new car.*

ă rat / ā pay / â care / ä father / ĕ pet / ē be / ĭ pit / ī pie / î fierce / ŏ pot / ō go / ô paw, for / oi oil / ŏŏ book

ep·i·sode (ĕp´ ĭ sōd) *n.* An incident that forms a distinct part of a story: *The story was divided into six episodes for television.*

ev·i·dent (ĕv´ ĭ dənt) *adj.* Easy to see or notice; obvious: *From the dark clouds, it was evident that it would soon rain.*

ex·cep·tion (ĭk sĕp´ shən) *n.* The act of leaving out or the condition of being left out: *All of our guests have arrived, with the exception of two.*

ex·pe·di·tion (ĕk´ spĭ dĭsh´ ən) *n.* A group making a journey for a specific purpose: *The expedition cheered when they reached the top of Mt. Everest.*

ex·ploit (ĕk´ sploit´) *n.* An act or deed, especially a brilliant or heroic one: *The exploits of Robin Hood helping the poor are legendary.*

ex·tend (ĭk stĕnd´) *v.* To stretch out; reach: *We saw a clothesline extending from the tree to the house.*

F

fac·tor (făk´ tər) *n.* Something that brings about a result: *A willingness to work hard is an important factor in achieving successes.*

faith·ful (fāth´ fəl) *adj.* Loyal and dutiful; trustworthy: *My dog is a faithful friend.*

fare (fâr) *v.* To get along; progress: *How are you faring with your project?*

fa·tal (fāt´l) *adj.* Causing death: *Disease can prove fatal to humpback whales.*

fea·ture (fē´ chər) *v.* To give special attention to; offer prominently: *The exhibit will feature Native American pottery.*

fe·ro·cious (fə rō´ shəs) *adj.* Extremely savage; fierce: *The tiger's ferocious roar frightened the deer.*

flaw (flô) *v.* To make defective: *The report was flawed with several errors.*

flour·ish (flûr´ ĭsh) *v.* To do well; prosper: *Their business flourished and they became rich.*

foe (fō) *n.* An enemy, opponent, or adversary: *Foes of the new city dump met to fight the plan.*

for·mal (fôr´ məl) *adj.* Structured according to forms or conventions: *The board of directors met in a formal meeting.*

for·mu·la (fôr´ myə lə) *n.* A method of doing something; procedure: *The teacher gave us the formula for writing a good research paper.*

fran·tic (frăn´ tĭk) *adj.* Very excited with fear or anxiety; desperate; frenzied: *She was frantic with worry.*

flaw

Flaw comes from the Norse word *flaga*, which originally meant "stone slab, flake." The word was first used to refer to a defect of character in 1586, and a defect in material things in 1604, probably referring to a fragment, or piece, broken off of a slab of stone.

ferocious

ōō **boo**t / ou **out** / ŭ **cut** / û **fur** / hw **wh**ich / th **th**in / *th* **th**is / zh vi**s**ion / ə **a**go, sil**e**nt, penc**i**l, lem**o**n, circ**u**s

household

Household is made up of *house,* meaning "a building made for people to live in," and *hold,* meaning "possession."

identical

Identical comes from a Latin word meaning "identity," the physical and personality characteristics that make up who a person is. Other English words relating to someone's identity come from the same Latin word root: *identity,* of course, *identify,* and *identification.*

inflate

ful·fill (fŏŏl fĭl´) *v.* To carry out: *Sharon fulfilled her responsibility when she finished cleaning her room.*

func·tion (fŭngk´ shən) *v.* To perform one's normal or proper activity: *The lungs function to take in oxygen.*

G

gor·geous (gôr´ jəs) *adj.* Dazzlingly beautiful or magnificent: *The snowcapped mountains were gorgeous in the sunset.*

grad·u·al·ly (grăj´ ōō əl lē) *adv.* Occurring in small stages or degrees, or by even, continuous change: *The water level in the lake changed gradually.*

grant (grănt) *v.* To give or allow (something asked for): *The teacher granted us permission to leave early.*

guar·di·an (gär´ dē ən) *n.* A person or thing that guards, protects, or watches over: *Courts act as guardians of the law.*

gush (gŭsh) *v.* To flow forth suddenly in great volume: *Water gushed from the broken pipe.*

H

hes·i·tate (hĕz´ ĭ tāt´) *v.* To be slow to act, speak, or decide: *We hesitated about whether to go over the rickety bridge.*

hos·tile (hŏs´ təl) *adj.* Not friendly: *Don't give me such a hostile look.*

house·hold (hous´ hōld´) *n.* The members of a family and others living together in a single unit: *Every household has its own rules.*

I

i·den·ti·cal (ī dĕn´ tĭ kəl) *adj.* Exactly equal and alike: *We're riding identical bicycles.*

ig·no·rance (ĭg´ nər əns) *n.* The condition of being unaware; lack of knowledge: *Ignorance of the law is no excuse for breaking it.*

im·press (ĭm prĕs´) *v.* To have a strong, often favorable effect on the mind or feelings of: *The worker impressed his manager and was promoted.*

in·cred·i·bly (ĭn krĕd´ ə blē) *adv.* Hard to believe; unbelievable: *The winner of the race ran incredibly fast.*

in·flate (ĭn flāt´) *v.* To cause to expand with air or gas: *She inflated the tires on her bicycle.*

in·flu·en·tial (ĭn´ flōō ĕn´ shəl) *adj.* Having or exercising influence: *Our city has an influential newspaper.*

in·sight (ĭn´ sīt) *n.* The perception of the true nature of something: *The movie critic's review had brilliant insights about the meaning of the movie.*

ă rat / ā pay / â care / ä father / ĕ pet / ē be / ĭ pit / ī pie / î fierce / ŏ pot / ō go / ô paw, for / oi oil / ōō book

in·ten·sive (ĭn **tĕn′** sĭv) *adj.* Complete and carried out with care: *After the accident, Mary needed intensive care for a few days.*

in·ter·rupt (ĭn tər **ŭpt′**) *v.* To do something that hinders or stops the action or conversation of; break in on: *I was about to finish my joke when my brother interrupted me.*

in·tim·i·date (ĭn **tĭm′** ĭ dāt) *v.* To fill with fear; frighten, or discourage: *The rough water intimidated us in our light canoe.*

is·sue (**ĭsh′** o͞o) *n.* A subject being discussed or disputed; a question under debate: *The senator spoke about the issue of reforming campaign laws.*

J

ju·ve·nile (**jo͞o′** vĕ nīl′) *adj.* Young: *The juvenile humpback played with the other young whales.*

K

keen (kēn) *adj.* Acute; sensitive: *The keen eyes of the owl help him to see at night.*

L

lack (lăk′) *v.* To be without: *The neighborhood lacked streetlights.*

launch (lônch) or (länch) *n.* The act of starting or setting into action: *The company was ready for the launch of its new research program.*

lec·ture (**lĕk′** chər) *v.* To give an explanation or a scolding: *My father lectured me about going out after dark.*

leg·en·dar·y (**lĕj′** ən dĕr′ ē) *adj.* Very well-known; famous: *Paul Revere's ride is legendary.*

lunge (lŭnj) *v.* To make a sudden forward movement: *She was lunging for the ball.*

M

mag·nif·i·cent (măg **nĭf′** ĭ sənt) *adj.* Outstanding of its kind; excellent: *Jackie Robinson was a magnificent athlete.*

mar·gin (**mär′** jĭn) *n.* An edge or border: *Weeds grew around the margins of the pond.*

ma·rine (mə **rēn′**) *adj.* Living in or connected to the sea: *Whales are marine mammals.*

mas·ter (**măs′** tər) *v.* To become the master of; bring under control: *He mastered a foreign language.*

---

o͞o bo**o**t / ou **ou**t / ŭ c**u**t / û f**u**r / hw **wh**ich / th **th**in / *th* **th**is / zh vi**s**ion / ə **a**go, sil**e**nt, penc**i**l, lem**o**n, circ**u**s

ma·ture (mə **tyŏŏr´**) or (mə **tŏŏr´**) or (mə **chŏŏr´**) *v.* To grow older: *Most puppies **mature** into full-grown dogs in a year or two.* *adj.* Having reached full growth or development: *A **mature** redwood can be hundreds of feet tall.*

men·tal (**měn´** tl) *adj.* Occurring in or done in the mind: *Good writing creates a **mental** image in the reader's mind.*

midst (mĭdst) or (mĭtst) *n.* The middle position or part; the center: *They planted a tree in the **midst** of the garden.*

mim·ic (**mĭm´** ĭk) *adj.* Acting as an imitation: *A snowman is a **mimic** person.* *v.* To resemble closely; simulate: *Children often **mimic** the mannerisms of their parents.*

min·i·mum (**mĭn´** ə məm) *n.* The smallest amount or degree possible: *We need a **minimum** of an hour to make dinner.*

mi·rage (mĭ **räzh´**) *n.* An optical illusion in which something that is not really there appears to be seen in the distance: *In the desert we saw **mirages** that looked like lakes.*

mis·hap (**mĭs´** hăp´) *n.* An unfortunate accident: *The trip ended without a **mishap**.*

mock (mŏk) *v.* To treat with scorn or contempt; deride: *I felt bad for Tom while his brother was **mocking** him.*

numb

Numb comes from the Old English word niman, which literally means "to take." When you are numb, you cannot feel or move normally; feeling has been taken from you.

N

nerve (nûrv) *n.* Courage or daring: *It took all my **nerve** to talk to the new student in our class.*

no·ble (**nō´** bəl) *adj.* Having or showing qualities of high moral character, as courage, generosity, or honor: *The knight performed a **noble** deed.*

numb (nŭm) *adj.* Deprived of the power to feel or move normally: *The boy's toes were **numb** with cold.*

O

ob·ject (əb´ **jěkt´**) *v.* To be opposed; express disapproval: *We **objected** to the loud noises downstairs.*

ob·vi·ous (**ŏb´** vē əs) *adj.* Easily perceived or understood; evident: *Large football players have an **obvious** advantage.*

of·fi·cial·ly (ə **fĭsh´** əl lē) *adv.* By or in a way relating to an office or post of authority: *The winner was **officially** declared.*

op·er·a·tor (**ŏp´** ə rā´ tər) *n.* A person who operates a machine or device: *The backhoe **operator** dug a ditch.*

op·po·nent (ə **pō´** nənt) *n.* A person or group that opposes another in a battle, contest, controversy, or debate: *The two runners were **opponents** in the race.*

ă rat / ā **pay** / â **c**are / ä father / ĕ **pet** / ē be / ĭ **pit** / ī **pie** / î **fie**rce / ŏ **pot** / ō g**o** / ô p**aw**, f**or** / oi **oil** / ŏŏ b**ook**

or·deal (ôr **dēl'**) *n.* An experience so difficult that it tests the ability to keep trying. *The wind was so strong that walking was an ordeal.*

or·di·nance (ôr' dn əns) *n.* A statute or regulation, especially one enacted by a city government: *The ordinance requires that every dog be on a leash.*

or·gan·ize (ōr' gən īz') *v.* To put together or arrange in an orderly, systematic way: *She was told to organize her messy room.*

o·rig·i·nal (ə **rij'** ĭ nəl) *adj.* Existing before all others; first: *Virginia is one of the original thirteen Colonies.*

P

pace (pās) *n.* Speed of motion or progress: *I love the fast pace of city life.*

par·tic·u·lar (pər **tĭk'** yə lər) *adj.* Separate and different from others of the same group or category: *The painter wanted the walls a particular shade of blue.*

peal (pēl) *n.* A loud burst of noise: *A peal of thunder frightened the baby.*

per·son·al·ly (**pûr'** sən əl lē) *adv.* In person or by oneself; without the help of another: *I thanked her personally.*

per·suade (pər **swād'**) *v.* To cause (someone) to do or believe something by arguing, pleading, or reasoning; convince: *He tried to persuade them to come with us.*

pic·ture (**pĭk'** chər) *v.* To form a mental image of; visualize; imagine: *He pictured himself winning the bike race.*

pierce (pîrs) *v.* To pass into or through (something) with or as with a sharp instrument: *The arrows pierced the target.*

plague (plāg) *v.* To annoy; pester; harass: *The manager was plagued with complaints from angry customers.*

plunge (plŭnj) *v.* To thrust, throw, or place forcefully or suddenly into something: *The farmer plunged the pitchfork into the hay.*

pre·lim·i·nar·y (prĭ **lĭm'** ə nĕr' ē) *adj.* Prior to or preparing for the main matter, action, or business; introductory: *The architect showed preliminary sketches for a building.*

press·ing (**prĕs'** ĭng) *adj.* Demanding immediate attention; urgent: *Hunger is one of the world's most pressing problems.*

pierce

ōō b**oo**t / ou **ou**t / ŭ c**u**t / û f**u**r / hw **wh**ich / th **th**in / *th* **th**is / zh vi**s**ion / ə **a**go, s**i**lent, penc**i**l, lem**o**n, circ**u**s

provisions

pre·vi·ous·ly (prē´ vē əs lē) *adv.* Before something else in time or order: ***Previously***, *the girls lived in New Orleans.*

prod (prŏd) *v.* To stir to action; urge: *She continually **prodded** him to do his homework.*

pro·duce (prə dōōs´) *v.* To create by mental or physical effort: *It takes time to **produce** a painting.*

pro·hib·it (prō hĭb´ ĭt) *v.* To forbid by law or authority: *The pool rules **prohibit** diving in the shallow end.*

pros·per (prŏs´ pər) *v.* To be fortunate or successful; thrive: *The man **prospered** after graduating from college.*

pro·vi·sions (prə vĭzh´ ənz) *n.* Stocks of foods and other necessary supplies: *Soldiers at war are given **provisions**.*

pub·li·ca·tion (pŭb lĭ kā´ shən) *n.* An issue of printed or electronic matter, such as a magazine, offered for sale or distribution: *The school's monthly **publication** is very informative.*

Q

quake (kwāk) *v.* To shiver or tremble, as from fear or cold: *I was so frightened that my legs were **quaking**.*

qual·i·fy (kwŏl´ ə fī´) *v.* To make eligible or qualified, as for a position or task: *She received all high grades, **qualifying** her for the Honor Society.*

quest (kwĕst) *n.* A search, especially for something held valuable or precious: *Space exploration represents the latest **quest** for knowledge of the universe.*

R

range (rānj) *n.* An extended group or series, especially a row or chain of mountains: *The Rocky Mountain **range** is in the western United States.*

re·al·i·za·tion (rē əl ĭ zā´ shən) *n.* The act of realizing or the condition of being realized: *The **realization** that he lost his wallet panicked him.*

rea·son (rē´ zən) *v.* To use the ability to think clearly and sensibly: *I **reasoned** that I should stay inside because it was raining outside.*

re·bel·lious (rĭ bĕl´ yəs) *adj.* Prone to or participating in a rebellion: *The **rebellious** farmer fought in the Revolutionary War.*

re·cite (rĭ sīt´) *v.* To repeat or say aloud (something prepared or memorized), especially before an audience: *The players **recite** the Pledge of Allegiance before each game.*

ă rat / ā pay / â care / ä father / ĕ pet / ē be / ĭ pit / ī pie / î fierce / ŏ pot / ō go / ô paw, for / oi oil / ŏŏ book

rec·ord (rĕk´ ərd) *n.* The highest or lowest measurement known, as in sports events or weather readings: *Death Valley holds the record for least rainfall in a year in the United States.*

reg·u·late (rĕg´ yə lāt) *v.* To control or direct according to a rule or a law: *Rangers regulate park activities.*

re·peal (rĭ pēl´) *v.* To withdraw or cancel officially; revoke: *The Senate voted to repeal the law.*

rep·re·sen·ta·tive (rep´ rĭ zĕn´ tə tĭv) *n.* A person who acts for one or more others: *Rob and Peter were elected as class representatives.*

re·quire (rĭ kwīr´) *v.* To be in need of; need: *Practice is required for a person to become better at a sport.*

re·sem·ble (rĭ zĕm´ bəl) *v.* To have similarity or likeness to; be like: *Some house cats resemble cougars.*

res·i·dent (rĕz´ ĭ dənt) *n.* A person who lives in a particular place: *Residents of the building had to leave because the power was out.*

re·spon·si·bil·i·ty (rĭ spŏn´ sə bĭl´ ĭ tē) *n.* Something that one is responsible for; a duty or obligation: *The two cats are my responsibility.*

re·store (rĭ stôr´) *v.* To bring back to an original condition: *The carpenter wanted to restore the old building.*

re·sume (rĭ zōōm´) *v.* To continue: *Classes resumed after school vacation.*

re·treat (rĭ trēt´) *v.* The act or process of withdrawing, especially from something dangerous or unpleasant: *Patriots forced the Hessians to retreat from battle.*

rev·o·lu·tion (rev´ ə lōō´ shən) *n.* The overthrow of one government and its replacement with another: *The goal of the American Patriots during their revolution was to overthrow British rule.*

romp (rŏmp) *n.* Lively or spirited play: *The girls took their dogs for a romp in the park.*

rou·tine (rōō tēn´) *n.* A series of activities performed or meant to be performed regularly; a standard or usual procedure: *They were delayed by the guards' routine of checking their passports.*

ru·mor (rōō´ mər) *n.* A story or report, usually spread by word of mouth, that has not been established as true: *I heard a rumor that Peter is moving to China.*

rur·al (rōōr´ əl) *adj.* Of, relating to, or characteristic of the country: *Farms are found in rural areas.*

rural

ōō b**oo**t / ou **out** / ŭ c**u**t / û f**u**r / hw **wh**ich / th **th**in / th **th**is / zh vi**s**ion / ə **a**go, sil**e**nt, penc**i**l, lem**o**n, circ**u**s

rus·tle (rŭs´əl) *v.* To make a soft fluttering sound: *A **rustling** in the woods scared me away.*

S

sal·va·tion (săl vā´shən) *n.* Someone or something that saves or rescues: *The spring was the **salvation** of the thirsty traveler.*

scan (skăn) *v.* To examine (something) closely: *She **scanned** the report card.*

se·cure (sĭ kyŏor´) *v.* To cause to remain firmly in position or place; fasten: *We **secured** the ship's hatches.*

seep (sēp) *v.* To pass slowly through small openings; ooze: *Cold air could **seep** in through the cracks.*

shake (shāk) *v.* To make uneasy; disturb; agitate: *She was **shaken** by the bad news.*

shat·ter (shăt´ər) *v.* To break into pieces by force; smash: *The **shattered** glass was unfixable.*

shift (shĭft) *v.* To move or transfer from one place or position to another: *She **shifted** the heavy basket in her arms.*

shim·mer (shĭm´ər) *v.* To shine with a subdued, flickering light: *The **shimmering** candle could be seen in the darkness.*

shoul·der (shōl´dər) *v.* To place on the shoulder or shoulders for carrying: *The dad **shouldered** the boy so he could see over the crowd.*

shuf·fle (shŭf´əl) *v.* To walk slowly, while dragging the feet: *I **shuffled** my feet because I was so tired.*

sim·u·late (sĭm´yə lāt´) *v.* To have or take on the appearance, form, or sound of; imitate: *We saw a device that **simulates** space flight.*

spare (spâr) *v.* To show mercy or consideration to: *I **spared** your feelings by not telling you about the problems.*

spe·cial·ty (spĕsh´əl tē) *n.* A special pursuit, occupation, talent, or skill: *His **specialty** is portrait painting.*

sprawl·ing (sprôl´ĭng) *adj.* Spreading out in different directions: *I looked over the **sprawling** meadow.*

squal·ling (skwôl ĭng) *n.* Loud crying: *The mother stopped her baby's **squalling** by singing him to sleep.* *adj.* Crying loudly: *They found the **squalling** kitten under a bush.*

squash (skwôsh) *v.* To beat or flatten into a pulp; crush: *He was **squashing** the peach on the pavement.*

shattered

ă rat / ā pay / â care / ä father / ĕ pet / ē be / ĭ pit / ī pie / î fierce / ŏ pot / ō go / ô paw, for / oi oil / ŏŏ book

G14

stag·ger (**stăg´** ər) *v.* To move or stand unsteadily, as if carrying a great weight; totter: *Carrying the large boxes, she staggered clumsily.*

stall (stôl) *v.* To slow down or stop the process of; bring to a standstill: *The traffic stalled because of the accident ahead.*

strain (strān) *v.* To work as hard as possible; strive hard: *The boy strained to lift the heavy bag.*

strat·e·gy (**străt´** ə jē) *n.* The planning and directing of a series of actions that will be useful in gaining a goal: *General George Washington came up with a strategy for the battle.*

stride (strīd) *n.* A single, long step: *The giraffe took long strides.*

strug·gle (**strŭg´** əl) *v.* To make strenuous efforts; strive: *She struggled to stay awake.*

stun (stŭn) *v.* To make someone or something unable to sense what is going on: *The loud noise of the boat engine stunned the fish.*

stunt·ed (**stŭn´** tĭd) *adj.* Slowed or stopped abnormally in growth or development: *The stunted tree did not grow because there was no water.*

sum·mon (**sŭm´** ən) *v.* To call forth; muster: *The smell of turkey summons memories of past Thanksgiving dinners.*

sup·pos·ed·ly (sə **pō´** zĭd lē) *adv.* Seemingly: *Until she lied, she was supposedly my friend.*

surge (sûrj) *v.* To move with gathering force, as rolling waves do: *The crowd surged forward.*

sur·vey (sər **vā´**) or (**sûr´** vā´) *v.* To look over the parts or features of; view broadly: *We surveyed the neighborhood from a hilltop.*

sus·pense (sə **spĕns´**) *n.* The state or quality of being undecided or uncertain: *The movie left us in suspense.*

sweep·ing (**swēp´** ĭng) *adj.* Moving in, or as if in, a long curve: *The castaways waved to the rescue plane with sweeping gestures.*

T

tech·nique (tĕk **nēk´**) *n.* A procedure or method for carrying out a specific task: *Jason learned techniques for carving wooden toys.*

te·di·ous (**tē´** dē əs) *adj.* Tiresome because of slowness, dullness, or length; boring: *He didn't like math, so he thought the lecture was tedious.*

suspense
The word *suspense* comes from the Latin prefix *sub-*, meaning "from below," and the Latin word root *pendere*, "to hang." A *suspension bridge* is a bridge on which the roadway hangs from cables. The related word *depend*, which means "to rely on" or "be determined by," comes from the Latin prefix *de-*, "down from," and *pendere*.

---

o͞o b**oo**t / ou **ou**t / ŭ c**u**t / û f**u**r / hw **wh**ich / th **th**in / th **th**is / zh vi**s**ion / ə **a**go, sil**e**nt, penc**i**l, lem**o**n, circ**u**s

tem·po·rar·y (tĕm´ pə rĕr´ ē) *adj.* Lasting, used, serving, or enjoyed for a limited time; not permanent: *The man was given a **temporary** license until he could get a permanent one.*

ten·ta·tive (tĕn´ tə tĭv) *adj.* Not fully worked out, concluded, or agreed on: *The publisher created a **tentative** production schedule.*

teth·er (tĕth´ ər) *v.* To fasten or restrict: *As a safety measure, the astronaut was **tethered** to the spaceship.*

thrust (thrŭst) *n.* A forceful shove or push: *The knight killed the dragon with a **thrust** of the sword.*

thumb (thŭm) *v.* To scan written matter by turning the pages with the thumb: *She **thumbed** through the magazine.*

tor·ment (tôr´ mĕnt´) *n.* Great physical or mental pain: *I was in a state of **torment** listening to the teacher explain the homework assignment.*

trans·form (trăns fôrm´) *v.* To change the nature, function, or condition of; convert: *The caterpillar **transformed** into a butterfly.*

treat (trēt) *v.* To give medical care to a person or animal or for an illness: *Some doctors make a specialty of **treating** birds only.*

trek (trĕk) *n.* A long, hard journey, especially on foot: *Settlers made the **trek** to the West.*

trib·u·tar·y (trĭb´ yə tĕr´ ē) *n.* A river or stream that flows into a larger river or stream: *People enjoy boating on **tributaries** of the Mississippi River.*

typ·i·cal·ly (tĭp´ ĭ kəl lē) *adv.* In a way that is usual for a kind, group, or category: ***Typically**, school begins early in the morning.*

U

un·doubt·ed·ly (ŭn dou´ tĭd lē) *adv.* Beyond question; undisputedly: *He was **undoubtedly** glad he made it to the meeting on time.*

un·e·vent·ful (ŭn´ ĭ vĕnt´ fəl) *adj.* Having no significant events: *The trip was **uneventful**.*

u·ni·form (yōō´ nə fôrm´) *adj.* Being the same as another or others: *He built the porch out of planks of **uniform** length.*

u·nique (yōō nēk´) *adj.* Being the only one of its kind: *The puppy had a **unique** mark on his back.*

un·i·son (yōō´ nĭ sən) or (yōō´ nĭ zən) *n.* At the same time; at once: *The rowers must work in **unison** to win.*

un·ob·served (ŭn´ əb zûrvd´) *adj.* Not seen or noticed: *We crept up the walkway **unobserved**.*

---

uni-

The basic meaning of the prefix *uni-* is "one." It comes from the Latin prefix *uni-*, which in turn comes from the Latin word root *unus*, "one." The word *unicorn*, a mythological one-horned horse, comes from *uni-* and the Latin word root *cornu*, "horn." *Uniform, unique, unison,* and *unicycle* all have "one" in their definitions.

ă **r**at / ā **p**ay / â **c**are / ä **f**ather / ĕ **p**et / ē **b**e / ĭ **p**it / ī **p**ie / î **fie**rce / ŏ **p**ot / ō **g**o / ô **p**aw, **f**or / oi **oi**l / ōō **b**ook

up·right (ŭp′ rīt′) *adv.* Straight up: *I taught my dog to sit **upright** and beg for a biscuit.*

urge (ûrj) *v.* To entreat earnestly and repeatedly; exhort: *The coach continues to **urge** us to stay in shape over summer vacation.*

V

vain (vān) *adj.* Having no success: *Firefighters made a **vain** attempt to save the burning building.*

var·y (vâr′ ē) *v.* To be different or diverse: *His diet will **vary** from day to day.*

veg·e·ta·tion (vej′ ĭ tā′ shən) *n.* The plants in an area or region; plant life: *There is little **vegetation** at the North Pole.*

ver·sion (vûr′ zhən) *n.* A type: *This new car is a reworked **version** of an older model.*

view·point (vyoo′ point′) *n.* A position from which something is observed or considered; a point of view: *From the **viewpoint** of the British, their navy was the best.*

vil·lain (vĭl′ ən) *n.* A wicked or very bad person; a scoundrel: *The evil brothers were the **villains** of the movie.*

vi·o·la·tion (vī ə lā′ shən) *n.* The act or an instance of breaking or ignoring or the condition of (a law or rule) being broken or ignored: *She was fined for traffic **violations**.*

W

wheel (hwēl) *v.* To turn or whirl around in place: *She **wheeled** to see what had made the loud sound behind her.*

wob·ble (wŏb′ əl) *v.* To move unsteadily from side to side: *The old table **wobbled**.*

villain

The meaning of *villain* has changed over the centuries. The word comes from the Latin word root *villa*, which means "country house." It originally meant a peasant or serf who lived in the country. It gradually changed to mean a person with coarse feelings or a foolish person, and then a wicked person.

vegetation

Acknowledgments

The Birchbark House written and illustrated by Louise Erdrich. Copyright © 1999 by Louise Erdrich. Reprinted by permission of Hyperion Books. All rights reserved.

Can't You Make Them Behave, King George? by Jean Fritz, illustrated by Tomie dePaola. Text copyright © 1977 by Jean Fritz. Illustrations copyright © 1977 by Tomie dePaola. Reprinted by permission of Coward-McCann, a division of Penguin's Young Readers Group, a member of Penguin Group (USA). Inc., and Gina Maccoby Literary Agency.

Cougars by Patricia Corrigan, illustrated by John F. McGee. Copyright © 2001 by Northword Press. Reprinted by permission of T & N Children's Publishing.

Dangerous Crossing by Stephen Krensky, illustrated by Greg Harlin. Text copyright © 2005 by Stephen Krensky. Illustrations copyright © 2005 by Greg Harlin. All rights reserved including the right of reproduction in whole or in any form. Reprinted by permission of Dutton Children's Books, a member of Penguin's Young Readers Group, a division of Penguin Group (USA) Inc., and The Gersh Agency.

Darnell Rock Reporting by Walter Dean Myers. Copyright © 1994 by Walter Dean Myers. Reprinted by permission of Random House Children's Books, a division of Random House, Inc.

"Deanie McLeanie" by Walter Dean Myers. Copyright © 1994 by Walter Dean Myers. Reprinted by permission of Miriam Altshuler Literary Agency.

"Disturbed, the cat" from *The Penguin Book of Japanese Verse* (1967). Translated by Geoffrey Bownas and Anthony Thwaite. Reprinted by permission of Geoffrey Bownas.

"The Dog Newspaper" from *Five Pages a Day: A Writer's Journey* by Peg Kehret. Text copyright © 2005 by Peg Kehret. Reprinted by permission of Albert Whitman & Company and Curtis Brown, Ltd.

Don Quixote and the Windmills, a retelling by Eric A. Kimmel from *The Ingenious Don Quixote De La Mancha* by Miguel de Cervantes Saavedra, pictures by Leonard Everett Fisher. Retelling copyright © 2004 by Shearwater Books. Pictures copyright © 2004 by Leonard Everett Fisher. Reprinted by permission of Farrar, Straus & Giroux, LLC.

El Diario de Elisa by Doris Luisa Oronoz. Text copyright © by Doris Luisa Oronoz. Reprinted by permission of the author.

Everglades Forever: Restoring America's Great Wetlands by Trish Marx, photographs by Cindy Karp. Text copyright © 2004 by Trish Marx. Photographs copyright © 2004 by Cindy Karp. Reprinted by permission of Lee & Low Books, Inc., NY, NY 10016.

"Genius" from *A Dime a Dozen* by Nikki Grimes. Copyright © 1998 by Nikki Grimes. Reprinted by permission of Dial Books for Young Readers, a division of Penguin Young Readers Group, a member of Penguin Group (USA) Inc. All rights reserved.

"Good Sportsmanship" from *All in Sport* by Richard Armour. Copyright © 1972 by Richard Armour. Reprinted by permission of Geoffrey Armour.

Interrupted Journey: Saving Endangered Sea Turtles by Kathryn Lasky, photographs by Christopher G. Knight. Text copyright © 2001 by Kathryn Lasky. Photographs copyright © 2001 by Christopher G. Knight. Reprinted by permission of Candlewick Press, Inc.

"James Forten" from *Now Is Your Time! The African-American Struggle for Freedom* by Walter Dean Myers. Copyright © 1991 by Walter Dean Myers. Reprinted by permission of HarperCollins Publishers.

"Karate Kid" by Jane Yolen from *Opening Day: Sports Poems*, published by Harcourt Brace & Co. Copyright © 1996 by Jane Yolen. Reprinted by permission of Curtis Brown, Ltd.

"LAFFF" by Lensey Namioka from *Within Reach: Ten Stories* edited by Donald P. Gallo. Copyright © 1983 by Lensey Namioka. Reprinted by permission of Lensey Namioka. All rights reserved by the author.

Lewis and Clark by R. Conrad Stein. Copyright © 1997 by Children's Press®, a division of Grolier Publishing Co., Inc. All rights reserved. Reprinted by permission of Scholastic Library Publishing.

Lunch Money by Andrew Clements. Text copyright © 2005 by Andrew Clements. Reprinted by permission of Simon & Schuster's Books for Young Readers, a division of Simon & Schuster's Children's Publishing Division, and Writer's House, LLC, acting as agent for the author.

"A Package for Mrs. Jewls" from *Wayside School is Falling Down* by Louis Sachar, illustrated by Adam McCauley. Text copyright © 1989 by Louis Sachar. Illustrations copyright © 2003 by Adam McCauley. Reprinted by permission of HarperCollins Publishers.

Off and Running by Gary Soto. Text copyright © 1996 by Gary Soto. Reprinted by permission of the author and BookStop Literary Agency. All rights reserved. Jacket cover reprinted by permission of Random House Children's Books, a division of Random House, Inc.

Old Yeller by Fred Gipson. Copyright © 1956 by Fred Gipson. Reprinted by permission of HarperCollins Publishers and McIntosh & Otis, Inc.

Rachel's Journal written and illustrated by Marissa Moss. Copyright © 1998 by Marissa Moss. All rights reserved. Reprinted by permission of Houghton Mifflin Harcourt Publishing Company and the Barbara S. Kouts Agency.

"Rockett Girls" from *Double Dutch: A Celebration of Jump Rope, Rhyme and Sisterhood* by Veronica Chambers. Copyright © 2002 by Veronica Chambers. Reprinted by permission of Hyperion Books for Children and the Sandra Dijkstra Literary Agency. All rights reserved.

"A Seeing Poem" from *Seeing Things* by Robert Froman, published by Thomas Y. Crowell, 1974. Copyright © 1974 by Robert Froman. Reprinted by permission of Katherine Froman.

Storm Warriors by Elisa Carbone. Copyright © 2001 by Elisa Carbone. Cover illustration copyright © 2001 by Don Demers. Reprinted by permission of Alfred A. Knopf, an imprint of Random House Children's Books, a division of Random House, Inc.

They Called Her Molly Pitcher by Anne Rockwell, illustrated by Cynthia von Buhler. Text copyright © 2002 by Anne Rockwell. Illustrations copyright © 2002 by Cynthia von Buhler. Reprinted by permission of Alfred A. Knopf, a division of Random House Children's Books, a division of Random House, Inc.

"Tiger" from *All the Small Poems and Fourteen More* by Valerie Worth. Copyright © 1987, 1994 by Valerie Worth. Reprinted by permission of Farrar, Straus and Giroux, LLC.

"A Tomcat Is" by J. Patrick Lewis from *Cat Poems*, published by Holiday House. Copyright © 1987 by J. Patrick Lewis. Reprinted by permission of Curtis Brown, Ltd.

"To Write Poetry/ Para escribir peosia" from *Iguanas in the Snow and Other Winter Poems/Iguanas en la nieve y otras poemas de invierno* by Francisco X. Alarcón. Copyright © 2001 by Francisco X. Alarcón. Reprinted by permission of Children's Book Press, San Francisco, CA, www.childrensbookpress.org

"Tucket's Travels" from *Tucket's Gold* by Gary Paulsen. Copyright © 1999 by Gary Paulsen. Reprinted by permission of Flannery Literary.

Ultimate Field Trip 5: Blasting Off to Space Academy by Susan E. Goodman, photographs by Michael J. Doolittle. Text copyright © 2001 by Susan E. Goodman. Photographs copyright © 2001 by Michael J. Doolittle. Reprinted by permission of Atheneum Books for Young Readers, an imprint of Simon & Schuster Children's Publishing Division.

We Were There, Too! by Phillip Hoose. Text copyright © 2001 by Phillip Hoose. All rights reserved. Maps by Debra Ziss. Reprinted by permission of Farrar, Straus and Giroux, LLC.

Credits

Photo Credits

Placement Key: (t) top; (b) bottom; (l) left; (r) right; (c) center; (bg) background; (fg) foreground; (i) inset.
TOC 4 (b) ©Michael J. Doolittle; **TOC 6** (b) ©Michael H. Francis; **TOC 8** ©Don Farrall/Photodisc/Getty Images; **17A** ©Fancy Photography/Veer; **17B** (spread) ©Fancy Photography/Veer; (inset) ©Siede Preis; **18** (tl) ©Jim West/Alamy; (tr) ©Blend Images/Alamy; (bl) ©Patrick Giardino/Getty Images; (br) ©Inspirestock/Jupiter Images; **19** (tl) ©Charles Gupton/CORBIS; (tc) ©Tom Morrison/Getty Images; (tr) ©Blend Images/Alamy; (bl) ©Ableimages/Getty Images; (bc) ©Rick Gayle/Corbis; (br) ©Digital Vision Ltd./SuperStock; **20-21** ©Masterfile; **20** (inset) ©Masterfile; **22** (b) ©Courtesy of Bruce MacPherson; (t) ©HANDOUT/Newscom; **37** (t) ©Ron Levine/Getty Images; **39** C Squared Studios/Photodisc; **42** (tl) ©Digital Vision/Getty Images; (tr) © NASA/epa/CORBIS; (bl) ©NASA/Handout/epa/Corbis; (br) ©NASA/Roger Ressmeyer/CORBIS; **43** (tl) ©Mike Dunning/DK IMAGES; (tc) ©Roger Ressmeyer/CORBIS; (tr) ©NASA/Roger Ressmeyer/CORBIS; (bl) ©CHARLES W LUZIER/Reuters/Corbis; (bc) © Bloomimage/Corbis; (br) ©Corbis; **44-45** (bkgd) ©Corbis; **46** (t) ©Courtesty of Susan E. Goodman; **46-47** ©Michael J. Doolittle; **48-59** (t)

©Taxi/Getty Images; **48** (l) ©Michael J. Doolittle; **49** ©Michael J. Doolittle; **50** ©Michael J. Doolittle; **51** ©Michael J. Doolittle; **52** (b) ©Michael J. Doolittle; **53** ©Michael J. Doolittle; **54-55** ©Michael J. Doolittle; **55** (r) ©Michael J. Doolittle; (c) ©Michael J. Doolittle; **56** ©Michael J. Doolittle; **57** (b) ©Michael J. Doolittle; **58-59** ©Jeff Greenberg/PhotoEdit; **58** (inset) ©Nasa; **59** (tr) Photo Royalty Free; (br) Getty Images/PhotoDisc; **60** (inset) ©NASA; **61** (br) ©NASA Marshall Space Flight Center; **62-63** (bkgd) ©NASA/Getty Images; (starry sky) ©Ian McKinnell/Photographer's Choice/Getty Images; **63** (t) ©PhotoLink/APEX; **65** ©Plain Pictures/Jupiter Images; **68** (tl) ©Tony Freeman/PhotoEdit; (tr) ©Image Source Black/Alamy; (bl) ©Corbis; (br) ©Age Fotostock/SuperStock; (graph) ©Beard & Howell/Getty Images; **69** (tl) ©Amy Meyers/Shutter Stock; (tc) ©Paul Conklin/PhotoEdit; (tr) ©Spencer Grant/PhotoEdit; (bl) ©Mary Kate Denny/PhotoEdit; (bc) ©Adam Taylor/Getty Images; (br) ©LWA-Dann Tardif/CORBIS; **70** ©Michael Newman/PhotoEdit; **70-71** (bkgd) ©J. Schwanke/Alamy; **72** (b) ©Courtesy of Eric Velasquez; **86** (yellow button) ©1995 PhotoDisc; **88** (bkgd) ©Age fotostock/SuperStock; **91** ©David Young-Wolff/PhotoEdit; **94** (tl) ©BananaStock/SuperStock; (tr) ©Marc Vaughn/Masterfile; (bl) ©PNC/Getty Images; (br) ©Tom Rosenthat/SuperStock; **95** (tl) ©WireImageStock/Masterfile; (tc) ©David Sanger Photography/Alamy; (tr) ©Rudi Von Briel/PhotoEdit; (bl) ©Tim Pannell/Corbis; (bc) ©David Madison/Getty Images; (br) ©LWA-Dann Tardif/CORBIS; **96-97** ©John Fletcher/www.usajumprope.org; **98-99** ©John Fletcher/www.usajumprope.org; **98** ©Courtesy Hyperion Books for Children; **100** (t) ©Lawrence Manning/Corbis; **100-101** ©Debbie Egan-Chin; **102-103** ©Debbie Egan Chin; **103** (t) ©Debbie Egan-Chin; **104-105** (t) ©Bob Jacobson/Corbis; **104** ©Debbie Egan-Chin; **105** ©Debbie Egan-Chin; **106-107** ©Ron Tarver; 108 ©Ron Tarver; **109** (tr) PhotoDisc - royalty free; **109** (br) Stockbyte/Getty Images Royalty-Free; **110-111** (bkgd) ©George Shelley/CORBIS; 110 (inset) ©Tom Carter/PhotoEdit; **112-113** ©Warren Morgan/CORBIS; (tr) ©D. Hurst/Alamy; (br) ©www.imagesource.com; **115** ©Michael Newman/Photoedit; **118** (tl) ©ImageState/Alamy; (tr) ©Mike Powell/Allsport Concepts/Getty Images; (bl) ©Galina Barskaya/Shutter Stock; (br) ©Arco Images/Alamy; **119** (tl) ©Jamal A. Wilson/Stringer/AFP/Getty Images; (tc) ©Alistair Berg/Taxi/Getty Images; (tr) ©Nick Garbutt/npl/Minden Pictures; (bl) ©Andrew Fox/Alamy; (br) ©Peter Beck/Corbis; (bc) ©Digital Vision/Alamy; **120-121** ©Tom Carter/PhotoEdit; **122** (b) ©Courtesy of Jim Tsinganos; (t) ©Courtesy of Terry Trueman; **133** (tr) Brand X Pictures/GettyImages; (tr) Stockbyte Photo; (br) Corbis; **134-135** (t) © www.photo-hartmann.de; **136** (inset) © www.photo-hartmann.de; **137** (b) ©George S. de Blonsky/Alamy; **139** ©Susanna Price/Dorling Kindersley/Getty Images; **144** (b) ©Jeff Greenberg/Alamy; **145A** ©Richard Cummins/Lonely Planet Images; **145B** (spread) ©Judy Bellah/Lonely Planet Images; (inset) ©Richard Cummins/Lonely Planet Images; (title) ©Siri Stafford/Getty Images; **146** (tl) ©Roger Bamber/Alamy; (tr) ©Gerry Ellis/Getty Images; (bl) ©David Frazier/Corbis; (br) ©Raymond Gehman/CORBIS; **147** (tl) ©Kari K. Greer/911 Pictures; (tc) ©Mike Mcmillan/Spotfire Images; (tr) © Bruce

Illustration